TOWER HAMLETS
91 000 001 084 85 4

D1627541

THE INDISPENSABLE BOOK OF PRACTICAL LIFE SKILLS

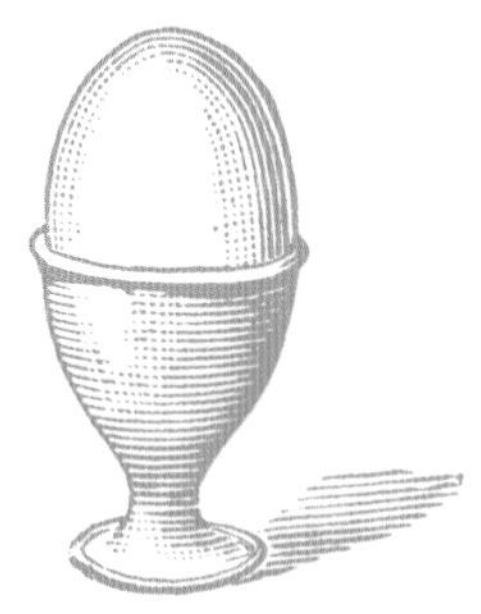

A
B
C

THE INDISPENSABLE BOOK OF PRACTICAL LIFE SKILLS

NIC COMPTON KIM DAVIES DAVID MARTIN SARA ROSE

Published in 2009 by
New Holland Publishers (UK) Ltd

London • Cape Town • Sydney • Auckland
www.newhollandpublishers.com

Garfield House, 86–88 Edgware Road,
London W2 2EA, United Kingdom

80 McKenzie Street, Cape Town 8001,
South Africa

Unit 1, 66 Gibbes Street, Chatswood,
NSW 2067, Australia

218 Lake Road, Northcote,
Auckland, New Zealand

10 9 8 7 6 5 4 3 2 1

A catalogue record for this book is available from the British Library

ISBN 978-1-84773-500-3

Printed in China

This book was created by
Ivy Press
210 High Street
Lewes, East Sussex BN7 2NS, UK

CREATIVE DIRECTOR Peter Bridgewater
PUBLISHER Jason Hook
EDITORIAL DIRECTOR Caroline Earle
ART DIRECTOR Michael Whitehead
PROJECT EDITOR Sanaz Nazemi
DESIGN JC Lanaway
CONCEPT DESIGN Joerg Hartmannsgruber
ILLUSTRATION Ivan Hissey, Coral Mula
PICTURE MANAGER Katie Greenwood
PICTURE RESEARCH Lyana Lanaway, Lynda Marshall
CONSULTANTS Christine Evans, paramedic; Marie-Eve Foisy, Parks Canada; Vivienne Macey, midwife; Dr Christopher Van Tilburg, wilderness physician; Tony Wafer, RNLI; Professor Greg Whyte, Professor of Applied Sport and Exercise Science, John Moores University, Liverpool.

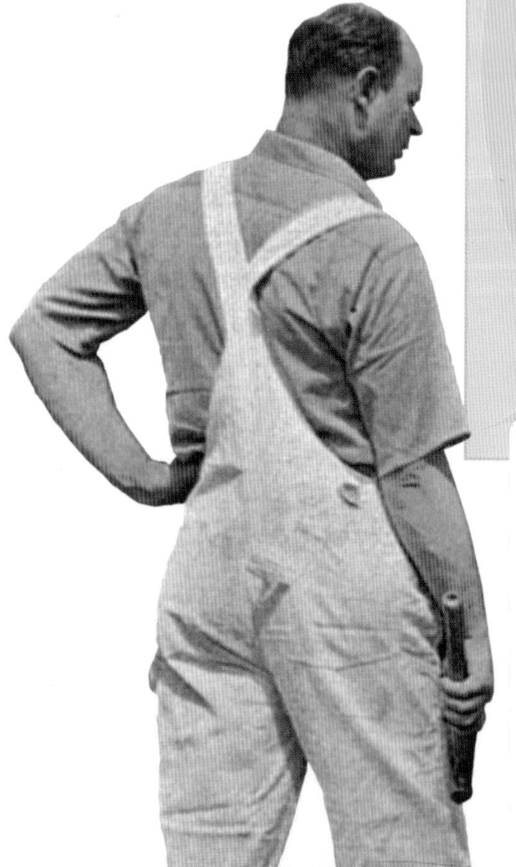

DISCLAIMER

The authors and publisher expressly disclaim responsibility for any liability, loss, injury or risk (personal, financial or otherwise) that may be incurred (or claimed) as a consequence directly or indirectly from the use and/or application of any of the contents of this publication. If you suffer from any health problems or special conditions, you should use proper discretion, in consultation with a health care practitioner, before undertaking the techniques described in this book. The publisher does not condone illegal activity of any kind.

CONTENTS

HOME & GARDEN

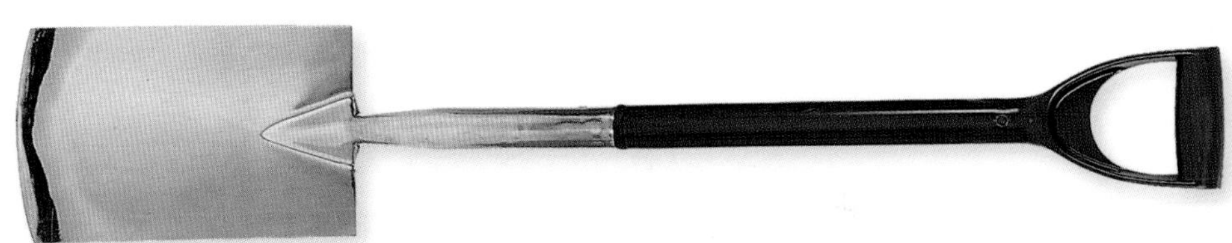

HEALTH & BEAUTY

TRAVEL & SPORTS

ON THE ROAD 177

FUN & GAMES 195

IN THE WILD

ACCIDENT & EMERGENCY

GOING TO THE RESCUE 265

DEALING WITH EMERGENCIES 295

SURVIVING IN EXTREMES 319

HOW TO USE THIS PRACTICALLY INDISPENSABLE BOOK

The INDISPENSABLE BOOK OF PRACTICAL LIFE SKILLS is packed with essential techniques and must-have methods, organized into an easy-to-navigate format and clearly explained with illustrated step-by-step instructions. You can quickly find the essential skill that fits your situation, read it, absorb it and get ready to ride to the rescue. It's indispensable. It's practical. And soon you will be, too...

ENTRIES

Whether it's fixing a puncture or chopping an onion, it's easy once you know how. Each entry talks and walks you through a skill that every fully functioning adult should have in their locker.

INTRODUCTION

Every topic and subject is introduced and explained, so that you're fully prepared to take all the information on board.

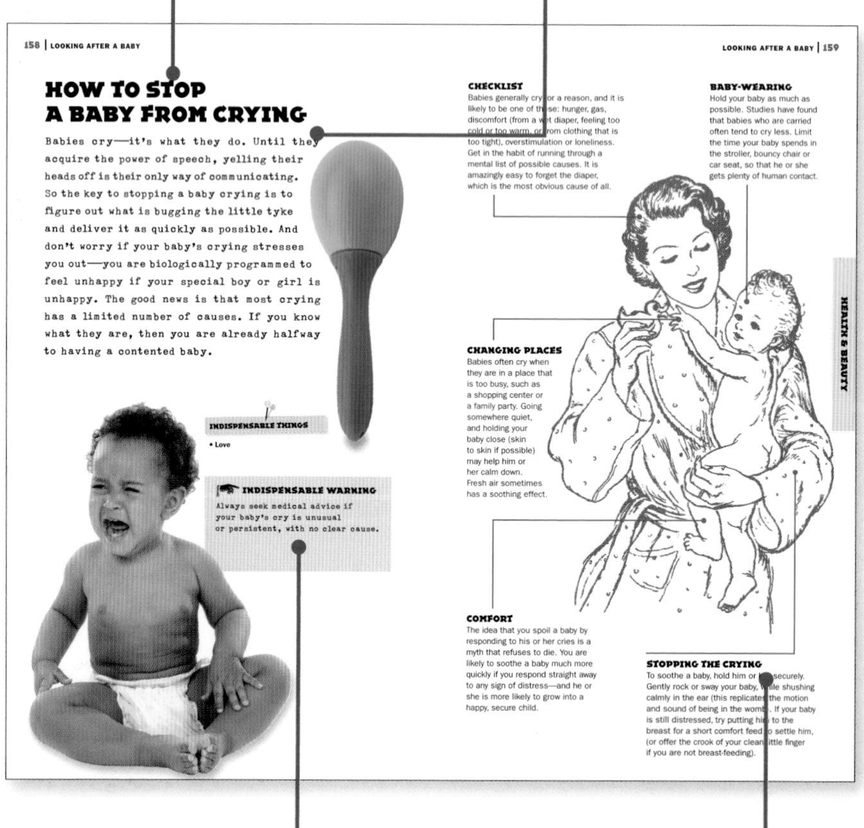

158 | LOOKING AFTER A BABY

HOW TO STOP A BABY FROM CRYING

Babies cry—it's what they do. Until they acquire the power of speech, yelling their heads off is their only way of communicating. So the key to stopping a baby crying is to figure out what is bugging the little tyke and deliver it as quickly as possible. And don't worry if your baby's crying stresses you out—you are biologically programmed to feel unhappy if your special boy or girl is unhappy. The good news is that most crying has a limited number of causes. If you know what they are, then you are already halfway to having a contented baby.

INDISPENSABLE THINGS

- Love

INDISPENSABLE WARNING

Always seek medical advice if your baby's cry is unusual or persistent, with no clear cause.

LOOKING AFTER A BABY | 159

CHECKLIST

Babies generally cry for a reason, and it is likely to be one of these: hunger, gas, discomfort (from a wet diaper, feeling too cold or too warm, or from clothing that is too tight), overstimulation or loneliness. Get in the habit of running through a mental list of possible causes. It is amazingly easy to forget the diaper, which is the most obvious cause of all.

BABY-WEARING

Hold your baby as much as possible. Studies have found that babies who are carried often tend to cry less. Limit the time your baby spends in the stroller, bouncy chair or car seat, so that he or she gets plenty of human contact.

CHANGING PLACES

Babies often cry when they are in a place that is too busy, such as a shopping center or a family party. Going somewhere quiet, and holding your baby close (skin to skin if possible) may help him or her calm down. Fresh air sometimes has a soothing effect.

COMFORT

The idea that you spoil a baby by responding to his or her cries is a myth that refuses to die. You are likely to soothe a baby much more quickly if you respond straight away to any sign of distress—and he or she is more likely to grow into a happy, secure child.

STOPPING THE CRYING

To soothe a baby, hold him or her securely. Gently rock or sway your baby, while shushing calmly in the ear (this replicates the motion and sound of being in the womb). If your baby is still distressed, try putting him to the breast for a short comfort feed to settle him, (or offer the crook of your clean little finger if you are not breast-feeding).

HEALTH & BEAUTY

PRACTICAL TIPS & INDISPENSABLE WARNINGS

Skills can be made easier with a little inside information. Tips provided will help keep you safe, and there are some dire warnings, too.

INSTRUCTIONS

Each procedure is divided into clear steps so that even the most impractical will find it easy to grasp the basics.

CHAPTERS

Each section is subdivided into chapters, to narrow down the area of interest. You can navigate your way into the Home & Garden section (In the Home, In the Kitchen, In the Garden); Health & Beauty (Looking After Clothes, Looking After You, Looking After a Baby); Travel & Sports (On the Road, Fun & Games, In the Wild); and Accident & Emergency (Going to the Rescue, Dealing with Emergencies, Surviving in Extremes).

SECTION DIVIDERS

The book is divided into four colour-coded sections by theme: Home & Garden (green), Health & Beauty (yellow), Travel & Sports (blue), Accident & Emergency (purple). The coloured tabs on the right-hand side of the pages make each section instantly accessible.

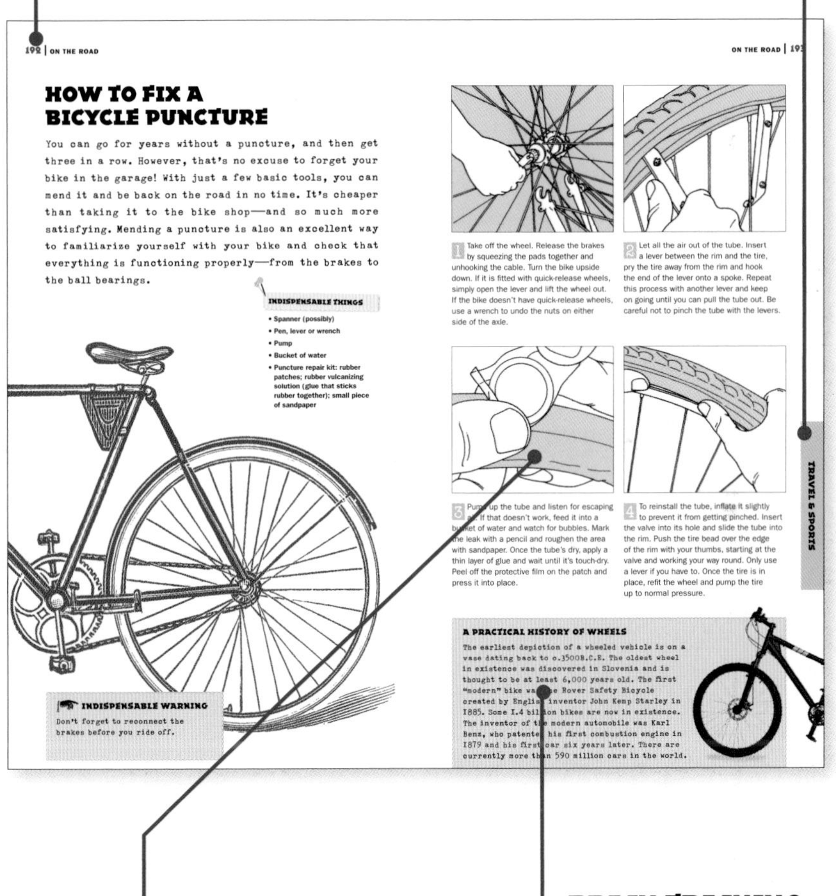

192 | ON THE ROAD

HOW TO FIX A BICYCLE PUNCTURE

You can go for years without a puncture, and then get three in a row. However, that's no excuse to forget your bike in the garage! With just a few basic tools, you can mend it and be back on the road in no time. It's cheaper than taking it to the bike shop—and so much more satisfying. Mending a puncture is also an excellent way to familiarize yourself with your bike and check that everything is functioning properly—from the brakes to the ball bearings.

INDISPENSABLE THINGS

- Spanner (possibly)
- Pen, lever or wrench
- Pump
- Bucket of water
- Puncture repair kit: rubber patches; rubber vulcanizing solution (glue that sticks rubber together); small piece of sandpaper

INDISPENSABLE WARNING

Don't forget to reconnect the brakes before you ride off.

ON THE ROAD | 193

1 Take off the wheel. Release the brakes by squeezing the pads together and unhooking the cable. Turn the bike upside down. If it is fitted with quick-release wheels, simply open the lever and lift the wheel out. If the bike doesn't have quick-release wheels, use a wrench to undo the nuts on either side of the axle.

2 Let all the air out of the tube. Insert a lever between the rim and the tire, pry the tire away from the rim and hook the end of the lever onto a spoke. Repeat this process with another lever and keep on going until you can pull the tube out. Be careful not to pinch the tube with the levers.

3 Pump up the tube and listen for escaping air. If that doesn't work, feed it into a bucket of water and watch for bubbles. Mark the leak with a pencil and roughen the area with sandpaper. Once the tube's dry, apply a thin layer of glue and wait until it's touch-dry. Peel off the protective film on the patch and press it into place.

4 To reinstall the tube, inflate it slightly to prevent it from getting pinched. Insert the valve into its hole and slide the tube into the rim. Push the tire bead over the edge of the rim with your thumbs, starting at the valve and working your way round. Only use a lever if you have to. Once the tire is in place, refit the wheel and pump the tire up to normal pressure.

A PRACTICAL HISTORY OF WHEELS

The earliest depiction of a wheeled vehicle is on a vase dating back to c.3500B.C.E. The oldest wheel in existence was discovered in Slovenia and is thought to be at least 6,000 years old. The first "modern" bike was the Rover Safety Bicycle created by English inventor John Kemp Starley in 1885. Some 1.4 billion bikes are now in existence. The inventor of the modern automobile was Karl Benz, who patented his first combustion engine in 1879 and his first car six years later. There are currently more than 590 million cars in the world.

TRAVEL & SPORTS

ILLUSTRATIONS

Step-by-step illustrations demonstrate and instruct so that you can follow the whole process visually from start to finish making it easy to learn and impossible to forget.

BRAIN TRAINING

A panel contains historical facts and trivia, for those who like their practical learning accompanied by a quick exercise in brain training.

HOME & GARDEN

IN THE HOME

Save money on paying professionals and rise to the challenge of home maintenance and repair with this indispensable chapter on easy fixes around the house. From keeping your home clean to unblocking a sink, all the essential tasks are covered, with easy-to-follow instructions, equipment checklists and top tips.

HOW TO CLEAN THE OVEN

Cleaning the oven is an arduous, dirty job that few people relish, so practise prevention to save yourself some elbow grease. Line the bottom of the oven with aluminium foil to catch crumbs and splatters, and wipe away any spills as soon as you can. But even the most vigilant will still need to deep-clean the oven regularly — once a month is best before there's too much build-up and food becomes baked on and difficult to shift.

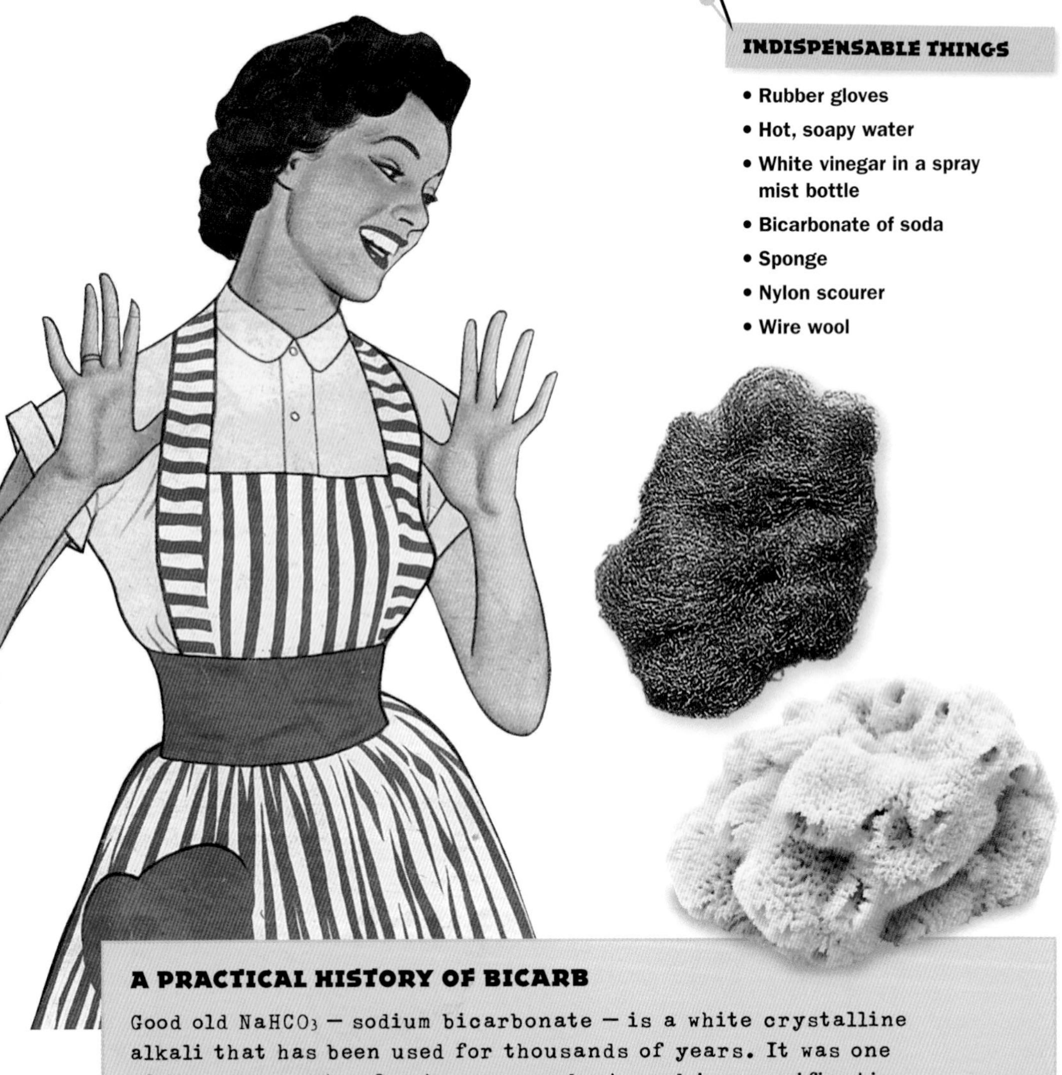

INDISPENSABLE THINGS

- Rubber gloves
- Hot, soapy water
- White vinegar in a spray mist bottle
- Bicarbonate of soda
- Sponge
- Nylon scourer
- Wire wool

A PRACTICAL HISTORY OF BICARB

Good old $NaHCO_3$ — sodium bicarbonate — is a white crystalline alkali that has been used for thousands of years. It was one of the components of natron, a product used in mummification, and used to be taken medicinally to treat a variety of minor ailments. Best known today as a raising agent in baking, the fizzy, scouring action of bicarbonate of soda also makes it the perfect ingredient in an amazing array of commercial household products, from toothpaste to toilet cleaners. Its continued popularity arises from a combination of its proven effectiveness and the fact that it's a natural, environmentally safe substance.

SURFACES
Prevent grease build-up by wiping all outside surfaces with hot, soapy water.

HOOD
Put metal filters from the hood in the dishwasher or scrub clean with hot, soapy water.

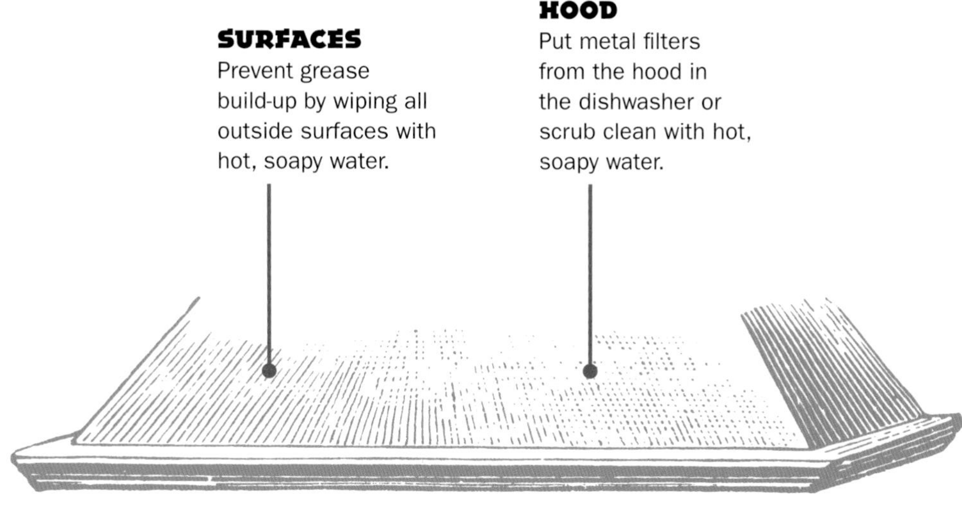

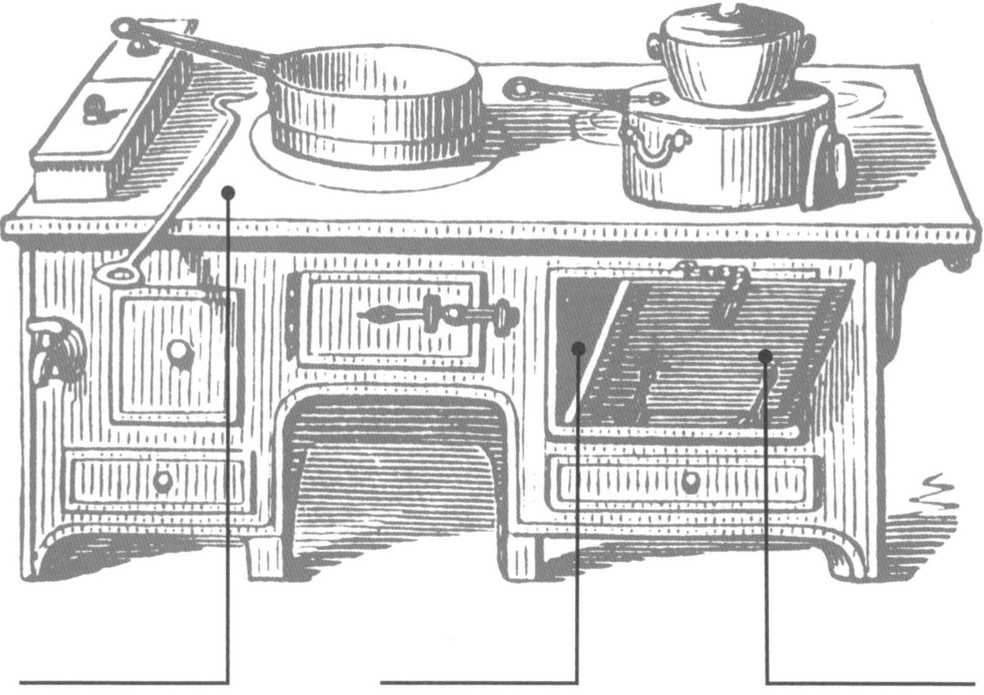

HOB
Wipe up spills when they occur (taking care not to burn yourself) and always wipe down the hob after cooking. Depending on the type of hob you have, dismantle gas rings and use a nylon scourer and hot, soapy water; ceramic hobs can simply be wiped clean with a cloth dipped in hot, soapy water.

OVEN
Before you begin, make sure the oven is completely cool. Put on your rubber gloves. If you don't want to use harsh chemicals, a mixture of bicarbonate of soda and white vinegar will do the trick. Lightly moisten the oven interior with water, then sprinkle with a thick layer of bicarbonate of soda. Leave for about 3 hours, then spray with the vinegar. Leave for a couple more hours, then simply wipe out with a damp sponge and warm water. You still need to rinse out the oven, but at least the next time you cook there won't be a residual smell or taste of oven cleaner!

OVEN DOOR
Make a paste of bicarbonate of soda and water and apply to stains. Leave for 10 minutes, then scrub clean with wire wool and rinse off with a clean sponge and hot water.

HOW TO KEEP THE HOUSE CLEAN AND TIDY

A clean and tidy home will help you feel more relaxed, calm and organized, but it's essential to find the cleaning system that suits your personal schedule so you can stick to it. Some people like to do a major blitz once a week, others prefer little and often. Kitchens and bathrooms are the rooms that make your house look dirty, so try to keep these sparkling, then follow a room-by-room to-do list so you can put your feet up sooner rather than later.

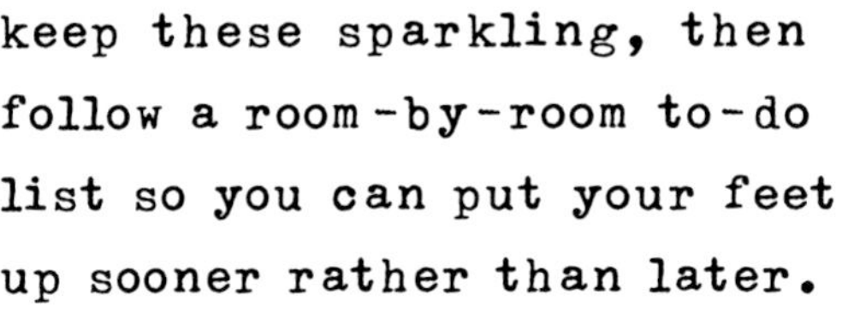

INDISPENSABLE THINGS

- Dustpan and brush
- Broom
- Bucket and mop
- Vacuum cleaner
- Paper towels
- Spray cleaner
- Disinfectant
- Non-abrasive cream cleaner
- Dusters and microfibre cloths
- Polish
- Sponges
- Scourers
- Rubber gloves

A PRACTICAL HISTORY OF THE VACUUM CLEANER

The Victorian era brought with it an increased understanding of the connection between cleanliness and germs, and various machines were invented to clean carpets, including huge horse-drawn contraptions that had to be parked outside the house. In 1907 James Murray Spengler invented a portable electric vacuum cleaner, which was little more than a pillowcase attached to a fan and a box, but crucially it incorporated a rotating brush. He sold the patent to his cousin's husband, William Hoover, the following year, and today the word 'hoover' is synonymous with vacuuming.

BATHROOM
Make cleaning the sink part of your daily routine, just like brushing your teeth. Rinse out the bath or shower, wipe the mirror, and pour some cleaner round the toilet bowl. Change and replace wet or dirty towels.

KITCHEN
Always start with the sink. Keep it empty and clean, and you'll be inspired to load plates into the dishwasher, wipe down surfaces and remove kitchen clutter from worktops. Sweep and mop the floor.

BEDROOM
Always make the bed. Fold and put away clothes and clear clutter from your bedside table. Invest in good-quality cleaning products such as microfibre cloths, which are much more effective than old tea towels.

HALLWAY
Institute a house rule whereby everyone leaves their shoes by the door – this will keep unwanted bacteria, chemicals and dust and dirt from being trodden all over the house. Make spot-cleaning a habit: wipe away smudges on walls, skirting boards and floors as and when you see them.

LIVING ROOM
Plump up cushions, recycle newspapers and remove objects from the floor. Put felt pads under items of furniture so you can move them easily for cleaning. When dusting, always put a dab of polish on the cloth, otherwise you'll just shift the dirt around.

HOW TO PUT UP SHELVES

If you lack storage space, putting up a few shelves can make all the difference, but it's essential to put them up right. An improperly put-up shelf won't last long and can be a safety hazard. To reduce the chance of sagging, shelves need to be at least 18mm (3/4in) thick and have brackets every 600mm (24in) for adequate support. Plywood and timber shelves are less likely to sag than chipboard or MDF.

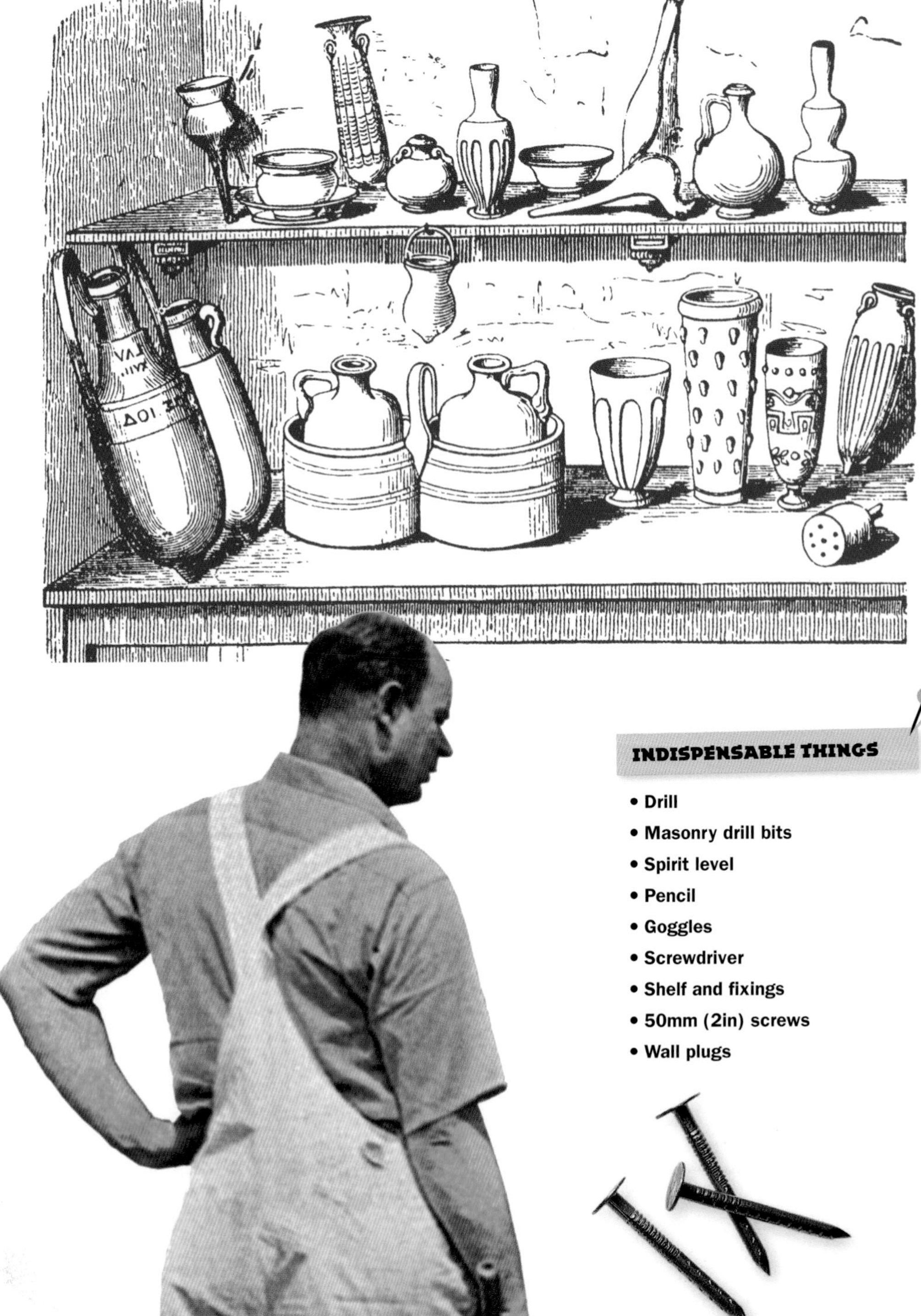

INDISPENSABLE THINGS

- Drill
- Masonry drill bits
- Spirit level
- Pencil
- Goggles
- Screwdriver
- Shelf and fixings
- 50mm (2in) screws
- Wall plugs

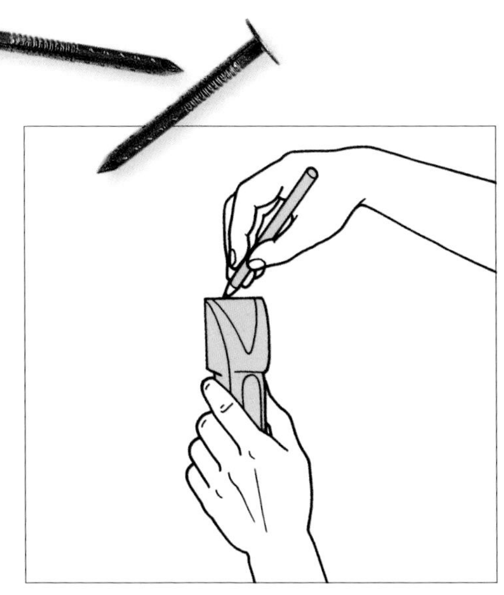

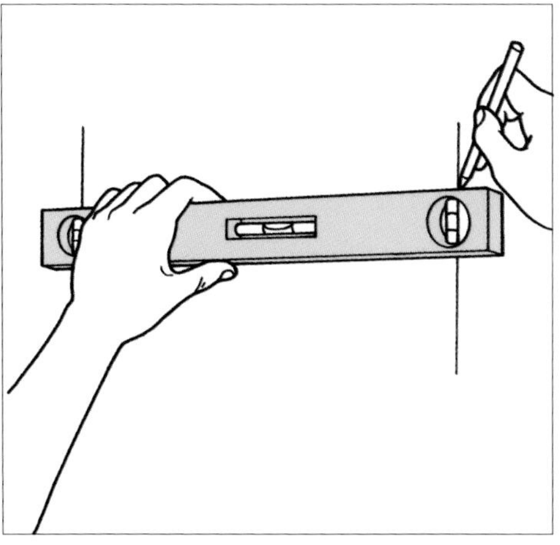

1 The most important step is to establish how much weight the shelf will bear, because shelves that will hold heavy loads can only be fixed to a masonry wall. If you have plasterboard walls, you must secure shelving to the studs in the wall – use a studfinder or knock along the wall with your knuckles until you hear a solid thud.

2 Paint the shelves before fixing them to the wall. Decide the position of each shelf, depending on what you want them to hold. Use a spirit level and a pencil to mark a pencil line on the wall where the shelf is to go. Mark the bracket positions on the line.

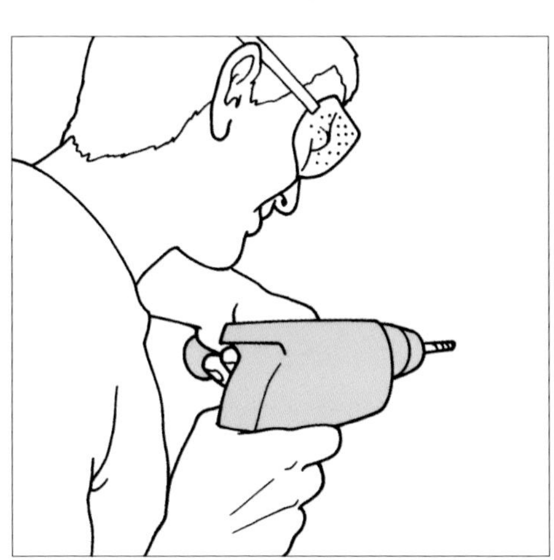

3 Put on your goggles, choose a masonry drill bit that matches the wall plug fixing size, and drill into the wall – but never start drilling until you are sure there are no electrical cables or pipes hidden behind the plaster. Drill holes to the depth of the plug.

4 Insert the plug, if using, and screw the fixing brackets to the wall. Make sure the screws grip firmly. If not, try using a larger wall plug or cavity fixing. Attach shelves with screws or panel pins so that they cannot tip forward when loaded.

A PRACTICAL HISTORY OF SHELVES

The simple and utilitarian nature of the humble shelf means they can be found in nearly every home. The existence of open wooden shelving can be traced back thousands of years to ancient Mesopotamia, where they were used to store official documents inscribed on clay tablets. However, it wasn't until the development of the printing press in the Middle Ages that books, and shelves to house them securely, became more commonplace. The oldest bookshelves in existence, dating from the end of the 16th century, are in the Bodleian Library, Oxford University.

HOW TO DRAUGHTPROOF THE FRONT DOOR

For lower bills and fewer chills, draughtproofing your front door is a simple DIY job that can make a big difference in cold weather. There is often a gap between the door and the frame, and even more air is let in by cat flaps, keyholes and letterboxes. So take a little time to draughtproof your front door, and keep in the heat, save energy and reduce your impact on the environment.

INDISPENSABLE THINGS

- Nylon brush draught excluder
- Hacksaw
- Phillips screwdriver
- Self-adhesive foam strip
- Escutcheon plate
- Letterbox cover

DOORFRAME
Wash down with warm, soapy water and leave to dry. Then press self-adhesive foam strip into place along the top and side of the door frame and cut to fit. This compresses to eliminate draughts when the door is shut. It's a cheap option, but will need replacing every couple of years.

DOOR
Hold the draught excluder along the inside of the bottom of the door and mark the length required from edge to edge, less about 5mm (1/4in). Cut the draught excluder with a hacksaw to fit. Secure to the bottom of the door with the screws provided with the draught excluder.

KEYHOLE
Fit an escutcheon plate to cover the keyhole.

LETTERBOX
Fit a letterbox cover to the inside of the door, making sure your post can still pass through the gap.

HOW TO FIX A WOBBLY CHAIR

There are usually two reasons why a chair is wobbly. One of the legs may have worn down more than the others, and all you need to do is sand away until all legs are of equal length. In other cases, the joints have become loose through wear and tear, which takes a little longer to fix.

INDISPENSABLE THINGS

- Newspaper or tarpaulin
- Different grades of sandpaper
- Tape measure and pencil
- Hammer
- Wood glue
- Damp cloth
- Clamp

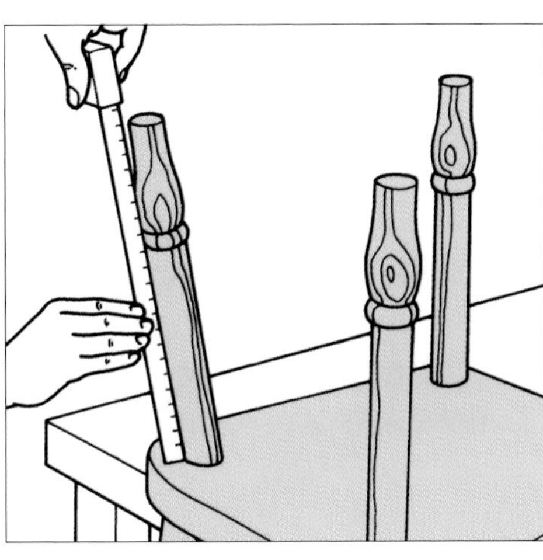

1 Spread a table with newspaper or tarpaulin and place the chair on it, turned upside down. Carefully measure the length of each leg to find out which is the short one, mark the other three legs to the same length, then sand down with coarse sandpaper until all are equal.

2 For loose joints, remove whatever has lost its grip (the wobbly leg or arm) and sand the top of it with fine sandpaper until all the old glue is removed. Use fine sandpaper to lightly sand the inside of the joint, then wipe away the wood dust.

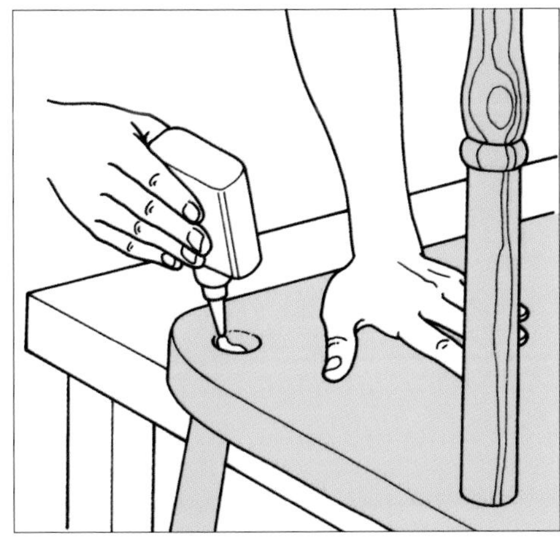

3 Squeeze some wood glue into the hole and insert the arm or leg, turning it a couple of times to make sure the glue is evenly distributed. Wipe away any excess glue with a damp cloth and clamp the joint to keep it in place until it dries. Don't sit on the chair for a day or two.

HOW TO HANG CURTAINS

How you hang your curtains can make a huge difference to the way a room looks. Not only will they reflect your style and personality, but there are also tricks that can make your room look bigger and let in the maximum amount of light, if that is the effect you want. You will need at least one curtain hook or ring per 10cm (4in) of fabric, so although these are usually supplied with the track or pole, buy extra. Make sure you have a sturdy stepladder to stand on and someone standing at ground level to take the weight of the curtains as you hang them.

INDISPENSABLE THINGS

- Stepladder
- An extra pair of hands
- Drill, wall plugs and screws
- Curtain pole or track
- Curtains
- Extra hooks and rings

1 Hanging the rod above the moulding makes the window and ceiling appear taller, and prevents the messy heading of the curtain being visible to the outside world. Mark the position of the pole on the wall at least 8cm (3½in) above the window and drill, plug and screw the pole brackets into place. Slide the pole into the brackets, then hang your curtains.

2 For a look that maximizes light, hang the curtains wide of the actual window frame by extending the rod anywhere from 25–40cm (10–18in) on each side. This way, when you push back the curtains, you will be able to see the whole window.

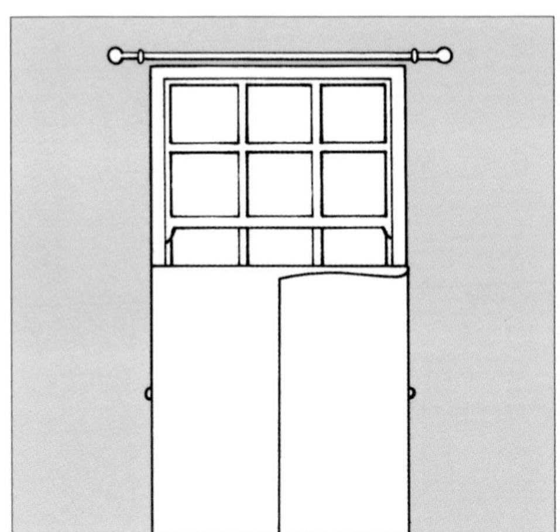

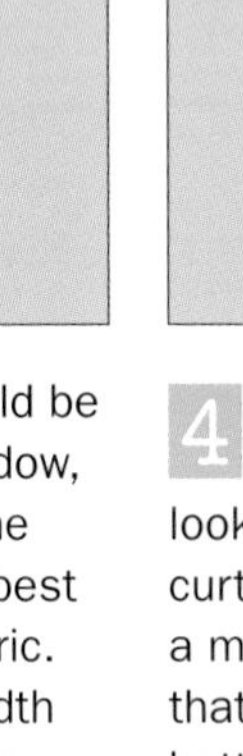

3 Calculating how wide a curtain should be involves not only the size of the window, but how much fullness you want when the curtains are closed. Curtains look their best when there is a generous amount of fabric. Standard curtains use 1½ × window width for each panel. If your curtains hang wide of the window, each curtain should be twice the window width.

PRACTICAL TIP

Always take the time to iron your curtains before hanging them up – they'll look much neater. For heavy drapes, choose sturdy curtain poles that won't sag.

4 Small variations in curtain length can make a big difference to how your room looks. For a streamlined, tailored look, your curtains should just hit the floor. If you prefer a more homely look, add 4cm (1½in) so that the fabric bunches up a bit at the bottom. If your curtains have heading tape at the top, draw the threads to make gathers. Put one curtain up and adjust the threads until the curtain is halfway across the pole or track. Tie the threads loosely together. Repeat with the other curtain. This ensures that the curtains will meet in the middle when closed.

HOW TO HANG A PICTURE

Putting your pictures up properly is more important than you might think – one that is crooked or misplaced will always draw the eye, and not in a good way. First, decide where to hang the picture. If in doubt, make a template the same size as your picture and place it where you think you might like to hang the real thing. Avoid hanging one small picture on a huge expanse of wall – small pictures will look better when grouped together.

INDISPENSABLE THINGS

- Tape measure
- Pencil
- Picture hooks or hangers
- Hammer and nails
- Spirit level

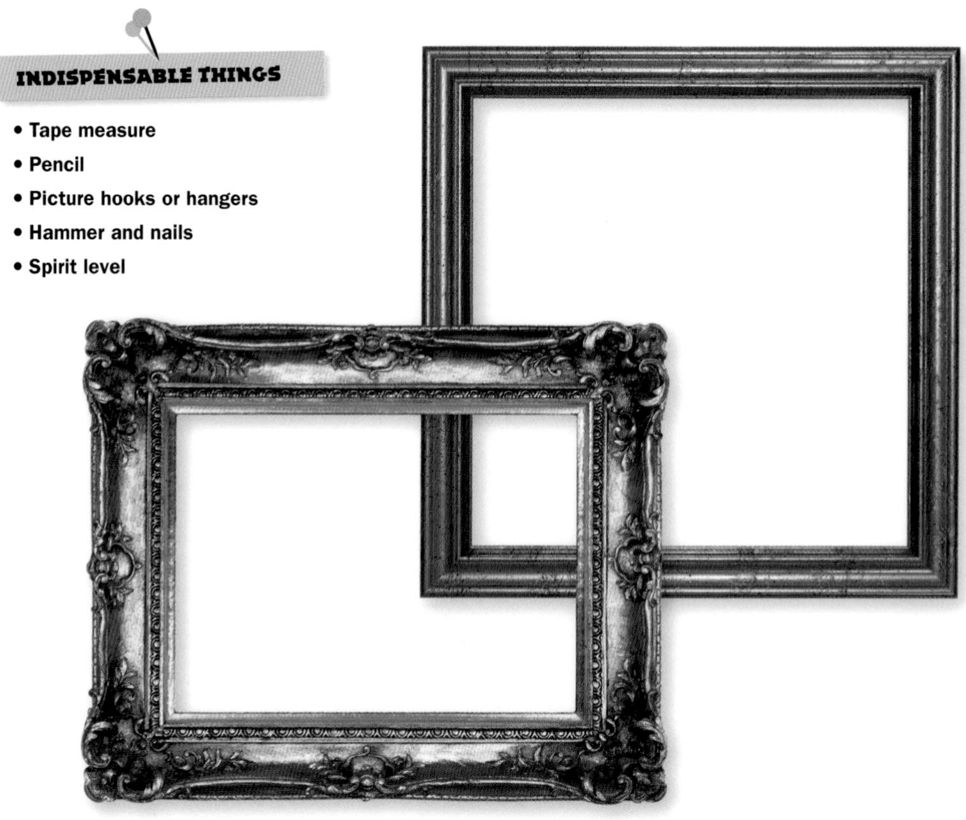

A PRACTICAL HISTORY OF HANGING ART

Museums have often hung pictures upside down by mistake, particularly if the art is abstract. The most famous case is that of Matisse's *Le Bateau*, which hung upside down at the Museum of Modern Art in New York for 47 days in 1961. *Long Grass with Butterflies* by Van Gogh briefly hung upside down in London's National Gallery in 1965. But in the 2008 Rothko exhibition at the Tate Modern in London, two of the artist's best-known works were deliberately displayed on their side, contrary to the artist's original intentions.

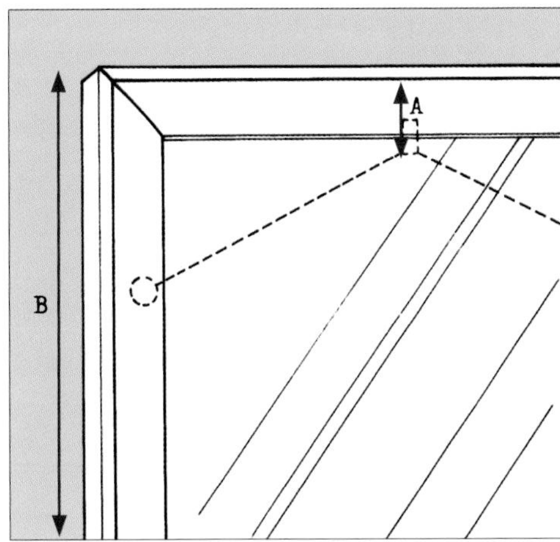

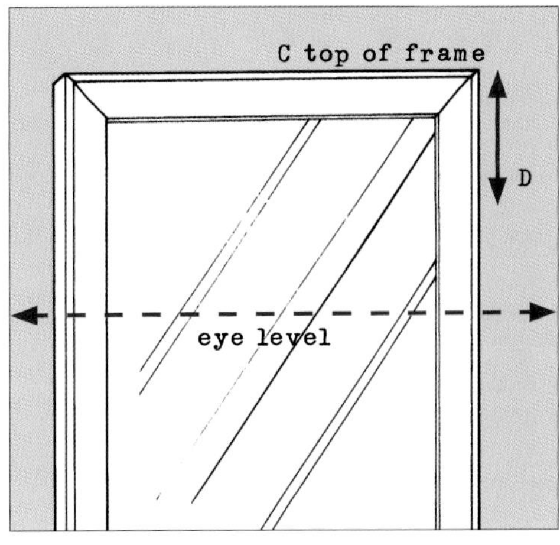

1 Measure the distance between the wire at full tension – or from the hanging tab if that's what the picture has – to the frame's top edge (A). Large pictures will need two hangers instead of one for stability, so when you measure this distance, spread the wire out to two different points where the wire will rest on hangers. Measure from the top of the frame to both points of tension to get your height. Measure the height of your frame (B) and halve the result.

2 From the floor, measure up the wall to 170cm (66in), the average adult eye-level, and make a pencil mark. From this mark, measure upwards half the height of the frame and make a second pencil mark (C). From the second mark, measure downwards the distance recorded in step 1 (from the wire at full tension to the frame's top edge) and make a third mark (D). Place nail and hanger here.

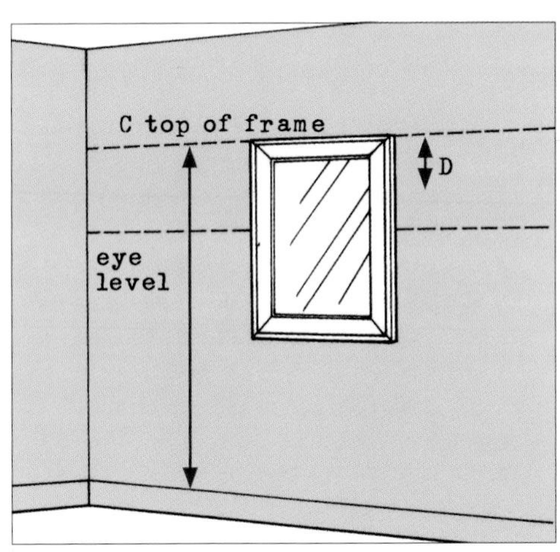

3 Make sure that the bottom of your hanger, rather than the nail point, is resting on the third pencil mark (D) when you hammer your nail in because this is where your wire will rest. If you are hanging a heavy picture, make sure you use the right hangers: standard sizes generally support 2.2–4.5kg (5–10lb) of weight. Use a spirit level to make absolutely sure your picture is hanging straight.

HOW TO LAY A FIRE

The key to laying a successful fire is to use materials that are perfectly dry and to arrange them so as to leave plenty of air space – if the supply of oxygen is cut off, the fire will not burn. But take care: fires get very hot! Use a mesh guard on an open fireplace, and never leave children unsupervised by a fire.

INDISPENSABLE THINGS

- Fireplace
- Newspaper, firelighters or cinders
- Kindling
- Logs (and coal)
- Matches

LIGHTING THE FIRE

Make sure the flue is open or you will fill the house with smoke. Light a match and hold it to the newspaper or firelighters. Blow slightly at the base of the kindling to spread the fire. When the crackling has died down and the flames are large and well established, add some larger logs or coal.

BOTTOM LAYER

Place two or three firelighters or a few sheets of crumpled-up newspaper on the bottom of the grate. Some cinders (small pieces of partly burnt coal or wood from the previous fire) will help the fire start quickly and easily.

KINDLING

Place small kindling (thin twigs or wood shavings) on top of the bottom layer and criss-cross it so there is plenty of air space between each piece. The more kindling you have, the better.

LOGS

Create a tent shape on top of the kindling with two of your smaller logs. Hardwoods such as oak, cherry or apple burn much hotter and longer than softwoods (pine, cedar).

HOW TO CHANGE A LIGHT BULB

To carry out this simple task, make sure you've got the right bulb for the job. Keep a supply of spare bulbs of appropriate wattage in the house, then you'll never be left in the dark. Turn off the light or lamp at the wall or mains socket and let the bulb cool. Hold the bulb in a cloth when changing it, in case it shatters in your hand.

INDISPENSABLE THINGS

- **Replacement light bulb**
- **Clean, dry cloth**

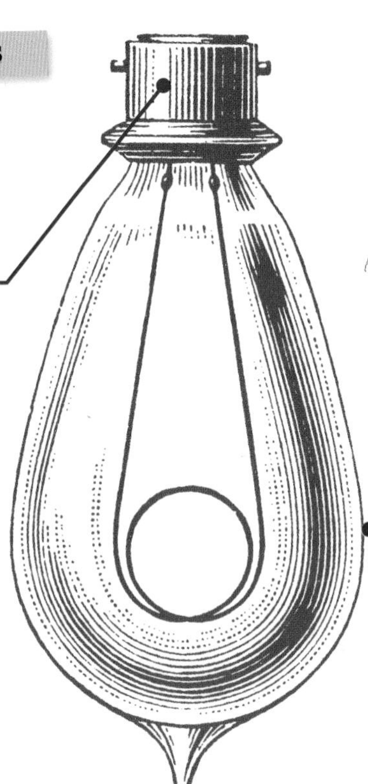

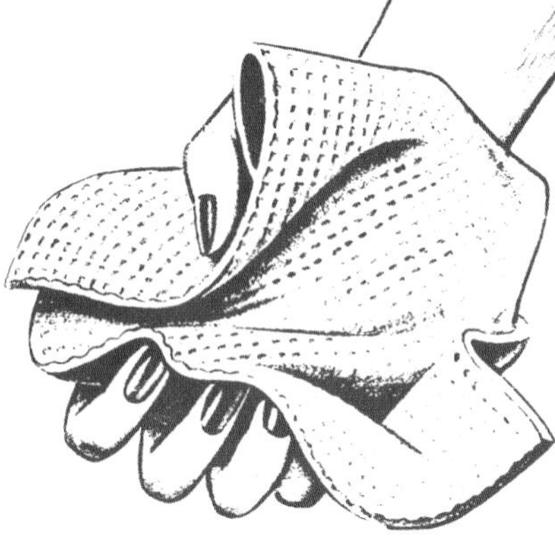

INSERTING

Insert a new bulb and turn it clockwise until secure. Turn the lamp back on to make sure the bulb works. Wrap the old bulb in newspaper before putting it in the bin, so you can dispose of it safely.

REMOVING

Cover the bulb with a cloth, grasp the bulb firmly and twist it gently in an anti-clockwise direction until it is released from the socket.

A PRACTICAL HISTORY OF THE LIGHT BULB

Until the 19th century, artificial lighting came in the form of candles, oil lanterns and gas lamps. The American inventor Thomas Edison didn't invent the light bulb, but he did develop the first light bulb for home use that was practical, safe and economical. In 1879, using a small, carbonized filament, an improved vacuum inside the globe and a lower current of electricity, he introduced a reliable, long-lasting source of light.

HOW TO HANG WALLPAPER

Nothing changes the appearance of a room quite as dramatically as a well-chosen wallpaper. For a professional look, a little preparation goes a long way. Always remove any old wallpaper and clean the surfaces to be covered, repairing any holes or cracks, then size the walls (apply a coat of diluted wallpaper paste). Do any painting (e.g. ceiling, woodwork) first because it's easier to remove paste than paint, and calculate how many rolls of paper you need before you begin.

INDISPENSABLE THINGS

- Wallpaper
- Tape measure
- Pasting table
- Pasting brush
- Wallpaper paste
- Paper-hanging brush
- Scissors
- Plumb line
- Seam roller
- Sponge

A PRACTICAL HISTORY OF WALLPAPER

During the Middle Ages, wealthy people used fabric to cover walls and windows to keep draughts out. Wallpaper came into being as a cheap substitute for tapestry and wood panelling, and its use in Europe is thought to date back to the 1400s. The first wallpapers were small squares with images on them printed by wood blocks, which were then coloured in by hand. The paper was not attached directly to the wall, but was pasted on to sheets of linen that were then attached to the walls with tacks.

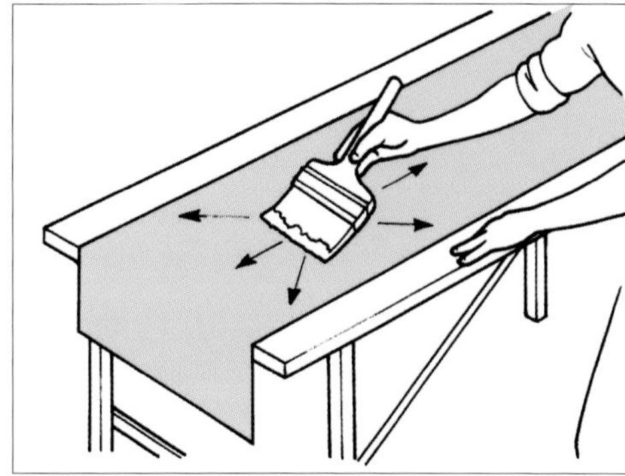

1 Cut your first length of wallpaper so it overlaps the ceiling and skirting by at least 5cm (2in) at each end. When you cut each subsequent length, take into account any patterns. Using a pasting table and pasting brush, apply wallpaper paste to the paper, making sure you paste right up to the edges.

2 Begin with your least noticeable wall. Use a plumb line to guide you so that you know where the strips of wallpaper should meet. Slide the paper on to the wall, but take care not to stretch the paper while you are positioning it.

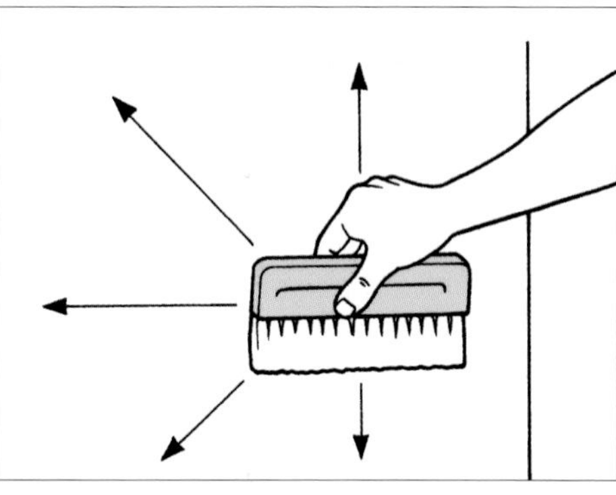

3 Use a paper-hanging brush to smooth out any air bubbles, working from the centre out. If air bubbles remain, or the paper doesn't appear to be straight, gently pull back the paper and smooth it down again.

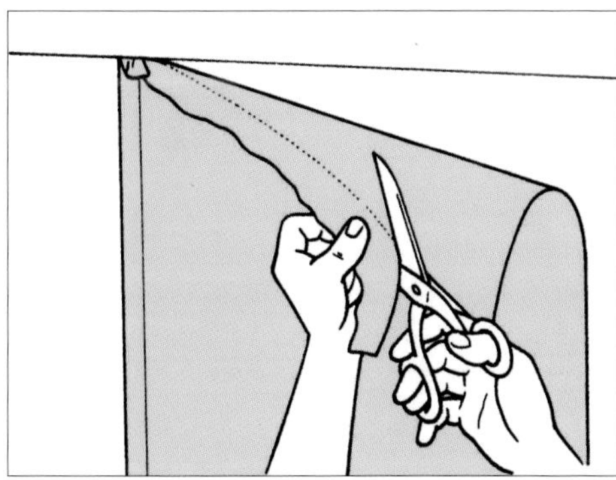

4 Using your scissors, carefully trim off any excess at the top and bottom. Follow the same procedure to put up subsequent strips of wallpaper, making sure you match the pattern exactly.

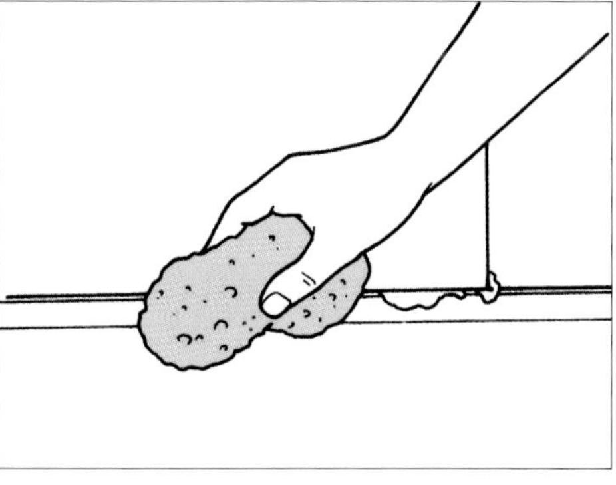

5 Wipe off any excess paste with a damp sponge as you go along, and seal the matching edges with a seam roller after hanging each piece of wallpaper. Make sure that you wipe off any excess paste from the woodwork as well.

HOW TO ARRANGE FLOWERS

You can put fresh flowers in almost any container to make an attractive and stylish arrangement. Choose flowers in different stages of development, from bud to full bloom, and use different shapes, colours and textures for a more interesting look. For maximum freshness, lightly spray your arrangement with water occasionally, to create a humid atmosphere around the flowers. Add flower food when you first arrange them and then every time after changing the water. Keep flowers out of direct sunlight and away from heat because these will speed up the wilting process. Remove and discard dying blooms when necessary.

INDISPENSABLE THINGS

- Flowers and foliage
- Container
- Waterproof mat
- Secateurs or sharp knife
- Water
- Household bleach
- Sugar
- Spray mist bottle

PREPARING THE FLOWERS

Cut at least 2.5cm (1in) from the bottom of each stem at an angle; this will give a larger surface area so the flowers can take up water with ease. With woody stems such as hydrangeas, cut a slit at the end of the stem to facilitate water intake. Remove any leaves that will lie below the level of the water as this will help to keep the flowers fresh.

LINES, GLOBES AND FILLER

Put the larger, more dominant flowers (lines) in first to create the focus of the arrangement. Then add the smaller flowers (globes). Turn the flowers to different angles to add interest to the display. Keep the colours balanced and use foliage (filler) to fill any gaps, but don't overdo it.

WATER

Partially fill the container with water at room temperature and add flower food. Don't overfill the vessel; you can always top it up later. Change the water every three days and re-cut the stems.

FLOWER FOOD

Make your own with a few drops of household bleach and a tablespoon of sugar. The bleach will kill the bacteria and the sugar will help feed the flowers, making them open and bloom faster. Dissolve in a mug of hot water and add to the container.

CONTAINER

Choose a container that's appropriate for your flowers – anything from a jam jar to a teapot or a bottle if you don't have a vase, but remember that smaller flowers look best in shorter, wider vessels whereas longer flowers look elegant in taller ones. Make sure the container has been thoroughly cleaned, and put down a waterproof mat if you intend to place it on a polished surface (never put on top of electrical appliances).

HOW TO FIX A DRIPPING TAP

A tap that drips is annoying, can leave nasty stains in the sink or bath, and is extremely wasteful – litres of water a day will go straight down the plug hole – so fixing a dripping tap is a job that needs to be done. If a tap drips from the spout, even after being turned off tightly, then it's likely that the washer needs replacing. But sorting out the problem yourself is easier than you think and you'll save on an expensive plumber's fee.

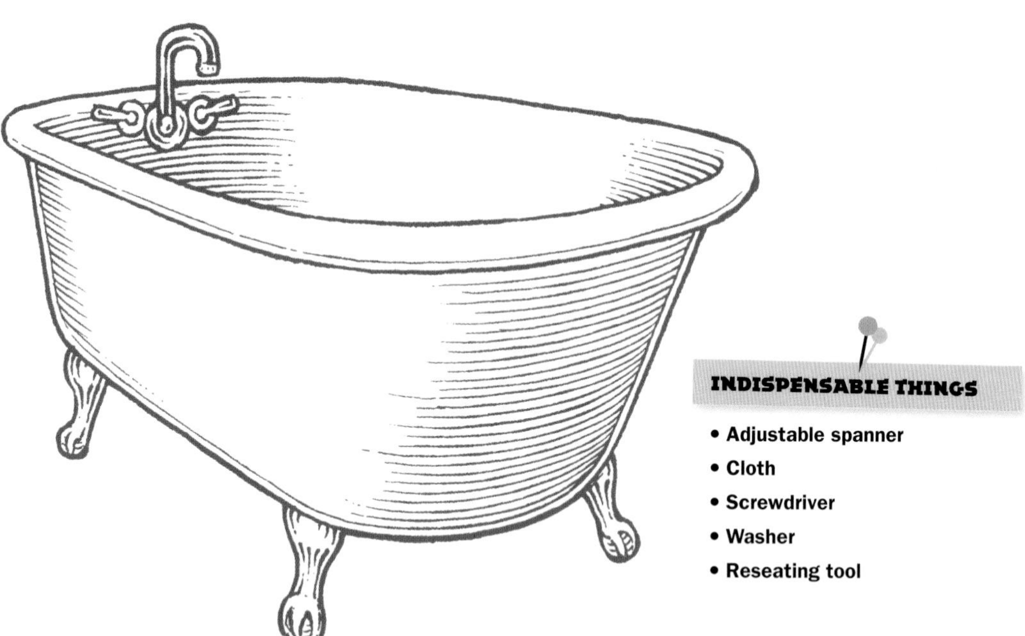

INDISPENSABLE THINGS

- Adjustable spanner
- Cloth
- Screwdriver
- Washer
- Reseating tool

A PRACTICAL HISTORY OF PLUMBING

Ancient civilizations in Egypt, Babylon, Greece, India and China had systems of providing potable water and waste drainage. The word 'plumber' comes from the Latin *plumbus* (lead) – the Romans developed lead piping, and public baths helped to spread a culture of cleanliness throughout their empire. As Western civilization stagnated during the Dark Ages, so did plumbing, and very little progress was made until the 19th century, when the importance of clean water and sanitation was once again recognized. The first screw-down tap was patented by Guest and Chrimes, a Rotherham brass foundry, in 1845.

PRACTICAL TIP

Remember to turn off the water supply or you will get drenched later on. Look under the sink or at the main water valve and turn the valve anti-clockwise. Turn on the tap to let out any water left in the pipes. Once it stops flowing, replace the plug to catch any small parts you may accidentally drop.

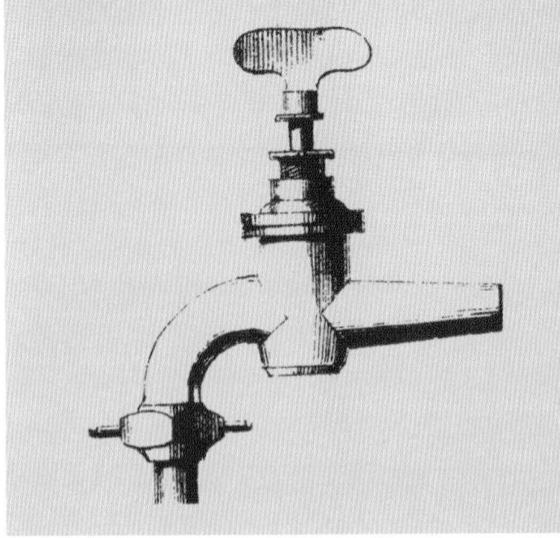

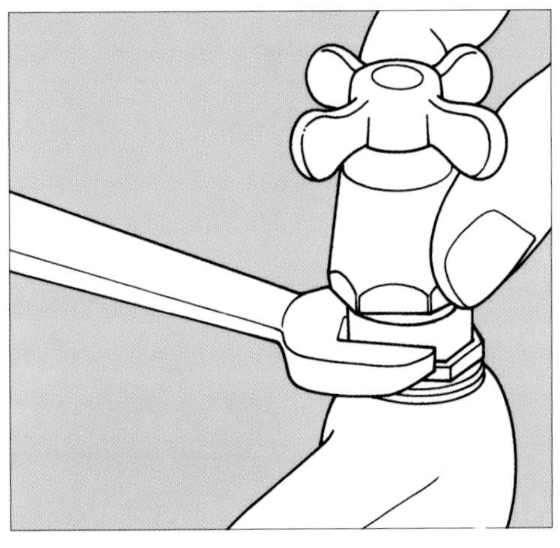

1 Take off the top of the tap. You may need to use an adjustable spanner to unscrew the large headgear nut, in which case, pad the jaws of the spanner with a cloth to avoid scratching the tap's metallic surface.

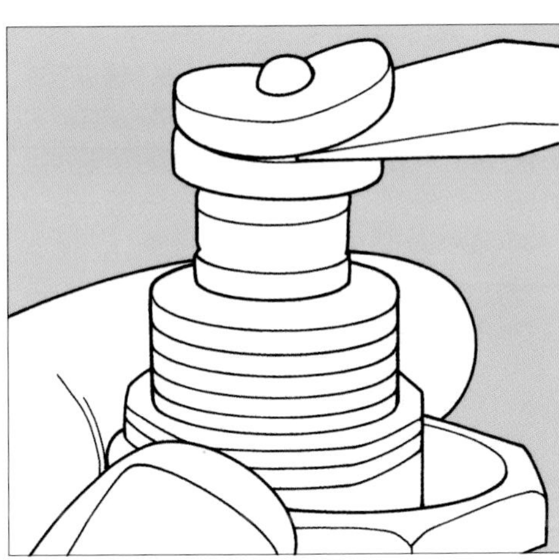

2 Using a screwdriver, prise off the old washer from underneath the headgear nut. Push a new washer of exactly the same size into place and screw the headgear back on to the tap, but do not over tighten. Replace the top of the tap and turn the water supply back on.

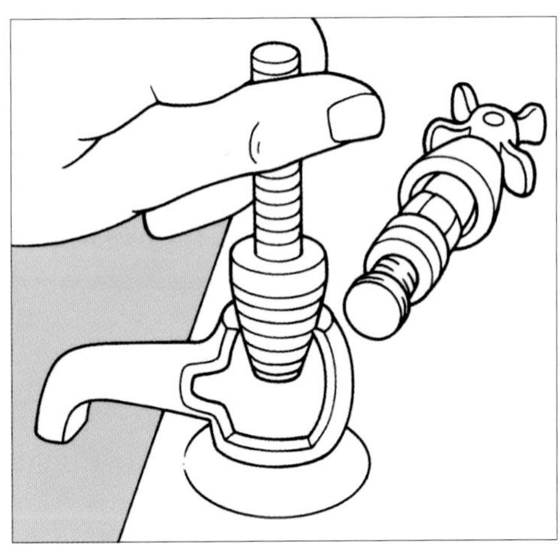

3 If the tap still drips, grit or general wear and tear has probably worn the seating. Buy a tap reseating tool, which is available from DIY stores. Push the end of the tool into the tap, adjust the cutter so it touches the seat and rotate it to grind down the metalwork. Reassemble the tap.

HOW TO CLEAN WINDOWS

Windows look best if cleaned on a regular basis, and sparkling clean windows can really make a difference to your home. Part of what makes window washing such a chore is that people insist on doing it with lots of suds, wads of newspaper and a ton of elbow grease. All that rubbing is a bad idea, because you're just moving dirt around from one spot to another and putting a static charge on the glass, which attracts dust and dirt.

INDISPENSABLE THINGS

- Water
- Toothbrush or cotton buds
- Washing-up liquid
- 2 plastic buckets
- Sponge
- Rubber gloves
- Squeegee
- Lint-free cloth or paper towels

A PRACTICAL HISTORY OF THE SQUEEGEE

The squeegee dates back to the Middle Ages, when fishermen scraped fish guts and water off boat decks with long-handled, wooden-bladed tools called 'squilgees'. It wasn't until the turn of the 20th century that window cleaners in America adopted a rubber-bladed version of the tool, which was needed to clean the windows of the newly developed skyscraper buildings. In 1936 Italian immigrant Ettore Steccone invented a light, brass-handled tool with a very flexible and sharp single rubber blade. The 'Ettore' squeegee remains a favourite among professional window cleaners.

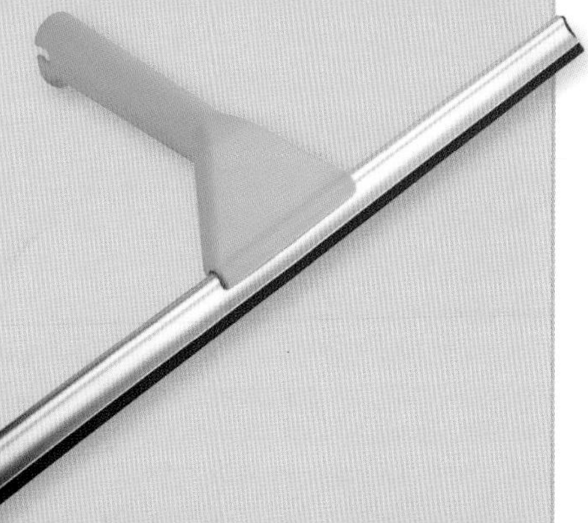

SILLS AND FRAMES

Make sure that the windowsills and frames are cleaned first. Dust and vacuum before wiping with a damp cloth to get rid of dirt and grime. Use a damp soft toothbrush or cotton bud to clean corners.

SPONGE CLEAN

Prepare a cleaning solution of just a squirt of washing-up liquid in a bucket of warm water. Dip a sponge into the bucket and wash the surface of the window, starting at the top and working down to the bottom. Never clean windows in direct sunlight, because the sun will dry the cleaner before it can be wiped away and there will be streaks.

SQUEEGEE

After sponging, dip a squeegee into a bucket of clean water. Press the squeegee lightly onto the surface of the window, starting at the top and pulling down vertically. Wipe the squeegee with a lint-free cloth or paper towel. Continue this process until the entire surface of the window has been cleaned, then pull the squeegee horizontally across the bottom section of the window. Wipe off the water at the bottom of the window frame.

AVOIDING STREAKS

Clean windows with up and down strokes on one side and side to side strokes on the other. This way, you can see which side has the streaks, instead of having to redo the whole window.

HOW TO UNBLOCK A SINK

You know you've got a blocked drain when the water drains away sluggishly or not at all. A blocked drain can be smelly and unhygienic, but the good news is that most of the time you don't need a plumber and it only takes a few minutes to get the water washing away freely again. You won't have to use expensive, toxic drain cleaners either, and these methods can also be used to clear blocked toilets. Begin by pouring boiling water into the sink. This will often clear the blockage – if this fails, follow these steps.

INDISPENSABLE THINGS

- Boiling water
- Plunger, drain auger or vacuum pump
- Bucket
- Brush
- Disinfectant
- Wrench (possibly)

PRACTICAL TIP

Prevention is better than cure, so to keep drains clear, pour a cup of washing soda crystals down the drain once a week followed by a kettle of boiling water to dissolve grease and prevent blockages from forming.

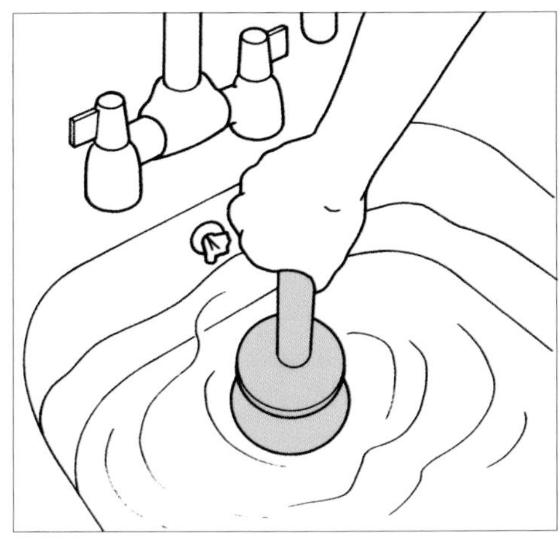

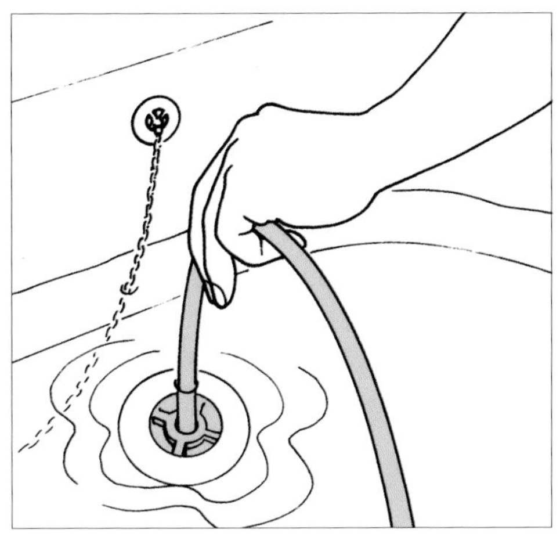

1 The plunger method involves, as you'd expect, an old-fashioned plunger, which is simply a rubber cup on the end of a stick that creates pressure in the waste pipe. Cover the plug hole with the sink plunger. Push until suction holds the cup in place. Plunge up and down quickly several times to create pulses of air and water that should suck or push the blockage out of the way. Remove the plunger and run the hot tap to clear out any remaining debris.

2 An auger is a coil of flexible wire that you insert into the plug hole. Push it down as far as it will go. Twirl the wire round, and this should dislodge any matter stuck in the trap and push it out into the waste pipe.

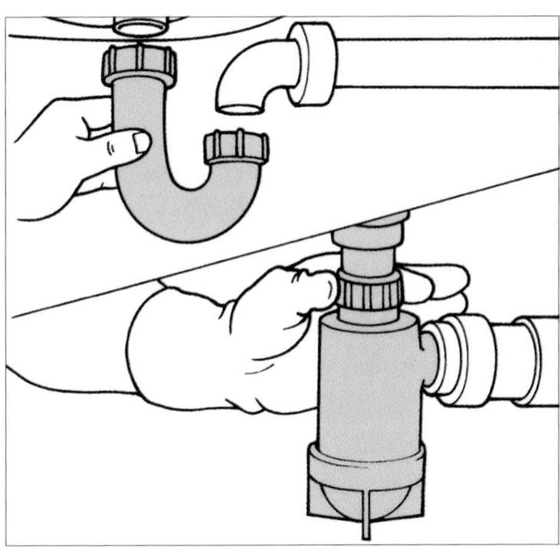

3 Alternatively, cover the plug hole with the end of a vacuum pump. Pull the pump handle up and push down to free the blockage. Remove the pump and run the hot tap to rinse away any debris.

4 If the plunger, auger and pump methods fail to clear the blockage, you'll need to remove the trap. Remove as much water from the sink as possible and put in the plug. Place the bucket under the trap. If you have a u-bend trap, loosen the fixings at either end (you may need to use a wrench) and gently pull the u-bend away from the other pipes. Empty any water from the u-bend into the bucket. Clean out the pipe with a brush and some disinfectant, then replace. If you have a bottleneck trap, untwist the fixings to remove the trap, empty the contents into the bucket and clean out the bottleneck with a brush and disinfectant. Replace the trap.

HOW TO REMOVE STAINS FROM CARPET

Most carpet stains can be removed with water and ordinary household items, although you may occasionally need to buy a specialist stain remover or have the carpet professionally cleaned. Many carpets have been treated with stain-resistant materials, so spills can be removed if you get them right away. However, the longer you delay, the more difficult removing carpet stains becomes. When treating stains, simply dab the offending spot – do not rub or scrub, or you will spread the stain and may damage the carpet. If you're not sure how to remove a carpet stain, always try plain water first.

INDISPENSABLE THINGS

- Water
- White vinegar
- Washing-up liquid
- Paper towels
- Ice cube
- Spoon or knife
- Hairdryer
- Clingfilm or plastic bag
- Brown paper bags
- White wine
- Milk

CHEWING GUM

Scrape as much of the residue off as you can with a knife or spoon. Leave an ice cube on the gum for a minute to freeze it. The gum should harden sufficiently so that it can be broken up and removed from the carpet. An alternative treatment is to heat the gum with a hairdryer, being careful not to melt the carpet fibres. Place a piece of clingfilm or a plastic bag on top of the gum, then pull up and discard.

AFTER-CARE

After all treatments, rinse the area well with clean water and dry with paper towels. Place a weight on top of the paper to speed up water absorption, or blow a fan or hair dryer over the top of the carpet. Brush clean and vacuum the carpet when the stain is dry to pick up any lingering particles.

RED WINE AND INK STAINS

For red wine, blot the remaining liquid with kitchen paper. Apply white wine to the spot. This recreates the initial conditions, especially on old stains, making it easier to remove. Mop up with paper towels and repeat. To treat ink stains, dab the area with a small amount of milk.

CANDLE WAX

Using a spoon or knife, scrape off as much wax as you can. Put a clean brown paper bag over the spot, and place a clothes iron on it, set on low. The wax will liquefy and transfer to the paper. Apply a new paper bag as often as necessary until all of the wax has been removed.

COFFEE STAINS

Soak up the excess with paper towels. Mix a few drops of washing-up liquid with 1 cup lukewarm water. Sponge the area with the detergent solution. Another method is to mix 1/3 cup white vinegar with 2/3 cup lukewarm water. Sponge the stained area with the vinegar solution.

HOW TO REMOVE HEAT STAINS FROM WOOD

If something hot, such as a coffee cup, sits directly on wood furniture, a heat mark is almost inevitable. The wood will gradually change colour as it warms, until you're left with a white mark that mars the look of the furniture and will have you reaching for the tablecloth. But fear not, just follow these simple, indispensable tips.

INDISPENSABLE THINGS

- Toothpaste
- 2 damp cloths
- Clean white cloth
- Iron
- Dry cloth and furniture polish

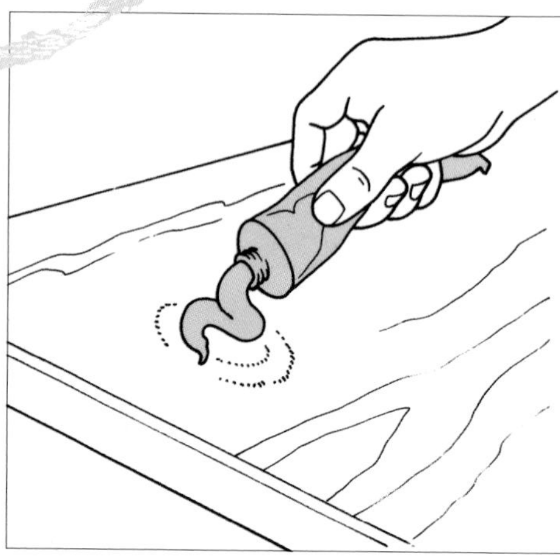

1 Apply some toothpaste (not gel) to the stain and rub with a clean, damp cloth, using a circular motion. Remove the toothpaste from the surface with a second damp cloth. You may have to repeat the process several times to lift the mark. Polish as usual.

2 Double-fold a clean white cloth and place over the scorch mark. Turn your iron to a low or medium setting and let it heat up. Press the iron back and forth over the cloth. Tap the steam release on the iron so that a burst of steam hits the cloth over the stain. Remove the cloth and wipe up any moisture.

INDISPENSABLE WARNING

If your furniture is antique, be extremely careful, because depending on the type of finish used to seal the wood, the above treatments may do more harm than good. Ask an expert first.

IN THE KITCHEN

Impress your friends and family with this indispensable guide to kitchen competence. From the basics of boiling an egg to sharpening a knife and setting a formal table, you'll find practical advice and labour-saving tips to help you achieve culinary success and entertain in style.

HOW TO OPEN A JAR

Jars are vacuum-sealed to keep food fresh, but this also makes the lids stick like wasps to flypaper. Some people try to break the vacuum by stabbing the top with a knife, but if you'd rather avoid a trip to A&E and want to use the lid again, follow these indispensable steps instead.

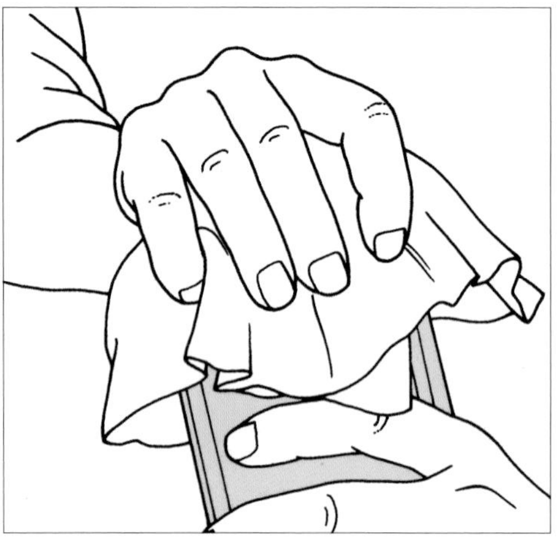

1 First of all, simply tap the top of the jar with a wooden spoon to break the vacuum. If this fails, wrap the lid in a dish cloth to give your hands traction. Make sure that you have a firm grip on the jar lid and press down on the lid as you twist.

INDISPENSABLE THINGS

- **Wooden spoon**
- **Dish cloth**
- **Rubber bands**
- **Rubber gloves**

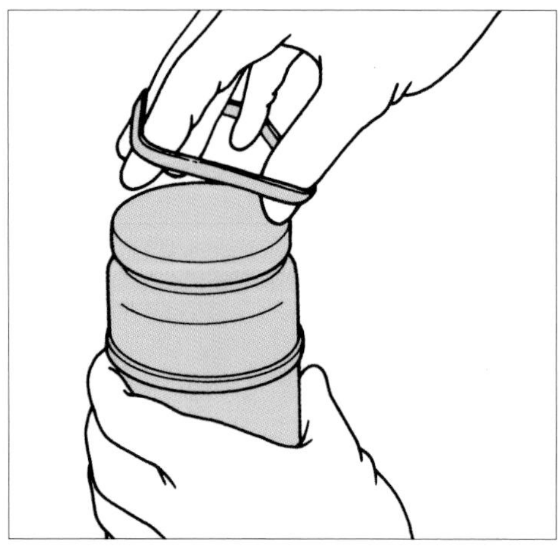

2 Alternatively, try placing rubber bands around the jar or hold it while wearing rubber gloves. Use one hand to grip the jar and the other to grip the lid. Twist the hand holding the jar clockwise and the one holding the lid anti-clockwise.

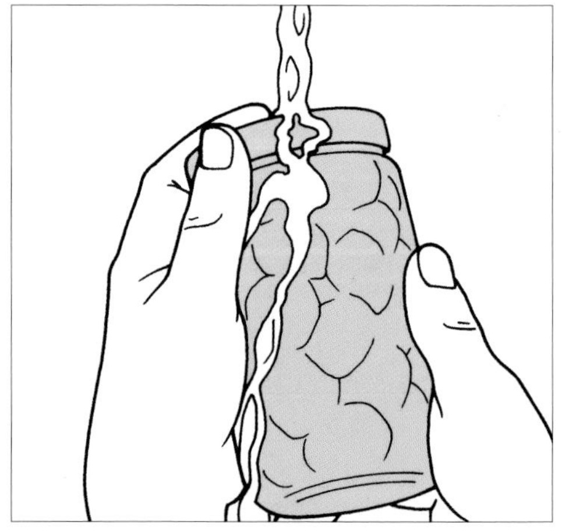

3 If mechanical force fails, run the lid under warm (not boiling) water for a minute to make the metal expand. This increases the radius of the lid, making it a little bigger and looser, and therefore easier for you to open the jar.

HOW TO SHARPEN A KNIFE

It's essential to keep your knives sharp: a blunt knife is dangerous because it requires more pressure and is more likely to slip and cut you. A sharp knife also means a better, faster and easier job. Test for sharpness on a firm, ripe tomato – it should slice through easily rather than crush it. Be very careful when sharpening knives.

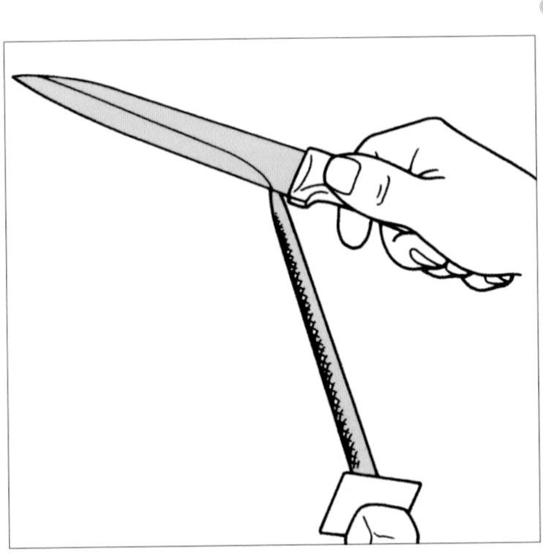

INDISPENSABLE THINGS

- **Sharpening steel**
- **Knife**
- **Sharpening stone**

1 A sharpening steel is a metal rod designed for sharpening knives. Hold it in one hand and hold the knife in the other. Place the knife just above the handle of the steel. With the knife at a 10–25-degree angle to the steel, draw the knife blade away from you down the steel.

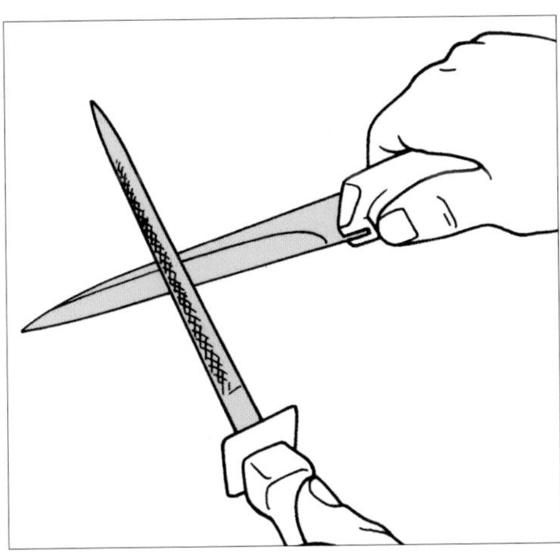

2 Do the same on the other side and repeat several times until the entire blade of the knife has been drawn across the steel on both sides.

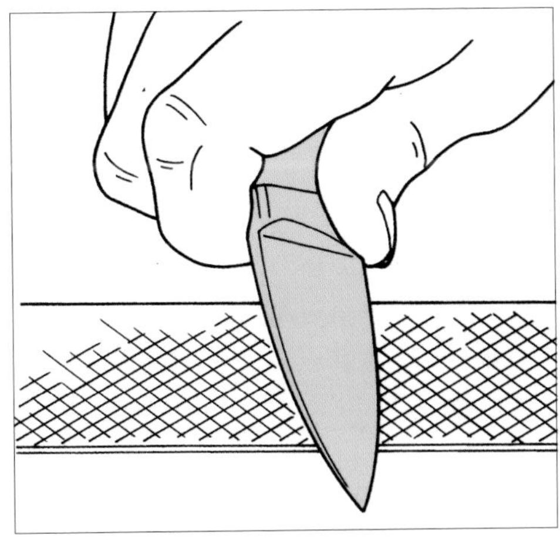

3 If using a sharpening stone, place it in front of you. Lay the edge of the blade nearest to the knife handle on the stone at a 45-degree angle. Slowly scrape the knife blade along the stone in an even motion, keeping the blade at the same angle. Repeat several times on each side. Turn the stone over and repeat on the smoother side.

HOW TO FRY AN EGG

For the perfect fried egg, make sure your egg is as fresh as possible. You can use a teaspoon of oil instead of butter, but it should have a mild flavour so it doesn't affect the taste of the egg. For eggs 'over easy', turn over with a spatula when the whites are just about done and cook for a further 15 seconds.

INDISPENSABLE THINGS

- Egg
- Frying pan
- Spatula
- Butter or mild-tasting oil (such as groundnut)

PAN
Use a small non-stick frying pan. This means that you will need to use less oil (which is better for you) and that the egg will slide easily out of the pan once it is cooked.

FAT
Only add a little fat to the pan – approximately 1 dessertspoon per egg. Heat the fat for several minutes until sizzling – if it is not hot enough, the egg will spread out and take longer to cook, becoming rubbery.

EGG
Crack the egg against the side of the pan and slide it in. Tilt the pan and baste the top of the egg with the fat. Fry for a couple of minutes or until the white is firm and the yolk has started to thicken, but is not rock solid.

HOW TO BOIL AN EGG

The perfect boiled egg is mostly down to timing, but there are a few tricks that can help you achieve great results every time. Serve with buttered bread or toast cut into strips (soldiers) for a simple treat.

INDISPENSABLE THINGS

- Eggs
- Pan
- Water
- Slotted spoon

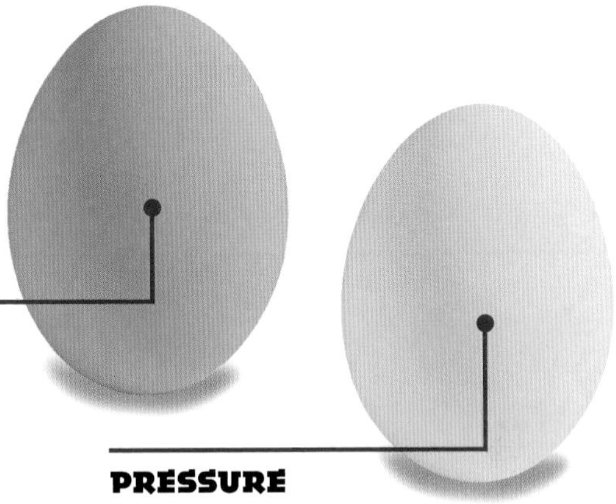

TEMPERATURE

The egg should be at room temperature before cooking or it will crack when added to the boiling water. Remove the egg from the refrigerator an hour beforehand or run under the hot tap.

PRESSURE

Prick the big end of the egg with a needle. This will let steam escape during cooking, so it doesn't crack the shell.

WATER LEVEL

This should be 2.5cm (1in) higher than the egg. Add a teaspoon of salt as this makes the eggs easier to peel.

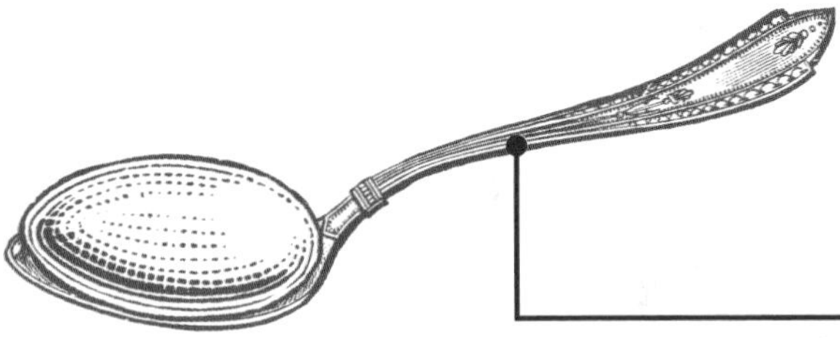

BOIL

Using a tablespoon, lower the eggs one at a time into a pan of boiling water. Cook for 4 minutes for a soft-boiled egg; 6 minutes for a hard-boiled one.

PAN

The pan should just be large enough for the amount of eggs you are cooking. This is to prevent them from breaking as they bump into each other or the side of the pan while cooking.

PLUNGE

As soon as the cooking time is up, plunge the eggs briefly into a bowl of cold water to stop cooking and prevent discoloration of the egg yolk.

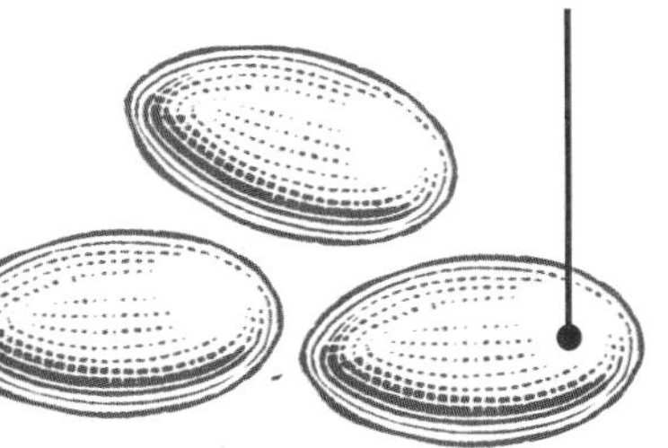

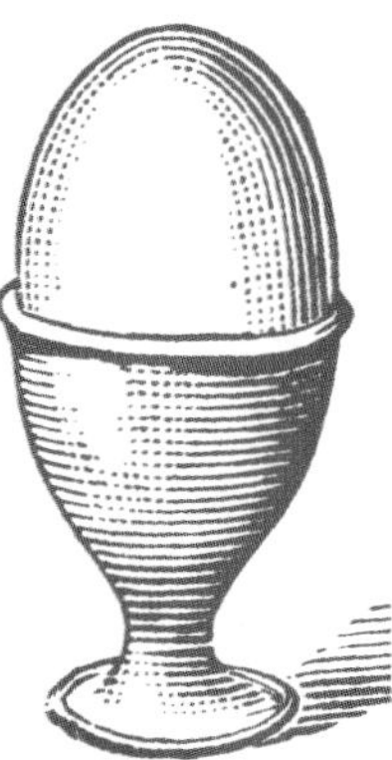

HOW TO MAKE AN OMELETTE

The perfect omelette is one that is just tinged with gold on the outside and very soft and squidgy on the inside. The number-one rule is not to over-mix the eggs. The size of the pan is also vital: too large and the eggs will spread like a pancake and become dry and tough; too small and the omelette will be spongy and difficult to fold. You can vary the basic recipe by using different fillings.

INDISPENSABLE THINGS

- 2 large eggs
- Salt & pepper
- 1/2 teaspoon butter
- 1/2 teaspoon olive oil
- Bowl
- Fork
- Non-stick frying pan measuring 15cm (6in) in diameter
- Fish slice
- Plate

PRACTICAL TIP

Popular fillings include grated cheese, chopped tomatoes, ham, mushrooms and cooked onion — use any combination or all, adding at the end of step 3 (mix in any herbs in step I). Eggs cook quickly so have all the ingredients ready before you start.

A PRACTICAL HISTORY OF THE OMELETTE

The practice of cooking beaten eggs in butter in a pan is an ancient one. According to the *Larousse Gastronomique* (1938), some scholars claim that the omelette derives from *ova mellita*, a classic Roman dish consisting of beaten eggs cooked on a flat clay dish with honey. However the word 'omelette' did not enter the English language until the early 17th century, when it was thus defined by Randle Cotgrave in *A Dictionarie of the French and English Tongues* (1611) as: 'Haumelette, an Omelet, or Pancake of Egges'.

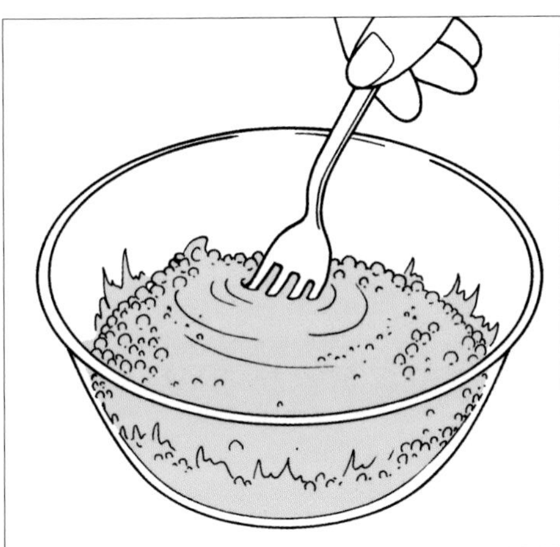

1 Break the eggs carefully into a bowl and season with salt and pepper. Blend the egg yolks and whites with a large fork. Place the pan on the heat and let it get quite hot.

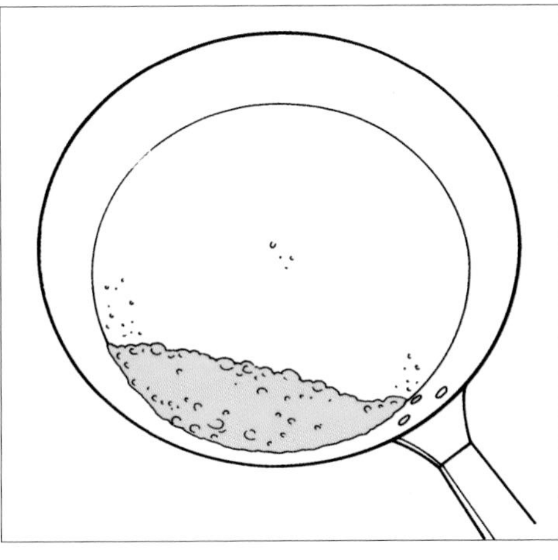

2 Add the butter with the oil and when melted swirl around the pan to coat the base and the sides. Turn the heat up as high as possible, then, when the butter is foaming, pour the eggs into the pan, tilting it to spread them evenly over the base. Leave the pan on the heat without moving it for a count of five.

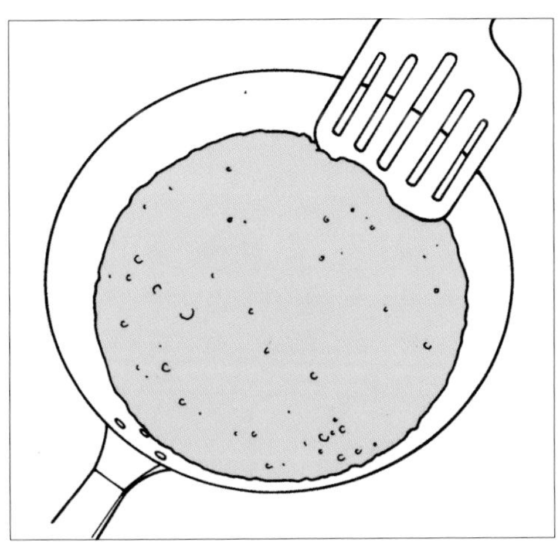

3 Tilt the pan to 45 degrees and, using the fork, draw the edge of the omelette into the centre. The runny egg will flow into the space. Tip the pan the other way and repeat. Keep tilting the pan backwards and forwards, lifting the edges with a fish slice so the runny egg flows underneath and cooks.

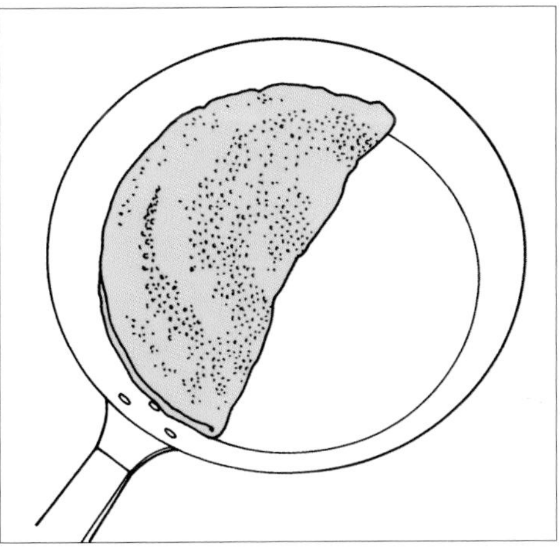

4 When there is just a small amount of liquid left, on the surface, tilt the pan again, loosen the edges of the omelette and fold it in half. Slip the omelette on to the plate and serve immediately.

HOW TO MAKE BREAD

A home-baked white loaf is hard to beat. Just follow these steps, or simply place all the ingredients in a food processor with a dough hook and knead for 3 minutes. The longer you leave the dough to rise, the better the bread will be. Dough will also rise at a cold temperature, so if more convenient, pop in the lowest part of the fridge and leave overnight. All bread recipes are approximate guides only – the amount of liquid the flour absorbs depends on the type of flour you use and even the weather!

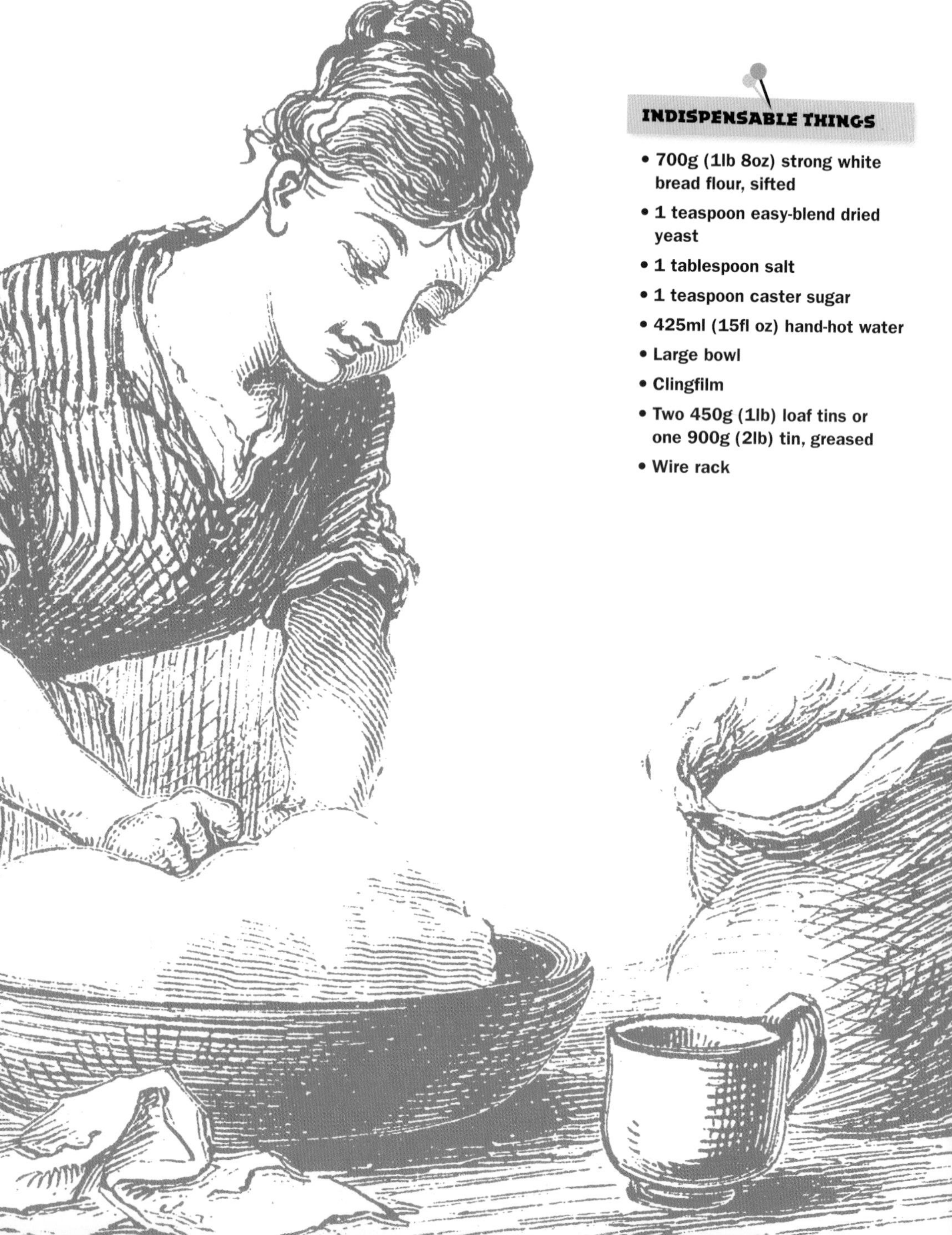

INDISPENSABLE THINGS

- 700g (1lb 8oz) strong white bread flour, sifted
- 1 teaspoon easy-blend dried yeast
- 1 tablespoon salt
- 1 teaspoon caster sugar
- 425ml (15fl oz) hand-hot water
- Large bowl
- Clingfilm
- Two 450g (1lb) loaf tins or one 900g (2lb) tin, greased
- Wire rack

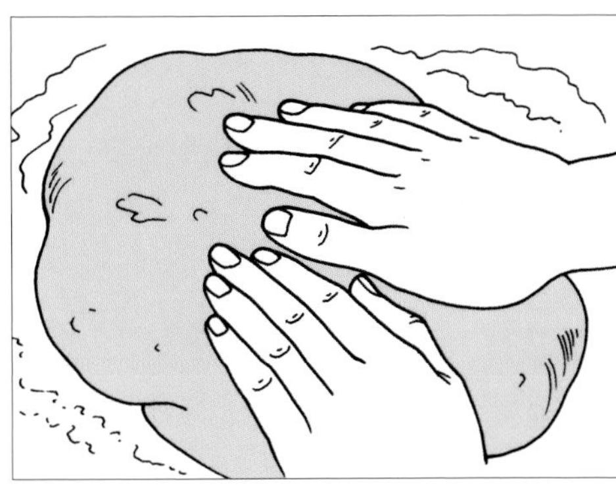

1 Put the flour, yeast, salt and sugar in a bowl. Make a well in the centre and add enough water to make a soft dough. Place the dough on a flat work surface, then stretch it away from you, using the heel of one hand to push from the middle and your other hand to pull the other half towards you. Then lift the edges over and back to the middle.

2 Repeat the process, turning the dough slightly with each movement. When the dough becomes very smooth and springy and appears blistery on the surface (anything from 5 to 15 minutes), it's ready to rise.

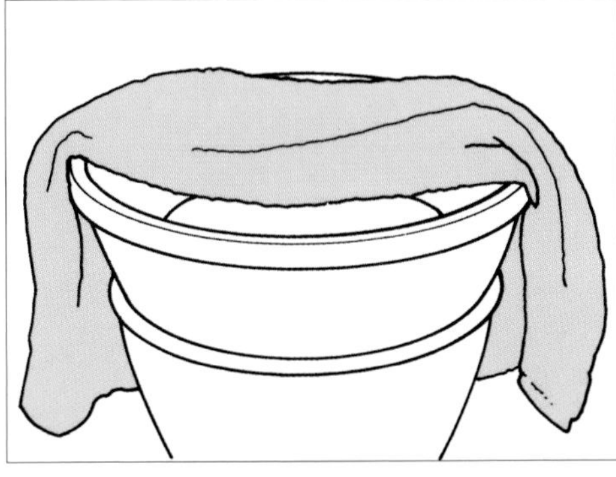

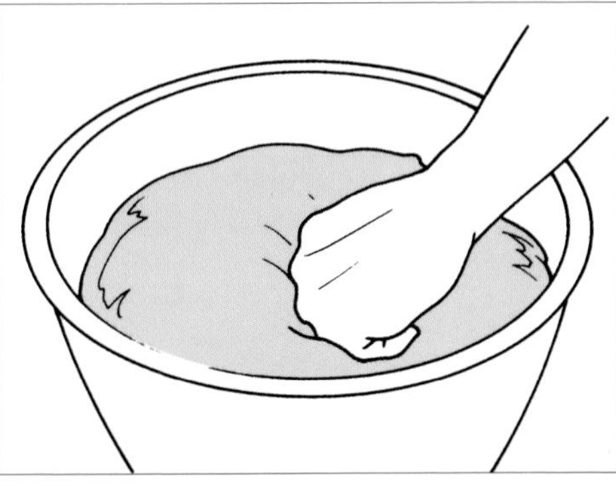

3 Form the dough into a ball and place in a large, warm, oiled bowl, turning to coat evenly with grease. Cover with lightly oiled clingfilm or a damp cloth and leave to expand. When risen, the dough should have doubled in size and should spring back, feeling slightly sticky when touched.

4 Knock back the dough by punching all the air out of it with your fists until it's back to its original size. Put the dough into the loaf tin, cover as before and leave for 20 minutes for a second rising.

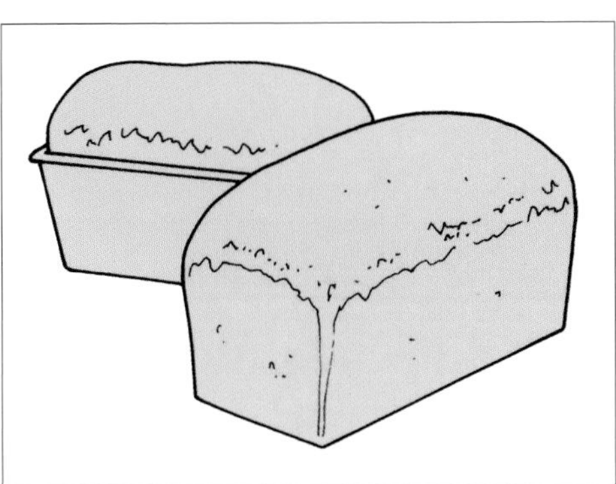

5 Remove the cover and put the bread on the centre shelf of a preheated oven (230°C/450°F/Gas Mark 8). Bake for 30–40 minutes. Remove from the tin and give the bottom of the loaf a quick tap with your knuckles. If cooked, it will sound hollow; if not, put back in the oven for a few minutes. Leave on a wire rack to cool.

HOW TO ROAST BEEF

A succulent slice of roast beef is one of life's simple pleasures. Take the joint out of the fridge to bring it to room temperature before cooking. Season with salt and pepper or rub with garlic, herbs or mustard powder, according to taste. Place the meat in a shallow roasting tin with the fattiest side on top.

INDISPENSABLE THINGS

- Joint of beef
- Roasting tin
- Seasoning
- Foil
- Spoon
- Skewer

TEMPERATURE & TIME

Put the beef in a very hot pre-heated oven (240°C/475°F/Gas Mark 9) for 15 minutes. Lower the heat to 190°C/375°F/Gas Mark 5. Cook for another 17 minutes per 450g (1lb) for rare beef and add a further 15 minutes for medium or 30 minutes for well done.

BASTING

While the beef is cooking, baste at least three times to keep it moist. Take the tin out of the oven, tip the juices to one end and spoon over the meat.

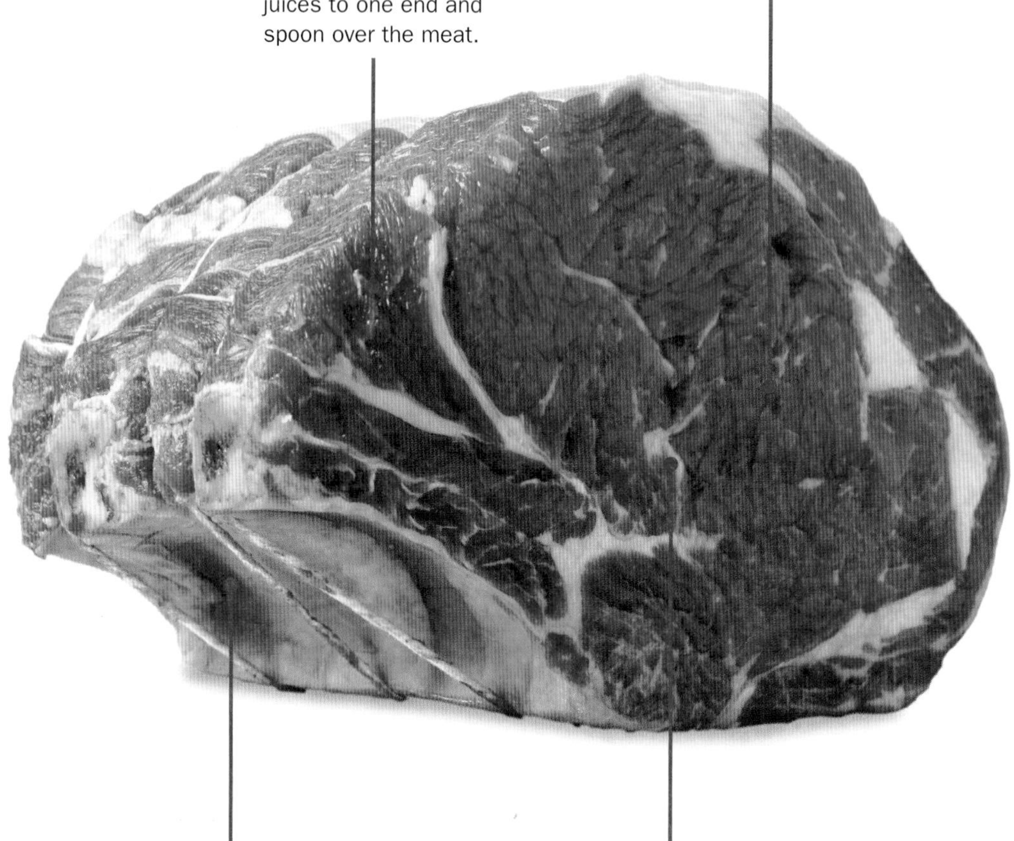

STANDING

When the beef is cooked, cover with foil and let it stand for at least 10 minutes to enhance its flavour and make carving easier.

JUICES

Stick a skewer into the middle of the joint to find out if it's cooked. If the juices are clear, it's well done; pink indicates medium, and red shows it's rare.

HOW TO CARVE A JOINT OF BEEF

Meat is made up of thousands of tiny strands of muscle, and the way you carve it can determine how tender or tough the meat turns out. Carving is an art that can easily be mastered, provided that you have a suitable sharp knife and some practice! Let the joint 'rest' for at least 10 minutes before carving.

INDISPENSABLE THINGS

- Cooked joint of beef
- Carving knife
- Sharpening steel
- Carving fork with guard
- Board or spiked plate

KNIFE AND FORK

The blade of the carving knife should be slightly flexible. Sharpen the knife each time it is to be used for carving, so that it will cut straight through the meat instead of sawing and tearing. You also need a carving fork with a guard, in case the knife slips.

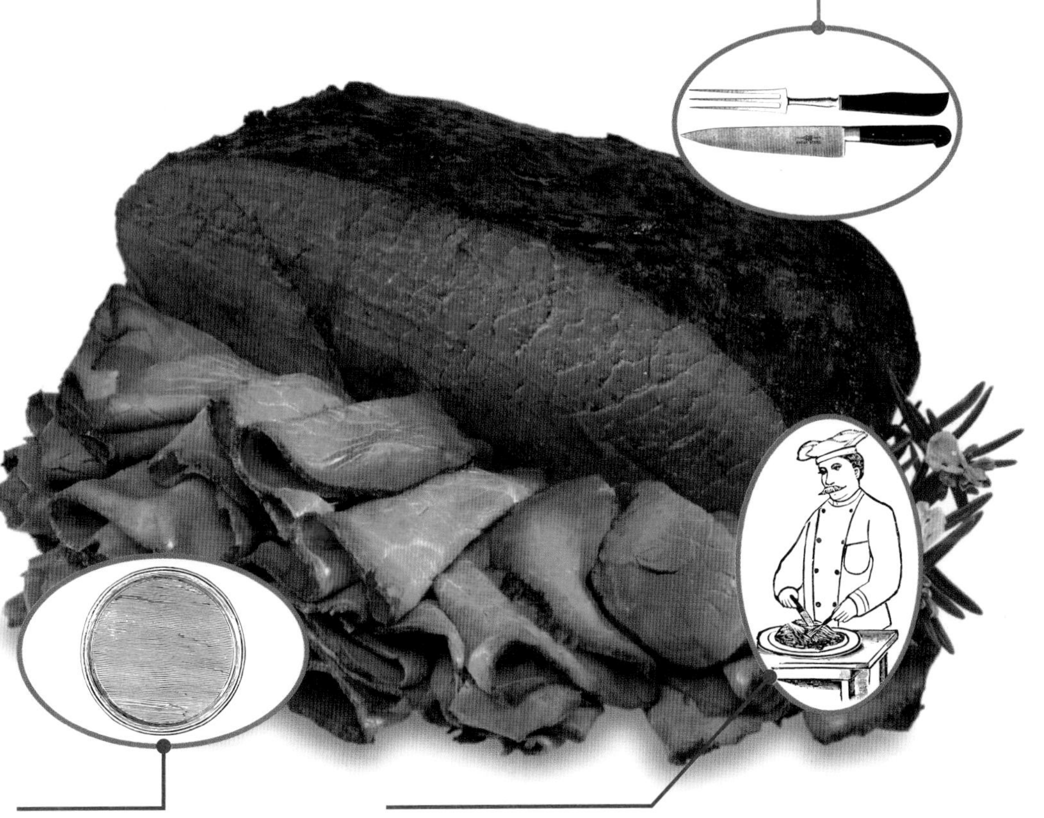

FLAT SURFACE

Stand the joint on a flat slip-proof surface, such as a wooden board, or on a plate with spikes to hold it in position. Remove any string and/or skewers that will be in the way.

CARVING

You'll find it much easier to carve while standing up. Create a flat base by slicing away one end of the roast. Cut even-sized slices across the grain of the meat to shorten the fibres and make the meat seem more tender.

HOW TO MAKE CHOCOLATE SOUFFLÉ

Impress your friends with this fabulously easy and delicious chocolate dessert. The perfect soufflé should be light, crisp on top and slightly moist in the middle. This soufflé may shrink a little on its journey from oven to table, but it won't collapse. Use good-quality chocolate, but note that chocolate with a high content of cocoa solids (over 55 per cent) will make the soufflé too bitter. This recipe makes one large soufflé to serve 6, or 4-6 individual ramekins, and you can make it an hour or two ahead, unbaked, and keep in the fridge until ready to go.

INDISPENSABLE THINGS

- 115g (4oz) dark chocolate
- Melted butter, for greasing
- 55g (2oz) caster sugar
- 4 large egg yolks
- 5 large egg whites
- Pinch of salt
- Icing sugar, for dusting
- Baking tray
- 3 bowls
- Saucepan of hot water
- Wooden spoon
- Soufflé dish or individual ramekins
- Whisk
- Metal spoon
- Palette knife

1 Preheat the oven to 200°C/400°F/Gas Mark 6 and pop in the baking tray to heat up. Break the chocolate into a heatproof bowl and melt it over a saucepan of simmering water, making sure the base of the bowl doesn't touch the water. Leave until the chocolate is just soft, which will take about 5 minutes.

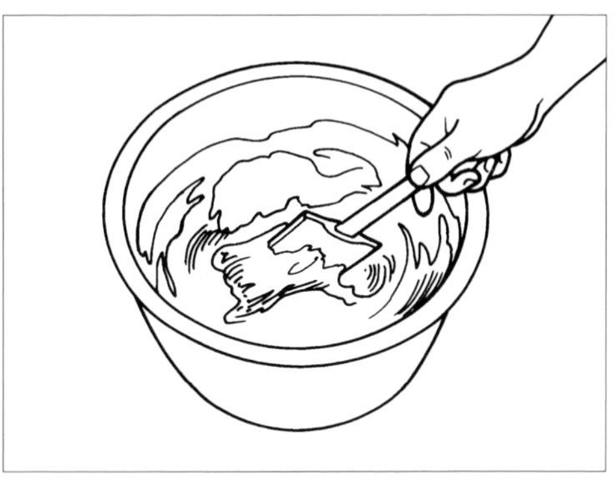

2 Remove the chocolate from the heat and beat with a wooden spoon until smooth and glossy. Leave the melted chocolate to cool slightly. Meanwhile, grease the soufflé dish lightly and sprinkle with a little of the caster sugar.

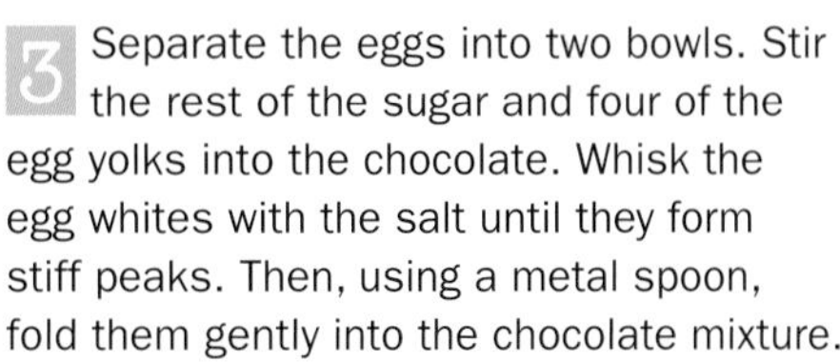

3 Separate the eggs into two bowls. Stir the rest of the sugar and four of the egg yolks into the chocolate. Whisk the egg whites with the salt until they form stiff peaks. Then, using a metal spoon, fold them gently into the chocolate mixture.

4 Fill the soufflé dish or individual ramekins until they are nearly full. Take a palette knife and pull it across the top of the dish so the mixture is completely flat. Wipe any splashes off the outside of the dish, or they will burn while cooking.

5 Place on the baking tray in the oven and bake for about 20 minutes until the soufflé rises and puffs up. It should have risen by about two-thirds of its original height and wobble when moved, but be set on top. Serve straight from the oven, dusted with icing sugar, accompanied by chocolate sauce or whipping cream.

HOW TO MAKE A SPONGE CAKE

Successful cake-making is immensely satisfying, but it requires strict attention to detail. All ingredients should be at room temperature when you start. Careful weighing and measuring, precise oven temperatures and timing are also crucial to success. A cake should be baked as soon as it is mixed and you should never open the oven door until at least three-quarters of the cooking time has elapsed, because the temperature will drop suddenly and the air in the cake will contract, causing the cake to sink. For a really easy recipe, just pop all the sponge ingredients in a food processor and whisk.

INDISPENSABLE THINGS

- Oil, for brushing
- 115g (4oz) butter or margarine
- 115g (4oz) caster sugar
- 2 medium eggs
- Vanilla essence
- 115g (4oz) self-raising flour
- 1–2 tablespoons hot water or milk
- Jam
- Whipped cream
- Icing sugar, for dusting
- 2 x 15cm (6in) sandwich tins
- Greaseproof paper
- Wooden spoon
- Large mixing bowl
- Sieve
- Palette knife
- Wire rack

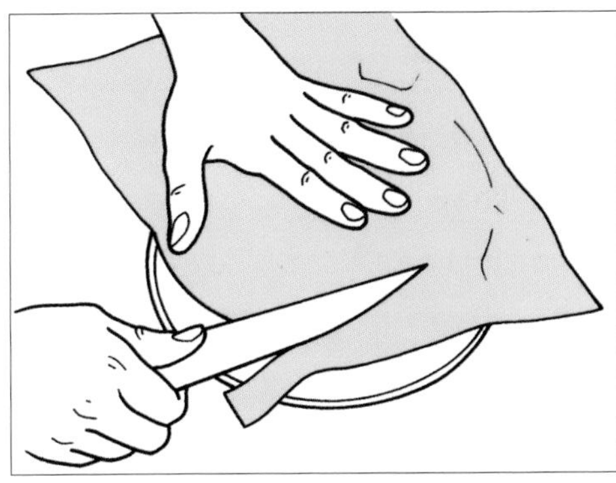

1 Gather all your ingredients and utensils and preheat your oven to 200°C/400°F/ Gas Mark 6. Line the base of each sandwich tin with a disc of greaseproof paper and brush the sides with oil.

2 Cream the butter until light in colour, then beat in the sugar, a little at a time, and beat until the mixture has a mousse-like consistency. The creaming incorporates air and is the secret of the sponge's lightness.

3 Mix the eggs together in a separate bowl and gradually beat into the creamed mixture a little at a time. If the mixture begins to curdle, simply sift in some of your flour and give it a stir, then carry on.

4 Sir in a few drops of vanilla essence. Fold the sifted flour into the mixture. You should have a mixture that drops off the spoon easily, but if the consistency is not right, add a little hot water or milk.

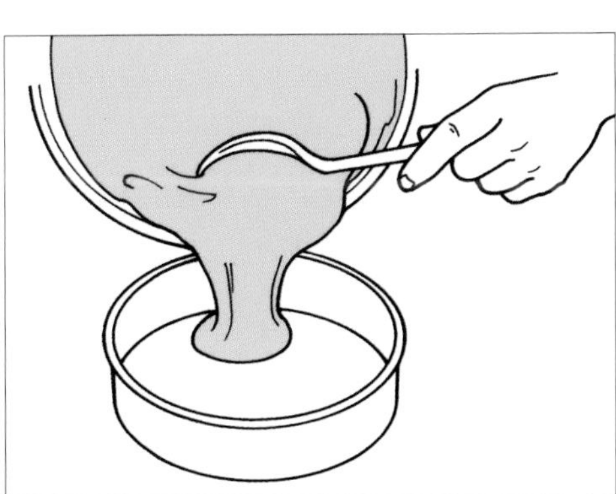

5 Divide the mixture into the two sandwich tins. Push the mixture towards the edges of the tins and smooth out the tops with a palette knife. Put the cakes into the oven for 20 minutes.

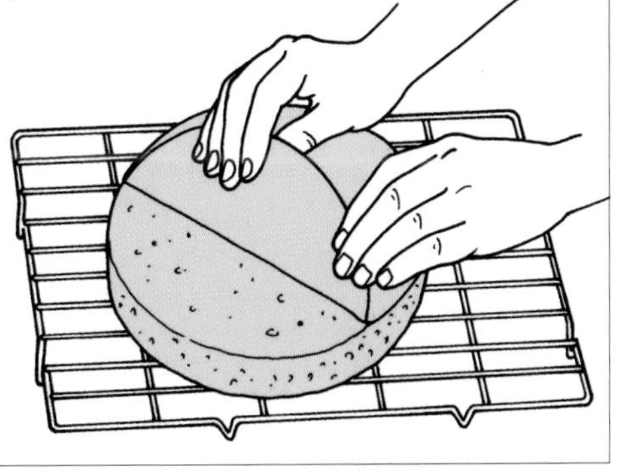

6 If the sponges are cooked, they will have come away slightly from the sides of the tin and, when you gently press the top of the cakes, they will spring back. If they are not ready, give them another 3–5 minutes but no longer. When the sponges are cooked, turn them out on to a wire rack and peel off the greaseproof paper. Leave to cool, then sandwich together with a layer of jam and whipped cream. Dust the top with icing sugar.

HOW TO MAKE A BLT

A BLT is an irresistible combination of bacon, lettuce and tomato between two pieces of bread. This delicious sandwich is very simple to make, and the trick is to use good-quality ingredients and get the balance between them just right. The BLT is known and loved throughout the world, but is generally regarded as an American classic. The world's biggest BLT was assembled in Sonoma County, California, in 2003, and was 31.6m (104ft) long and covered an area of 9.7m^2 (about 105ft^2).

INDISPENSABLE THINGS

- 4 slices smoked or unsmoked bacon, preferably dry cured
- 2 slices bread, lightly toasted
- 2 lettuce leaves, washed
- 1 firm tomato, sliced
- Mayonnaise
- Paper towel
- Palette knife or spatula

A PRACTICAL HISTORY OF THE SANDWICH

John Montague, the 4th Earl of Sandwich, was an 18th-century aristocrat whose name is immortalized in this humble snack. History records him as an inveterate gambler who preferred playing cards to eating his dinner. Snacks of meat served between slices of bread satisfied his hunger and enabled him to stay longer at the card table. The less colourful account is that he was a hard-working peer who didn't have time to stop for lunch, so ate a meat and bread snack at his desk. Whatever the truth, this type of fast food soon became very popular among the English gentry and later among the whole of society.

TOMATO

Use a firm, ripe tomato, cut into thick slices and sprinkled lightly with salt. Many prefer a beefsteak variety for its firm flesh and fewer seeds – this makes the BLT a seasonal treat. Tile the slices of tomato so they overlap slightly.

BREAD

This can be white, brown or sourdough, according to preference, but it's best to go with something that tastes mild and that doesn't compete with the flavour of the bacon (this rules out rye bread and wholegrains). It is usually lightly toasted.

BACON

This is regarded as the magical ingredient that transmutes a basic sandwich into gold. Many would argue that standard supermarket bacon just isn't good enough, but whatever sort you use, fry until crisp, then place on a paper towel to blot up excess grease.

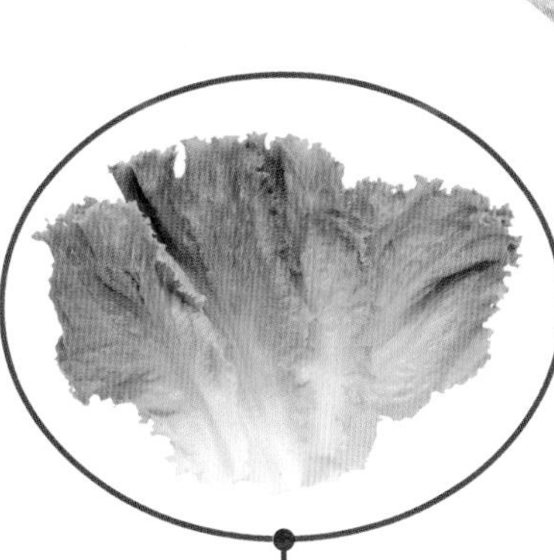

LETTUCE

You will need a couple of leaves of a crisp, bland variety – cos, little gem or iceberg are all perfect. Strong-tasting lettuces change the nature of the BLT.

MAYO

Use good-quality mayonnaise, but not too much or it will mask the other flavours. Spread this on both slices of bread using a palette knife or spatula, and dab it on rather that rub it in.

HOW TO MAKE A MARTINI

This legendary cocktail is a drink long associated with sophistication, glamour and power. Aficionados included Ernest Hemingway, Winston Churchill, Frank Sinatra and, of course, the ultra-suave fictional James Bond, although he used vodka and gin. In a classic Martini you need only three things: gin, dry vermouth and an olive or two. Other alcohols, garnishes and methods can be used for different variations, but to a purist, they wouldn't be considered true Martinis.

INDISPENSABLE THINGS

- Cocktail shaker
- Long-stemmed, cone-shaped cocktail glass
- Crushed ice
- Few drops to 15ml (1/2fl oz) dry vermouth
- 60ml (2fl oz) good-quality dry gin
- Angostura bitters (optional)
- Olives or twist of lemon, skewered on a cocktail stick

A PRACTICAL HISTORY OF THE MARTINI

There are as many supposed origins of the Martini as there are ways to make it, but the first written reference to a Martini is found in the *Bon Vivant's Companion: or How to Mix Drinks* (1887), a bartender's manual that lists sweet vermouth among the ingredients. The Martini rose in popularity in America during the Prohibition period of the 1920s, when gin was quick and easy to produce, but was of such poor quality that it needed the addition of vermouth to disguise its taste.

1 For absolute purists, everything should be at room temperature before you make the cocktail. However, many favour storing the gin in the freezer to make it syrupy, although this will result in a blunter, more oily taste. Never put vermouth in the freezer because it will partially freeze, ruining its taste.

2 Add lots of ice to the cocktail shaker to chill and blend the ingredients. Add the vermouth – from a few drops to a full shot, according to taste. Some prefer just to roll the vermouth around a chilled cocktail glass to form a coating, then tip out the vermouth. This makes a Dry Martini.

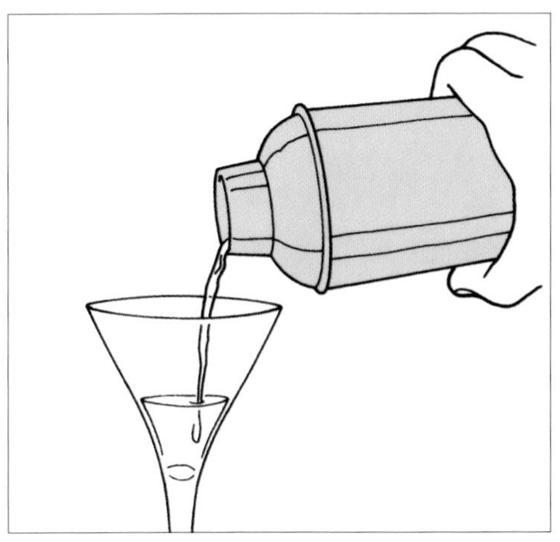

3 Place the gin in the cocktail shaker and stir for 20 seconds or shake vigorously. Shaking will make the gin temporarily cloudy, and some people believe this technique bruises the gin. Strain into the glass, and add a dash of Angostura bitters if desired. Garnisn with the olives or lemon twist.

INDISPENSABLE VARIATION

There are countless variations on the classic cocktail:

- A Vodka Martini uses vodka instead of gin.
- A Gibson is a classic Martini garnished with cocktail onions instead of olives or a lemon twist.
- Adding a dash of olive brine — which creates what is known as a Dirty Martini — takes the edge off the harshness of the gin.

HOW TO OPEN A CHAMPAGNE BOTTLE

The secret of opening a champagne bottle without injuring your guests or showering the contents around the room is to make sure the wine is well chilled before opening and then to simply twist the bottle, instead of pulling on the cork. The best serving temperature is around 7°C (45°F). If you put your hand on the bottle it should feel very cold, not just cool – champagne that is too warm will foam and spill when you open the bottle.

INDISPENSABLE THINGS

- Bottle of champagne
- Kitchen towel
- Champagne glass

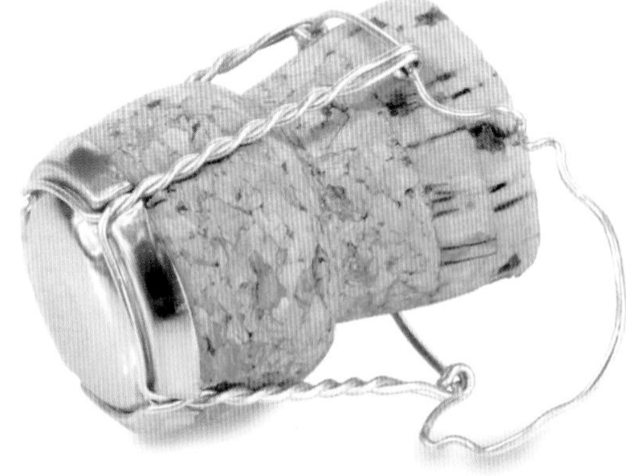

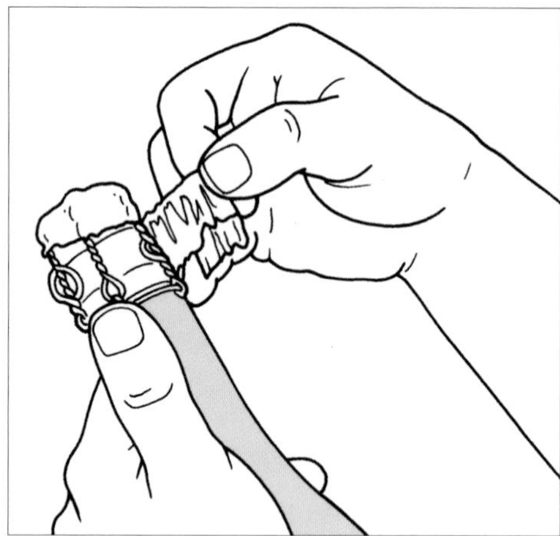

1 Never use a corkscrew on a champagne bottle because the contents are under pressure and may explode. Hold the bottle upright and remove the foil and wire cage.

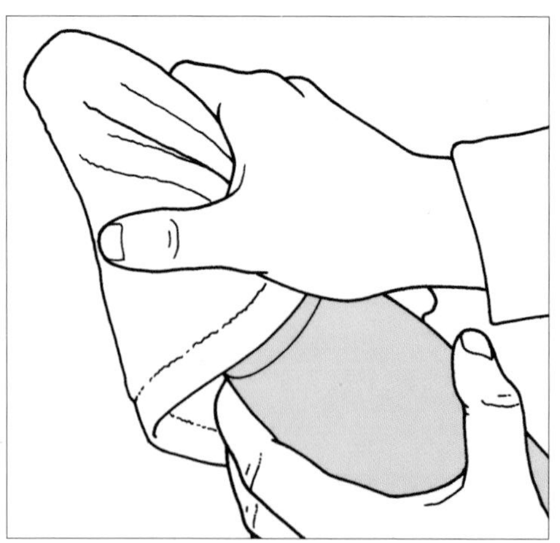

2 Drape a kitchen towel over the top of the bottle. If the cork pops before you're ready, the towel will stop it flying off and will also catch any wine spills. Grip the cork between fingers and thumb. Using your other hand, turn the bottom of the bottle until you hear a soft 'pop'.

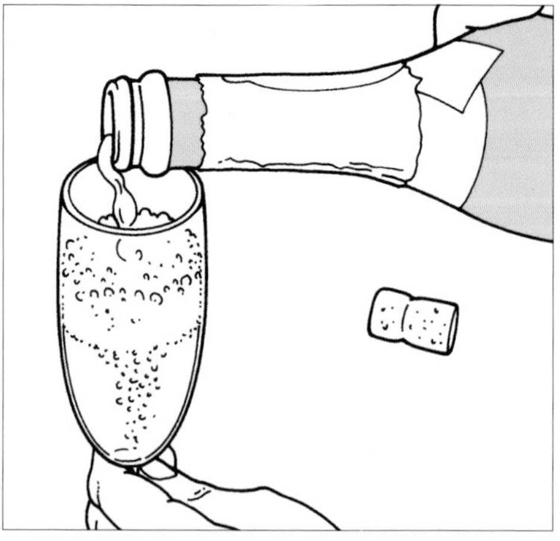

3 Remove the towel and cork, and pour a little champagne into a champagne glass. Wait for the foam to subside, then top up with more champagne until the glass is two-thirds full.

HOW TO MAKE OIL & VINEGAR DRESSING

An oil and vinegar dressing not only livens up salads, but also adds zing to pasta, fish and vegetables. Simply put all the ingredients in a screwtop jar, shake until well blended and drizzle over your dish. Oil and vinegar dressing will keep in the refrigerator for up to three days, but is best made fresh. It is an unstable emulsion and will separate after an hour – in this case, simply shake again to recombine.

INDISPENSABLE THINGS

- 6 tablespoons olive oil
- 2 tablespoons vinegar
- 1 teaspoon mustard
- Salt & pepper

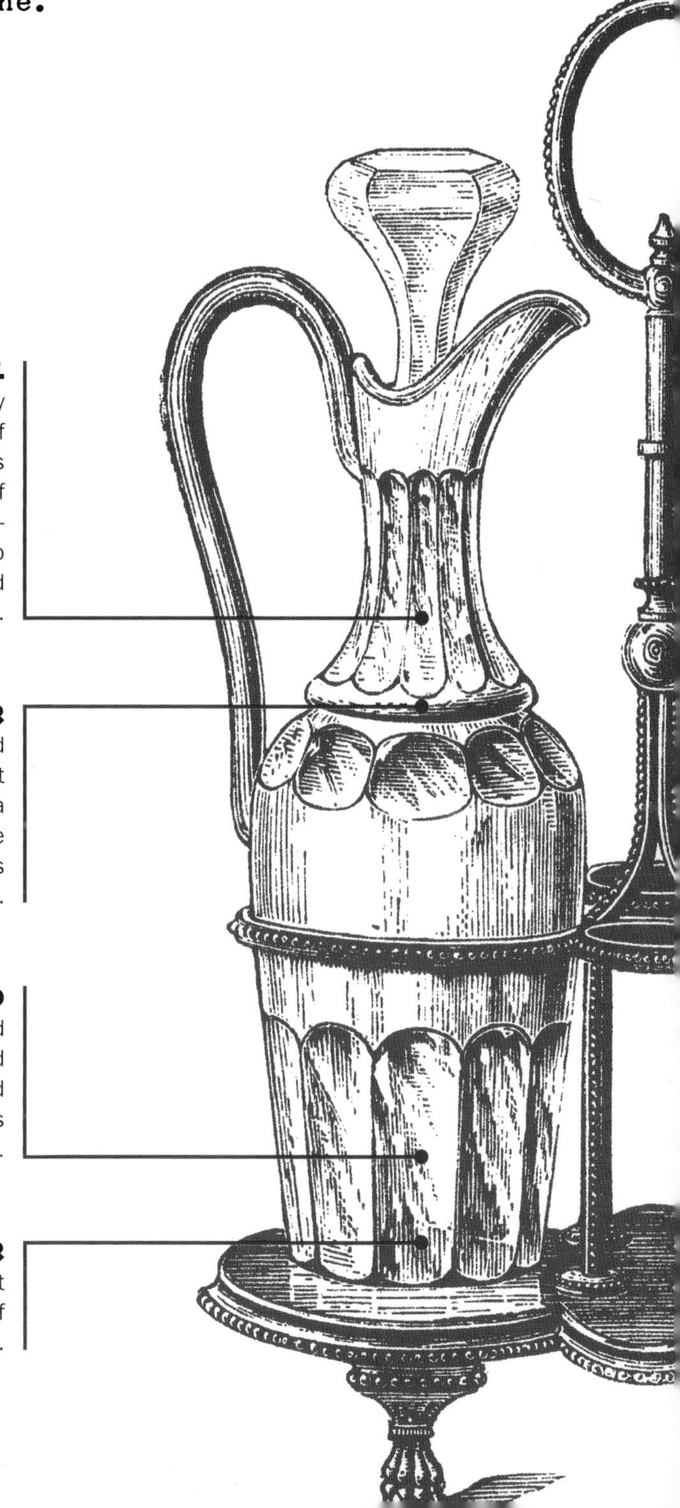

OIL

The ratio of oil to vinegar is usually 3:1, although less oil is used if a milder acid than vinegar is substituted. The better the quality of oil, the better the taste – use extra-virgin olive oil. Don't be afraid to experiment with different flavoured oils such as garlic-infused oil.

VINEGAR

Any good-quality vinegar will do. Red or white wine vinegar is the norm, but try balsamic or tarragon vinegar for a different taste. Vinegar can be replaced with another acid such as lemon or orange juice.

MUSTARD

Add a small amount of Dijon mustard to act as an emulsifying agent and bind the oil and vinegar together. Powdered mustard would add flavour, but does not emulsify the ingredients.

SALT AND PEPPER

Add salt and pepper – sea salt and freshly milled black pepper, if possible – according to taste.

HOW TO CHOP ONIONS SO YOU DON'T CRY

Onions make you cry because, when you cut them, you break apart cells that combine with enzymes to release gases that are dissolved by the water in the eyes. Oxygen in the air converts the dissolved gas into sulphuric acid, so your eyes form tears to wash the acid away. Try these indispensable tips for chopping onions without tears.

INDISPENSABLE THINGS

- Onions
- Sharp knife
- Swimming goggles or a mask
- Water
- Chewing gum

KEEP THEM COLD

Chilling is supposed to change chemical compounds in the onion, reducing the amount of gas that they release.

ABSORB THE GASES IN WATER

Cut the onions in a bowl of water, under running water or near a cloud of steam (from a kettle). Alternatively, chew gum to produce saliva in your mouth, which will reduce the virulence of the sting.

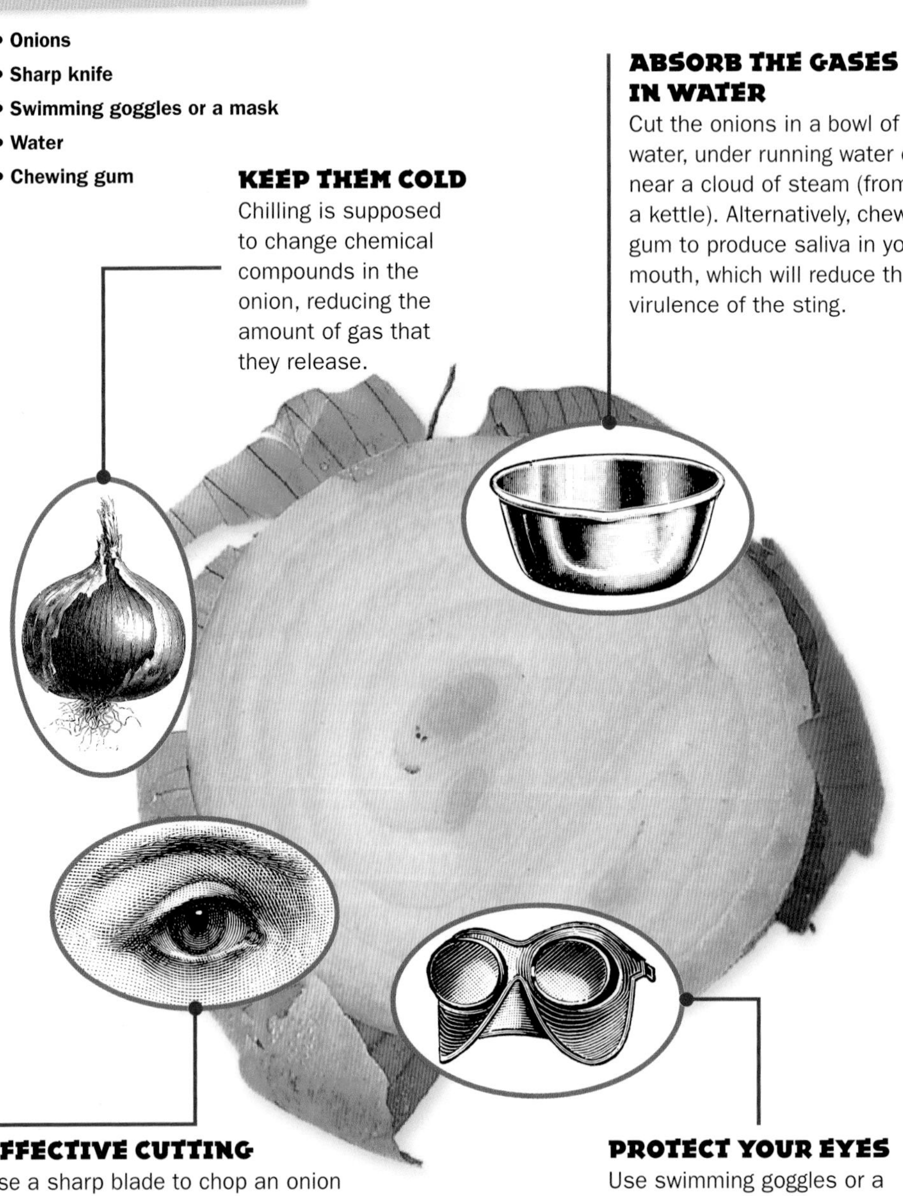

EFFECTIVE CUTTING

Use a sharp blade to chop an onion to minimize cell damage, and cut it quickly to reduce the time gases have to reach the eyes. Cut the root off last because it has the highest concentration of enzymes.

PROTECT YOUR EYES

Use swimming goggles or a mask with tight-fitting seals to prevent gases from entering the eyes. This is always effective.

HOW TO CRUSH GARLIC WITHOUT A PRESS

The cut of garlic affects its flavour, and crushing garlic releases more of its aromatic oils than simply chopping or slicing it. Garlic presses are effective, but fiddly to clean, so try these easy methods instead. To begin, take a clove of garlic and strip off its papery covering.

INDISPENSABLE THINGS

- Garlic cloves
- Wide-bladed knife
- Chopping board
- Paper towels
- Food tin (unopened)
- Pestle and mortar
- Wooden spoon

KNIFE

Position the garlic clove flat on a chopping board with the hollow side facing downwards. Place a knife with a wide blade flat over the garlic, taking care not to touch the sharp end of the blade. Press down strongly with the palm of your hand.

PESTLE AND MORTAR

Crush the garlic clove in a porcelain pestle and mortar – wood and stone versions absorb the scent of garlic and can taint the flavour of anything else you crush in it.

SPOON

Place the garlic clove on a chopping block. Use the back of a spoon to press down and apply pressure in order to crush the garlic.

TIN

Wrap the clove of garlic in a piece of paper towel. Place on the chopping board, then whack it with the base of an unopened food tin.

HOW TO SET THE TABLE

Planning a formal dinner party and need a reminder of how to set a table? Fear not – it's fairly straightforward. The basic rule is: cutlery is placed in the order of use; that is, from the outside in towards the plate. A second rule, with a few exceptions is: forks go to the left of the plate, and knives and spoons go to the right. Cups and saucers are put near the knives, or can be brought out after the meal. Finally, decide on a seating plan and, if you wish, put out cards with place names.

INDISPENSABLE THINGS

- Tablecloth
- Napkins
- Bread plates with butter knives
- Dinner plates
- Salad plates or soup bowls
- Water glasses
- Wine glasses
- Liqueur glasses
- Salad or fish forks
- Dinner forks
- Dessert forks
- Salad or fish knives
- Dinner knives
- Soup or melon spoons
- Dessert spoons

PRACTICAL TIP

It's a good idea to wear cotton gloves when handling silver cutlery to prevent the oils and acids in your skin from tarnishing the utensils. Rubber gloves contain sulphur that makes silver tarnish, so don't wear these when handling it.

GLASSES
Set out glasses in order of use above the knives. Usually this means placing the water glass to the left, then to its right the red wine, white wine and liqueur glasses.

TABLECLOTH
If you use a tablecloth, it should of course be spotlessly clean, ironed and with the middle crease arranged so that it runs in a straight line down the centre of the table.

NAPKINS
Napkins can be folded and placed at the side, on the plate, under the forks or inside one of the glasses, depending on your preference.

CUTLERY POSITION
The placement of cutlery is always guided by the menu, working from the outside in. Cutlery should be about 12mm (½in) away from the plate or each other, and should also be lined up evenly from the bottom. Each course should have its own utensils. Place forks to the left, knives to the right.

PLATES
Dinner plates need to be centred in front of each chair. Soup bowls or salad plates sit on top of each dinner plate. The bread plate should be placed to the side. Alternatively, bring out appropriate plates for each course and place on top of the dinner plate (which acts as an underplate or charger).

KNIVES
Knives should be placed with their cutting edge towards the dinner plate –except the butter knife, which should be laid flat on a bread plate.

SPOONS
Place soup or melon spoons to the right of the knives. The dessert spoon lies at the head of the plate, centred above it.

HOW TO POUR WINE

Pour wine like a professional with these simple tricks of the trade. Stemmed glasses are extremely important, because the stem enables the wine to be held without the palm of your hand heating it up too much. The shape of a glass can also affect the taste of the wine.

INDISPENSABLE THINGS

- Opened bottle of wine
- Wine glass

STILL WINE. Pour still wines slowly towards the centre of the glass. Fill up to just below the widest section, so that the guest can swirl the wine to release the aroma without risk of spillage. Finish pouring the wine, tilting the tip of the bottle upwards and slightly rotating your hand, so that the wine doesn't drip.

RED WINE. The best red wine glasses are rounded with a large bowl, which gives the wine a greater surface exposure. Swirling wine around in the glass aerates it and helps to remove sediment.

WHITE WINE. Tulip-shaped glasses that narrow at the rim are best for white wine because this helps to preserve more of the chill that enhances the wine.

SPARKLING WINE. Flute-type champagne glasses are ideal for sparkling wines because they provide a central point from which bubbles can rise. Hold the glass at an angle and pour the wine against the side, like a beer.

IN THE GARDEN

Make the most of your outdoor space with this indispensable guide to garden growth and maintenance. Covering everything from potting up your plants to making a cold frame or a compost heap, these clear instructions will guide you effortlessly through the practical tasks needed to help your garden flourish.

HOW TO DOUBLE DIG

This is an excellent way of cultivating soil. The deeper the planting soil, the deeper the roots can go, which leads to stronger plants and a higher yield at harvest. Hard work but straightforward, double digging usually only needs to be done once. You just need to remember that you have two layers: the top one dug with a spade and the bottom with a fork. The best time to do it is in autumn and winter, when the ground is moist, but not waterlogged or frozen. It then has time to settle before planting in spring.

INDISPENSABLE THINGS

- 2 garden canes or sticks
- String
- Wheelbarrow
- Spade
- Fork
- Organic matter (compost or well-rotted manure, about 1 bucket per $1m^2/10ft^2$)

PRACTICAL TIP

Make sure that you don't overdo it — you need a strong back for double digging and you don't have to dig it all in one day.

1 Make sure your bed is free of weeds and mark out the area you are going to dig with a piece of string stretched between two canes (1.5 x 6m/5 x 20ft is ideal). Begin at one end of the bed and dig a narrow trench, about 30cm (12in) wide and 30cm (12in) deep, along the length of the bed, placing the excavated soil in a wheelbarrow.

2 Work a garden fork into the floor of the trench, and wiggle it about to loosen the subsoil. This is why it's called double digging, because you're digging twice the depth of usual digging. Continue until the soil at the bottom of the trench is loosened. Add compost or well-rotted manure and fork in.

3 Dig a second trench directly next to the first. Place the excavated topsoil into the first trench you dug and enrich with compost or manure. Loosen the soil at the bottom of the second trench with the garden fork and add more compost or manure.

4 Dig a third trench next to the second trench. Backfill the second one with the excavated topsoil and enrich with compost or manure. Loosen the soil at the bottom of the third trench with the garden fork and add compost or manure. Continue this process until you have double dug the whole bed. Fill the last trench with the soil in the wheelbarrow. You'll end up with a raised bed because you have incorporated organic matter and broken up the soil.

HOW TO PLANT A SEED

Starting plants from seed is a great, inexpensive way to grow a huge variety of vegetables, herbs and flowers. Read the seed packet first to see if they require any special treatment – some seeds need soaking before sowing.

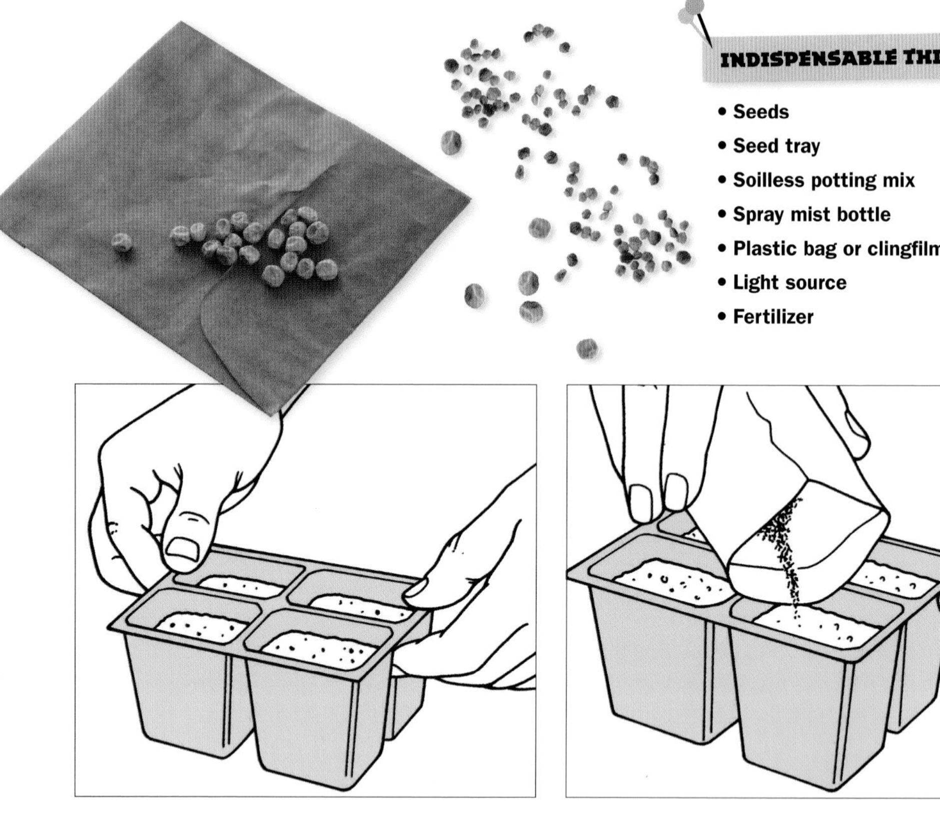

INDISPENSABLE THINGS

- Seeds
- Seed tray
- Soilless potting mix
- Spray mist bottle
- Plastic bag or clingfilm
- Light source
- Fertilizer

1 Pre-moisten the soil mix with a small amount of tepid water. Fill the seed tray with soil (about two-thirds full), but do not pack the soil down hard.

2 Plant your seeds shallow, not deep. Sprinkle tiny seeds on the surface. Spray the soil surface with water to settle the soil firmly over the seeds, but do not saturate it.

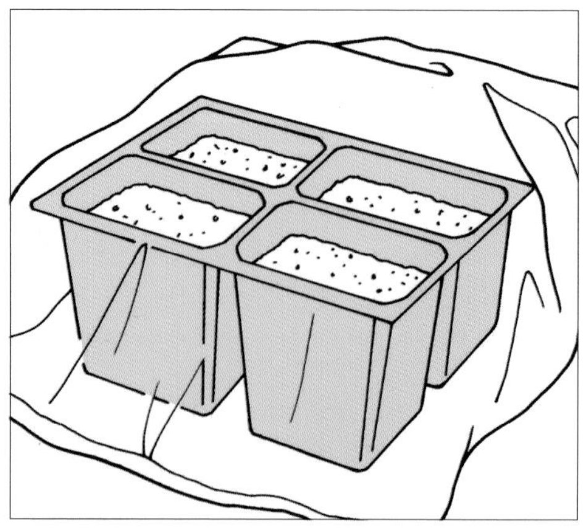

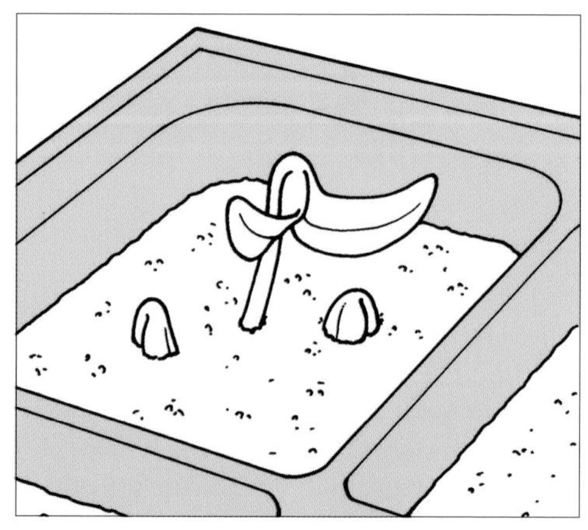

3 Cover your seed tray with clingfilm or put in a plastic bag to keep the soil evenly moist while the seeds germinate. Place the seed tray in a warm location somewhere that won't be in direct sunlight.

4 When the shoots appear, remove the plastic and place in direct sunlight. Water as needed and add fertilizer. Once there are a few leaves and the seedling is about 5cm (2in) high, transplant into individual pots.

HOW TO REPOT A PLANT

If your indoor potted plants appear to be stunted, deformed, pale and dull, or top-heavy, the reason for this is that they may be pot-bound and need to be moved to a larger pot. Pot-bound roots have outgrown their container and are starting to circle around the inside or poke out the drainage holes in search of more growing room.

INDISPENSABLE THINGS

- Plant
- Plant pot
- Potting soil

1 Take the plant out of its pot and knock off any old soil. Unwind circling roots and cut off any that look rotted or that need to be pruned back.

2 Choose a new pot that is only about 3–6cm (1–2 in) larger in diameter than the old one. Don't get too big a pot, because it will hold more soil and more water than the plant can use, which can lead to rot.

3 Put several centimetres of new potting soil in the bottom of the new pot, put the plant into the pot, and see if the level is high enough. The plant should be about 2.5cm (1in) below the top of the pot.

4 Fill in around the root ball with soil, tapping it down lightly with your fingers. Water the plant moderately.

HOW TO TAKE CUTTINGS

This is an easy way to increase the number of your garden plants. Plant cuttings can be taken from stems, roots or leaves on some plants. Cuttings taken from new shoots will root easily in spring to provide new plants for flowerbeds or pots. Alternatively, take cuttings of your favourite plants in late summer, keep them indoors in the winter, and plant outside in the spring. Always take cuttings in the morning, when the plants are at their freshest.

INDISPENSABLE THINGS

- Sharp knife or secateurs
- 10cm (4in) pot
- Potting compost
- Rooting hormone
- Dibber
- Spray mist bottle
- Clear plastic bag

1 Choose healthy, non-flowering shoots to use for cuttings. Use a clean sharp knife or secateurs to cut them from the parent plant. Cut below a single leaf joint or pair of leaves, aiming for a cutting of 7–10cm (3–4in) long. Remove any leaves from the bottom half of the cutting.

2 Fill a 10cm (4in) pot with compost. Dip the base of each cutting into rooting hormone to promote root development. Carefully tap off any excess liquid or powder. Use a dibber to make holes in the compost.

3 Insert the base of the cutting into the compost and firm in. Where possible, try to position cuttings so that their leaves don't touch each other. Water with a spray mist bottle, and label the pot so you know what the cuttings are.

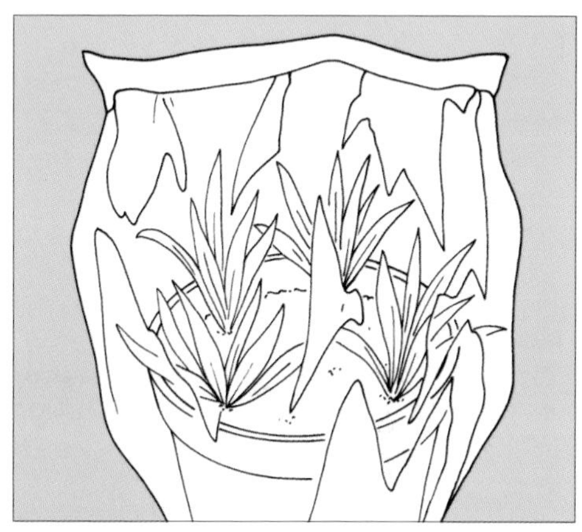

4 Cover the pot with a clear plastic bag and place the pot indoors out of direct sunlight. Mist regularly to keep the compost moist. Remove the bag once a day and shake out any excess water to prevent it becoming too humid inside. The cuttings should root in six to eight weeks. When the roots appear at the bottom of the pot, plant the cuttings up singly in pots of the same size.

A PRACTICAL HISTORY OF PLANT PROPAGATION

The Greek philosopher and disciple of Aristotle, Theophrastus (371–*c.*287BC) wrote *Enquiry into Plants* and *On the Causes of Plants*, two large botanical treatises that describe starting new plants from seed and from cuttings. The cuttings that he had most success with were actually rooted suckers that were separated or divided from the mother plant. The Romans worked out that using thin sheets of mica (glass) helped produce heat for protecting plants and encouraging them to grow. Ancient Chinese gardeners were also skilled in different methods of plant propagation.

HOW TO CHOP LOGS

Chopping wood for your fire can be a potential disaster, but with a little preparation and knowledge, you can safely produce a stack of logs. Always wear safety equipment, always place your log on a stable platform, and always make sure there are no bystanders or pets in the vicinity so they won't be hurt by flying splinters. Your goal is to hit the log directly in the centre: a glancing blow may result in injury to yourself, so aim carefully. Never use a dull or damaged axe, and don't attempt to chop logs at all if you have a back problem.

INDISPENSABLE THINGS

- Pile of logs
- Saw
- Hand axe
- Safety glasses
- Safety boots
- Chopping block

PRACTICAL TIP

Look after your tools and they'll last longer. When you've finished using the axe, lightly oil the blade to prevent rust and put a cover over it for safety reasons and to help keep it sharp.

SAFETY EQUIPMENT

This woodcutter should be wearing safety goggles to protect his eyes from flying splinters. Safety boots with steel toes are also recommended – the axe might miss the wood and hit your foot instead.

AXE

Use a hand axe with a sharp edge. Make sure that the head of the axe is attached securely to the shaft, otherwise the blade may fly off while you chop.

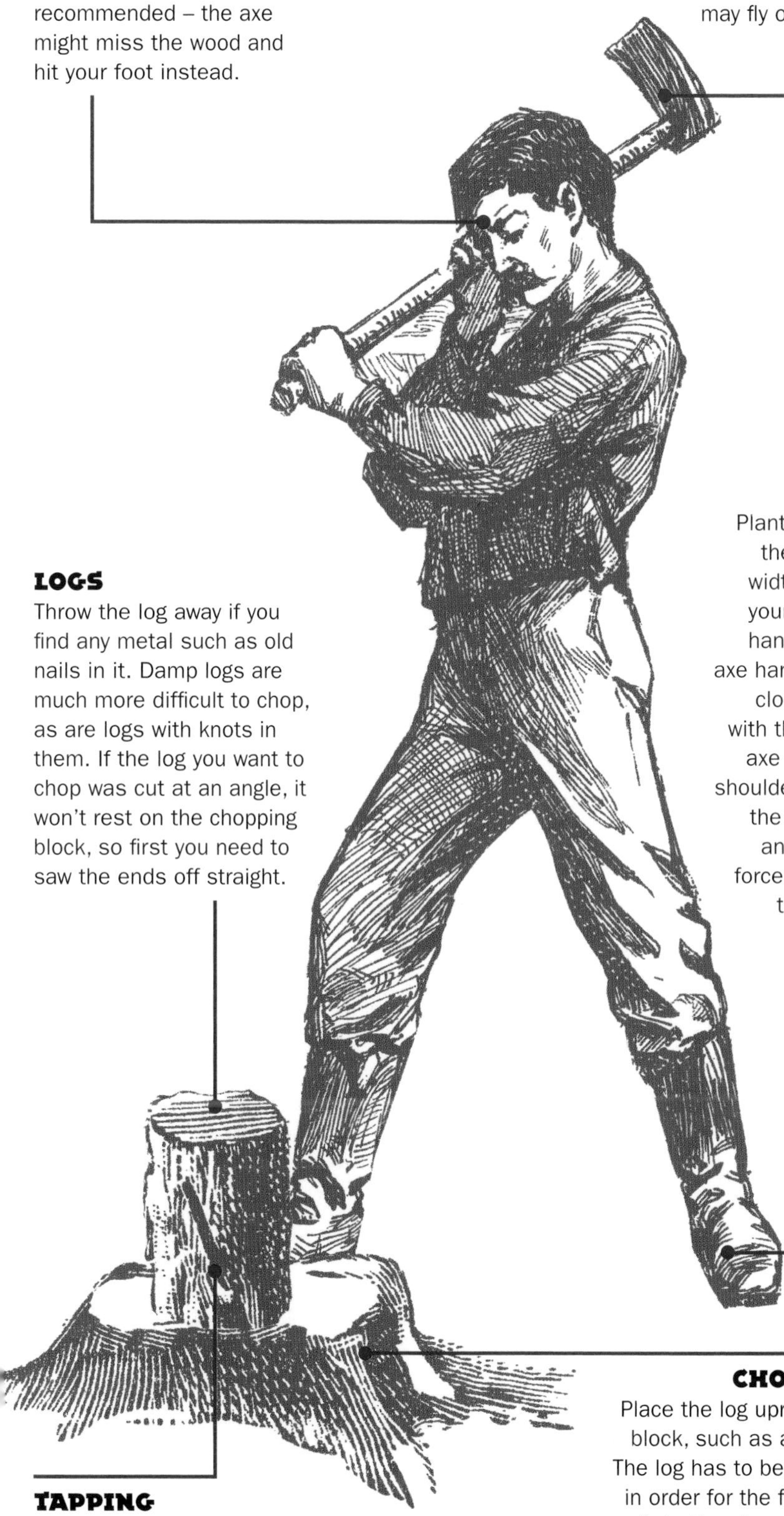

ACTION

Plant your feet firmly on the ground, shoulder-width apart to balance your weight. Place one hand at the end of the axe handle, and hold tight close to the axe head with the other. Raise the axe in an arc over your shoulder. Aim carefully for the centre, swing hard and follow through to force the axe head right through the log and imbed itself in the chopping block.

LOGS

Throw the log away if you find any metal such as old nails in it. Damp logs are much more difficult to chop, as are logs with knots in them. If the log you want to chop was cut at an angle, it won't rest on the chopping block, so first you need to saw the ends off straight.

CHOPPING BLOCK

Place the log upright on a chopping block, such as a large tree stump. The log has to be on a solid surface in order for the force of your axe to split it. The chopping block provides a solid base and raises the log so that your axe will meet it squarely.

TAPPING

If your axe doesn't chop the wood in half with the first hit, tap the axe (now embedded in the log) on the chopping block until it makes its way down the grain and splits the log in two.

HOW TO MAKE A TRELLIS

A trellis is nothing more than a grid for supporting plants, but it can range in size from a mere backdrop to a container to an elaborate structure running the length of a garden wall. Design a trellis to accommodate the climbing plant you have in mind – some vines will grab on to any surface; bushier plants may need to be tied on to a trellis. You'll get the best results from natural-born climbers like cucumbers, beans, squash, peas and tomatoes. If your soil is dry and hard, water deeply the day before you plan to build the trellis to make it easier to drive the poles or stakes into the ground.

INDISPENSABLE THINGS

- Bamboo, tree branches or broom handles
- Garden twine, raffia or cloth
- Spade
- Wooden mallet
- Wooden posts
- Wire, string or netting
- Staple gun

PRACTICAL TIP

Trellised plants can lose moisture quickly because they are exposed to wind and sun. Put a mulch on top of the soil to retain moisture and water regularly – the easiest way to do this is to entwine a tubing system through the trellis.

TEPEE TRELLIS

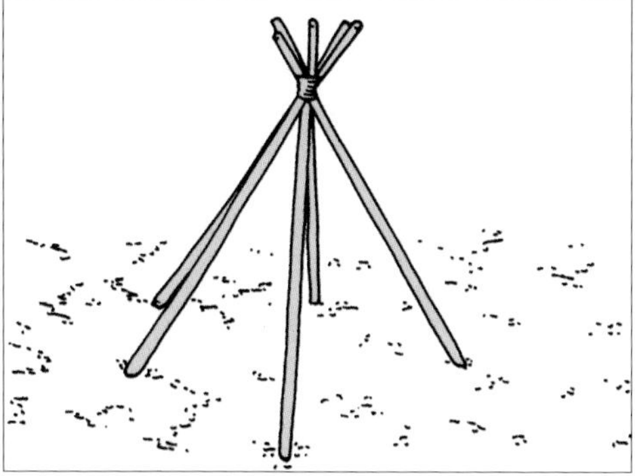

1 Tepee trellises make excellent supports for beans, peas and tomatoes, and for heavily fruited crops such as melon and squash. You will need three to six poles of equal length – bamboo, branches or broom handles – choose thin ones for lightweight plants and stouter ones for heavier crops.

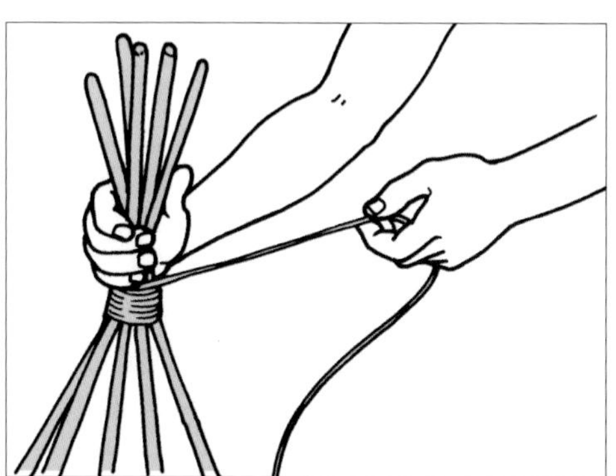

2 Use garden twine, raffia or strips of cloth to lash poles together near the top. Pull the poles into a tight bundle, wrap the twine around the bundle a few times and tie it snugly. Weave the twine in and out of the bundled sticks and make sure it's sturdy, stable and secure.

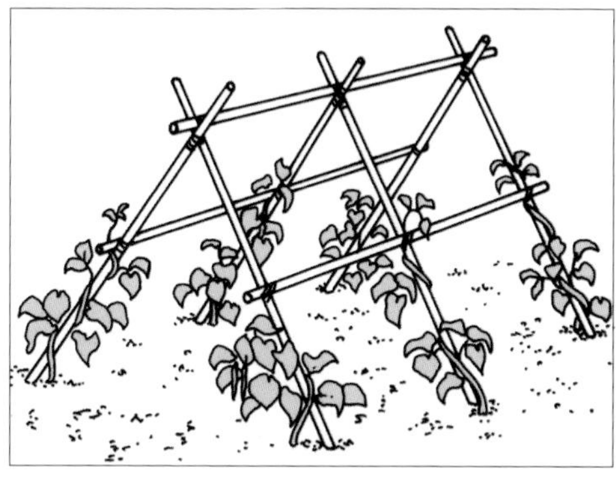

3 Prop the tepee over the planting area. Push the poles about 30cm (1ft) into the ground. Leave one area of the tepee plant-free so you can harvest produce easily. For a larger crop, space the poles in two rows and then place bamboo poles horizontally between them to add extra support.

FENCE TRELLIS

1 To make a fence trellis, dig two holes 60cm (24in) deep and 3m (10ft) apart. Use a mallet and drive a wooden post deeply into each hole. Tamp in with soil. Place other posts in between where needed.

2 Wrap wire or string tightly around one stake, then run it to the other fence post, wrap it around and tie it tightly. Wrap more wire horizontally around the posts at regular intervals, and vertically between the wires. Or attach mesh netting, using a staple gun.

HOW TO MAKE A BIRD BOX

This cheap and easy project is a great way of attracting birds into your garden. Specially constructed bird boxes imitate the cavities in trees and can be a real help to garden birds when rearing their young. Only make a perch if it is intended for house sparrows, because they will sit on it and peck at other birds using the box. Site your bird box in a north-east facing spot, high up in a tree or building away from predators, strong sunlight and wind. Avoid placing near other bird boxes, tables or feeders.

INDISPENSABLE THINGS

- Wood, 150mm wide x 1500mm long x 15mm thick (about 6in x 60in x 1/2in)
- Pencil and ruler
- Saw
- Hammer
- Galvanized 20mm (3/4in) nails
- Sealant
- Drill with cutting bits
- Hinge
- Screws
- Screwdriver
- Hook and eye fastener
- Linseed oil

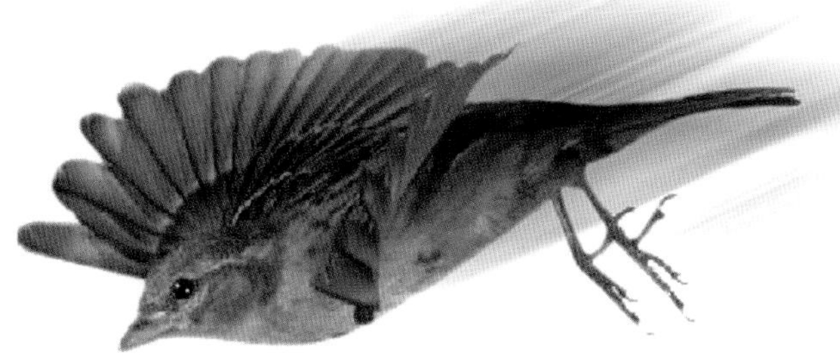

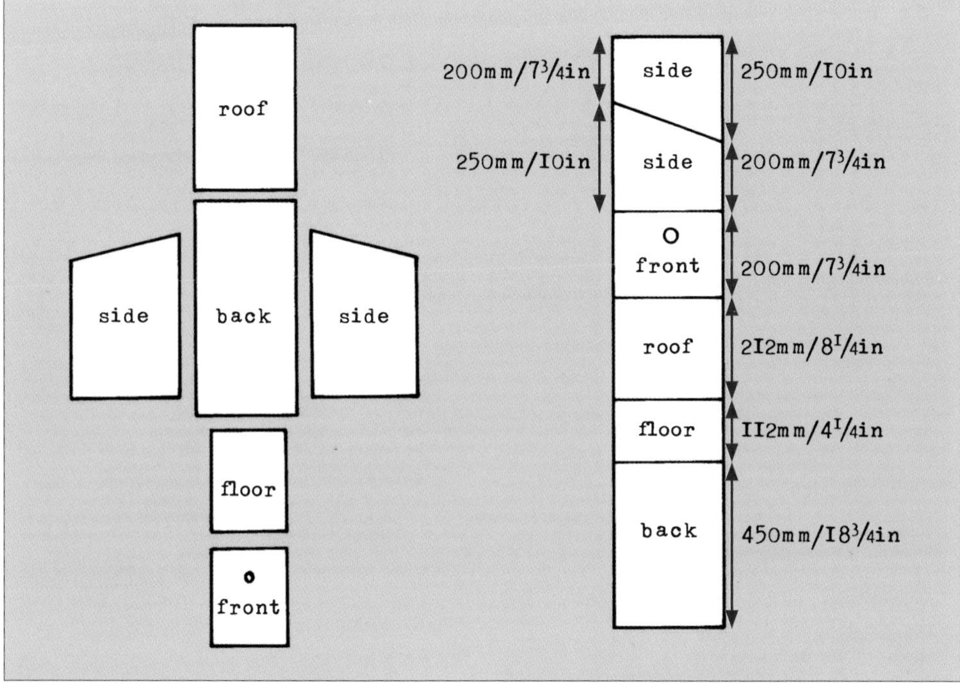

1 Any wood will do, but exterior-grade plywood is best. Mark out the six sections of the bird box with a pencil and ruler to the dimensions shown above, and write the name of each panel onto the marked-out wood to save confusion later. Where possible, try to ensure that the grain will run vertically in the finished box because this will help drainage.

Cut out the panels of wood. Make a small hole in the base to let liquid waste drain. The hole size for the entrance is important because some birds will oust others if they can get into the box. For blue tits and coal tits, make a 25mm (1in) hole; for great tits, make a 28mm (1$\frac{1}{10}$in) hole, for house sparrows, make a 32mm (1¼in) hole. Nail the sides, back and bottom together. To make the box waterproof and windproof, seal the sides with sealant as you build.

FINISHING TOUCHES

Fix the top to the sides of the box with a hinge so that it can be opened, and add a hook and eye fastener to keep it shut. You don't need to paint the box – indeed, some colours are known to scare birds off. A coat of linseed oil will keep the wood from drying out, but avoid wood preservatives because they can be poisonous to wildlife. Clean out the box every year, 2–3 weeks after birds have fledged (October–November). Remove any old nests or bedding and rinse out the box with boiling water to kill parasites. Do not use pesticides or flea powder, for obvious reasons.

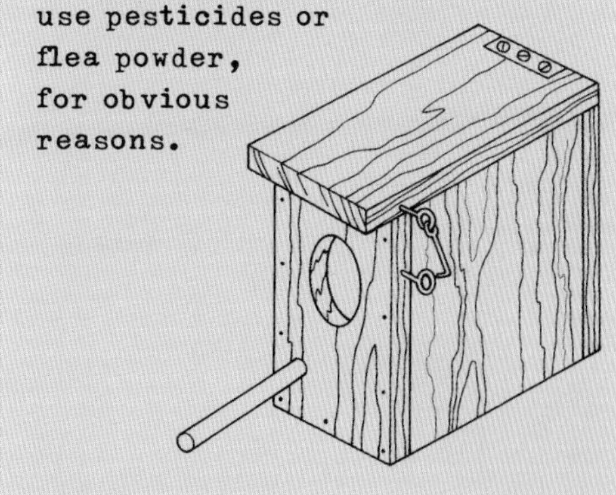

HOW TO PLANT UP A WINDOW BOX

A window box is a great way to smarten up the exterior of your home. Most plants will grow happily in containers if they are given the correct soil and watering conditions. A simple but effective design is to choose one type of plant that grows up, one that trails down and one bushy type to fill in the middle. Water your window box frequently to keep it moist, usually once a day during summer and autumn. Use liquid fertilizer once a fortnight when plants are established, and deadhead when necessary.

INDISPENSABLE THINGS

- Window box
- Clean crocks (pieces of broken crockery) for the base
- Multi-purpose compost, moistened with warm water
- Plants of your choice

PRACTICAL TIP

Flowers in window boxes grow away from the window, but if you want them to grow vertically instead of outwards, turn your window box around every few days (obviously you can't do this if it's fixed to the wall!).

LOCATION
Before buying, consider how the box will be fixed. Is the sill wide and strong enough for the box to sit securely? If in doubt, the box should be fixed to the wall. Window boxes can be fitted on walls facing any direction, but south and west-facing will require more watering. North-facing boxes will need shade-tolerant plants. If your box is in a very hot position, insert polystyrene tiles along the front to keep the inside cool.

CHOICE
There are a number of ready-made window boxes available, from simple plastic trays to metal, terracotta and ornate wood, but bear in mind that metal boxes may become too hot. Choose a window box that will blend in with your house wall – the more natural-looking, the better. Measure the windowsill before buying a window box to make sure it will fit.

LENGTH
For the best results in a window box garden, the box ought to be at least 1–1.25m (3–4ft) long but, not more than 2m (6ft). Any larger, and it will be too heavy to suspend and secure properly, and it will be very difficult to lift. Choose a container with good drainage holes, and cover the holes at the base with a layer of crocks.

PLANTING UP
Fill the container to three-quarters full with compost. Before planting, arrange the plants, while still in their pots, in the box to see how they will look best. Take into account structure, colour and foliage texture. Place taller plants in the middle and trailing plants such as ivy along the edge. When you're happy, knock them out of their pots and plant them at around 2cm (¾in) below the rim. Firm in and water.

HOW TO MAKE A COLD FRAME

A cold frame is a bottomless box with a see-through lid, used to protect tender plants throughout the winter months in cold regions and to extend the growing season. Relying solely on the heat and warmth of the sun, a cold frame costs nothing to use and very little to build. The size of the frame depends on the size of the window(s), but do not make your cold frame so wide that you cannot easily reach the plants at the back, especially if you're growing vegetables. A maximum width of 1–1.25m (3-4ft) is about right for most people to reach the back for weeding or harvesting their produce.

INDISPENSABLE THINGS

- Old window
- Heavy-duty hinges
- Tape measure
- Lengths of wood
- Saw
- 50mm (2in) stainless steel screws
- Phillips screwdriver
- Wood glue
- Hook and eye closure
- Paint

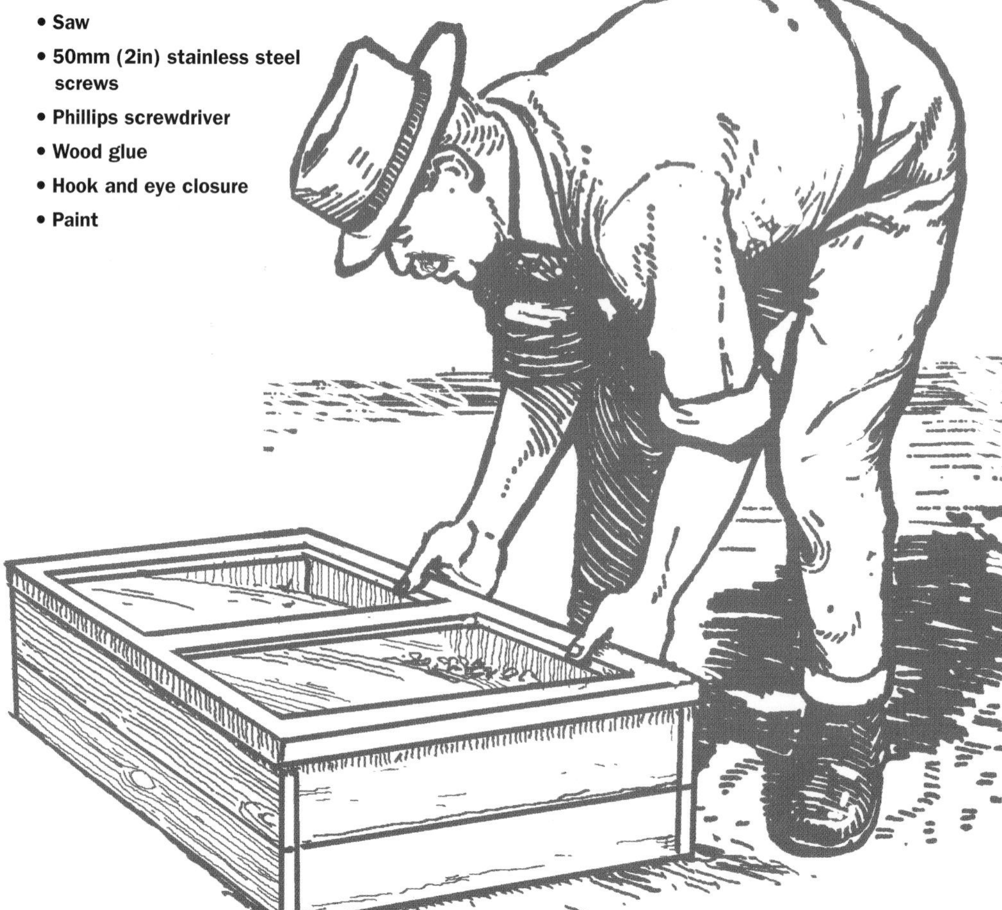

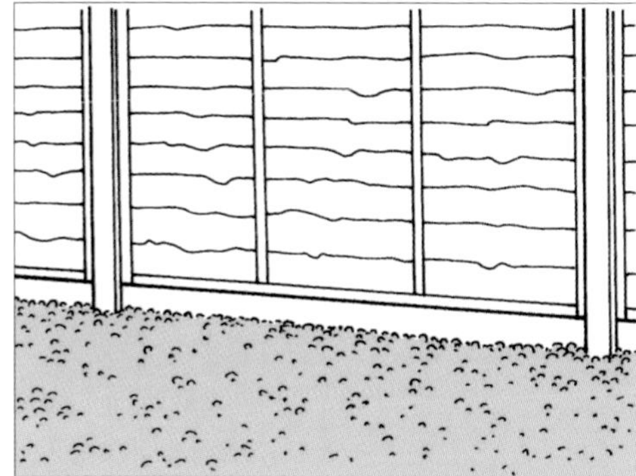

1 Before building a cold frame, choose a good location. You need a site that receives an ample amount of sunlight each day; one where you can butt the cold frame up against an existing structure to provide protection from winds and rain, and one with good drainage, to allow water to flow away from the cold frame.

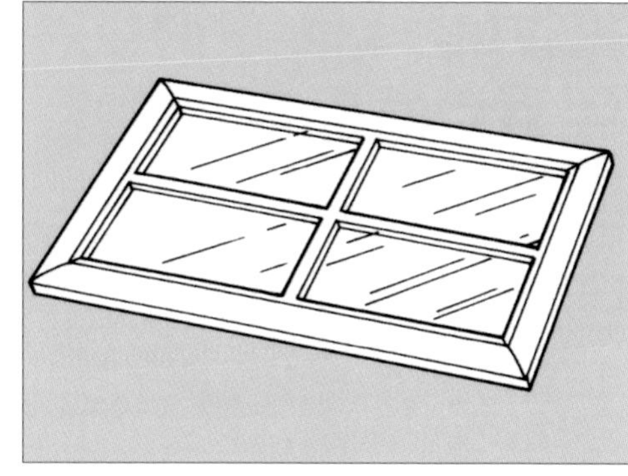

2 The top of most cold frames made at home are old windows (the glass lets the sunshine in), so the dimensions of the frame depend on the size of the window you use. You will need to hinge the window, so buy some heavy-duty hinges. You will need to build your frame to fit your window, making sure that the back is higher than the front.

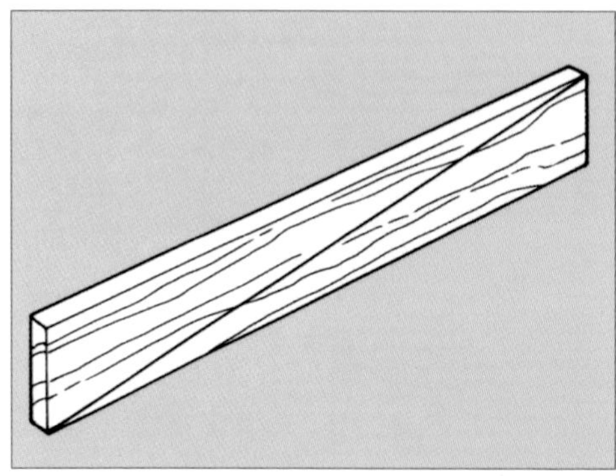

3 Measure the window's side length. Draw a line that length from top to bottom of a plank. Saw along this to make the angled top pieces. Cut 2 planks the same length as the flat edge of those angled top pieces to form the box sides and another 3 the same as the front length of the window (1 to make the front and 2 to make the back of the frame).

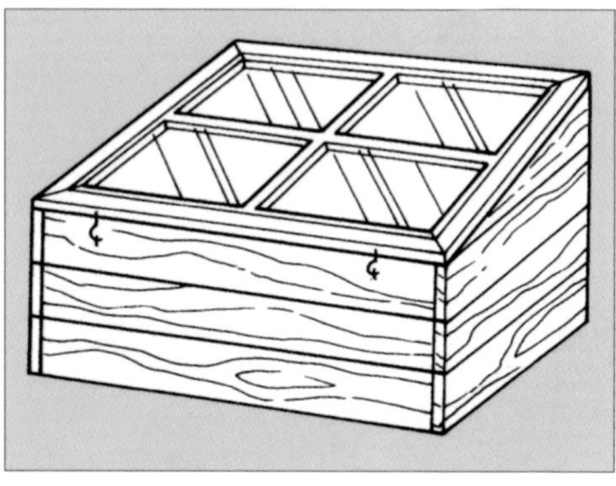

4 Glue the pieces of wood together and screw together at the joints for extra support. Place the old window over the top and attach with hinges on the back. If wind is likely to blow your window top open, add a simple hook and eye closure to the front.

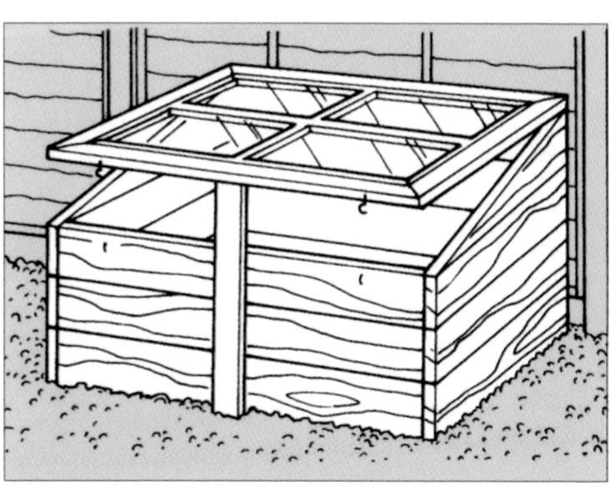

5 Paint the outside of the frame to make it weatherproof. You'll also want to include a way to keep the window open for ventilation during mild days when the temperature reaches above 7°C (45°F). A spare piece of wood can be used as a prop.

HOW TO PRUNE A ROSE BUSH

It is hard to kill a rose with pruning. Like a bad haircut, most mistakes will grow out quickly and it is better to prune than to let roses grow rampant. No pruning results in a mess of tangled stems bearing only a few flowers.

INDISPENSABLE THINGS

- Secateurs
- Loppers for longer stems
- Thick gloves (preferably long ones)

WHY

Roses need pruning to promote new growth, increase air circulation, shape the plant and remove dead, damaged or diseased stems.

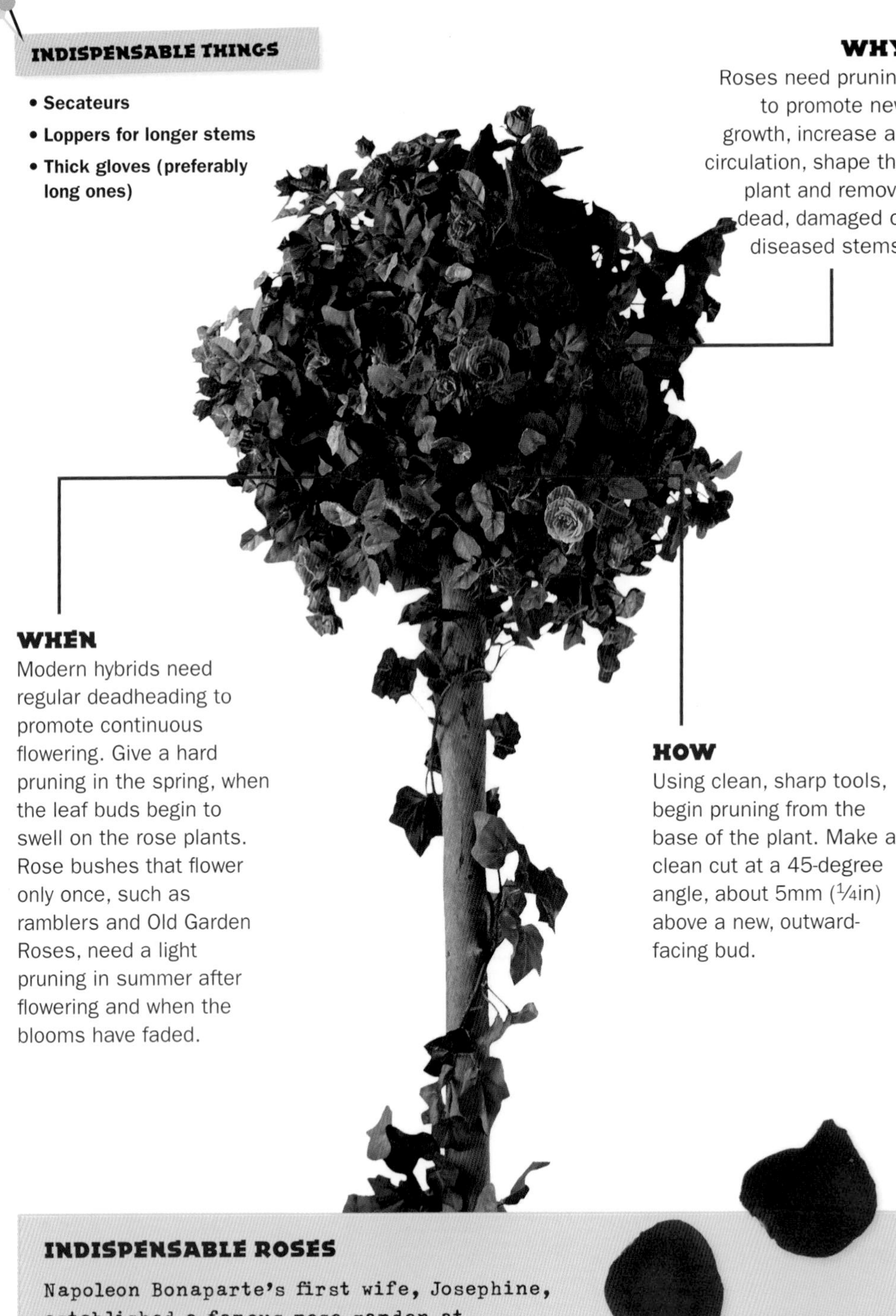

WHEN

Modern hybrids need regular deadheading to promote continuous flowering. Give a hard pruning in the spring, when the leaf buds begin to swell on the rose plants. Rose bushes that flower only once, such as ramblers and Old Garden Roses, need a light pruning in summer after flowering and when the blooms have faded.

HOW

Using clean, sharp tools, begin pruning from the base of the plant. Make a clean cut at a 45-degree angle, about 5mm (¼in) above a new, outward-facing bud.

INDISPENSABLE ROSES

Napoleon Bonaparte's first wife, Josephine, established a famous rose garden at Malmaison, in France. Apparently she liked to wander around with a rose, which she would hold near her mouth when conversing to conceal her rotten teeth.

HOW TO WATER A HOUSEPLANT

Most houseplants require a thorough soaking and then to be left alone until they almost dry out. Stick a small knife in the compost: if it comes out dry with no soil particles attached, then your plant needs watering. If the soil is very dry, leave the pot in a few centimetres (an inch) of water for 30 minutes until the top of the soil is moist.

INDISPENSABLE THINGS

- Houseplant
- Tap water

SEASON
Most plants grow faster in the spring and summer than in the autumn and winter. The faster a plant grows, the more water it needs.

LOCATION
A plant in a warm bright room requires more water than the same plant in a cool dark room.

POT
Plants in small pots dry out faster than those in large ones. A plant in a porous container such as terracotta will dry out faster than the same plant in a metal or plastic one.

WATER
Tap water is fine, but leave it in a jug for 30 minutes so the chlorine evaporates and it reaches room temperature (if water is too cold, the roots can't absorb it).

METHOD
Water thoroughly from the top until the water comes out the drip holes. This leaches out salts that have built up in the soil from fertilizers.

HOW TO MAKE COMPOST

Compost is used to feed and nourish the soil to help you grow healthy plants. To make your own compost, just provide the right ingredients and let nature do the rest. The finished product should be dark, crumbly and sweet-smelling. For best results, use a mixture of green and brown ingredients. Do not compost meat, fish, dairy products or cooked food (these will attract vermin), cat litter, nappies or weeds with seed heads. You will know that your compost heap is right if it becomes hot in the middle – this is important to sterilize the compost and kill off any pathogens that cause disease.

INDISPENSABLE THINGS

- Compost bin
- Water

BROWN INGREDIENTS

- Cardboard (cereal packets, egg boxes, toilet rolls)
- Wood shavings
- Prunings
- Fallen leaves

GREEN INGREDIENTS

- Grass clippings
- Vegetable peelings
- Cut plants and flowers
- Teabags
- Coffee grounds
- Vegetarian pet manure and bedding

INGREDIENTS

Green compost ingredients are those that are rich in nitrogen, and include urine, so yes, you can pee on the compost heap! A 2008 report from the Oregon State University Extension Service found that coffee grounds increased the heat of the compost heap, killing off pathogens and weed seeds and having much the same effect as manure.

FIRST STEPS

To start your compost, place a few woody plant stems or small twigs at the bottom of the container to improve the air circulation and drainage. Collect enough materials to make a layer of at least 30cm (12in) or more in the compost bin. Turn the compost every few weeks to keep things moving.

MAINTENANCE

Brown compost ingredients are rich in carbon. Roughly 40 per cent of the average dustbin contents are suitable for composting, so it helps to cut down on landfill, too. Continue to fill the container as and when you have ingredients. Remember that a thriving compost heap needs water – it should remain damp, but not be dripping wet. If you do not get enough rainfall, pour a bucket of water over it once a week to keep things moving.

LEAVE TO MATURE

When the container is full – which it may never be because the contents will sink as it composts – or when you decide to, stop adding any more. If the lower layers have composted, use this on the garden. Mix everything else together well. Add water if it is dry, or add dry brown material if it is soggy. Replace in the bin and leave to mature – this can take anything from a couple of months to a year.

HEALTH & BEAUTY

LOOKING AFTER CLOTHES

They say you shouldn't judge a book by its cover, but that's nonsense. Everything about your appearance — from the buttons on your coat to the shine of your shoes — speaks volumes about who you are. This chapter tells you how to use your clothes to show off your best side.

HOW TO MEND A HOLE IN YOUR POCKET

There's a hole in your pocket. You know there is because every time you put away some loose change, it gushes from your trouser leg like a small win on a fruit machine. Fortunately, the repair job is quick and easy. If the seam has come apart, turn the pocket inside-out, remove any loose threads and sew. If there's a hole in the fabric, then you can patch it. For the quickest fix, turn the pocket out and sew right across. You'll end up with a smaller pocket, but it will take barely a minute to ensure your pennies look after themselves.

INDISPENSABLE THINGS

- Patch or spare pocket
- Pins
- Needle
- Thread

PRACTICAL TIP

Put together a mini sewing kit so that you have the basics to hand. You need a variety pack of needles (a needle threader will save you bother); sharp scissors; all-purpose thread in black, white and a few basic colours; fusible web for superfast hemming repairs; safety pins – for emergencies; and all the spare buttons that came with your clothes.

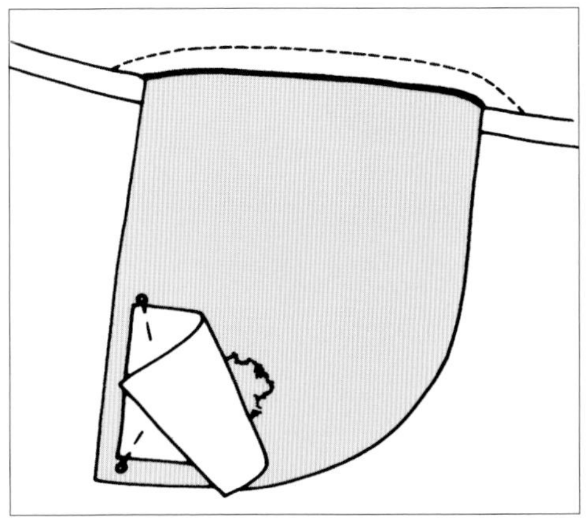

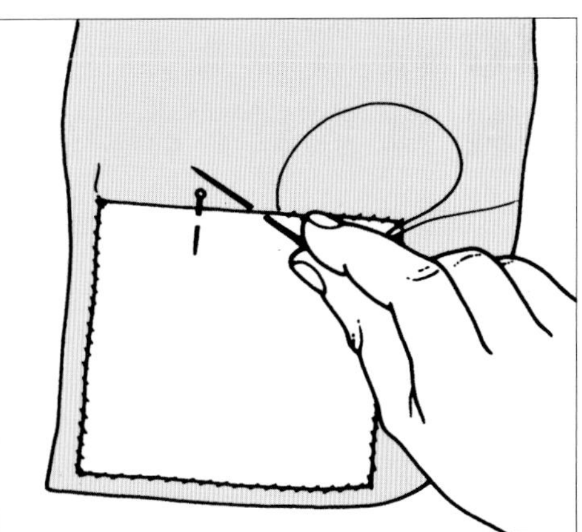

1 Find some fabric that is the same weight as the pocket. Cut a patch to cover the hole, leaving a 2cm (¾in) edge all the way around. Turn the pocket inside-out, then lay the patch over the hole so that the fabric is right-side up. Pin round the hole, turning under the edges of the patch as you go.

2 Sew the patch into place by hand, using a simple stitch (you'll need to back-stitch if the fabric is heavy). If using a machine, tack the patch into place first. Place the foot over the beginning of the tacking line. Use zigzag stitch to sew all around the pocket (pivoting at the corners), making sure that you don't sew through it.

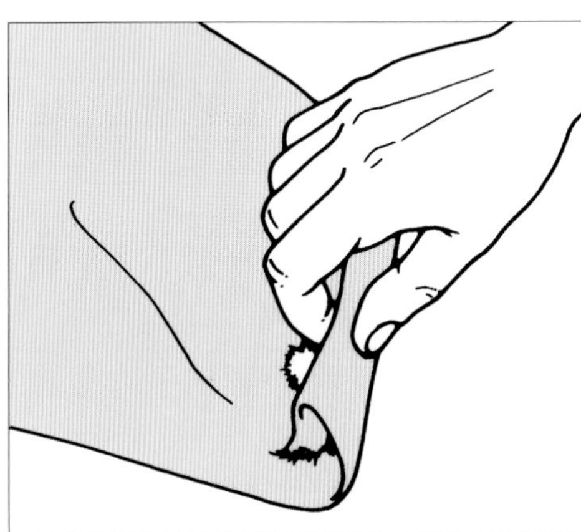

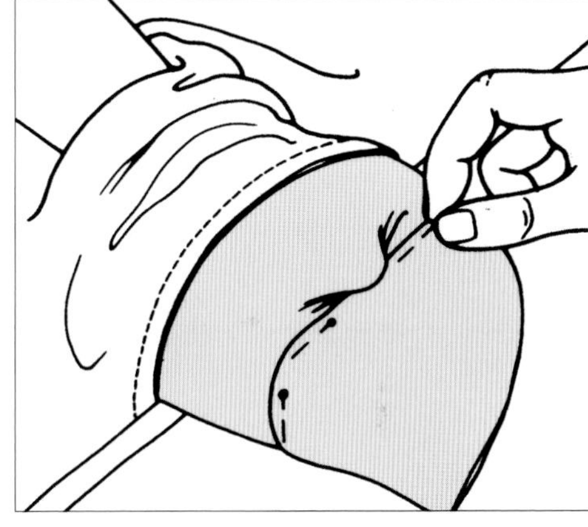

ALTERNATIVELY, if the hole is at the bottom of the pocket, you can simply fold up the pocket to cover the hole. Pin the fold into place, then tack if using a machine. Stitch right across the pocket, sewing through both sides at once. This method will make the pocket shorter than before.

ANOTHER REPAIR OPTION for a hole in the base is to use the base of a pocket from an unwanted item of clothing it (the fabric should be the same weight). Cut the repair-pocket so it will reach over the hole, then pin and hand-stitch into place, or use a machine as in step 2.

A PRACTICAL HISTORY OF POCKETS

The word pocket is related to 'pouch', and also to the defunct word 'poke', which meant 'sack' (as in 'pig in a poke'). Herein lies a clue to the origin of the modern pocket: it began life in the Middle Ages as a detachable money bag which was kept, for maximum safety, inside the clothes. In later centuries, as clothing technology improved, trousers were provided with a convenient tailored slit, so that people could reach their money without undoing their belt. From there it was a short step to stitching the little pouch (or 'poke-ette') permanently and invisibly into the fabric of a man's breeches.

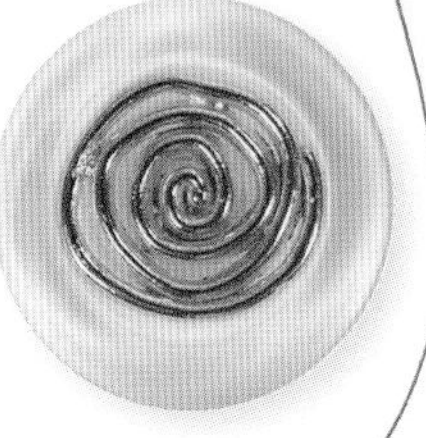

HOW TO SEW ON A BUTTON

Buttons can come off even the most expensive item of clothing, and nothing looks less stylish than a gaping shirtfront or a flapping sleeve. If you have an amenable grandmother to act as your personal seamstress, all well and good. If not, then it pays to know how to do this job yourself. The key thing is to make sure that you do not sew on your button either too loosely or too tight.

INDISPENSABLE THINGS

- Thread matching the fabric or button
- Needle
- Scissors
- Matchsticks (head removed)
- Spare button (two or four holes)

A PRACTICAL HISTORY OF BUTTONS

The Amish of Pennsylvania don't use buttons because they are not mentioned in the Bible. But buttons were part of tailoring technology well before New Testament times, and were known to the Romans. The buttonhole, on the other hand, was not conceived until the 14th century – and it revolutionized fashion by making it possible to cut clothes to fit a shapely body. Buttons became a status symbol, an early form of bling (another reason the godly Amish are opposed to them). Horn or clay buttons gave way to sparkling bijoux of gold, silver or glass. Mass-produced buttons arrived with the industrial revolution. For a time, clothes and even boots were festooned with so many rows of buttons that they couldn't be fastened by hand – hence the invention of the button hook.

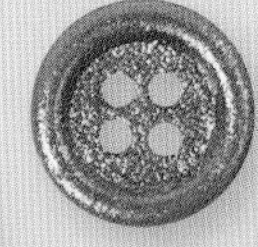

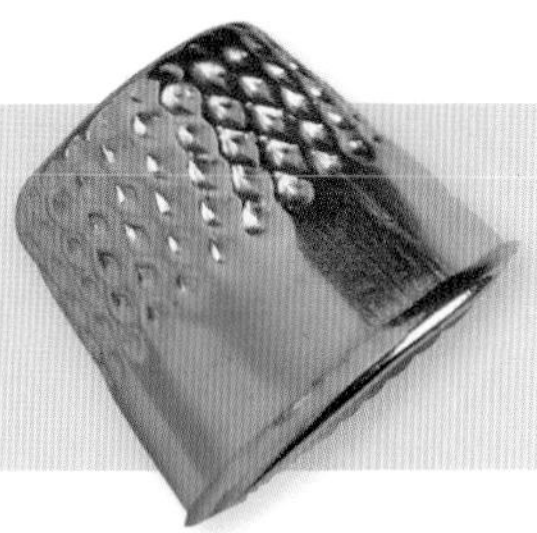

INDISPENSABLE WARNING

If you are sewing a button onto a jacket made from heavy fabric, use a thimble to protect your finger when pushing the needle through.

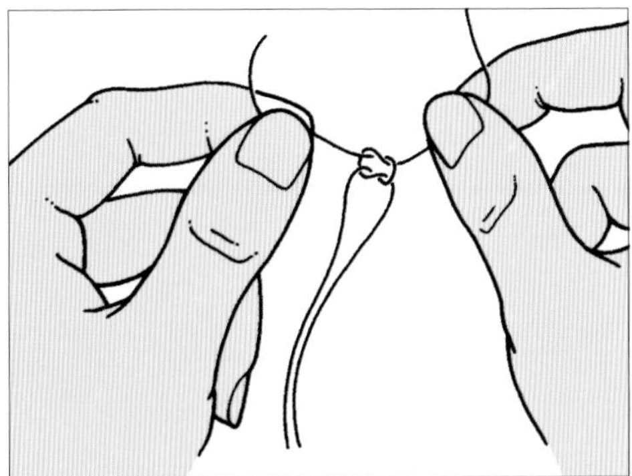

1 Cut a thread 45–60cm (18–24in) long and slip through the eye of the needle. Pull the ends together and tie in a double knot. Cut off the loose ends.

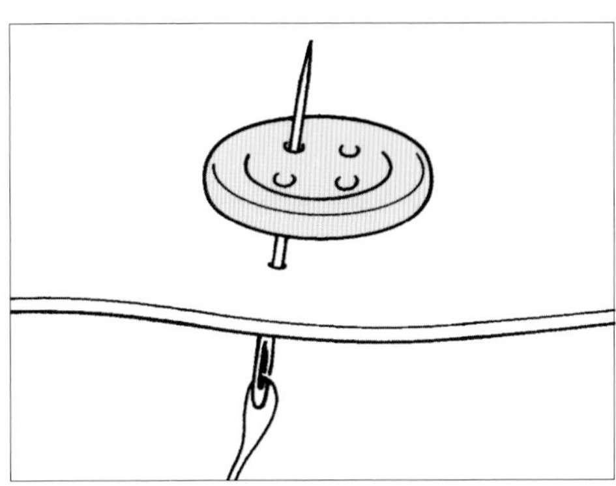

2 Line up the button with the other buttons and with the buttonhole. Insert the needle through the fabric and up through one of the button's holes and pull the thread through.

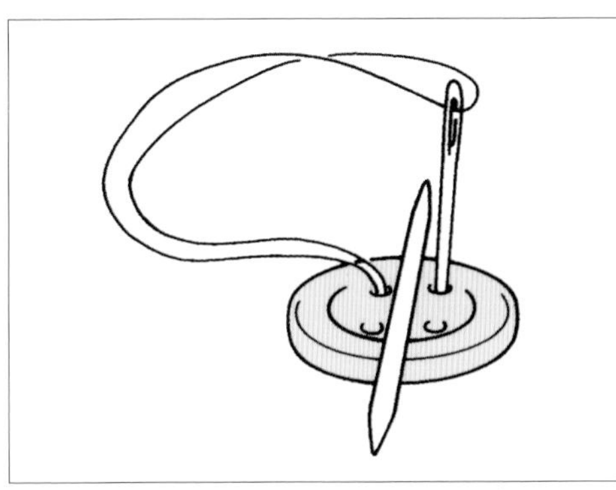

3 Place a matchstick across the button. Push the needle into the hole opposite the one you started with and through the fabric. Hold the matchstick as you pull the thread down, anchoring the button on the fabric.

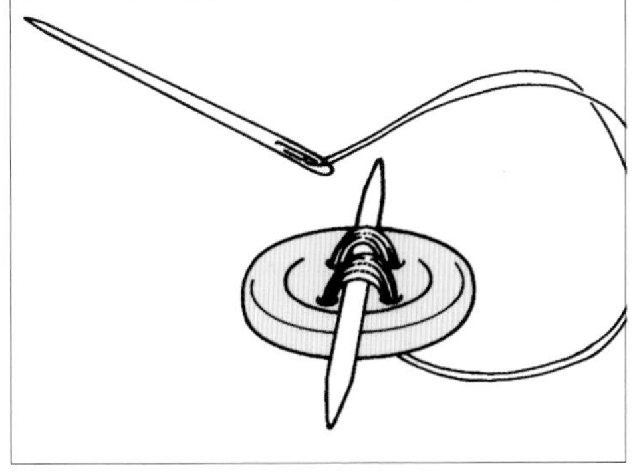

4 Repeat the stitch to secure the button. If you have a four-hole button, do the other side, again using two stitches. Then push your needle through the fabric and pull the thread up between the fabric and button.

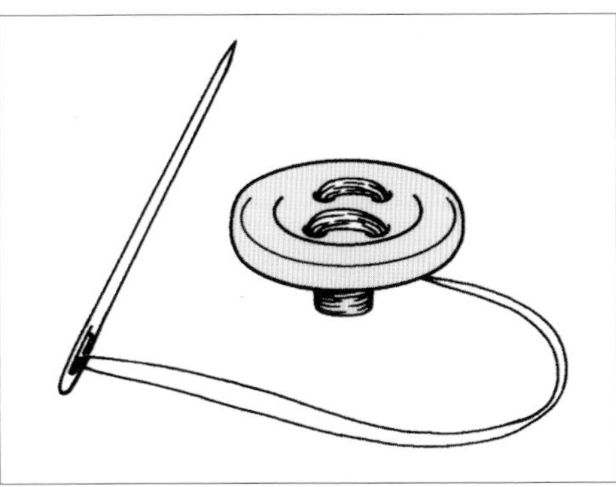

5 Remove the matchstick. Wind the thread around the thread between fabric and button three times (up to six if the material is thick). This creates a 'shank' that raises the button away from the fabric for easy fastening.

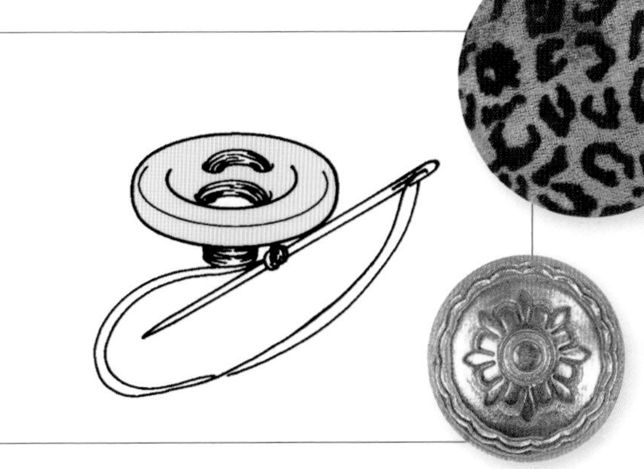

6 Now loop the thread around the shank again, but this time leave it loose. Pass the needle through the loop and pull the thread taut to create a knot. Repeat, then cut the thread close to the shank.

HOW TO WASH CASHMERE

Your cashmere jumper may say 'dry clean only', but that's often the manufacturer's lawyer talking – if the label says hand-wash and you plunge the jumper into boiling hot water, you are going to want a refund. Most cashmere garments (not quite all of them) can be washed, and if you do it right, then they will actually last longer than if you clean them chemically. And washing is cheaper than dry-cleaning, so you will not only preserve your cashmere, but you will also save cash.

INDISPENSABLE THINGS

- Specialist detergent
- Tepid water
- Two towels

INDISPENSABLE WARNING

Be very careful when washing a cashmere jumper; if you make any mistakes, then you could shrink or damage the item. Expensive cashmere may be dry-cleaned as a safeguard.

CASHMERE CLEAN

Use a specialist mild detergent to clean cashmere. Ordinary detergent is too harsh and can destroy the natural oils in cashmere. Add the soap to water that is just warm (not hot) and swish around to distribute. Submerge the jumper, then gently squeeze the suds through it.

SOAKING

Do not rub, twist or stretch the garment in any way. Soak for 10 minutes, then rinse carefully in cool clean water; repeat until the rinse water is clear.

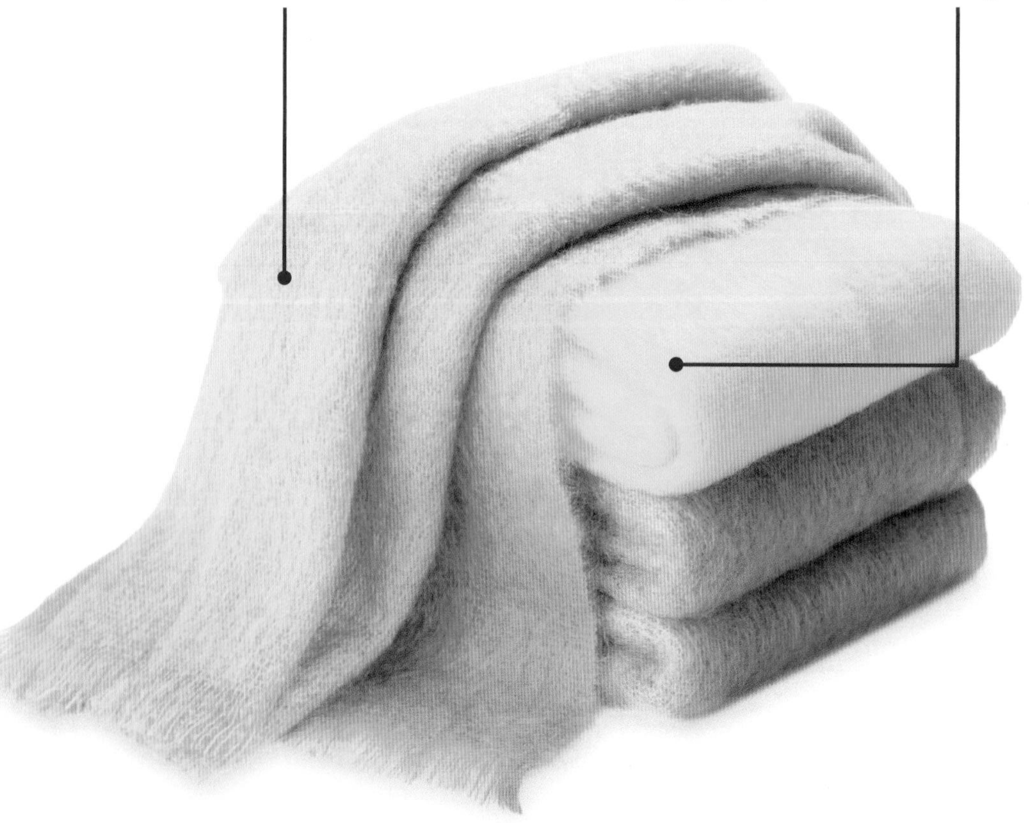

STORING CASHMERE

Your cashmere is delicate so treat it carefully. Wash and dry it before storing in a garment bag. Use cedar balls or lavender to keep moths away – because moths love cashmere.

SQUEEZE-DRYING

Very gently squeeze out the excess water. Lay a clean towel flat on the floor, then place the garment on top. Very carefully roll it up, pressing with the palms of your hands to squeeze the water into the towel. Reshape the garment and dry flat on another towel or drying rack, away from direct heat or sunlight. Do not line-dry cashmere; this will pull it out of shape. Never tumble-dry cashmere.

STAIN REMOVAL

If your garment has a grease stain, then it is best to take it to the dry-cleaners; rubbing the cashmere will harm it.

IN THE MACHINE

Some cashmere can be machine-washed (check the care label). Always fasten any buttons and turn the item inside-out first. Place in a cotton pillow case, and select the wool cycle on your machine. Again, use a specialist mild detergent. Select a very gentle, short spin before drying flat.

HOW TO IRON A SHIRT

Let's face it: shirts need ironing. Resign yourself to spending 5 minutes on each one. The up side is that you'll soon be good at it — and there is real satisfaction in a perfectly pressed shirt. For that brand-new crispness, invest in some spray starch: hang the shirt up, fasten the top button and lightly spray before ironing. A word of warning: always iron in a clean place. There's nothing worse than realizing that you have just dragged a spotless white sleeve through the cat's litter tray.

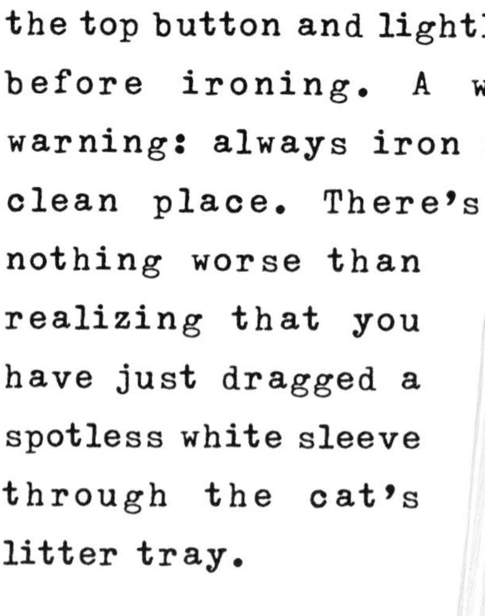

INDISPENSABLE THINGS

- Steam iron
- Ironing board
- A shirt
- Hanger

PRACTICAL TIP

If your shirt is very creased, use a spray mist bottle to spray it lightly with water. Roll up the shirt and wrap in a towel for 10 minutes so that the dampness spreads to every part of the shirt. Then iron as instructed.

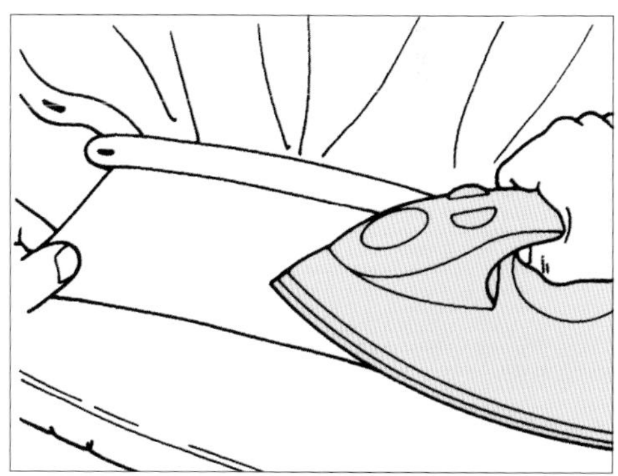

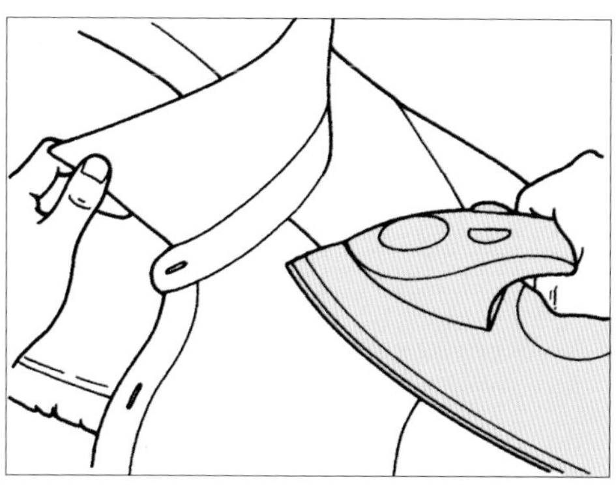

1 Heat the iron to the right temperature (check the manufacturer's label). If you are ironing linen or cotton, you'll need the steam function, so fill the iron with water. Start with the collar. Open it out flat, then position it underside-up on the ironing board. Iron from each point into the centre. Turn it over and do the other side.

2 Pull one shoulder of the shirt onto the tapered end of the ironing board, so that the back yoke is on the ironing board. Smooth it out and then press. Do the same on the other side.

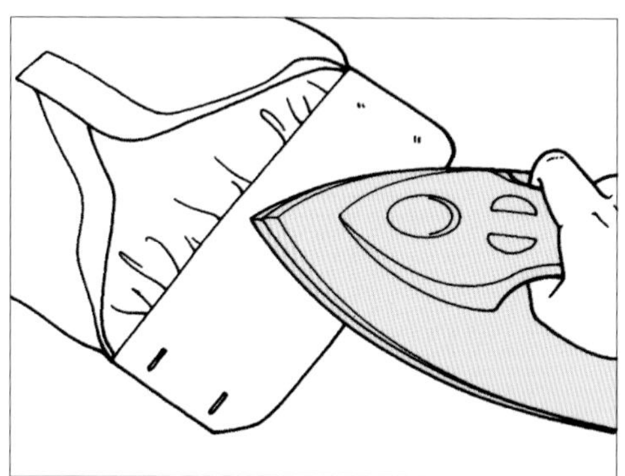

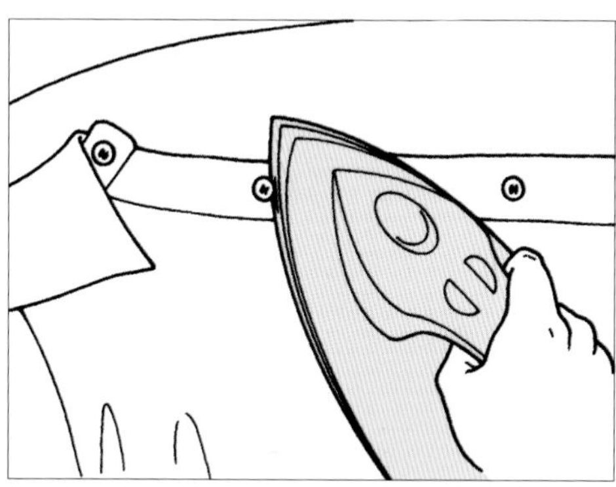

3 Open the cuff and press first the inside, then the outside. Lay the back of one sleeve on the board and smooth it flat. Press, working from the shoulder down to the cuff. Do the front of the sleeve in the same way. Repeat the process on the other sleeve.

4 Next do the button-side front panel. Slip the sleeve into the tapered end of the ironing board and press the top section first. Then move the panel so that it is flat on the board and press the remainder. Take extra care around the buttons.

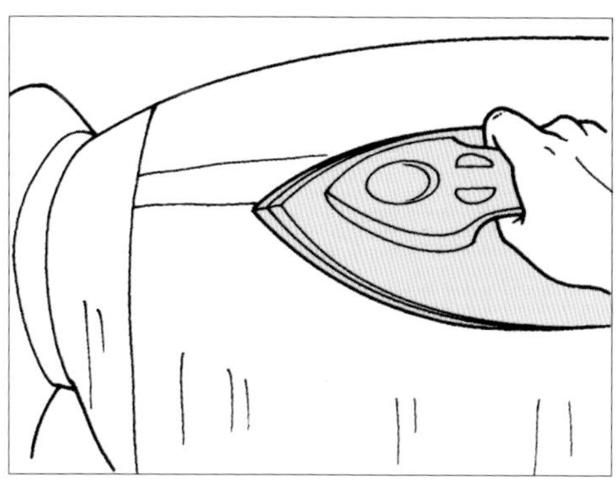

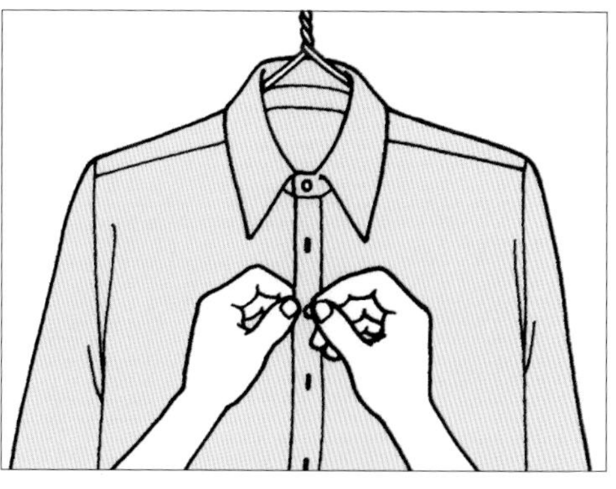

5 Iron the back of the shirt, working from the shoulder to the hem. Then do the remaining front panel.

6 Place on a hanger, making sure that the shirt is hanging straight with the sleeves over the front of the shirt. Button the first and third buttons, and hang in your wardrobe, leaving plenty of space around it.

HOW TO MEASURE YOUR BRA SIZE

Ladies – if you are wearing the correctly sized bra, then you are in a minority. As many as eight out of ten women are in the wrong one. We spend fortunes on our underwear, but when it comes to the bra, we have a one-size-fits-all mentality – often 34B. Generally speaking, we overestimate the band size (the numerical bit) and underestimate the cup size (the alphabetical bit). Wearing the right bra can make you stand better, look taller and appear slimmer.

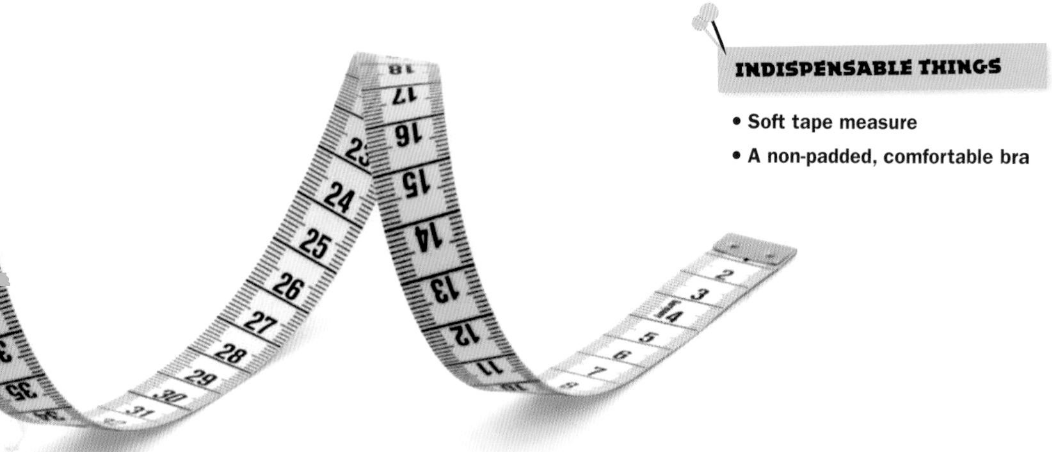

INDISPENSABLE THINGS

- Soft tape measure
- A non-padded, comfortable bra

A PRACTICAL HISTORY OF BRAS

In ancient Crete, women wore a garment that lifted bare breasts out of clothing – the antecedent of every support bra. The first modern bra was invented by Mary Phelps Jacob, an American debutante. She wanted an undergarment that was lighter than a corset and so would not show through her fitted evening gown. Her solution was two silk handkerchiefs attached to ribbon. Bras in the 1920s flattened the breast, to suit the fashion for a boyish figure. The first bras to support the bust and enhance a woman's natural curves were created by Ida Rosenthal, a Russian-American immigrant at the end of the decade. With her husband she founded the bra company Maidenform, and introduced the concept of cup sizes.

INDISPENSABLE BRA-CALCULATOR

Measure (in inches) just under your breasts, keeping the tape close-fitting and level all the way round. Add 4 to an even measure, 5 to an odd one, to get your bra size (32, 34, and so on). Next measure all around your body at the fullest part of the breasts – ideally wear a comfortable non-wired bra while doing this and do not squash the breast. To find your cup size, subtract the first measurement from the second: if the difference is 0, you're an A-cup; 1 inch less, AA cup; 1 inch more, B cup; 2 inches, C; 3 inches, D; 4 inches, DD; 5 inches, E; 6 inches, F; 7 inches, FF; 8 inches, G.

CHECKING THE CUPS

There should be no bulging flesh (indicating too-small cups) or fabric-wrinkling (too big). Any underwiring should curve around the breasts, and the centre of the bra should lie flat against your body.

TRYING ON

Bra-fitting is an inexact science, but it gives you a rough idea of what size to select. Enlist the help of a professional fitter in-store if you can. Manufacturers use different cuts and fabrics, so you'll probably need to try on lots of bras to find the perfect fit.

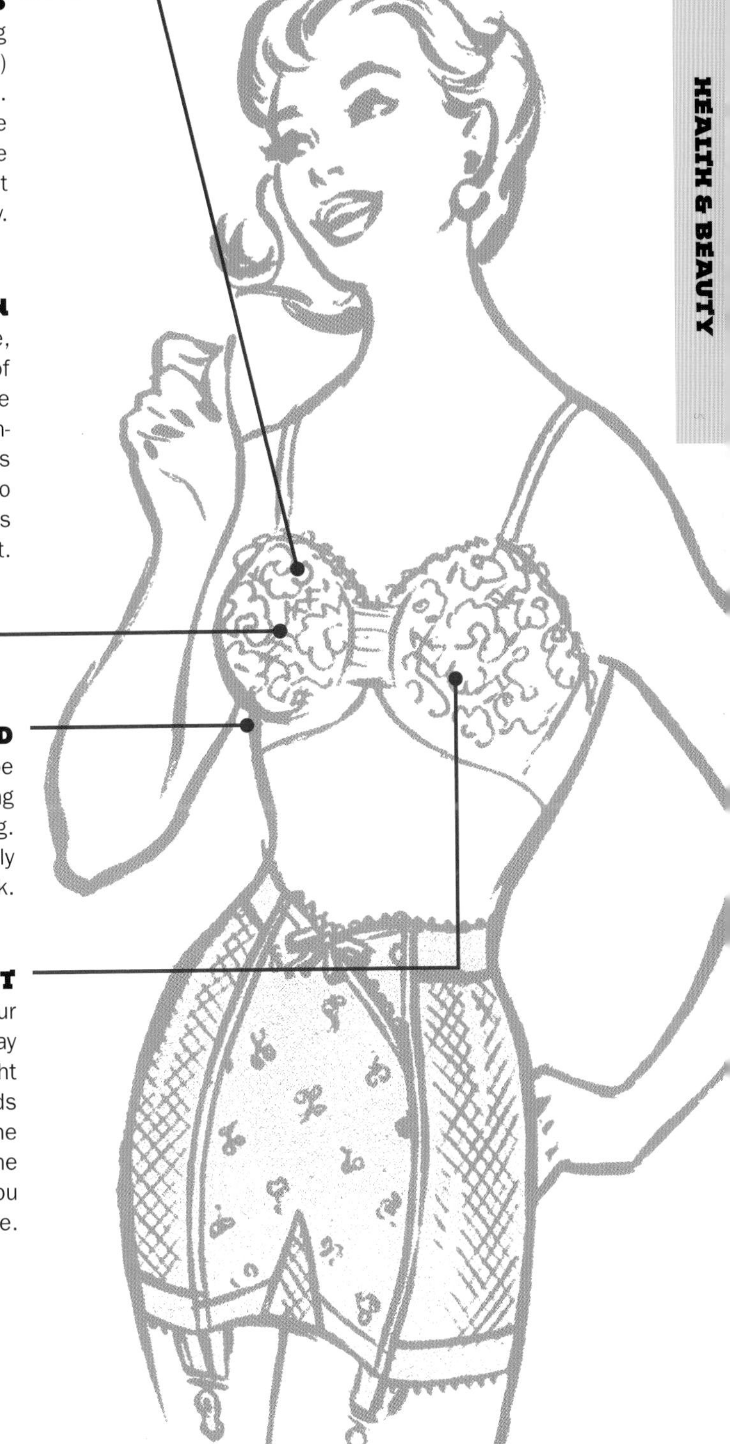

CHECKING THE BAND

The back of the band should be level with the front; if it is riding up, the bra is probably too big. Make sure the band fits snugly without leaving a red mark.

FINAL FIT

Slip the straps off your shoulders – the bra should stay put if it fits and gives the right support. Stretch up your hands and move around to check the fit. Check your new bustline under clothing to ensure you have a smooth line.

HOW TO POLISH YOUR SHOES

It is said that you can tell a lot about a person by their shoes. It was long held, for example, that only a cad would wear brown suede around town. It is certainly true that the state of your shoes sends a message. Scuffed, worn shoes say that you don't care much about yourself; well-maintained, polished shoes spell high self-esteem. But whether you believe in footwear psychology or not, you should polish your shoes regularly: that way, they will last you much longer.

INDISPENSABLE THINGS

- A pair of shoes
- Old newspaper
- 2 fine-bristled boot brushes
- Shoe polish to match the colour of your shoes
- Soft cotton cloth

A PRACTICAL HISTORY OF SHOE SHINING

Dubbin — a mixture of tallow (animal fat) and oil — has been used since the Middle Ages to make shoe leather soft and waterproof. In the 18th century, fashion poppets had their shoes shined with polishes incorporating beeswax or lanolin, which gave a better sheen. Blacking — made from

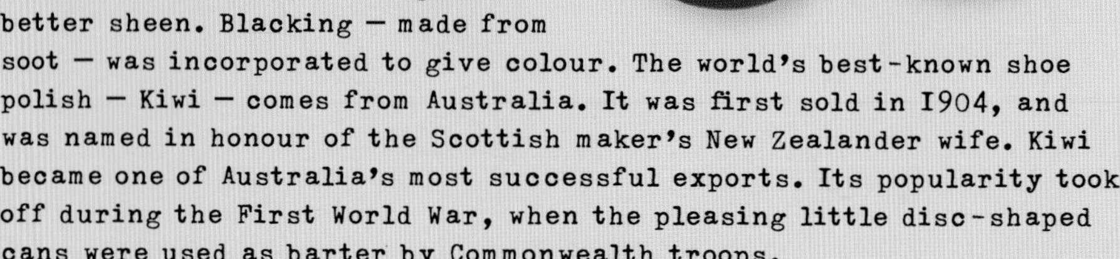

soot — was incorporated to give colour. The world's best-known shoe polish — Kiwi — comes from Australia. It was first sold in 1904, and was named in honour of the Scottish maker's New Zealander wife. Kiwi became one of Australia's most successful exports. Its popularity took off during the First World War, when the pleasing little disc-shaped cans were used as barter by Commonwealth troops.

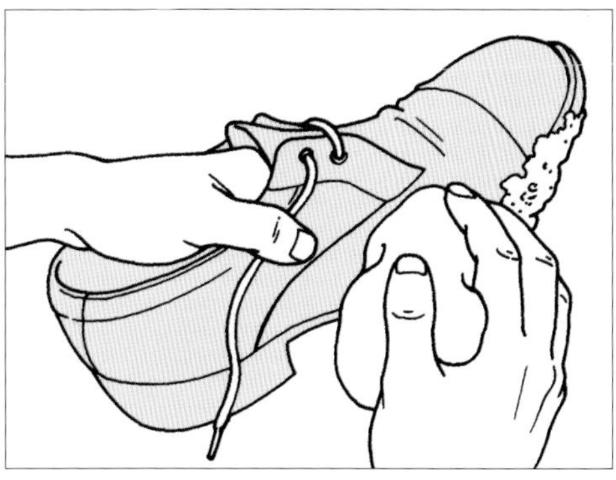

1 Clean any dirt off the shoes using warm water. Leave the shoes to dry. Cover the floor with old newspaper to protect it from polish. Remove laces from light-coloured shoes.

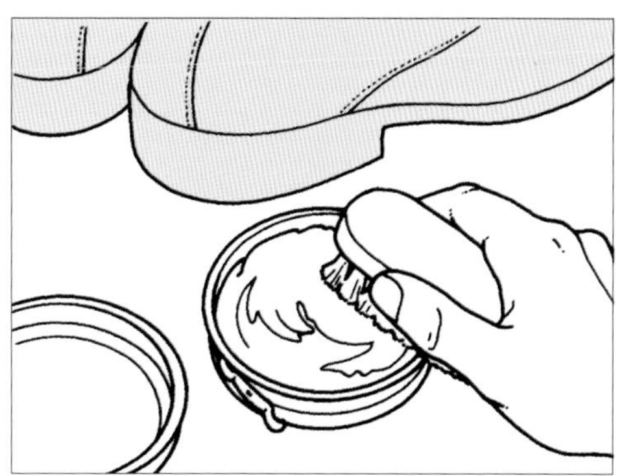

2 Rub a fine-bristled boot brush over the polish. Then brush over the shoes, applying it as evenly as you can (be sparing with the polish; you need only a fine layer).

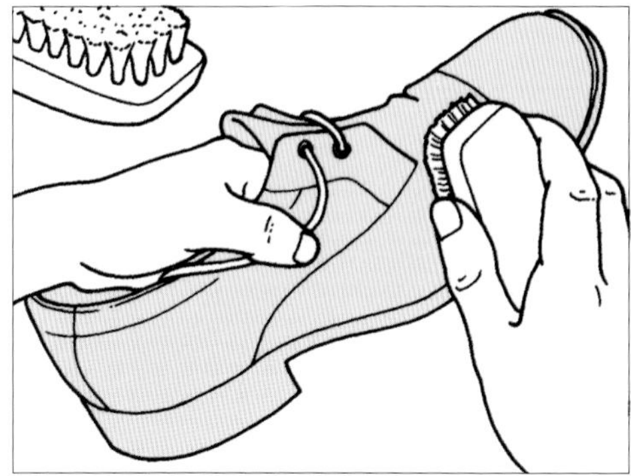

3 Put the shoes to one side for five minutes to let the polish sink in. Then rub a second boot brush all over the shoe, using a brisk back-and-forwards motion. This will remove any excess polish and give your shoes the first layer of shine.

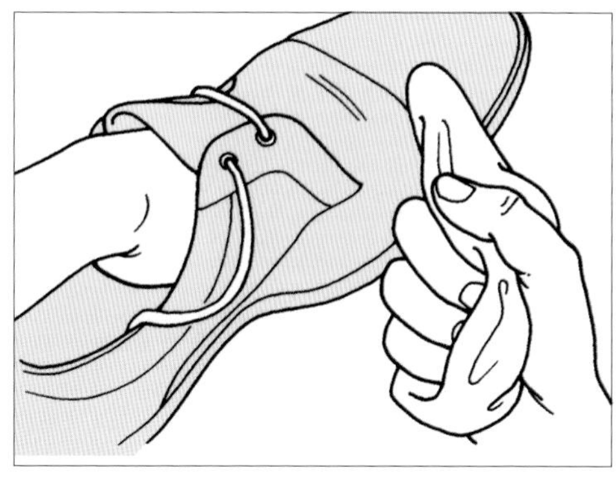

4 Take a damp cotton cloth and wrap tightly around the index finger, holding the rest tightly in your palm – the cloth over your fingertip should be smooth.

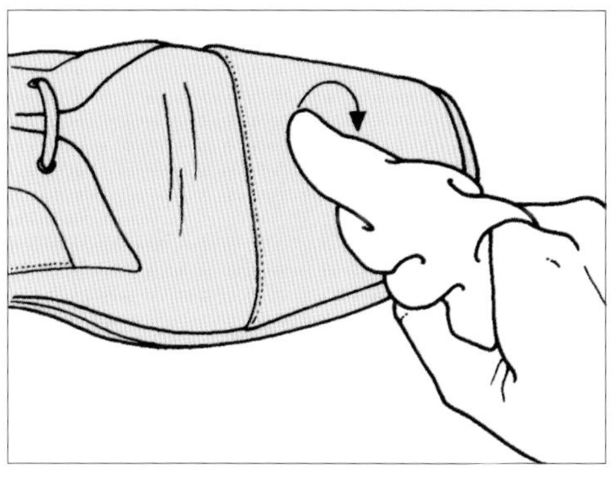

5 Apply a little polish to the cloth, then rub into the shoe using small circular movements – this is what the army calls 'bulling'. Dampen the cloth and re-apply polish as necessary. Work from toe to heel and then back down the other side, not forgetting any hard-to-reach areas such as round the stitches. Spend as long as you like to get the desired sheen – the more time you spend bulling, the higher the sheen will be.

PRACTICAL TIP

Always use one brush to put polish on and one to brush it off; do not mix them up.

HOW TO TIE A BOW TIE

If you want to wear a bow tie, you simply must know how to tie one. A clip-on bow tie is a sartorial abomination that instantly marks you out as a know-nothing arriviste. People think that tying a bow tie is fiendishly difficult – but that is a myth put about by the dinner-jacket-wearing elite. The fact is, tying a bow is no harder than tying your shoelaces. Yet it is a skill that, once mastered, immediately marks you out as a gentleman.

INDISPENSABLE THINGS

- Bow tie
- Shirt with wing collar
- Dinner jacket

A PRACTICAL HISTORY OF TIES

Neckties and bow ties alike are descendants of the cravat. These knotted kerchiefs came into fashion in the 17th century, when they were worn by swashbuckling Croatian mercenaries in the service of France (the term 'cravat' is derived from the French word for 'Croat'). Then as now, the cravat was worn inside the shirt. In later centuries, it migrated to the outside of the collar, and necessarily became a thin strip of coloured material. It is impossible to say why the bow tie became a more formal item than the necktie, but the practical advantage of the bow is that it does not dangle – hence its popularity with surgeons.

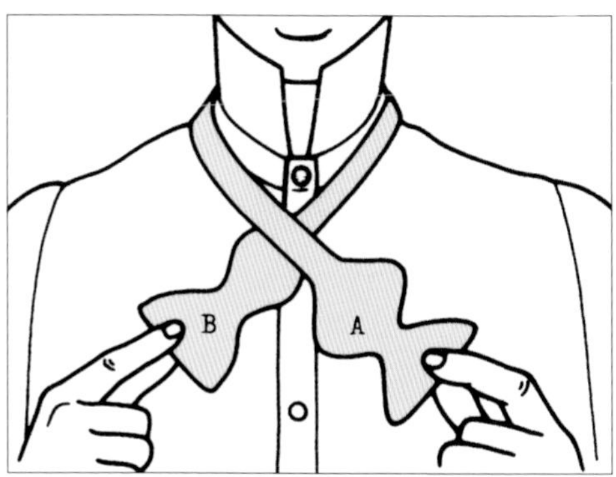

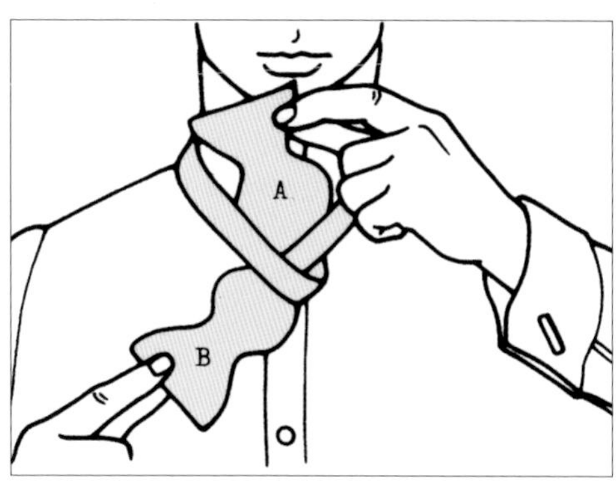

1 Place the tie around your neck so that one end (A) hangs lower than the other end (B). Then cross the longer end (A) over the shorter one (B), keeping the crossover close to your neck.

2 Take the longer end (A) through the loop to make a simple knot and hold it up and out of the way. Leave end B dangling down.

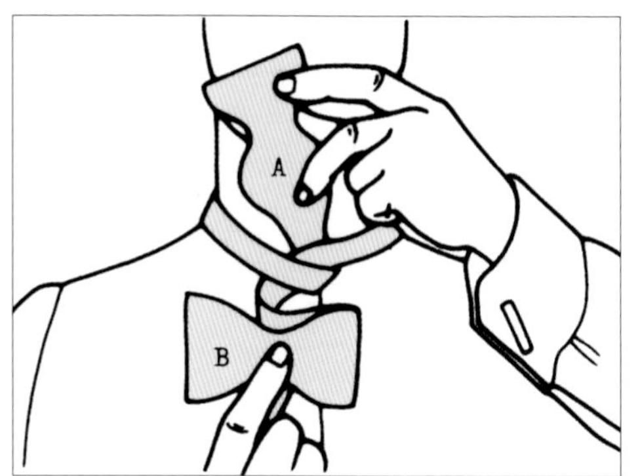

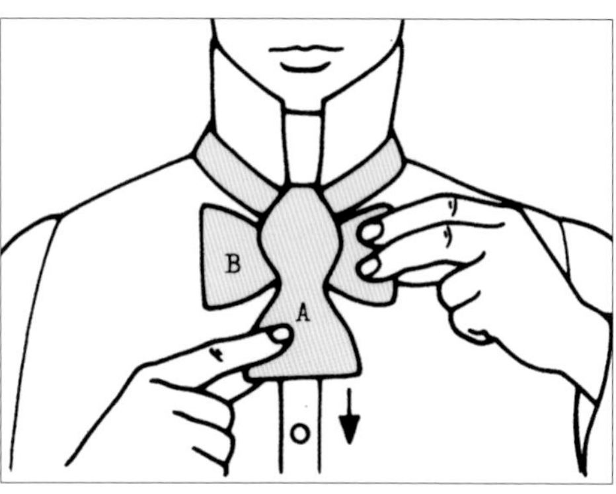

3 Now bend end B over itself. Holding it between your thumb and index finger, place the loop in a central position between the points of your shirt's collar – this is where the knot of the bow tie will be.

4 Now drop end A over both the crossover you made in step 1 and over the front of end B. It should hang down vertically.

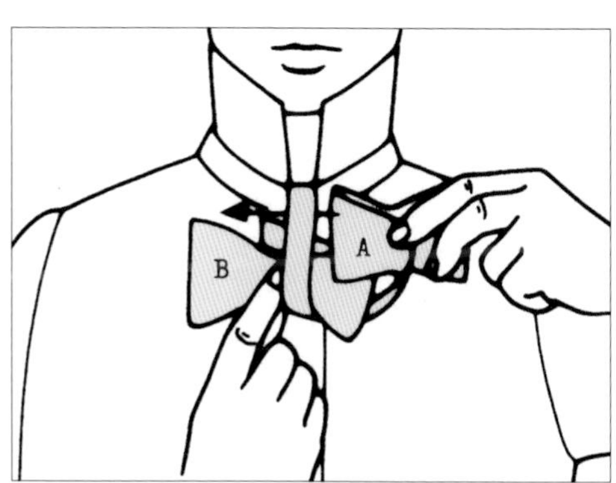

5 Hold the double-ended B with one hand while you fold end A over itself as shown. Then slide the loop you have formed with end A behind loop B, as shown – this is the tricky bit, but it gets easier with practice.

6 Pull gently on each loop at the same time to tighten the knot – then adjust to straighten. When you want to untie the bow, pull on the tails.

HOW TO WEAR A SUIT

To wear a suit well, you must first buy a suit well. Above all, it has to fit. This may seem obvious, but men are just as vain as women, and it is all too easy to buy the suit that fits the shape you would like to be. Nothing looks worse than a pair of formal trousers that cut into the gut like cheesewire, or a jacket that gapes like the jaws of a yawning hippo. So be honest with yourself — or better yet, take advice from a tailor or a plain-speaking friend.

INDISPENSABLE THINGS

- Formal suit
- Tie
- Shirt
- Polished shoes

CONSERVATIVE COLOURS

For a business suit, you can't go wrong with black, but other subdued colours are acceptable: charcoal grey, navy blue, dark shades of brown. A pinstripe looks good if it is subtle; if it is too strong you will look like a zebra. Striking colours (powder blue, white, shades of yellow) are all right if you are a children's entertainer, but not otherwise.

STAND TALL

You will naturally be more conscious of your posture when in formal wear, which is good. Hold your head high; pull back your shoulders; and when you walk, walk purposefully. These things will make you look better, and will show off your clothes to the best advantage.

SHIRT AND TIE

Shirt and ties are a besuited man's chance to show off his plumage. A splash of colour looks good. The shirt should generally be plain and contrast with the suit: go for pale pinks, lilacs and blues. Ties should match in a contrasting way: say, maroons and purples with an unobtrusive pattern. Ties depicting phalanxes of flying pigs are permissible on the first day back at work after the Christmas holidays, but at no other time.

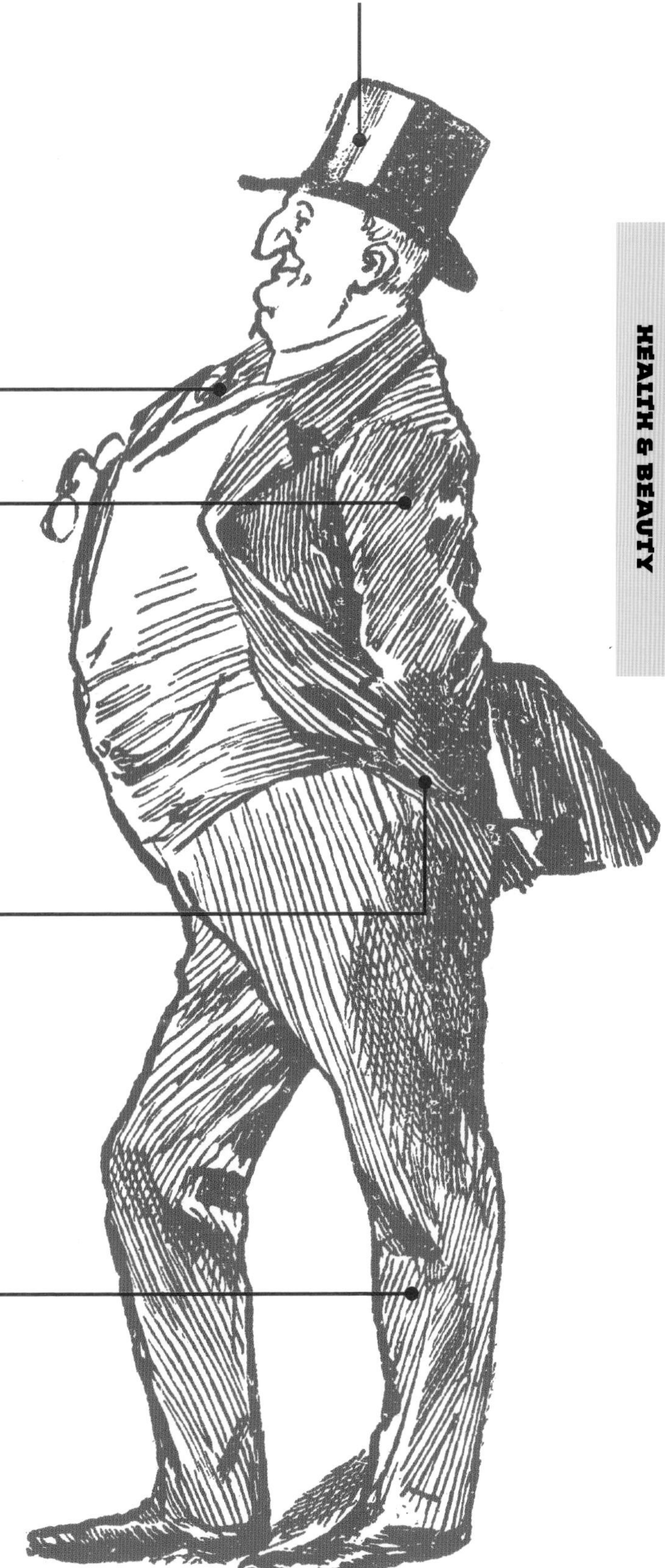

ARMS AND SLEEVES

Sleeve-length is vital to the overall look. The cuffs of your shirt should protrude about an inch from the end of your sleeve. The best way to make certain that they do is to wear a formal shirt when you go to buy your suit. Cufflinks are a classy touch that separates the CEO from the office junior.

LOSE YOUR KEYS

Your suit is not a rucksack, so don't treat it like one. Don't fill your pockets with car keys, mobile phones, loose change, breath mints... they will ruin the look. If you must have your wallet with you, make sure it as slim as can be, and keep it in your inside jacket pocket.

LEGS

If your trouser leg is too long you will look like a mess. If it is too short, you will look like your mum bought your suit before your last growing spurt. Your trouser leg should rest lightly on your (highly polished, black) shoes – with no bunching.

HOW TO PUT A CREASE IN A PAIR OF TROUSERS

No matter how casual a man's style, there will come an occasion – his wedding or some vital interview – when he needs to put a crease in his trousers. Trouser-pressing is a skill, like shaving, that every man should learn. And, as with shaving, when it goes wrong it looks terrible. The common trouser-press gaffs are the zigzag crease, the multiple crease and the off-centre crease. All of them are sartorial disasters, to be avoided at all costs. Here is how to go about getting the perfect crease.

INDISPENSABLE THINGS

- Pair of formal trousers
- Steam iron
- Ironing board
- Spray mist bottle
- Water
- Paper bag

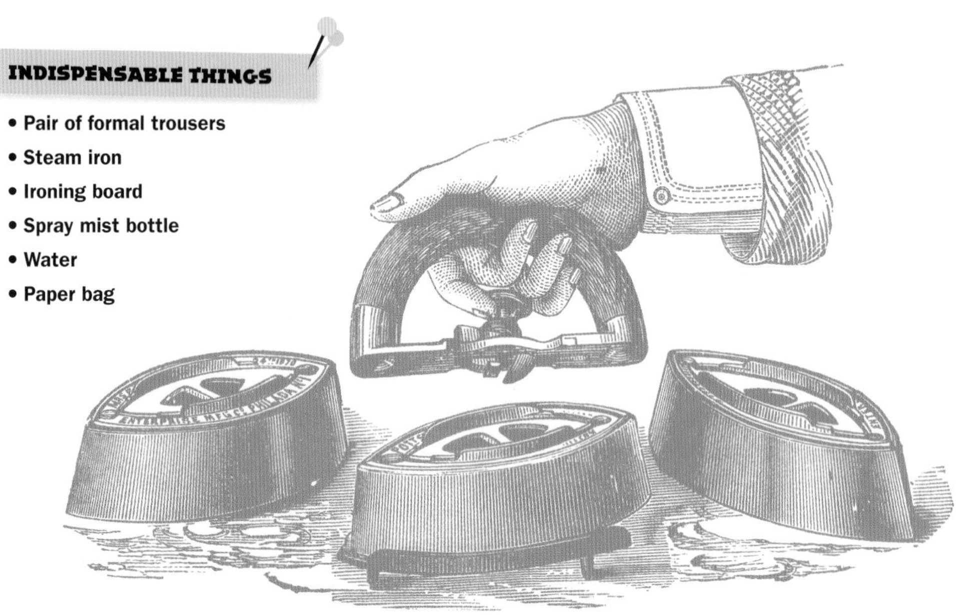

A PRACTICAL HISTORY OF IRONS

Vikings used flat stones to press and pleat their cloth. In the Middle Ages, similar tools were known as slickstones or sleekstones. 'Shee that wanteth a sleek-stone to smooth hir linnen, wil take a pebble,' wrote the Elizabethan dramatist John Lyly. About that time, blacksmiths began to make 'flat irons' – out of iron. You needed a pair to get the work done: one in hand and the other on the stove. It was hot, difficult work, and you had to keep the iron scrupulously clean to avoid marking the cloth. Ironing became easier once electric irons came into use – too easy for some. Hence the new sport of extreme ironing, in which people take an ironing board to some remote location such as a mountain top and do a spot of ironic ironing outdoors.

THE POSITION

Hold your trousers by the hems, and match up the inner and outer seams of both legs exactly. Then lay them on the ironing board, positioning one leg over the other. Put your hand in the pocket of the top leg, and extend your finger to the furthest corner: it should end exactly at the intended crease.

GETTING THE CREASE

Fold the top leg neatly out of the way, and smooth the bottom leg so it is perfectly flat. Dampen the intended crease by spraying with water, then lay a paper bag over the top and press hard; start at the hem and continue up the leg. If there are no pleats, fold the top section of the upper trouser leg back so that you can do the crotch area. Then flip the trousers over so that you can do the other leg.

PLEATS

If your trousers have pleats, iron your creases only as far as the end of the pleat. A single pleat should line up with the trouser crease; if you have a double pleat, the inner one should align. Pleats shouldn't have the razor-sharpness of a crease; use the iron to press the material in between the pleats rather than pressing down on them.

HANGING

If you are not wearing your trousers straight away, slip them onto a wooden (not wire) hanger and place in the closet with plenty of space around them.

HOW TO PACK A SUITCASE

It is smart to travel light, and not just because of strict airline rules on baggage. Dragging a suitcase the size of a garden shed behind you is a nuisance — to you and to everyone in your path. So pack clothing that you can layer, and concentrate on interchangeable outfits: you want trousers that work with several tops. Above all, do not pack too many shoes. Check that the clothes you are taking match your plans: if you are spending a week on the beach you can leave your tuxedo at home. You always need less than you think you do, so leave the just-in-case items at home. Squashed clothes become creased clothes, which is why the best packers are utterly ruthless.

INDISPENSABLE THINGS

- Suitcase
- Holiday clothes
- Toiletries and other items
- Plastic bags
- Coloured ribbon
- Tissue paper

PRACTICAL TIP

Tissue paper will help stop your clothes from wrinkling. Place a sheet in between each layer, and place another at the back of shirts or jackets before folding. A large ball of crumpled tissue paper inside the collar of a shirt will help protect it from crushing.

BELTS AND UNDERWEAR

Snake a thick belt around the inside edge of your suitcase to stop it getting crushed. Coil thin belts, placed in a bag, and tuck inside a shoe. Underwear can be rolled, bagged and placed in shoes or used to fill gaps in the case. If you have underwired bras, first place something soft in the cup – other underwear or crumpled tissue paper – and then fold.

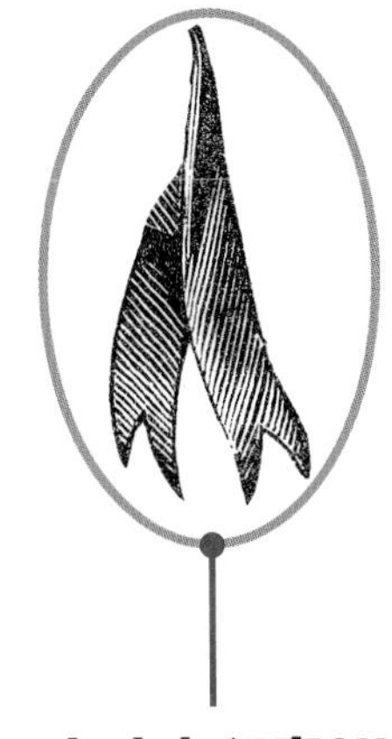

IDENTIFICATION

Tie a piece of coloured ribbon around the handle of your suitcase so you can spot it easily on the baggage carousel. And put your name and address inside; use the luggage label for your name and flight details only.

ROLL OR FOLD?

Roll T-shirts and use them to fill gaps in your suitcase. Fold shirts and blouses: first fold in the sleeves from a point a couple of centimetres in from the seam, then fold up the bottom of the sleeves and shirt, and finally bring the top and bottom together to make a neat rectangle.

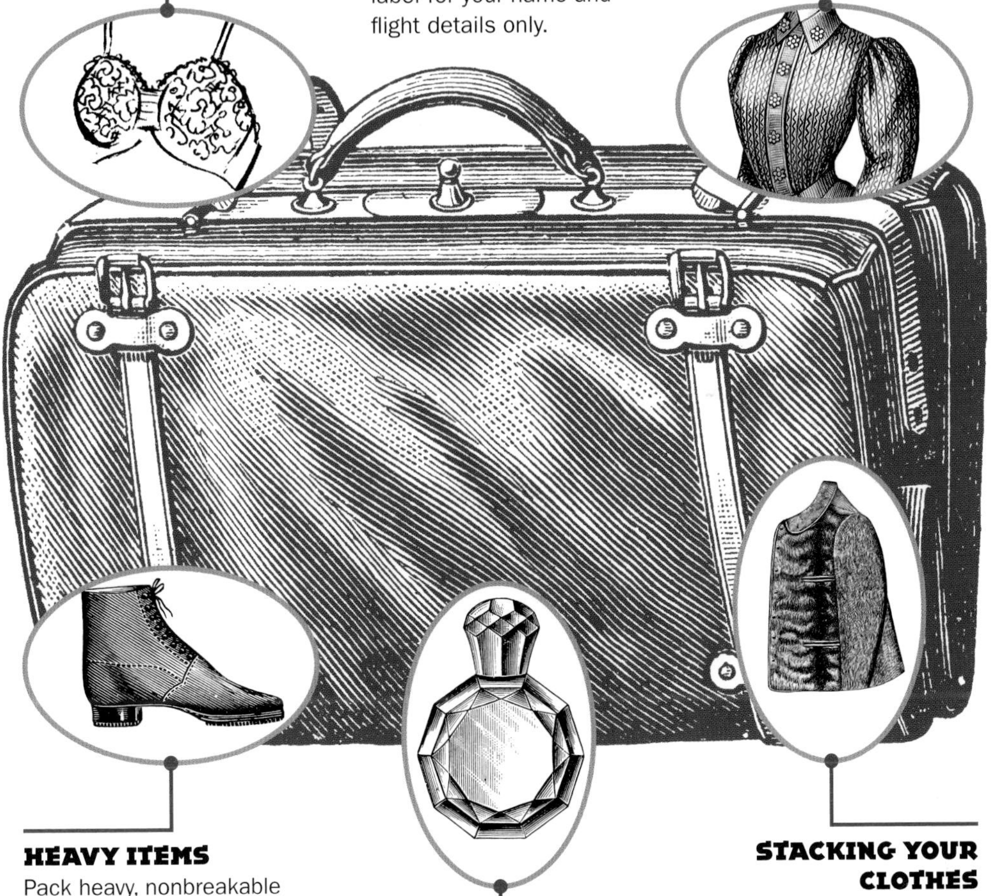

HEAVY ITEMS

Pack heavy, nonbreakable items such as shoes or books against the base of your suitcase (at the wheel end). This will stop them pushing your clothes down and creasing them while you are carrying or wheeling the suitcase. Put shoes into a plastic bag if they are dirty, and always wear your heaviest pair on the plane.

TOILETRIES

Wrap all your toiletries in heavy, sealed plastic bags. Pack the smallest size possible to save on weight and space – decant shampoo and so on into refillable plastic travel bottles. Be sure not to fill bottles to the top.

STACKING YOUR CLOTHES

Put the heaviest items – jeans, woollens and so on – at the base of the suitcase, follow with jackets and dresses, and put shirts and delicates on top. If you have more than one pair of trousers, lay them so that the top ends are at opposite sides of the case; this method avoids layering one bulky waistband over another.

HOW TO REMOVE A BLOODSTAIN

For some reason (maybe Lady Macbeth is to blame) blood is thought to be the indelible stain. In fact, blood is easy to remove if you get to it quickly; and there are ways to get rid of dried blood, too. The one thing to avoid is chucking your clothes in the wash without treating the stain first — once hot water hits the protein in blood, the stain will indeed set permanently.

INDISPENSABLE THINGS

- Cold water
- Liquid detergent
- Household ammonia
- Salt

INDISPENSABLE WARNING

Use these tips only on washable items. For dry-clean items, blot the bloodstain with a paper towel and take to the cleaner's straight away.

OUT AND ABOUT

If you can't whip off your shirt and wash it straight away, spit on the stain and rub in. The enzymes in saliva help to break down the proteins in blood.

INSTANT ACTION

Wash out a bloodstain as soon as possible using cold water and liquid detergent.

PERSISTENT STAINS

If the stain persists, rub a little salt into the spot (don't rub woollen items, though).

OLD STAINS

If the bloodstain is old or stubborn, soak the clothing for 20 minutes in a large bowl of cold water with 3 tablespoons of household ammonia. Then launder as usual.

LOOKING AFTER YOU

Your body is a well-oiled machine — but it is possibly not quite as well-oiled as it should be, or once was. This chapter shows you how to keep your physical self from going slightly rusty, and also how to maintain a shining mind and a gleaming spirit.

HOW TO SHARPEN YOUR MEMORY

The brain is a muscle: the more you use it, the fitter it gets. There are all kinds of mental press-ups and intellectual aerobics that you can do to make your brain bulge like a Schwarzenegger bicep. This is almost literally true: in taxi drivers, the part of the brain that deals with spatial knowledge is often larger than in other people. The memory is the part of the mind that is most likely to grow weak with age; the best way to stop this happening is to give it a daily workout. Use it or lose it.

A PRACTICAL HISTORY OF MEMORY TRICKS

The earliest memory feat was performed by Simonides of Ceos, who lived in the 5th century BC. He had left a banquet just before the roof collapsed, killing everyone inside. The bodies were crushed beyond recognition, but Simonides was able to recall who sat where. This led Simonides to develop a method in which physical spaces (loci) are used to remember things. Dominic O'Brien, eight times winner of the World Memory Championship, has used a similar technique to memorize the order of 10 shuffled decks of cards in the space of an hour. Even an elephant might struggle to match that feat of memory.

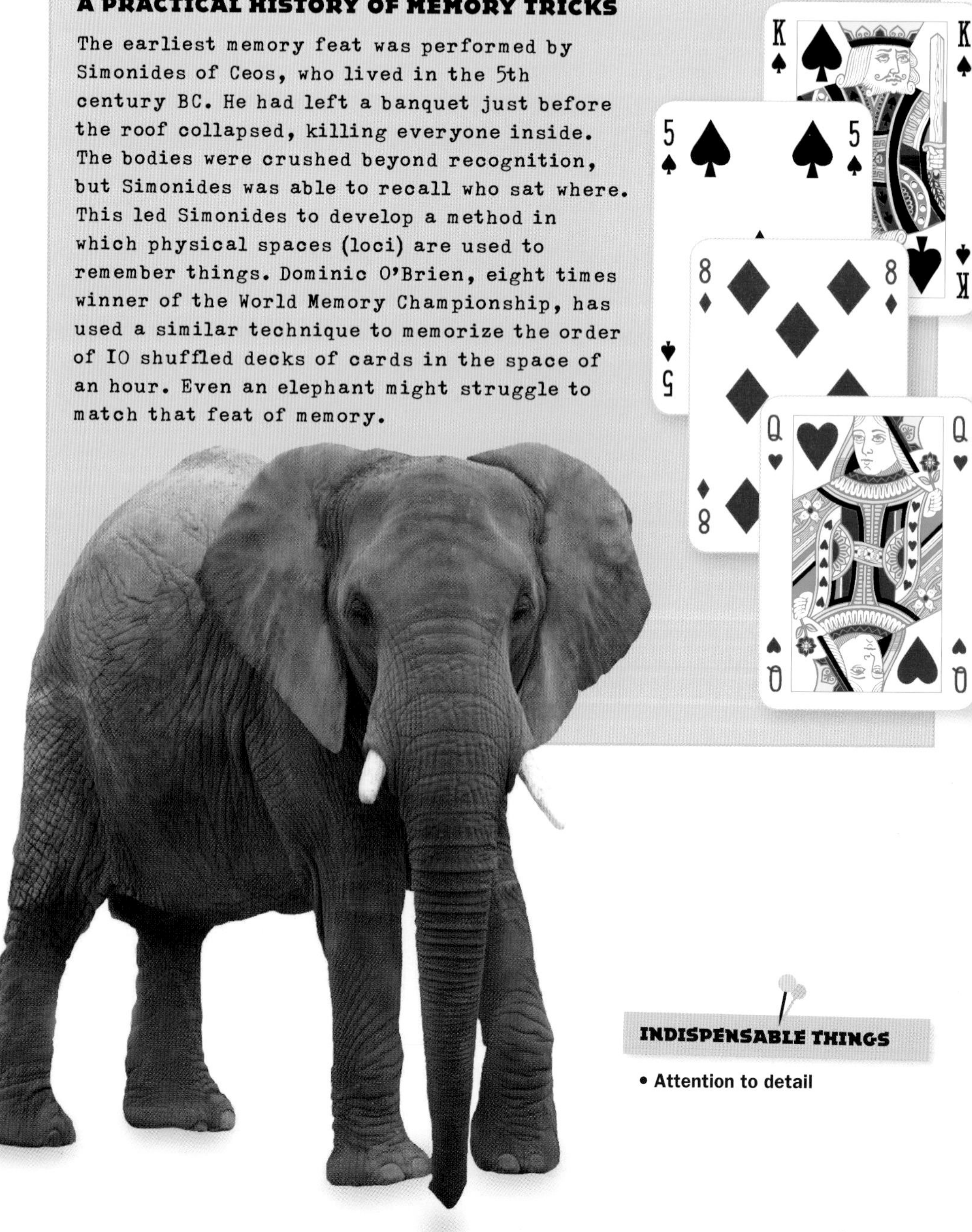

INDISPENSABLE THINGS

- Attention to detail

USE THE LOCI METHOD

To remember a series of things, bring to mind a familiar building (such as your house). Mentally place a visual reminder for each item in different rooms or areas (the more striking the image, the better). You could have a statue of the Madonna in the hallway (to remind you to call your mother), a flaming Olympic torch on the mantelpiece (to tell you to pay the gas bill). Take a mental stroll through the house when you need to remember what you have to do.

BREAK IT DOWN

Mentally divide a string of numbers down into chunks: the telephone number 775362 is more easily recalled as 77 53 62.

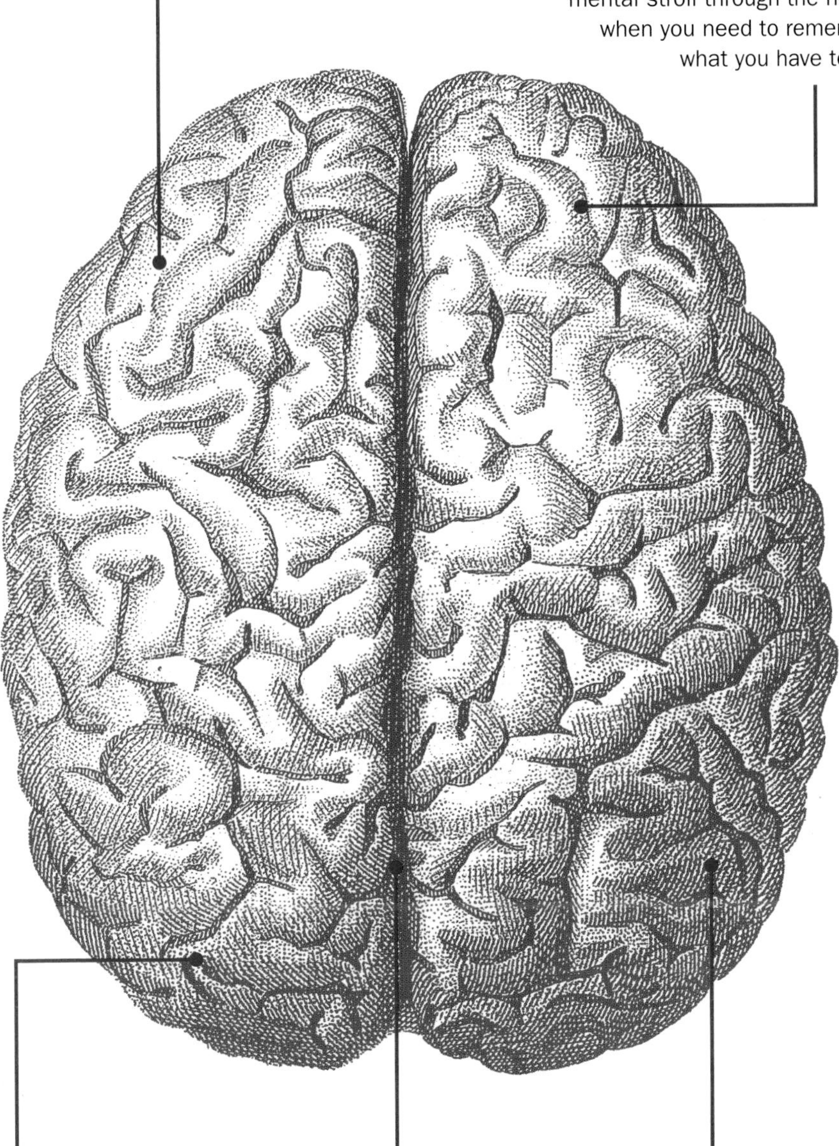

THINK VISUAL

Striking mental images can help you recall names or foreign words: for example, if you are introduced to a Mr Appleton, picture him sitting in a bath of apples, with a tonne weight falling on his head.

REPEAT IT

If you know that there is something you want to remember – like an address – repeating it out loud several times will make it easier to recall later on.

USE MNEMONICS

These handy devices are useful for remembering lists – for example, the six strings of a guitar are tuned to the notes EADGBE, which can be remembered using the phrase 'Even after dinner, greedy boys eat'.

HOW TO DO THE PERFECT SIT-UP

For toning the abdominals, there is nothing better than the old-fashioned sit-up. It requires no special equipment, but will rapidly build core strength, if done properly and regularly. You should notice the results within weeks: you will look trimmer around the midriff, and you will feel fitter and more powerful. But it's essential to do it right, or you risk hurting your back and neck. The key is to make sure that it really is your abdominals that are doing the work, not your neck or back muscles.

INDISPENSABLE THINGS

- A carpeted or padded floor, or exercise mat
- Warmed-up muscles
- Your doctor's permission, if in any doubt

INDISPENSABLE WARNING

Sit-ups should be practised with caution, especially if you have lower back problems. Stop if you feel any pain; if you feel strain in the neck or back, then stop and reassess your technique. Seek medical advice if the pain persists. If sit-ups feel too difficult, try alternative forms of abdominal work.

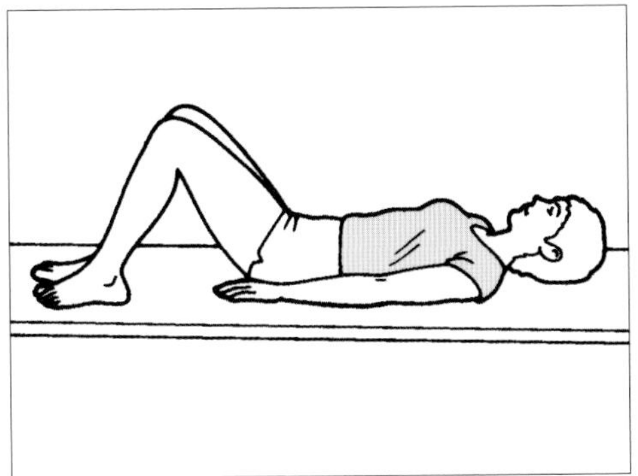

1 Lie on your back on the floor. Bend your legs so that they form a right angle at the knee, and so that your feet are resting flat on the floor, shoulder-width apart. Don't anchor your feet under a piece of furniture: you'll work the hip flexors and leg muscles rather than the abdominals.

2 Place your hands by your ears, or cross them over your chest. If you are a beginner, you'll find it easier to keep your arms by your side. Never lace your hands behind your head.

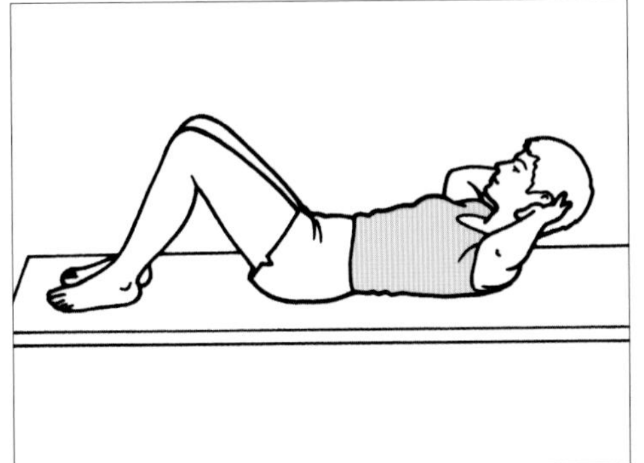

3 Slowly squeeze your abdominal muscles to bring your head, then shoulders and then trunk off the floor – work very slowly. Exhale as you come up to help the abdominal muscles contract. Be sure to keep your neck straight and relaxed.

4 Once you reach a point where your trunk is at an angle of 30 degrees to the floor, hold this position for a few seconds, and then slowly lower yourself back down. Breathe in as you come down. Keep your feet flat on the floor throughout.

5 Pause *before* your shoulders and head touch the floor, and raise yourself up for the next sit-up. Remember to exhale as you come up and inhale as you come down.

PRACTICAL TIP

Do a few sit-ups at a time. Build up the number you do very gradually, as your fitness improves. It's more important to do a few sit-ups well than to do lots with a poor technique.

HOW TO GO JOGGING

Jogging is no more or less than a good walk speeded up a bit. As such, it is one of the simplest and most satisfying forms of aerobic exercise you can do: just pull on your shoes and go. The main difference between jogging and running is attitude: when you run you want to be faster than the rest. But when you jog you are running against no one but yourself – the ideal non-competitive sport.

INDISPENSABLE THINGS

- **Running shoes**
- **A little motivation**
- **Your doctor's permission, if in any doubt**

GET GOOD SHOES

You can run in any old clothes, but you must invest in proper running shoes. They aren't cheap but you do not have to spend a fortune. Go to a specialist running shop, and take advice from a knowledgable salesperson. As with car tyres, you can't go far wrong if you choose a well-known, respected brand – so long as they fit properly.

INDISPENSABLE WARNING

Always take medical advice before starting any strenuous form of exercise. Warm up before your run, and cool down afterwards.

TAKE RESTS

Don't jog every day: your muscles need time to recover. Aim to run three or four times a week. If you are training for a race, you should 'go long' once a week – that is, increase the time or distance of your longest run. If you are struggling on a jog, then there is no shame in stopping and resting. The runner's mantra is 'train, don't strain'.

DRINK WATER

You should be thoroughly hydrated before you set out on a jog. Drink several glasses of water in the hour or two before you set out. Have another drink when you return. If you are running for more than half an hour, take a bottle of water with you.

GO SLOW

If you have never run before, or if you have not run for some months, then take it very easy to begin with. Ten minutes (with rests if need be) is long enough for a first outing. When jogging you should never be so out of breath that you can't hold a conversation.

DON'T HURT YOURSELF

Most runners get slight pains from time to time. You will soon learn to tell the difference between a wholesome muscle ache and a genuine hurt. Don't try to 'run off' an injury: you will only make it worse and put yourself out of action for a long stretch.

FIND A BUDDY

Motivation is hard to find: it is too easy to find an excuse to take a day off. So find a running buddy and make a definite date. Then you can't dodge your appointment with the pavement, and the companionship will make your run more fun..

HOW TO PRACTISE YOGA

Yoga is not just exercise for hippies. It's brilliant for strengthening muscles and improving flexibility. When it comes to all-round bodywork, yoga is unbeatable. The best way to learn is in a class with an experienced teacher — you definitely want someone who practises what they preach. There are various forms to choose from: if you want to work up a sweat, try astanga vinyasa. If gentle stretches are more your thing, seek out a scaravelli or viniyoga class. But remember: the correct mental attitude is as important as the physical pose. And yoga is not a competitive sport — you get no extra points for best downward dog.

INDISPENSABLE THINGS

- 'Sticky' yoga mat
- Comfortable clothing
- Bare feet
- Your doctor's permission, if in any doubt

PHYSICAL POSTURES

Don't expect to get into demanding postures straight away – it can take years to master advanced poses such as the lotus. Never force your body further than it wants to go; with regular practice, your muscles will gradually become more supple.

BREATHING

Breathe deeply and smoothly, through the nose. Try to coordinate your breath with your movements.

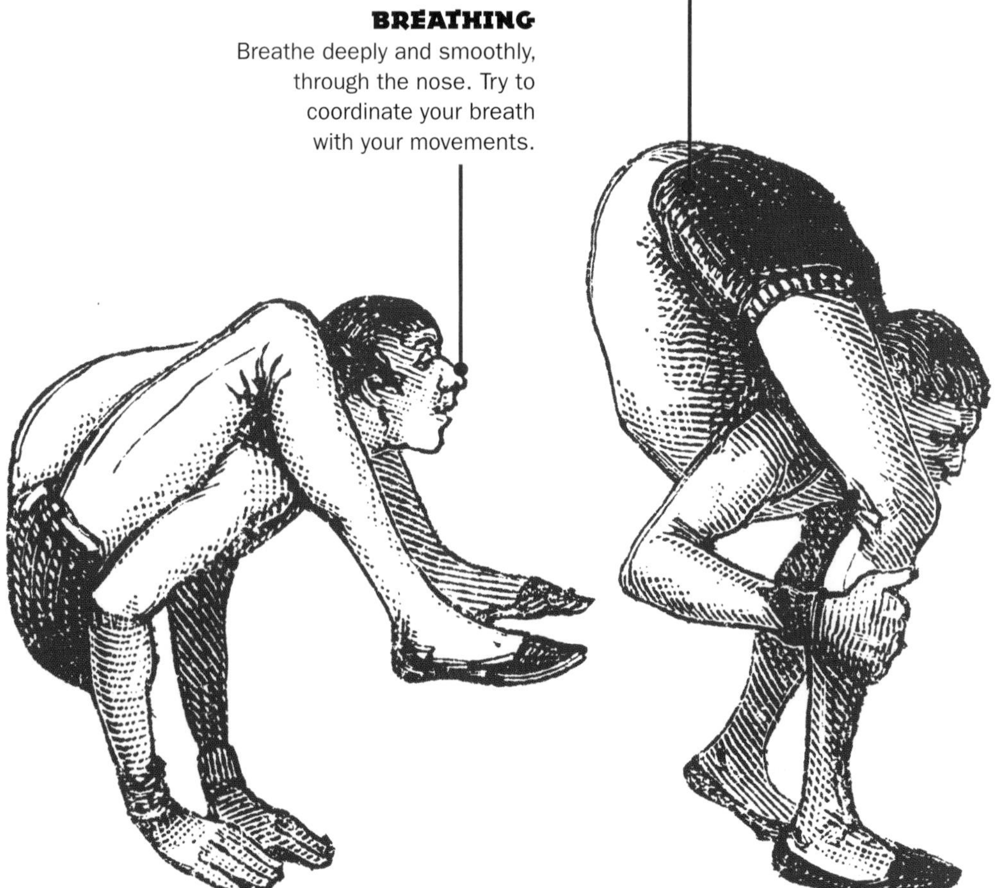

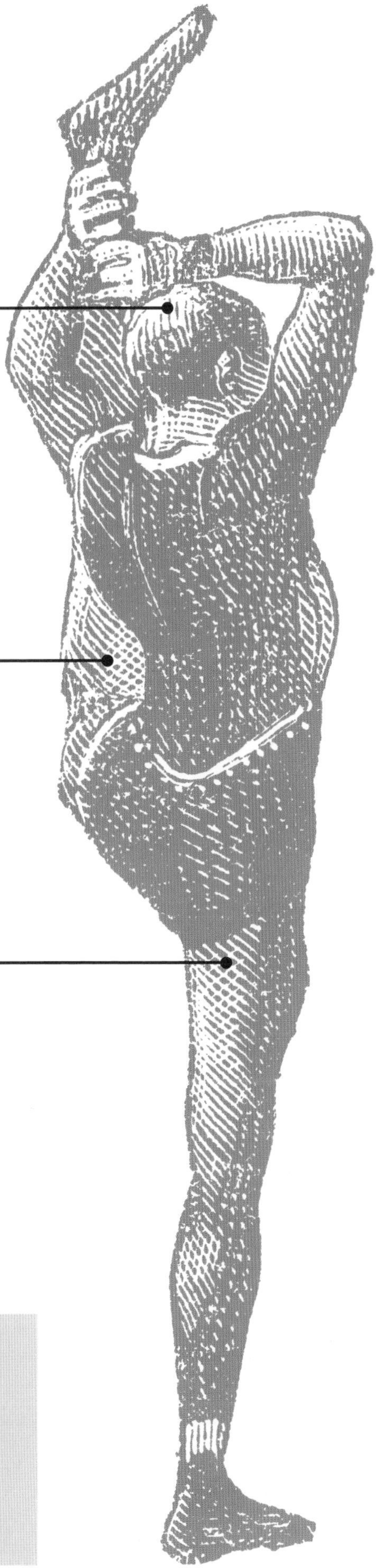

AWARENESS

Yoga integrates body and mind, and it is important to approach it with concentration and a calm mental attitude. Don't measure yourself against other people in your class; yoga is designed to help develop a non-judgemental, accepting state of mind.

WHERE TO PRACTISE

All you need is a quiet space, free from clutter. Make sure you have enough room to stretch out without knocking into anything. Avoid doing yoga directly under the sun, or next to a heat source.

WHEN TO PRACTISE

You can do yoga at any time of day. Many yogis opt for mornings, when the mind is alert and stiff muscles benefit from stretching, but you may find an evening session more practical. Wait two hours after eating a meal before practising yoga, and empty your bowels and bladder before you start.

PRACTICAL TIP

There are many different styles of yoga – go to a few classes to find a teacher and style that suit you. It's best to settle on one type of yoga and stick to it, rather than to chop and change.

HOW TO DO A HEADSTAND

The headstand has so many benefits that it is known as the king of postures (the elegant shoulderstand is the queen). It increases the flow of blood to the head, revitalizing body and mind. It also relieves back strain, promotes good circulation and encourages deep exhalation. It's also a great posture for improving sleep and concentration.

INDISPENSABLE THINGS

- Patience
- Concentration

STARTING OUT

A STRONG BASE
You don't have to be especially strong to do a headstand. The key is to create a tripod with your two elbows and clasped hands at the centre – and to conquer any natural fear of being upside down. Learn the pose in slow and easy stages, under the guidance of an experienced teacher. It is best practised at the end of a yoga session.

AN EASIER OPTION
Try doing a headstand in the corner of a room; press the backs of your hands into the corner and let each hip touch the walls.

INDISPENSABLE WARNING

See your doctor and a specialist yoga teacher to check that this pose is suitable for you. Headstands should not be practised by people suffering from high blood pressure, eye, heart, neck or back problems, by women who are pregnant or menstruating, or by those suffering from a headache or migraine.

1 Kneel down and clasp each elbow with the opposite hand – the elbows should be shoulder-width apart. Release your hands and place them on the floor with your fingers interlocked.

2 Place the crown of your head on the floor so that your little fingers are touching the back of your head – your hands and elbows should form a triangle.

3 Straighten your knees, pushing up on the balls of your feet and lifting your hips. Keep your thighs, knees and heels together, and walk your feet in until your neck and back form a straight line – this is a good place for beginners to stop.

4 Breathing out, bend your knees in towards the chest and slowly lift your feet off the floor. Bring your heels towards your buttocks, keeping your knees bent. Push your elbows down to the floor and lift your shoulders away from it. Stop here if you cannot do a full headstand.

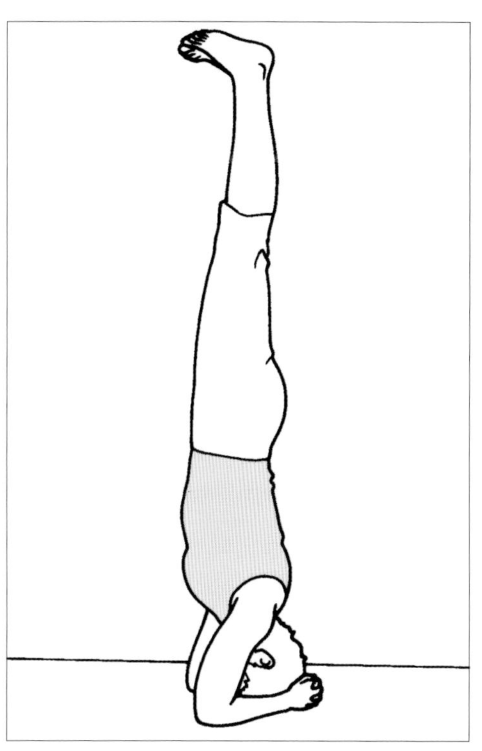

5 If you feel able, straighten your legs so that the soles of your feet (not your toes) face towards the ceiling. Press down into the forearms, and take a few slow breaths (gradually build the time you spend in the pose as you practise).

6 Come out of the pose slowly, reversing the sequence of going into it. To counterstretch the spine and normalize the circulation, kneel with your buttocks resting on your feet, your forehead on the floor, and your arms by your sides (child's pose). Rest here for a minute or so.

PRACTICAL TIP

If you feel yourself start to topple, drop your feet so that they hit the floor first.

HOW TO DO TAI CHI

Tai chi may look balletic, but every move is derived from the kind of punches and parries practised by the likes of Bruce Lee and Jackie Chan. Tai chi moves are performed in a strict sequence (the 'form'). The 'walk' is a simple meditative exercise that can easily be done at home. Be sure to keep a sense of softness in your posture – there are no tensed muscles in tai chi. Keep the mind concentrated, and breathe rhythmically and smoothly.

INDISPENSABLE THINGS

- Loose comfortable clothing
- Shoes with thin, flexible soles (such as plimsolls)
- Your doctor's permission, if in any doubt

INDISPENSABLE WARNING

Take care not to twist your knee in a different direction to the rest of your leg, or to bend it further than the toe. Tai chi is not suitable for people with knee problems.

START
Put your feet together, toes forward. Shift your weight onto the left foot, lift the right one and move it out to the side so that your feet are parallel, shoulder-width apart, and your weight equally balanced.

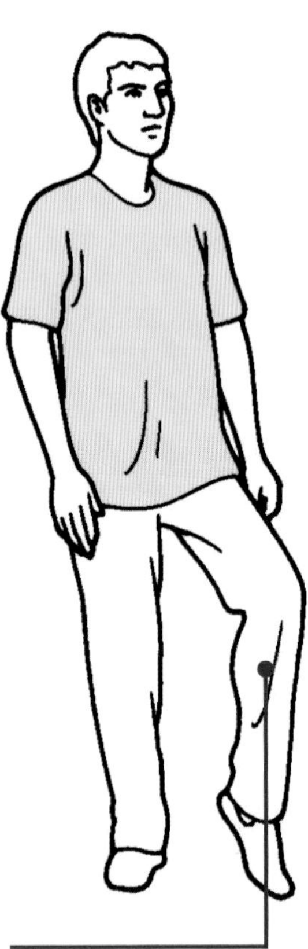

RAISE LEFT FOOT
Stand tall and breathe. Bring all of your weight onto the right leg. Raise up the heel of your left foot, leaving your toes resting on the ground for a moment.

SHIFT WEIGHT
Step forward with your left foot, maintaining an upright posture as you do so. Place the left heel on the floor, and then roll down the rest of the foot. Keep your weight on the back leg.

A PRACTICAL HISTORY OF TAI CHI

The founder of tai chi was a monk named Chang San Feng, who was born in China in 1247. His inspiration came from watching a snake fight a crane, where each animal used its natural movement to evade the other.

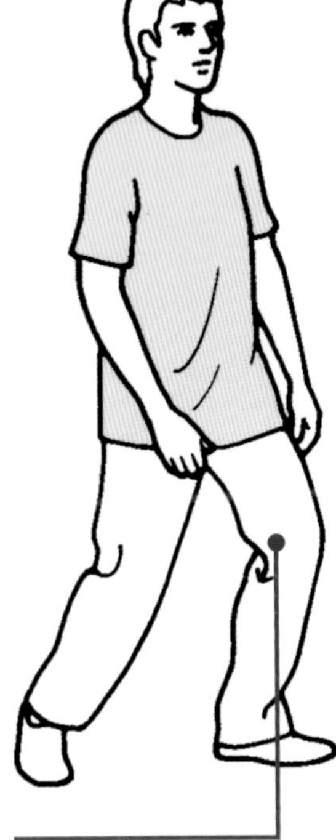

WEIGHT ON LEFT

Now slowly bring your weight onto the left leg, allowing the left knee to bend slightly while you straighten the right one. Do not lean forward.

FORWARD

When all of your weight is on the left leg, step forward with your right foot, heel first. Remember to keep your weight on the back leg.

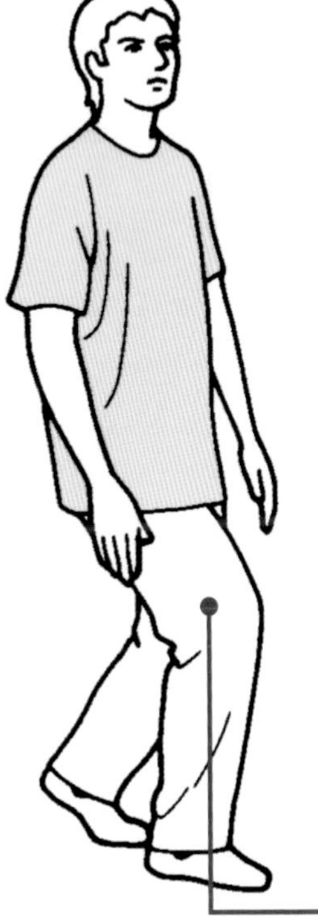

REPEAT

Repeat for 10 minutes or so. You can also try stepping backwards, in which case you should place the toes of the leading foot on the ground first, instead of the heel.

HOW TO SKIP

Skipping's not just for little girls. It's a great all-round sport for grown-ups: good for cardio-respiratory fitness, suppleness, endurance, balance and coordination. And it will help trim those hips, thighs and bottom. The world's greatest boxers – including three-times heavyweight champion Lennox Lewis – have routinely used skipping in their training. Don't think you can pinch the nearest child's skipping rope, though. You need a rope that is the right length for your height. Skipping with a rope that's too short is as pointless – and potentially damaging – as running a marathon in shoes that are too small.

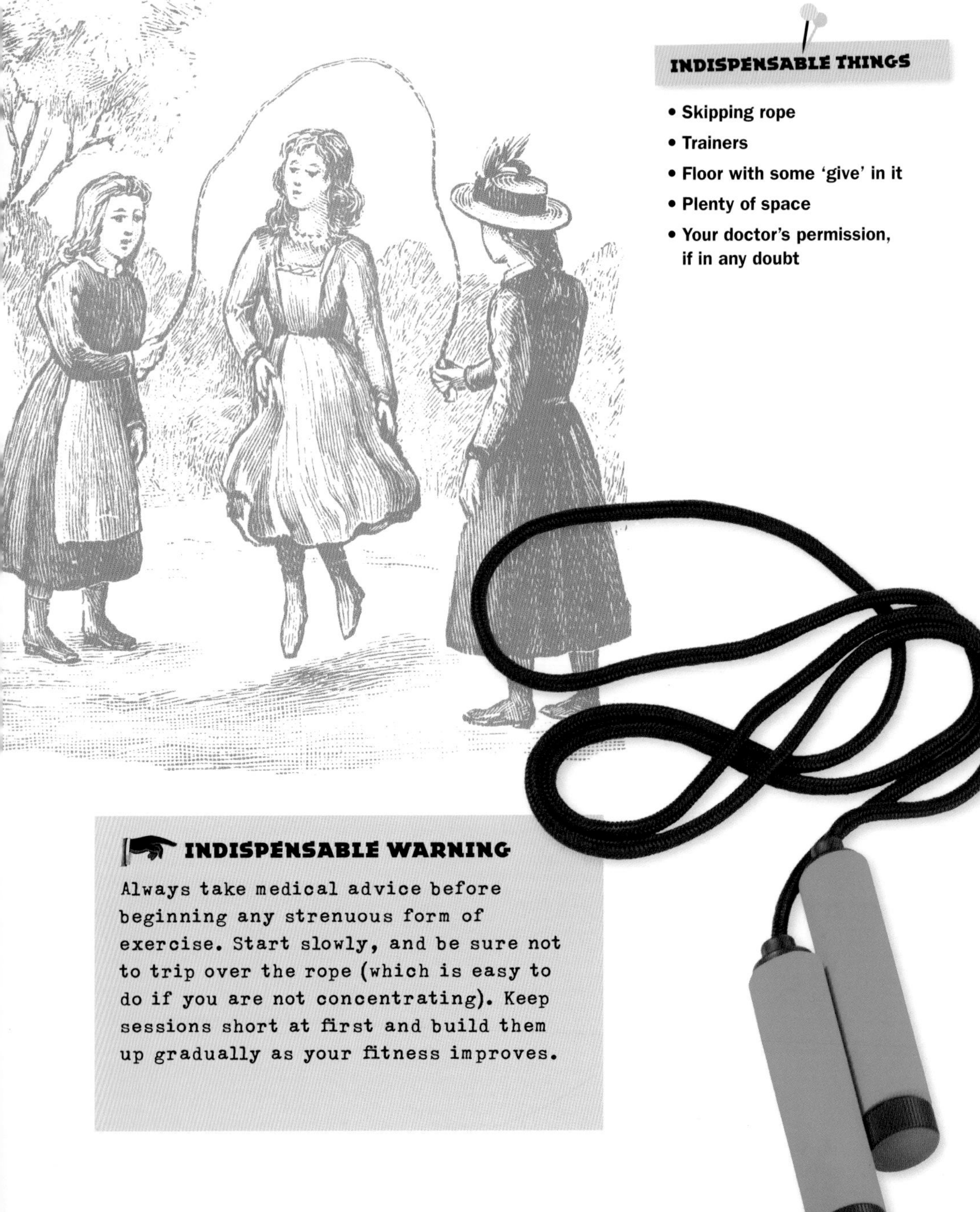

INDISPENSABLE THINGS

- Skipping rope
- Trainers
- Floor with some 'give' in it
- Plenty of space
- Your doctor's permission, if in any doubt

INDISPENSABLE WARNING

Always take medical advice before beginning any strenuous form of exercise. Start slowly, and be sure not to trip over the rope (which is easy to do if you are not concentrating). Keep sessions short at first and build them up gradually as your fitness improves.

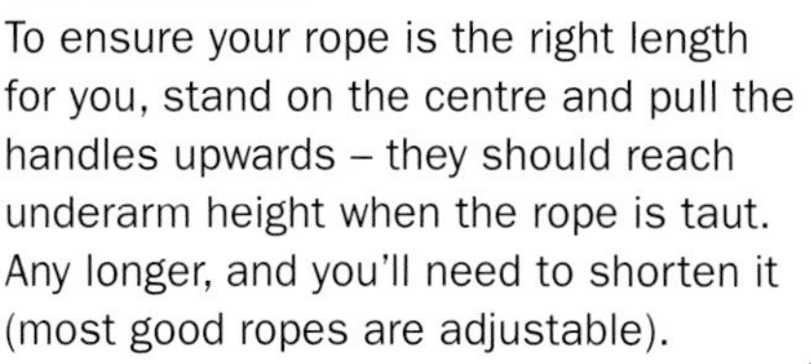

YOUR ROPE

To ensure your rope is the right length for you, stand on the centre and pull the handles upwards – they should reach underarm height when the rope is taut. Any longer, and you'll need to shorten it (most good ropes are adjustable).

BASIC TECHNIQUE

Have your feet slightly apart and drop the rope behind you. Bring it over your head and, when it gets to your feet, jump over it. Bend at the ankles rather than the knees as you jump, and keep your jumps low. Watch that you don't lean forwards (your back should be straight), keep your elbows close to your body and turn the rope smoothly.

BURN RATE

A 10-minute skipping session will burn between 70 and 110 calories, depending on your weight and on how much you exert yourself. One study found that a 10-minute session of jumping rope gave as many health benefits as a 30-minute run.

SKIPPING TRICKS

Once you have mastered the basic technique, try some skipping tricks. Try going backwards (back jump), using alternate feet to jump the rope (speed step), using one foot for several jumps and then the other (hop jump), crossing your hands as you bring the rope over (the criss cross), or alternate between one jump with the legs apart and one with the legs together (jack jump).

HOW TO SHAPE YOUR EYEBROWS

A well-defined eyebrow is a thing of wonder – provided that it matches its neighbour, of course. Your brows are no less expressive and personal a feature than your mouth or your eyes. And, like your mouth and your eyes, they will benefit from a little cosmetic attention. Shaping your eyebrows will enhance your good looks – but don't overdo it, because pencil-thin lines give your face a mean, cruel look. So tweeze cautiously and sparingly (and definitely leave waxing to the professionals).

INDISPENSABLE THINGS

- Flannel
- Cotton pad
- Witch hazel
- Eyebrow brush or clean old mascara wand
- Eyebrow pencil
- Tweezers with slanted ends
- Magnifying mirror

1 Wash your face, then place a warm flannel over your eyebrows for a minute, to help soften the hair follicles. Wipe a cotton pad soaked in witch hazel over the brows (repeat this regularly throughout the plucking process). Brush the hair of your eyebrows up and out, using your brush.

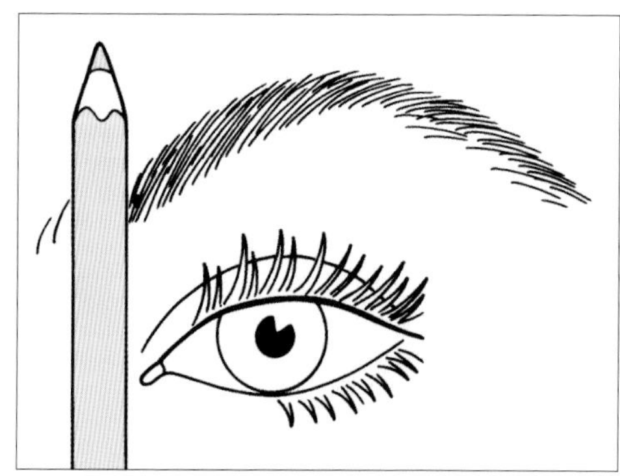

2 Assess the natural shape of your eyebrows in the mirror – it's best to follow this closely. Take an eyebrow pencil and hold it vertically at the side of your nose. Your eyebrow should start at the point where it intersects with the pencil – make a dot with an eyebrow pencil as a guide.

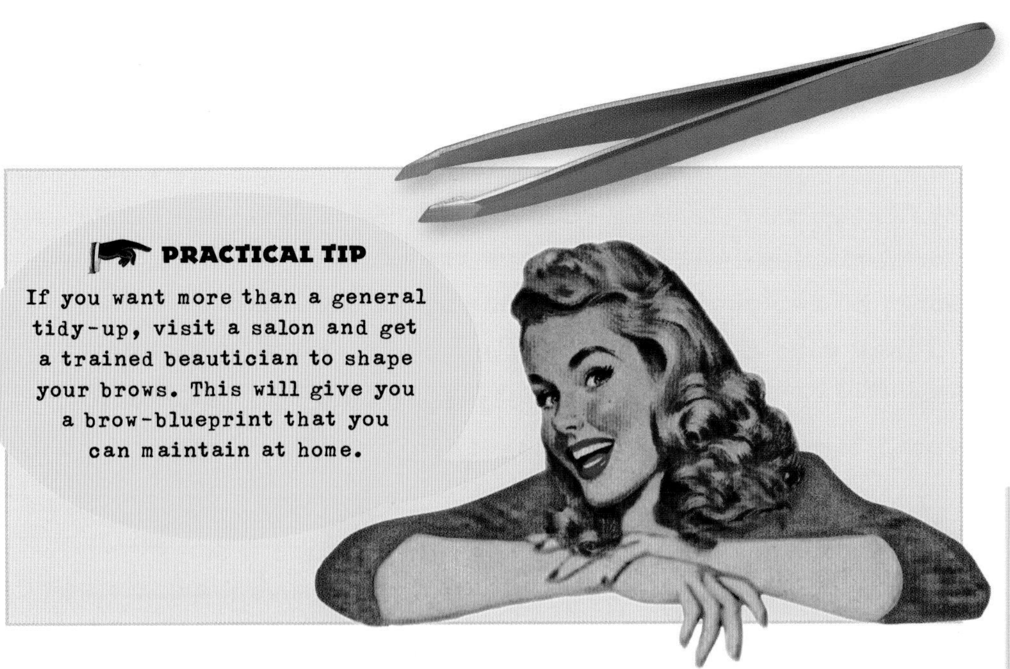

PRACTICAL TIP

If you want more than a general tidy-up, visit a salon and get a trained beautician to shape your brows. This will give you a brow-blueprint that you can maintain at home.

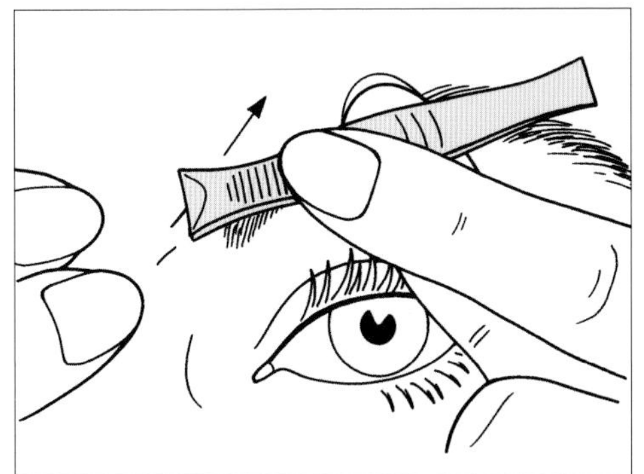

3 Remove any hairs that are on the nose-side of the dot. Use two fingers to keep the skin tight, and remove the hairs in the direction they are growing, using small sharp movements. Remove one hair at a time, then do the other side.

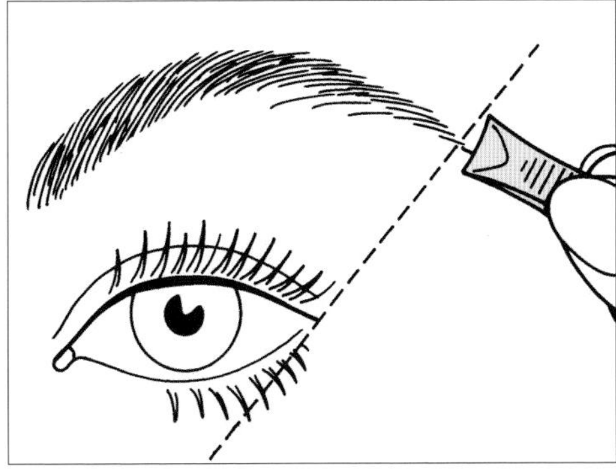

4 Take your pencil again and angle it from the outside edge of the nostril to the outer corner of the eye and beyond. The point where it hits the brow marks the end of your eyebrow. Again, make a dot and then remove any hairs beyond this point, being sure to pluck the hair in the direction it is growing.

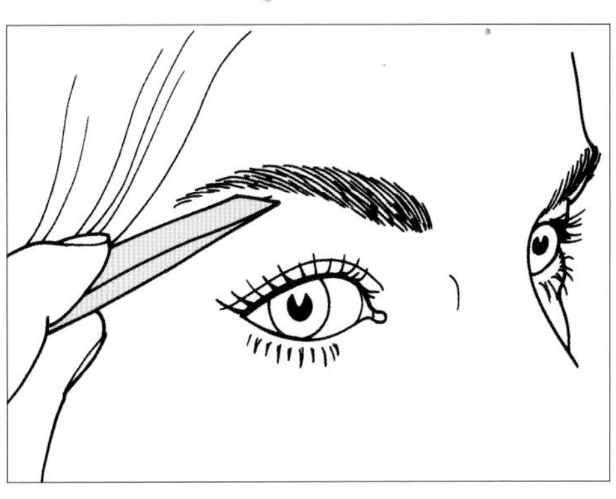

5 Now remove any other hairs that are obviously outside the natural curve of your brows. Always pluck from below not above. It's best to pluck a few hairs from each brow at a time, alternating between them in order to keep the shape symmetrical and avoid overplucking.

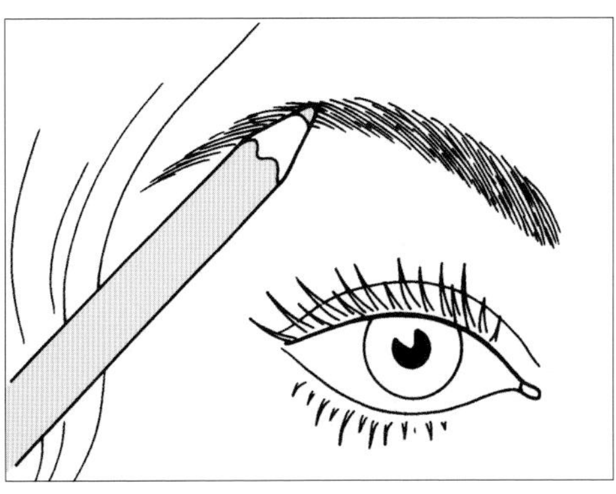

6 Wipe with the cotton pad again, to soothe any redness and swelling. To finish, use your pencil to fill in any gaps, using small light strokes, then brush again.

HOW TO LOSE WEIGHT

Sad to say, there are no miracle diets. To lose weight you must use up more calories than you take on board. The best way to do this — the only sensible way — is to eat a healthy balanced diet and to exercise regularly. Faddy diets don't work; 80 per cent of dieters end up fatter than they started. So take your time, and get slim slowly. You will be healthier and fitter, you will probably live longer — and you know what? — you will be an altogether happier person.

INDISPENSABLE WARNING

Always check with your doctor before embarking on a major change in your diet or starting a new exercise regime. Check that you really are overweight before starting a weight-loss programme.

INDISPENSABLE THINGS

- Your doctor's permission, if in any doubt
- Willpower
- Patience

GET ACTIVE

Regular exercise will help you to reach and maintain a healthy weight. Ideally, you should spend 30 minutes a day doing something that makes you slightly breathless and sweaty. Brisk walking is a good way to start. Be gradual about the way you build up the amount and the intensity of the exercise that you do.

EAT SMALL

Using a smaller plate at mealtimes can help you monitor how much you eat. Eat slowly, chewing each mouthful, so that you savour your food and notice when you are getting full (it takes 20 minutes for your body to signal that it has had enough). Take particular care when you eat out and cannot control your portion size.

EAT WELL

Eat a balanced diet: plenty of fruits and vegetables, as well as fibre-rich wholegrains, pulses, lean meat and low-fat dairy products (ask your doctor to refer you to a nutritionist if you need help with this). Choose healthy snacks such as raw nuts or plain homemade popcorn rather than crisps and biscuits. Avoid ready meals – even those labelled 'low-fat' can be loaded with sugar.

DRINK LESS, DRINK MORE

Alcohol and sugary drinks are high in calories – so cut them out. Drink plenty of water instead (2 litres/3½ pints) a day is the optimum). Hot (sugar-free!) drinks can make a good alternative to a snack. Try green tea; it is tasty, healthy and there is some evidence that it can help boost the metabolic rate, and so help you burn calories faster.

TAKE YOUR TIME

Don't expect to lose weight quickly. Aspire to lose no more than 0.5kg (1lb) a week. Watch yourself when you reach your target weight; this is the time when most people relax their regime and so backslide.

HOW TO GET A SIX-PACK

The six-pack has become the very cipher of sexiness for the modern man. But this wedge of abdominal muscle only looks like a six-pack – the bottom of a pack of beer cans – when it is highly developed, and when it is not hidden below a layer of fat. This means that acquiring one is much easier for younger adults and more challenging for those with a few years' indulgence under their belts. So leaner-bodied guys should concentrate on doing muscle-building exercises, while those carrying a few extra pounds must be sure also to eat healthily and do plenty of cardiovascular exercise if they want that washboard stomach.

INDISPENSABLE THINGS

- Your doctor's permission, if in any doubt
- A healthy diet
- Dedication
- Basic level of fitness

A PRACTICAL HISTORY OF MUSCLE-BUILDING

Body-building goes back to ancient times. The Egyptians used stones as weights to develop their muscles, and dumbbells dating from the 11th century have been found in India. In the late 19th century, strongmen showed off their prowess alongside bearded ladies at travelling shows. Later, men began 'sculpting' the body into an aesthetically pleasing form (the first body-building contest was held at London's Royal Albert Hall in 1901). The idea that every man can (and should) aspire to a muscle-bound physique was popularized by Charles Atlas. His advertisements, describing the transformation of a '97-pound weakling' into a muscleman, ran from the 1940s until the late 1970s.

INDISPENSABLE WARNING

Always consult an expert before doing strenuous exercise. Abdominal exercises such as sit-ups should be practised with caution, especially for those with lower back problems. A gym will advise you on which exercises are best for you and will help you with your technique.

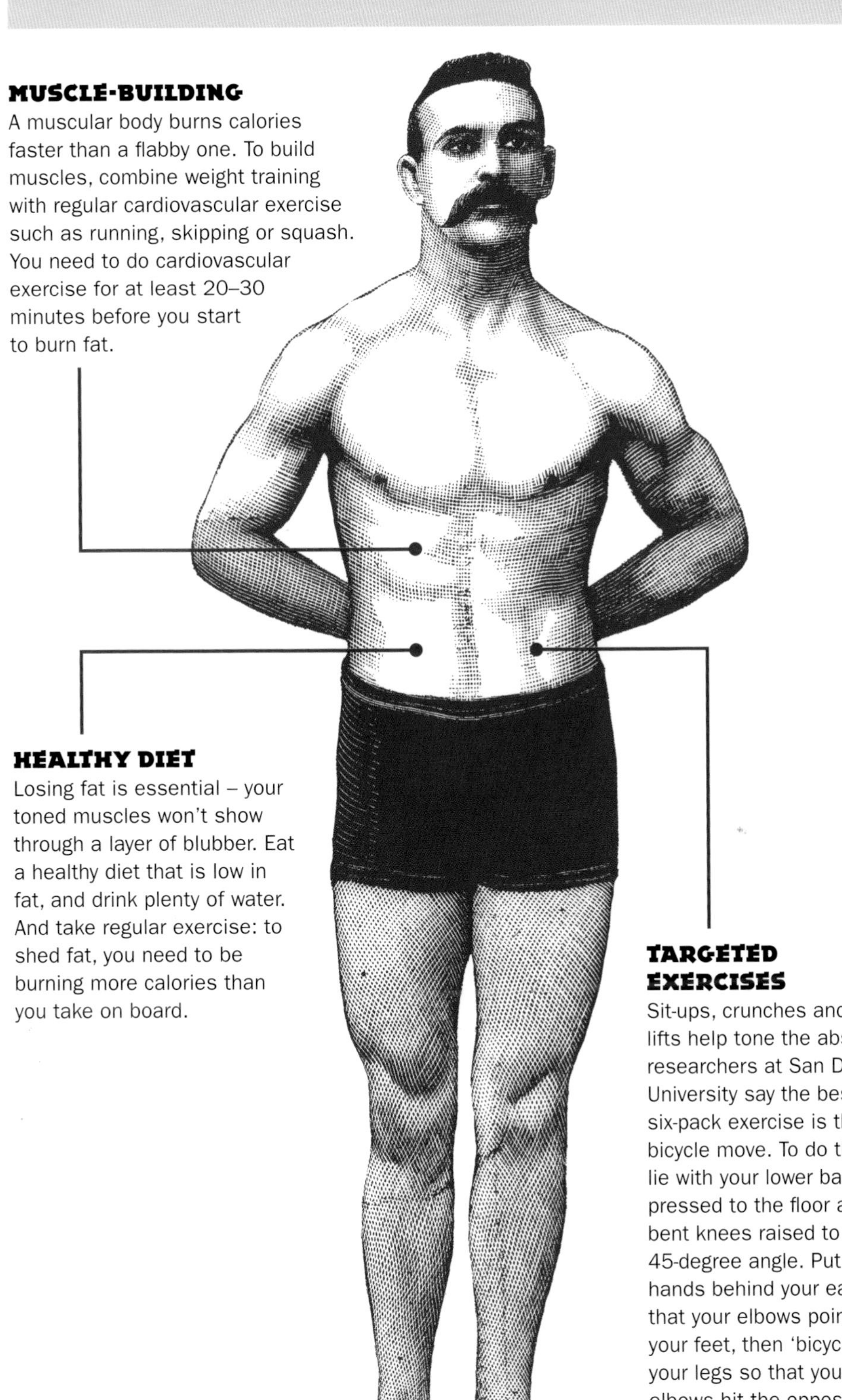

MUSCLE-BUILDING

A muscular body burns calories faster than a flabby one. To build muscles, combine weight training with regular cardiovascular exercise such as running, skipping or squash. You need to do cardiovascular exercise for at least 20–30 minutes before you start to burn fat.

HEALTHY DIET

Losing fat is essential – your toned muscles won't show through a layer of blubber. Eat a healthy diet that is low in fat, and drink plenty of water. And take regular exercise: to shed fat, you need to be burning more calories than you take on board.

TARGETED EXERCISES

Sit-ups, crunches and leg lifts help tone the abs. But researchers at San Diego University say the best six-pack exercise is the bicycle move. To do this, lie with your lower back pressed to the floor and bent knees raised to a 45-degree angle. Put your hands behind your ears so that your elbows point at your feet, then 'bicycle' your legs so that your elbows hit the opposite knee. Breathe steadily throughout the exercise.

HOW TO GET A CLOSE SHAVE

Designer stubble is so 1990s; beards really only suit saints and sea captains; moustaches of any kind are the hallmark of foreign despots. So let's face it: 99.9 per cent of men look best without facial hair. But even a clean-shaven face will not look good if the job is not done well, or if the process causes cuts and soreness or razor burn. To get a really pleasing, close shave you need to take some time and care over it. You also need to go down the wet route; electric razors just don't measure up.

A PRACTICAL HISTORY OF THE RAZOR

If you find shaving a bore, spare a thought for our prehistoric ancestors. Contrary to popular belief, they were not all beardies, but actually went to the trouble of shaving with flints, clam shells or sharks' teeth. One of the benefits of the Bronze Age was the invention of the metal razor. Blades made of copper or gold were used in India and Egypt 6,000 years ago. Steel 'cut-throat' razors were produced in Sheffield in the early part of the 19th century, but the safety razor with disposable blades was not mass-produced until the beginning of the 20th century. Its inventor was the magnificently named King Camp Gillette.

INDISPENSABLE THINGS

- Flannel
- Basin of hot water
- Shaving foam and brush, or other shaving lubricant
- Non-disposable razor
- Mirror
- Towel
- Aftershave balm

1 Have a hot shower – this will soften your stubble and open up the pores, making shaving much easier. If that isn't possible, wash your face with warm water and then hold a warm, damp flannel over the bearded part for a minute or two.

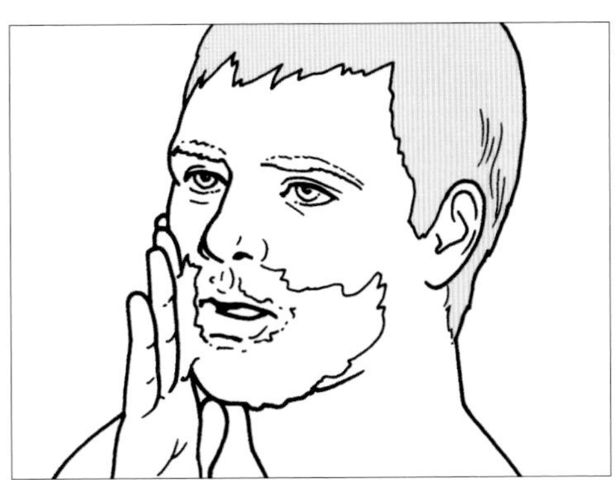

2 Half-fill the basin with hot water, wet your face and apply your lubricant. If using shaving cream, lather it up and apply with a shaving brush in circular strokes to make a thick, even layer. Alternatively, use shaving foam or gel. Don't skimp or you risk razor burn.

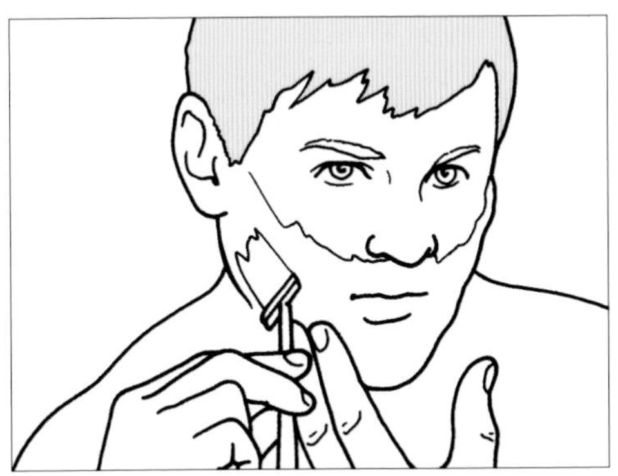

3 Take your razor, making sure that it is clean and sharp (a blunt razor is more likely to give you a nick or cause ingrowing hairs). Use one hand to pull the skin taut as you shave. Start with the sides of the face, using long, smooth strokes, working in the direction of the hair growth. Do not press down.

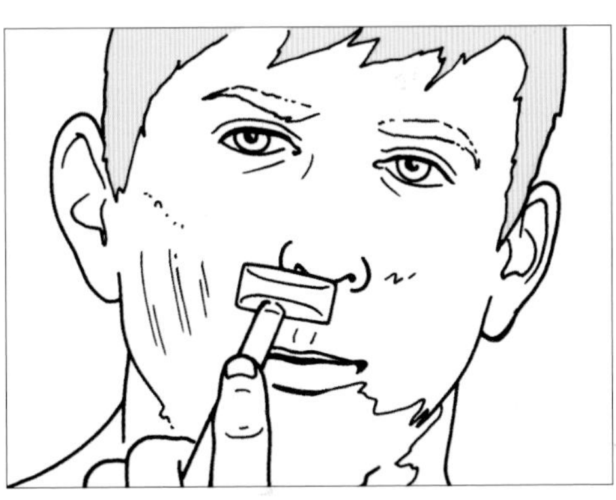

4 Rinse your razor in the basin after every stroke. Shave your moustache, chin area and neck, continuing to scrape the razor along the grain.

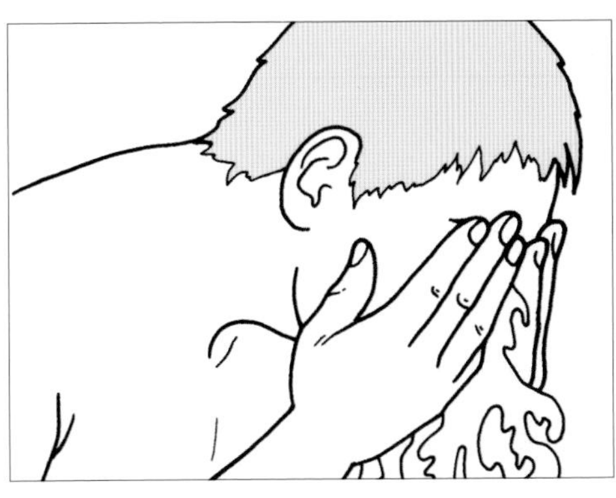

5 If you need a closer shave, wash your face, reapply your lubricant and then shave again, this time against the direction of the hair growth. Once your shave is complete, splash your face with clean, cold water, then pat dry with a towel. Apply a good-quality aftershave balm.

PRACTICAL TIP

Change your blade at least once a week to be sure of a close shave.

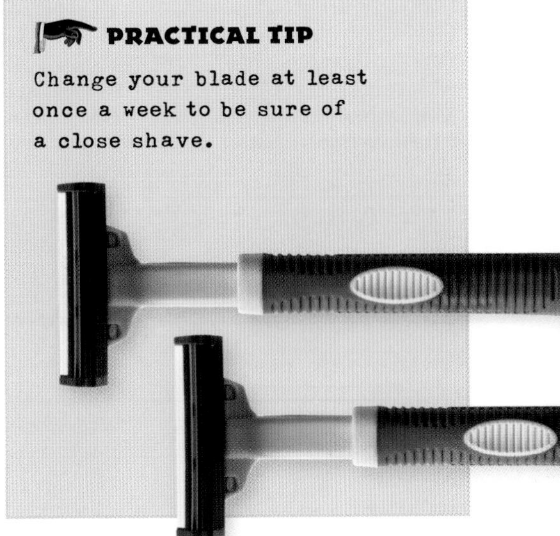

HOW TO HAVE PERFECT NAILS

You may not be all that bothered about your nails, but be sure that other people will be. Dirty, bitten and torn nails are instant turn-offs – they tell other people that you don't care about yourself. But over-embellished nails are just as woeful. As ever in matters of taste and fashion, simplicity is the best policy. Short and rounded nails will always look good so long as you keep up the maintenance: chipped nail varnish looks worse than no nail varnish.

INDISPENSABLE THINGS

- Hand and nail cream
- Rubber gloves
- Emery board
- Orange stick and cotton wool
- Base coat
- Nail polish
- Top coat
- Nail varnish remover
- Cotton bud

PRACTICAL TIP

Always wear rubber gloves when you are doing household chores: cleaning chemicals can weaken your nails. If you are digging or trying to prise off a lid, use an appropriate implement – never your nails.

CARING FOR CUTICLES

It's best not to cut your cuticles. Soak your hands before pushing back the cuticles using an orange stick covered in cotton wool.

SHAPING THE NAIL

Be sure to keep your nails filed to the same length; it looks odd when one nail is shorter than the rest. Use an emery board to shape (not a metal file), filing in one direction rather than going back and forwards. Keep the nails short and naturally rounded – square-ended or long nails are out.

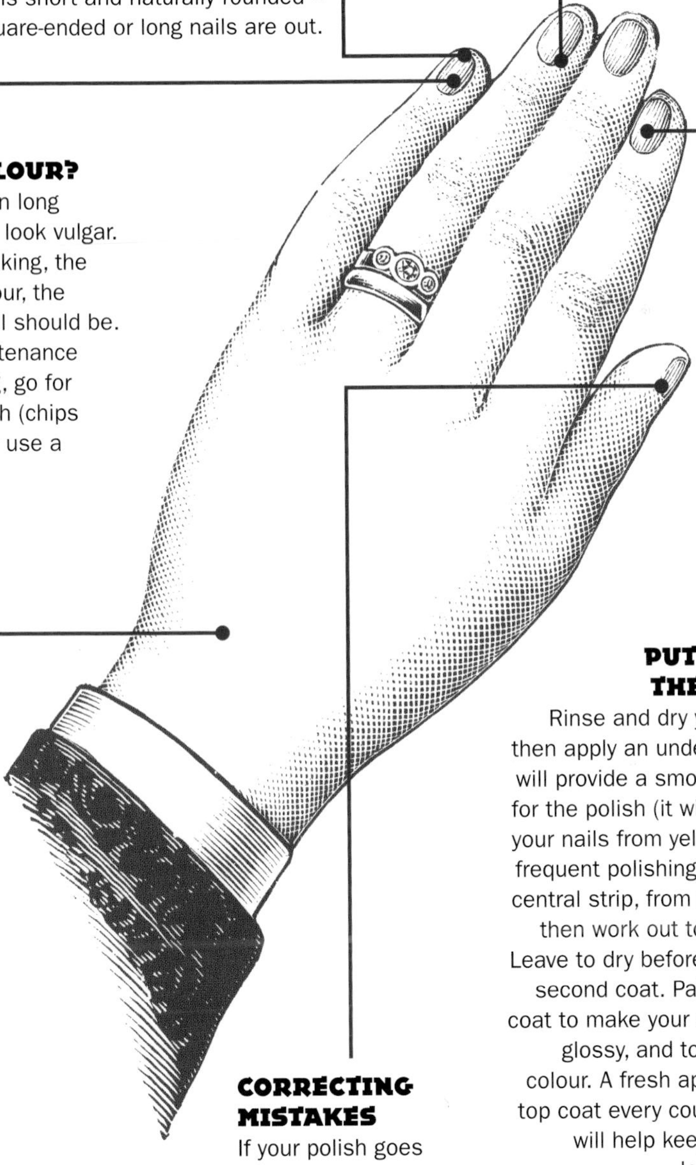

WHICH COLOUR?

Dark colours on long fingernails can look vulgar. Generally speaking, the darker the colour, the shorter the nail should be. If regular maintenance isn't your thing, go for clear nail polish (chips won't show) or use a buffer instead.

PUTTING ON THE POLISH

Rinse and dry your hands, then apply an undercoat. This will provide a smooth surface for the polish (it will also stop your nails from yellowing from frequent polishing). Paint one central strip, from base to tip, then work out to the sides. Leave to dry before applying a second coat. Paint on a top coat to make your nails super-glossy, and to seal in the colour. A fresh application of top coat every couple of days will help keep your nails looking good.

CORRECTING MISTAKES

If your polish goes onto the skin, dip a cotton bud in nail varnish remover and run down the sides of your nail to remove.

BASIC MAINTENANCE

Moisturize your hands and nails often – whenever you wash them and always before bed. It's a good idea to keep some cream by the sink, in the bathroom, in the glove compartment of your car and by your bed, so that you never forget. Keep your nails out of very hot water altogether.

HOW TO GET RID OF SPOTS

A zit raises its ugly head just when you are about to go on a big date. It's not the end of the world, but it feels like it. The temptation to squeeze a spot is almost overwhelming – but resist. A burst pimple may well look bigger, redder and altogether worse (not to mention the fact that it may get infected). There are cleverer ways to make a spot go away – or at least to render it invisible for the duration of a film or a romantic dinner.

INDISPENSABLE WARNING

Seek medical advice if you suffer from frequent outbreaks of spots, since this may well indicate that you have acne or some other skin condition.

INDISPENSABLE THINGS

- Mild cleanser
- Toner
- Soap
- Concealer
- Face powder
- Phone number of a dermatologist

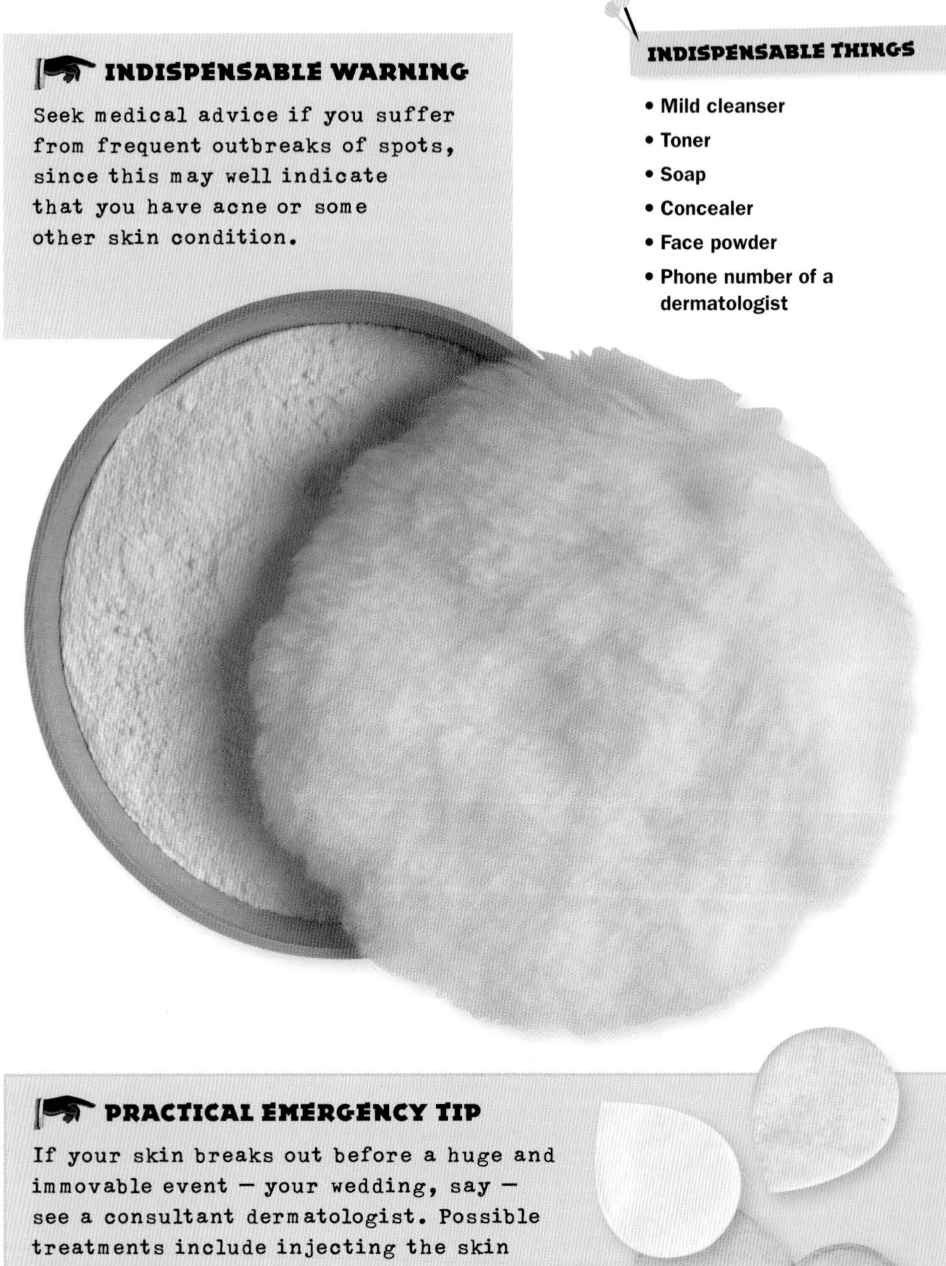

PRACTICAL EMERGENCY TIP

If your skin breaks out before a huge and immovable event – your wedding, say – see a consultant dermatologist. Possible treatments include injecting the skin with diluted cortisone.

AVOID MAKE-UP

Go bare-faced to promote healing – foundation clogs up your pores, so will keep the pimple from drying out. If you can't face the day without make-up, remove it as soon as you get home. High-factor sunscreens are also bad for people suffering frequent breakouts (you may want to consider wearing a hat that shades your face instead).

STAYING SPOT-FREE

Spots can break out at times of hormonal activity such as the end of the menstrual cycle. They're also more likely to occur when you are stressed. Eating a good balanced diet, getting plenty of sleep and drinking lots of water will help to keep the skin clear. But don't worry about eating the occasional bar of chocolate – it's not true that sugary, fatty foods cause acne.

HIDE THAT ZIT

Dab a little oil-free, antibacterial concealer on the spot and pat with powder. Wear a bright red lipstick or dramatic eye make-up to draw attention to all the fabulous things that happen on your face. Any zit is, after all, going to be much smaller and less interesting than your fascinating mouth or your luminous eyes.

KEEP CLEAN

Good hygiene is the best way to speed healing. Wash your face twice a day with a gentle cleanser, rinse well, pat dry, then follow with toner. Don't put moisturizer on a spot. Be sure to wash your hands often, and avoid touching your face as much as possible. Tie long hair back to keep it off your face, and change your pillow case regularly.

HOW TO GIVE UP SMOKING

Smokers are masters at ignoring bad news. Somehow the fact that the ciggy habit can give you cellulite or even gangrene in no way detracts from the sublime pleasure of lighting up. But there is no doubt that smoking is getting less glamorous. It is not just that so many people object or disapprove; the fact is there is nothing cool about huddling in a doorway in the rain taking furtive drags from a damp roll-up. It really is time to give up.

INDISPENSABLE THINGS

- Willpower

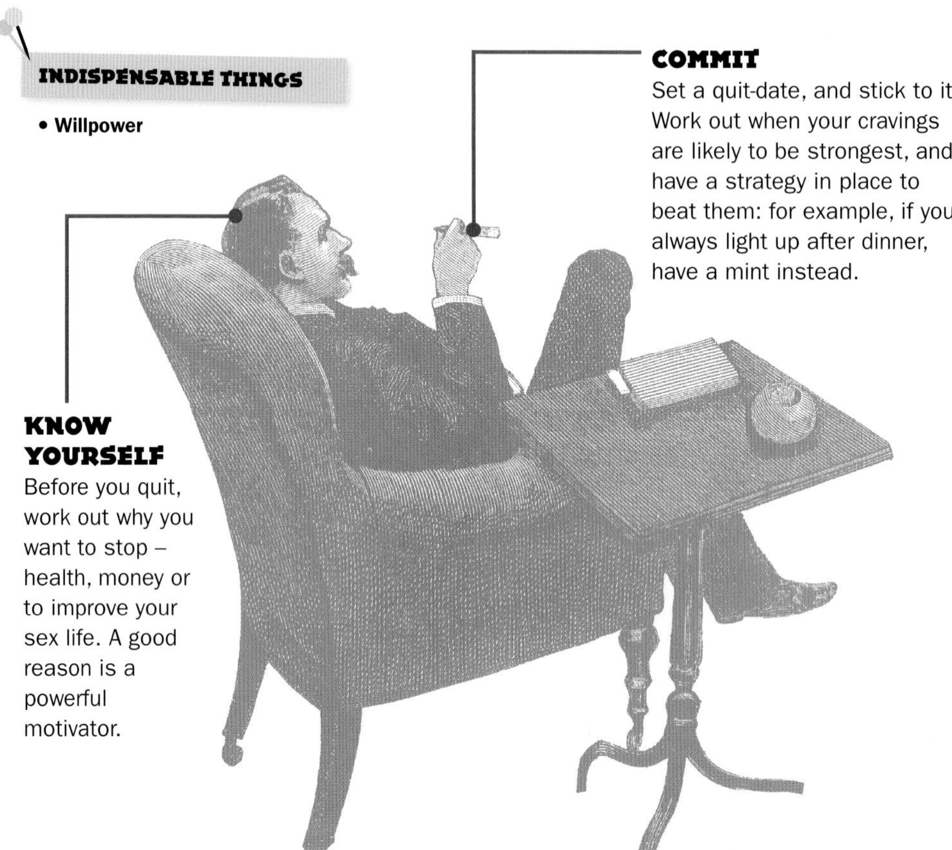

COMMIT

Set a quit-date, and stick to it. Work out when your cravings are likely to be strongest, and have a strategy in place to beat them: for example, if you always light up after dinner, have a mint instead.

KNOW YOURSELF

Before you quit, work out why you want to stop – health, money or to improve your sex life. A good reason is a powerful motivator.

A PRACTICAL HISTORY OF SMOKING

It's been known for years that smoking is bad for you. In 1604, within a generation of tobacco arriving in Europe, James I of England described it as 'a custom loathsome to the eye, hateful to the nose, harmful to the brain, dangerous to the lungs'. But for centuries, people smoked for the good of their health. In the 17th century, tobacco was believed to protect against plague – and boys at Eton College were beaten for not smoking their pipes. In 1950, scientists proved the link between lung cancer and smoking. The cigarette habit has been in long, slow decline ever since.

GET HELP
You don't have to do it on your own. Join a stop-smoking group or get some one-on-one counselling – see your doctor for a referral. Call a stop-smoking helpline, too (details from your doctor or the internet).

EXERCISE
If you are worried that your weight will balloon, kickstart your exercise programme. Going out for a run is a great way to divert those cravings into something truly health-giving.

GET DRUGS
Nicotine Replacement Therapy (NRT) has been shown to double your chances of quitting. You can get NRT over the counter or on prescription as gum, patches, lozenges or nasal spray.

REWARD YOURSELF
Quitting is a hard slog, so book yourself a facial as a treat, or buy some new CDs – your reward will be practically free if you take into account the money you are saving on ciggies.

HOW TO MEDITATE

If everyone meditated, the world would probably be a much happier place. But meditation is not a way to do nothing – sitting completely still for even a few minutes can be a detox for the mind. There are no guarantees when it comes to meditation, but it is likely that practising stillness on a regular basis will make you less stressed, more relaxed – and just possibly enlightened. One study found that regular meditators needed to visit their doctors less frequently than non-meditators – which is probably the reason many doctors recommend it.

INDISPENSABLE THINGS

- Quiet calm space
- Cushion or chair
- Patience

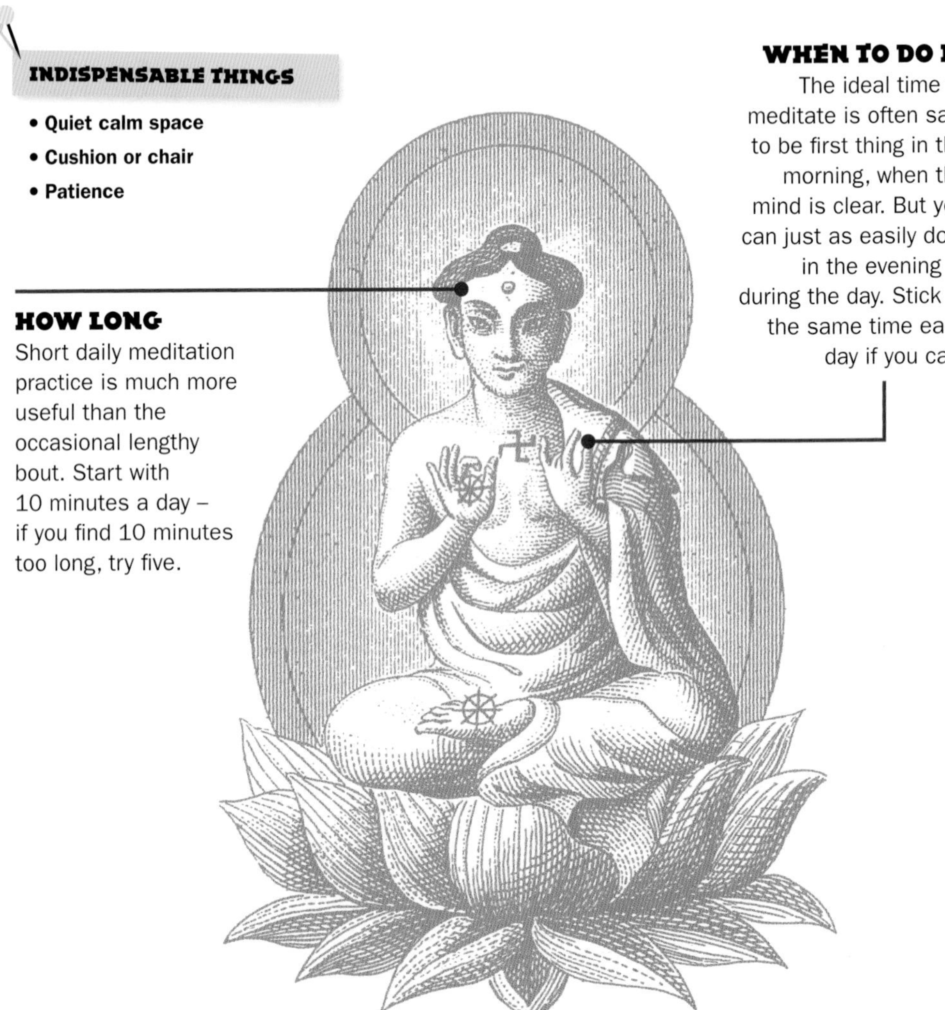

WHEN TO DO IT

The ideal time to meditate is often said to be first thing in the morning, when the mind is clear. But you can just as easily do it in the evening or during the day. Stick to the same time each day if you can.

HOW LONG

Short daily meditation practice is much more useful than the occasional lengthy bout. Start with 10 minutes a day – if you find 10 minutes too long, try five.

INDISPENSABLE WARNING

If you have experienced mental illness or recent emotional problems, talk to your doctor before practising meditation. It is advisable to learn meditation under the guidance of an experienced and reputable teacher. Be wary of self-styled 'gurus' and cults.

BASIC TECHNIQUE

Close your eyes. Focus your attention on the breath, either noticing the sensations when it passes in and out of the nostrils or the rise and fall of the chest (stick to one or the other focus, rather than switching between them). Don't try to breathe more deeply or regularly; this should happen naturally as you relax. Every time you notice yourself thinking (or falling asleep), gently bring your attention back to your breath.

MENTAL ATTITUDE

Meditation is a technique to enable you to notice the mind's activity without judging it. So don't be hard on yourself if you are distracted – it's normal to lose your focus many, many times. Practising meditation in a group, under the guidance of a good teacher, will help enormously with concentration and motivation.

SITTING POSITIONS

The lotus is the traditional pose for meditation – but it only suits those with years of yoga behind them. Less experienced meditators should sit on a cushion on the floor or on a straight-backed chair (both feet flat on the floor). The important thing is to keep your back straight and shoulders relaxed, and to be comfortable enough to maintain your pose.

HOW TO DO YOUR EYE MAKE-UP

They say that the eyes are the window of the soul, which means that eye make-up is window-dressing. Skilfully executed eye make-up can make your eyes look bigger, brighter and more beautiful. But you need to get the basic colours right. The salesperson at the cosmetic counter is a good person to ask – but check that you like her make-up first. And be prepared to invest in a decent set of brushes as you need the right tools to get a good result.

INDISPENSABLE THINGS

- Selection of eye make-up brushes
- Light, medium and darker eye shadows
- Shimmer shadow
- Mascara
- Concealer
- Eye liner

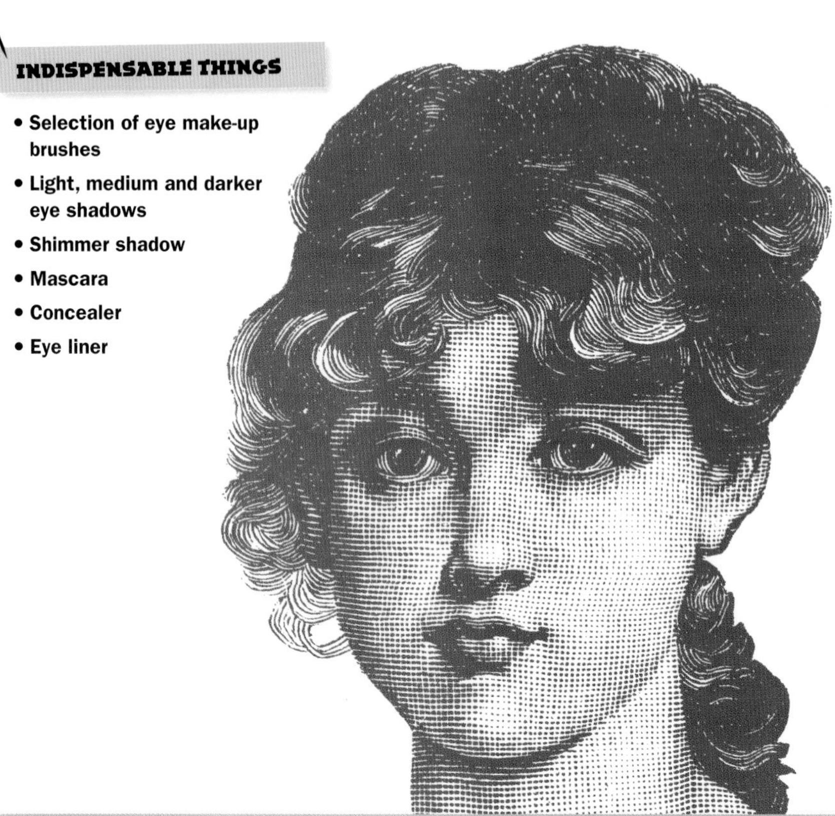

PRACTICAL TIP

Lots of women try to match their eye shadow to their eye colour, but you get a more interesting and vibrant effect if you go for contrast. If you have green eyes, purple shades such as violet look beautiful. For blue eyes, browns and golds are a good choice. Brown-eyed women should try blue or greenish hues. If you are using eye liner, make sure it complements the eye shadow – plum for violet, chocolate for brown, and dark green for green shades.

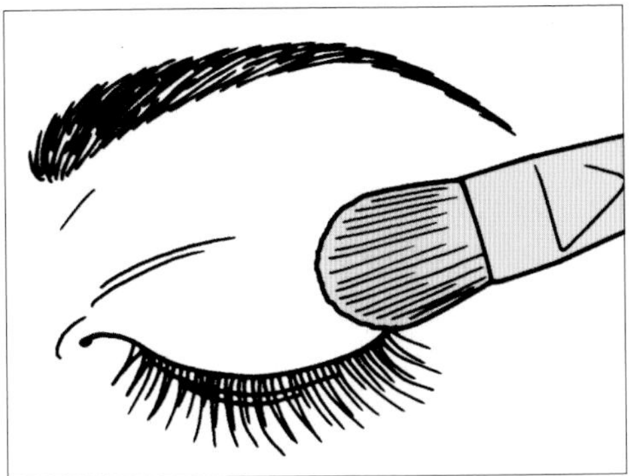

1 Use an all-over shadow brush to apply a light neutral colour over the entire lid of the eye. You could also use a sponge-tip applicator (often supplied free with an eye shadow) to do this.

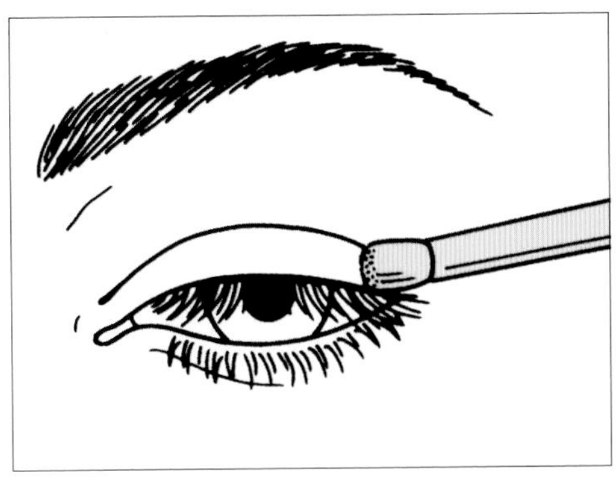

2 Brush a medium-toned shadow over the part of the lid that covers the eyeball. Again you can use a sponge-tip applicator for this, but a contour brush works best. Blend the colours where they meet.

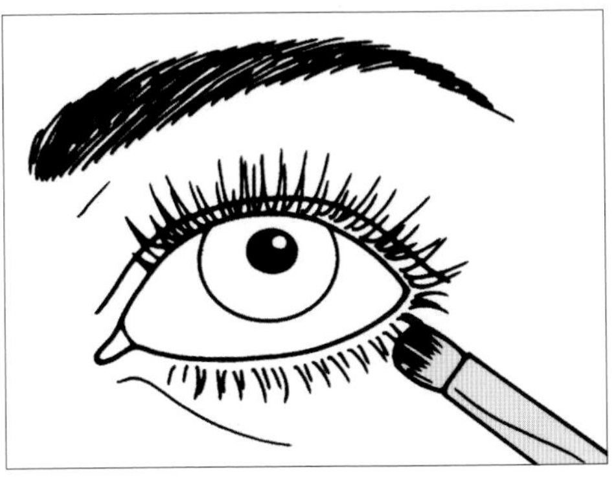

3 Now use a fine smudge brush to apply dark shadow along the lash line, blending it into the mid-tone. Apply under the bottom lashes, too.

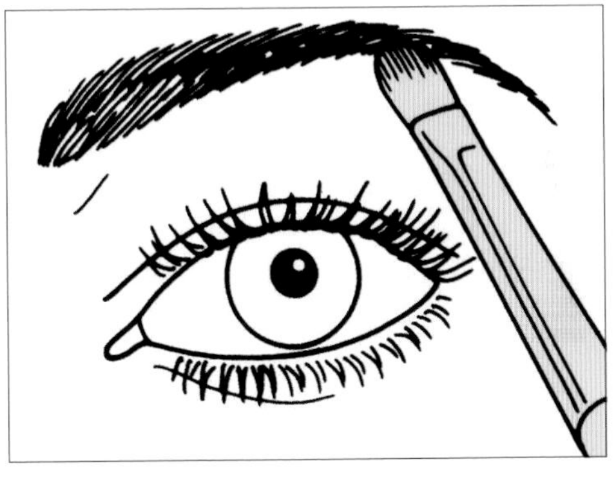

4 Then use a small shadow brush to apply a small amount of light-toned shimmer shadow to the brow bone. This will help the eyes to appear brighter.

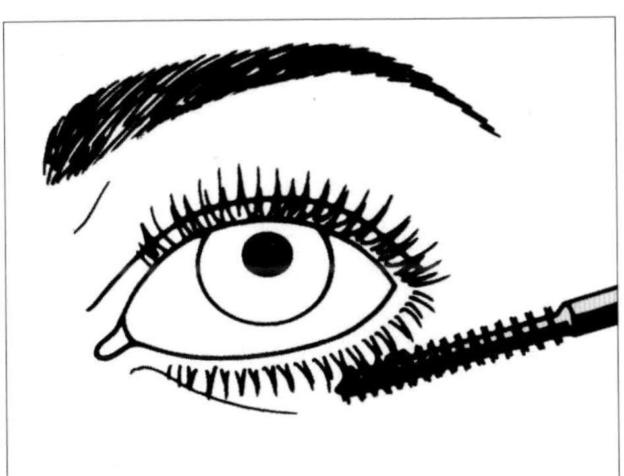

5 Apply mascara to the tips of both upper and lower lashes (your lashes will look better if you curl them first). Use repeated light brush strokes to extend them and build up the colour.

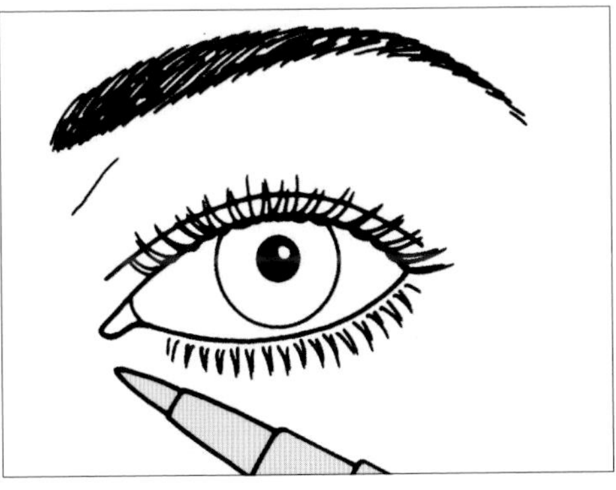

6 Finally, apply concealer to any dark areas under the eyes. Use your finger to blend the concealer in well.

HOW TO CLEAN YOUR TEETH

You would think that everybody brushes their teeth often enough to know what they are doing. But the very fact that we do it so frequently means that few of us give it the attention it requires. Brushing your teeth should take at least two minutes if you do it properly – the chances are you spend barely 30 seconds. The consequences of inadequate brushing are various and horrible: tooth decay, gum disease and bad breath. So whatever else you do, be sure to go the full 120 seconds to keep the tooth fairy from your door. And don't forget to floss.

INDISPENSABLE THINGS

- Soft-bristled toothbrush
- Fluoride toothpaste
- Dental floss

PRACTICAL TIP

Some people find that their gums bleed when they start to floss; this usually means that the gums are inflamed, and should stop happening if you floss regularly and in the correct way. If the bleeding continues longer than a week or two, see your dentist for advice.

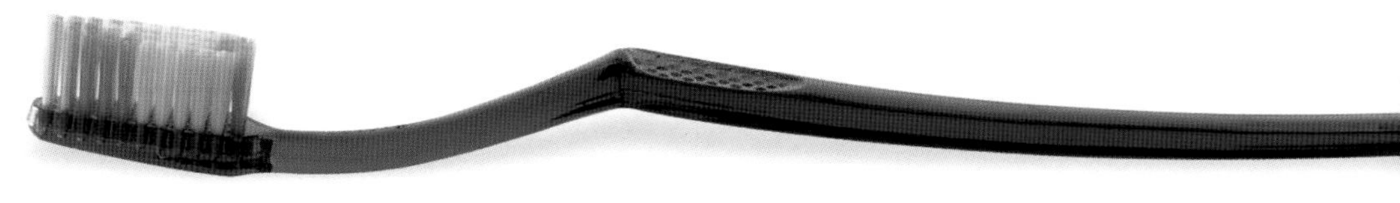

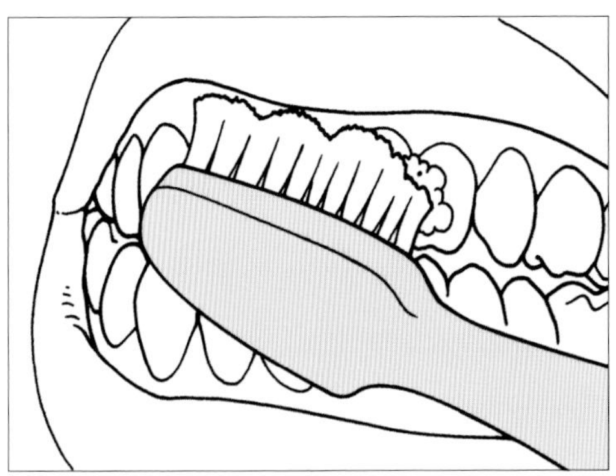

1 Clean first the outsides, then the insides of the teeth, using small circular movements. It helps to angle the brush against the gumline at about 45 degrees. Make sure you brush along the gumline, because this action stimulates blood flow to the gums.

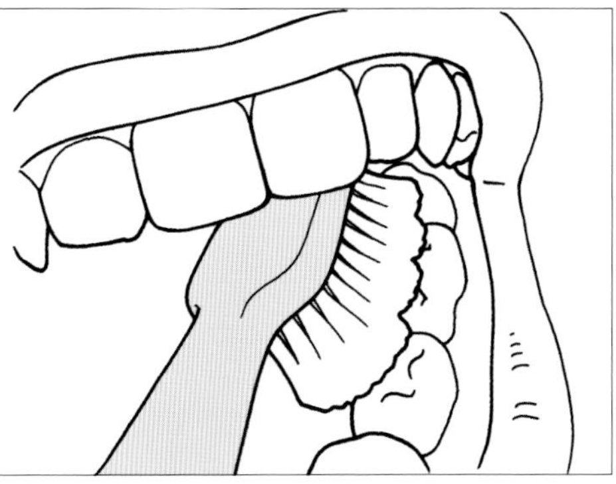

2 Clean the insides of the upper and lower middle teeth by tilting the brush vertically so that you can reach them. Finally brush along the biting surfaces, using a back-and-forth motion.

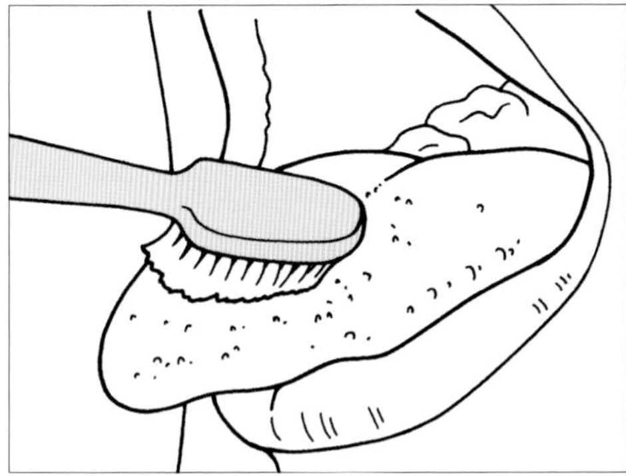

3 Give your tongue a clean using your brush or a special tongue cleaner – this will help get rid of bacteria and freshen the breath. Rinse your mouth, drawing the water through your teeth.

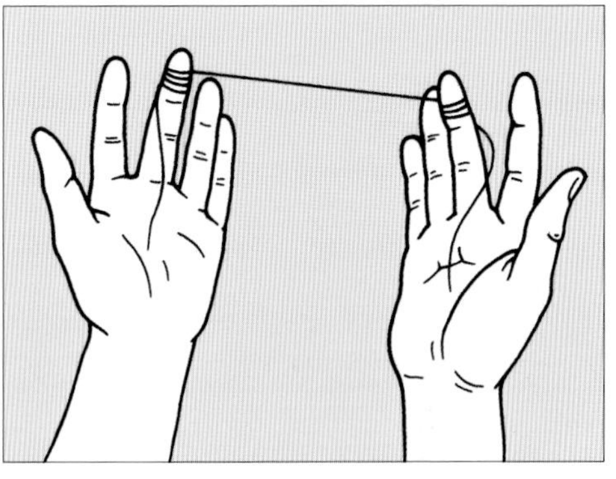

4 Take a 45cm (18in) length of floss and wind it around the middle finger of each hand. Use your thumbs and forefingers to hold the floss taut, leaving yourself about 2.5cm (1in) in between to work with.

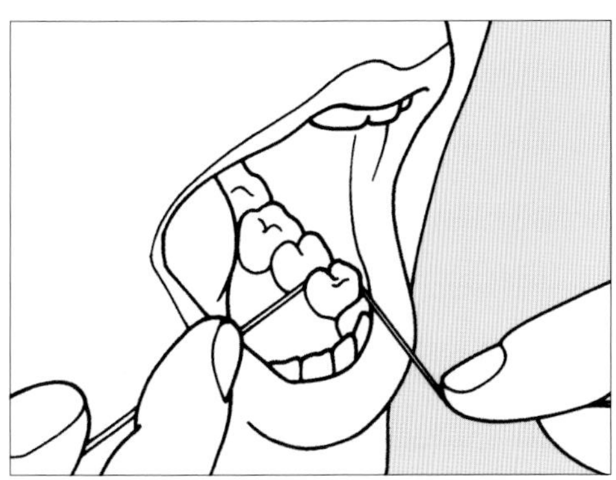

5 Gently guide the floss up around the tooth and under the gum line, in a smooth circular movement. Gently rub down the tooth a few times. Clean between all your teeth, remembering to do both sides. Wind the floss along so that you use a clean piece each time.

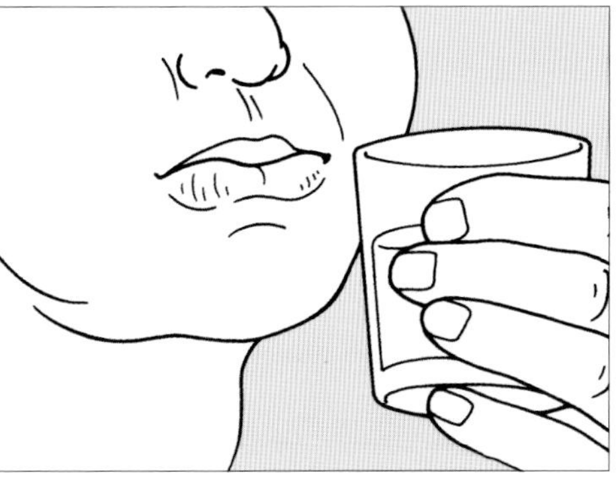

6 Give your mouth a good rinse, drawing the water through your teeth, to wash away any dislodged food particles.

HOW TO BLOW-DRY YOUR HAIR STRAIGHT

If you were blessed with straight hair as an infant, the chances are you spent your childhood longing for waves and ringlets. For grown-up women, however, curls are out and stick-straight is in – according to one survey, two-thirds of us prefer our hair to be sleek and smooth. If you don't want to shell out for hair straighteners, then blow-drying is the best way to straighten your hair. You'll need time and patience – it takes about 30 minutes – and also a good hairdryer to get a perfect flat-iron style.

INDISPENSABLE THINGS

- Damp, just-washed hair
- Wide-toothed comb
- Hairdryer with nozzle
- Heat protectant
- Straightening balm
- Large hairdressing clips
- Thick round brush

A PRACTICAL HISTORY OF HAIR

Hair – especially women's hair – has always had deep cultural significance. In many ancient cultures, long hair with vibrant colour was considered beautiful for a very sound anthropological reason. It advertised youth, and it proclaimed that the woman in question had enjoyed uninterrupted good health over an extended period. Blonde or brunette, a good head of hair was a visual indicator that the woman in question was a safe prospect as a mate. All the vast resources of modern beauticians and stylists – their many chemicals and colouring agents, their multifarious creams and conditioners – are aimed at evoking that same subliminal and primeval human response to an eye-catching set of locks.

1 Comb your hair with a wide-toothed comb. Rough-dry under a cool dryer while running your fingers through it – you want to get it about 80 per cent dry before you start straightening. Apply heat protectant and straightening balm, according to the manufacturer's instructions.

2 Divide your hair into several sections. Clip the sides and front of your hair on top of the head, leaving the back loose. Take a small section of the loose hair at the back in order to style it.

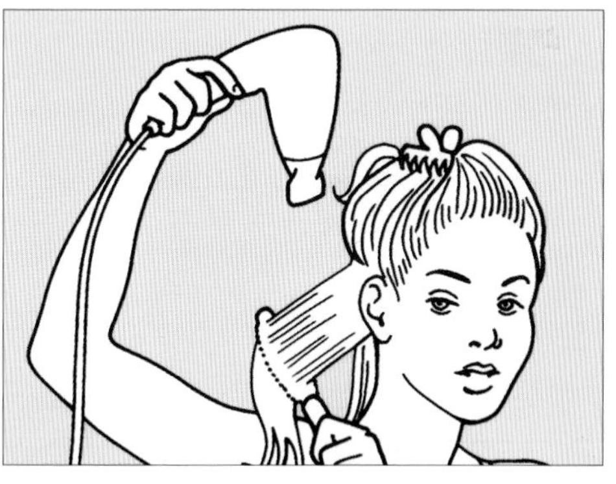

3 Use your brush to lift the hair at the roots and then pull it down to the ends at the same time as you dry it. Hold the hairdryer nozzle about 10cm (4in) away from the hair, and direct the air *down* the shaft, to encourage it to lie flat (don't let the dryer get too close).

4 Now do the upper side. Again, use your brush to pull the hair straight as you dry it, keeping the tension as even as possible. Keep the dryer moving to avoid burning the hair, and try not to overdry any areas.

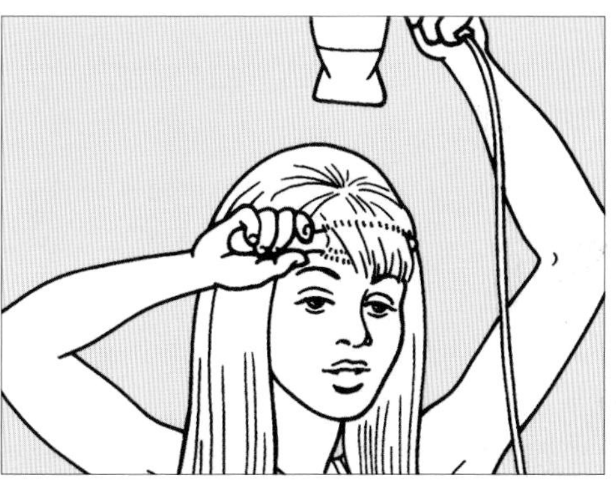

5 Make sure the hair is completely dry before moving onto the next small section of the back. Once you have done the back of the hair, do the sides, followed by the fringe and crown.

HOW TO DO A PRESS-UP

Press-ups are a way of using your body as a kind of dumb-bell. Every time you do a press-up you are lifting part of your own weight, and at the same time building the 'Popeye' muscles — your biceps and triceps. The press-up also works the chest, shoulders and abs — and builds overall upper body strength. It's a great exercise to do if you are into racket sports, because it helps you to get more power into every shot. And if a full press-up is too difficult, try the bent-knee version. It's sometimes dubbed the 'girl's press-up', which is a chauvinist's way of saying it's a good option for beginners.

INDISPENSABLE THINGS

- A carpeted or padded floor (or 'sticky' yoga mat)
- Comfortable, unrestrictive clothing
- Warmed-up muscles
- Your doctor's permission, if in any doubt

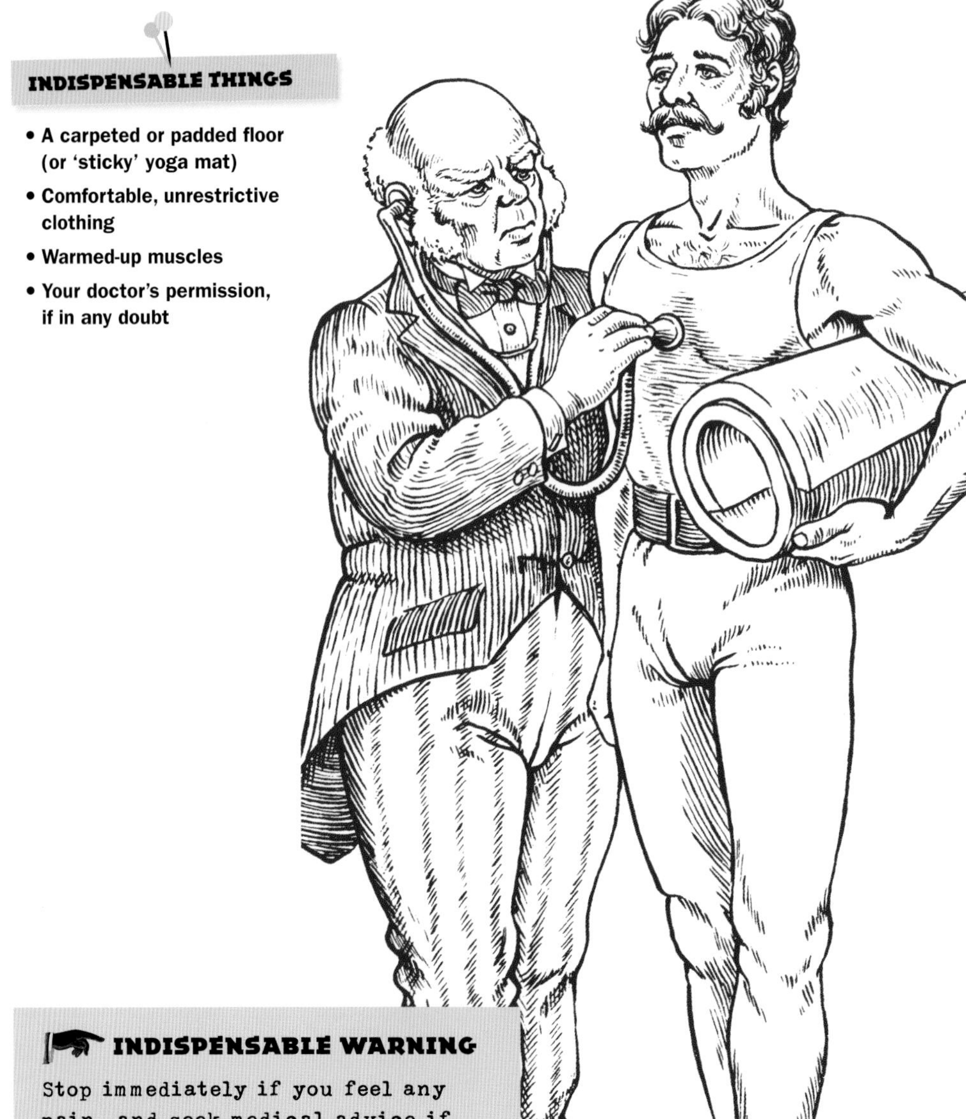

INDISPENSABLE WARNING

Stop immediately if you feel any pain, and seek medical advice if the pain persists.

FULL PRESS-UP

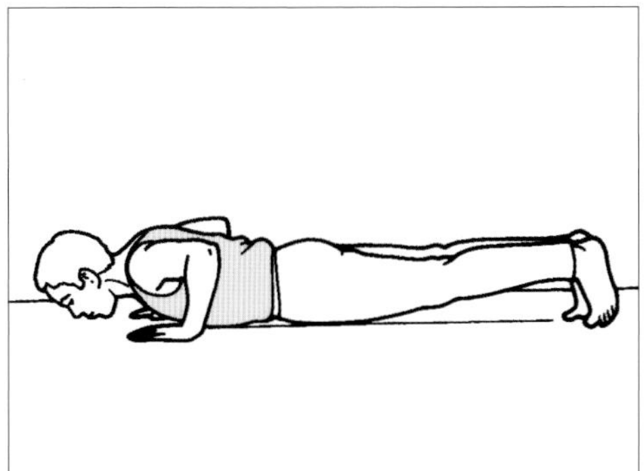

1 Lie face-down on the floor. Put your hands on the floor, either side of your chest and slightly further apart than your shoulders, with fingers facing forwards. Keeping your feet slightly apart, place them so that the toes and the balls of your feet are on the floor.

2 Raise yourself up until your arms are straight, breathing out as you do so. Keep your abdominals pulled in. Your neck, back and legs should form a straight line (or 'plank') – do not push your bottom in the air or arch your back. Hold this position.

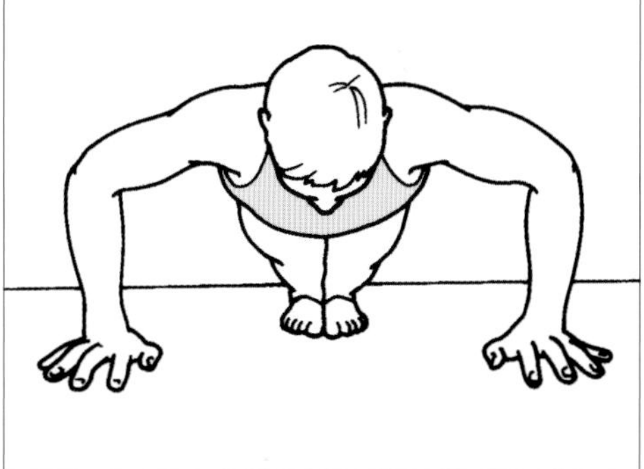

3 Now slowly lower your chest to the ground by bending the arms until the elbows form a right angle and your chest is about 5cm (2in) from the floor. Breathe in as you come down.

4 Repeat up to 10 times, working slowly and concentrating on your technique rather than on speed. Pause for a moment between each press-up. Stop if your lower back starts to sag or you get tired. Over time, you can build up the number of press-ups you do in each session.

BENT-KNEE PRESS-UP

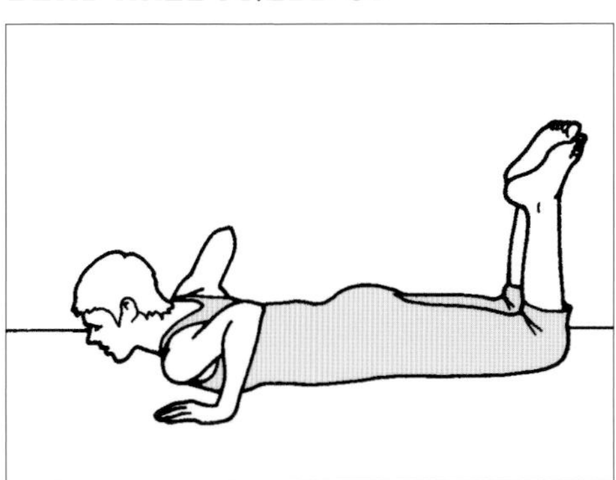

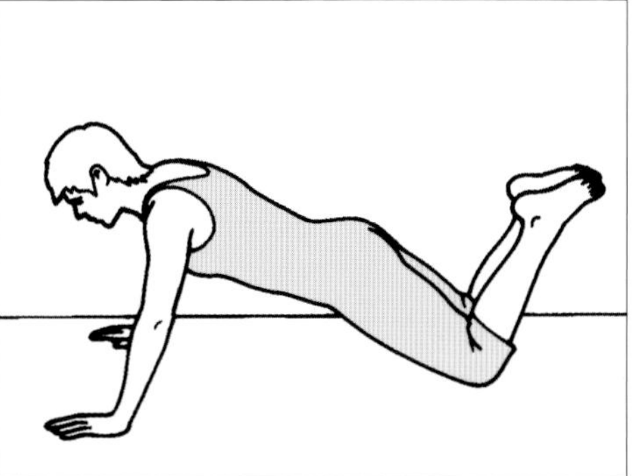

1 Lie on the floor, with your hands either side of your chest, fingers facing forwards and elbows bent. Bring your feet off the floor, bending your knees to form a 45-degree angle.

2 Breathing out, raise yourself up until your arms are straight. Keep your back and neck in a straight line and pause for a moment. Breathe in as you lower yourself back until your chest is about 5cm (2in) from the floor. Pause and repeat.

HOW TO IMPROVE YOUR POSTURE

Your mother was right when she told you to sit up straight. Most of us have faulty posture, and nine out of ten people suffer from back problems at some point in their lives. This is the inevitable result of years spent hunched over laptops or slouched on sofas – or else, more actively, carrying babies on one hip or lopsidedly toting bags of schoolbooks or shopping. You can add centimetres to your height, improve your health and even boost your confidence in an instant – simply by holding yourself properly.

INDISPENSABLE THINGS

- Body awareness

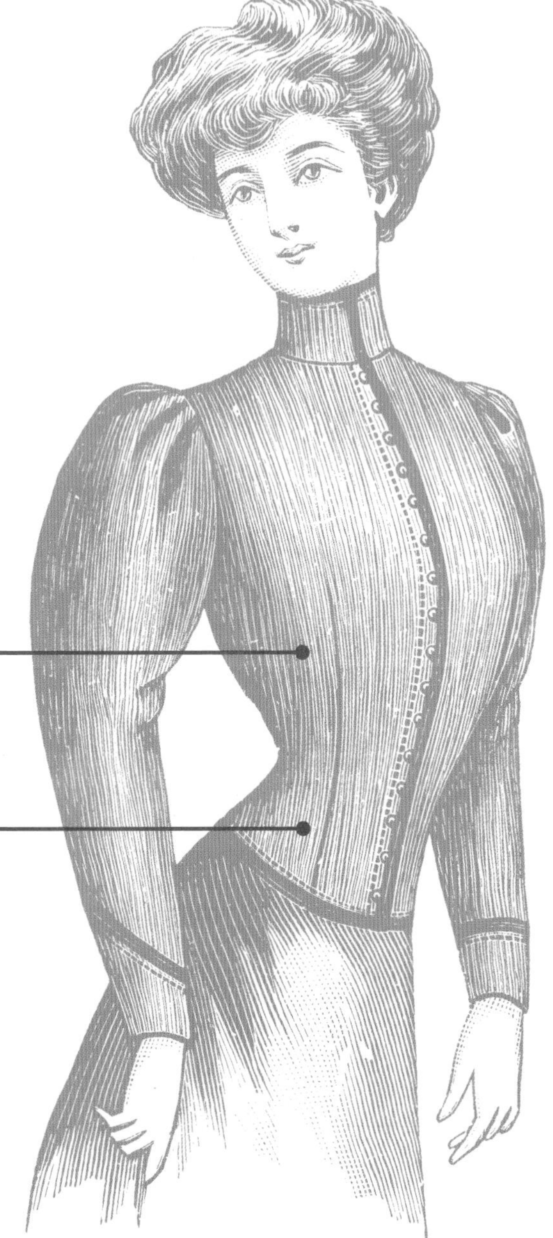

BE SPINE-FRIENDLY

Stand so that your spine tends towards its natural curve. This means keeping your head upright, relaxing your shoulders, pulling the blades in and down the back, pulling in your abdomen, keeping the hips level and tucking in the tailbone.

SEE AN EXPERT

Alexander Technique specifically targets your posture and helps to release you from unhealthy ways of moving and standing. It's best taught on a one-to-one basis, and you'll need several sessions, plus regular follow-ups.

GO EAST
Try eastern forms of exercise such as yoga and tai chi: they work on the whole body, so they naturally improve your posture. You may notice a difference in the way you stand after a few sessions. Pilates incorporates elements of yoga, and is known to encourage good postural habits. Or try dance – you don't often see a ballerina with a hump.

START AT THE TOP
Where the head leads, the rest of the body will follow. Jutting out the chin like a sergeant-major will pull your spine out of its optimal position. So, keep your head erect with your chin parallel to the floor and your neck soft – you'll feel the rest of the spine lengthen below. A good tip is to imagine there is a string attached to the centre of your crown, helping to lift you into an upright posture.

CHECK YOURSELF
Don't get stuck in the same pose for long periods – get in the habit of checking your posture and adjusting it regularly. If you use a computer, make sure you have a proper chair and that you keep both feet flat on the floor, knees slightly apart. Don't cross your legs: it twists the spine. Get up and walk around at regular intervals.

SHOE SENSE
If you want good posture, lose the high heels: they push the spine out of alignment. Wear comfy shoes with a low heel.

HOW TO SLEEP BETTER

One in three people has trouble sleeping. If you are one of them, take heart from the fact that most sleep problems are treatable. The key is not to spend your evenings on things that are vexatious to the spirit. Don't exercise at night, drink lots or watch much telly. Sleep is something you have to get yourself in the mood for.

INDISPENSABLE THINGS

- **A good mattress (less than 10 years old)**
- **Enough covers**

SET A ROUTINE

Going to bed and getting up at the same times every day – including weekends – helps set your body clock for good, regular sleep. So resist the lie-in.

STAY WARM

Keeping warm will help you to drop off; make sure you have a decent duvet or enough blankets. Having a warm bath an hour or so before bedtime can soothe you into a state of sleepiness.

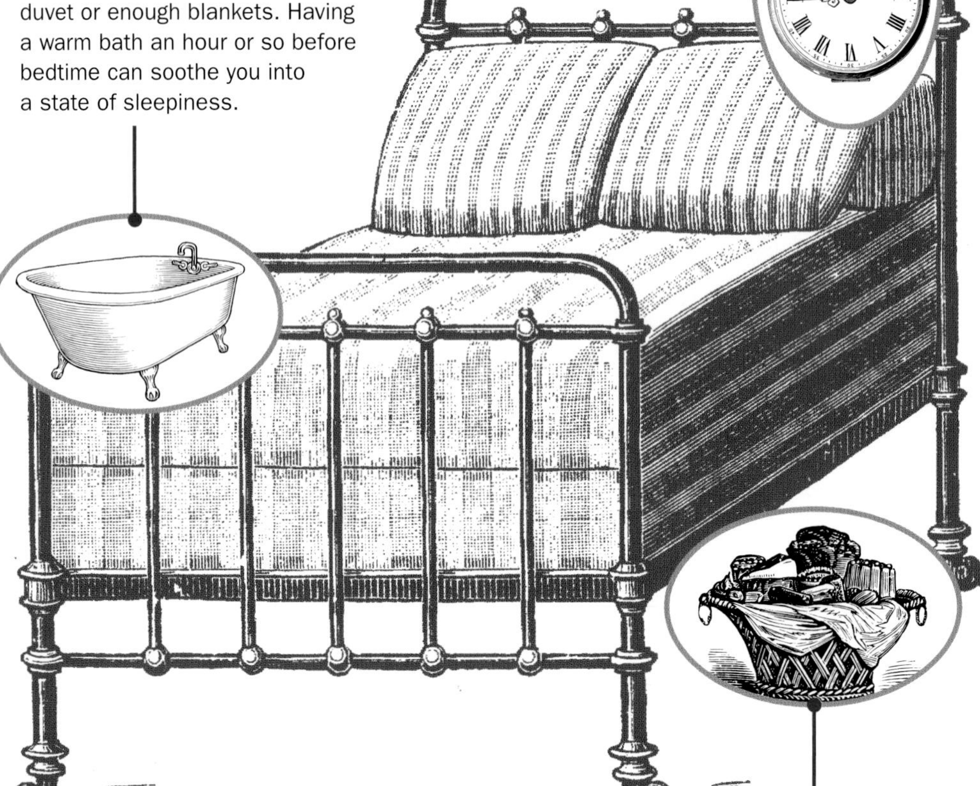

INDISPENSABLE WARNING

Seek medical advice if you constantly feel tired, or if you have trouble falling asleep on a regular basis.

EAT WELL, BUT NOT TOO WELL

Avoid a heavy meal before bedtime. Coffee late at night is another no-no, as are black tea, chocolate and cola. Try an old-fashioned mug of hot milk with some toast – carbs help trigger the release of serotonin, which makes you drowsy.

LOOKING AFTER A BABY

Most of the complicated items that you have in your home come with an instruction booklet. Not babies: the only way to learn how to manage one is to manage one. This chapter points you in the right direction with insider secrets, and with handy tips to help you avoid the rookie errors.

HOW TO HOLD A BABY

All new parents worry that they are going to drop their little darling – but they almost never do. The key things are to support the baby's head, since the neck muscles are too floppy to do the job themselves, and to keep the baby close to you so that he or she feels secure. Ignore grannies who warn you not to 'spoil' your baby by cuddling. Scientists have confirmed what mothers instinctively know: babies need bodily contact to help them grow, sleep better and be happy. It even strengthens the immune system and helps with brain development. A cuddled baby is a cleverer, more contented baby.

INDISPENSABLE THINGS

- A baby

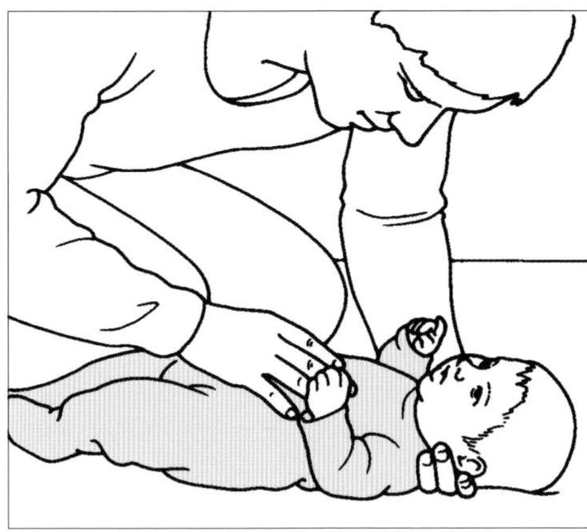

1 Make your baby aware of your presence by talking softly, and offering gentle touch before you pick him or her up. Lean towards the baby, and slide one hand under the neck and head.

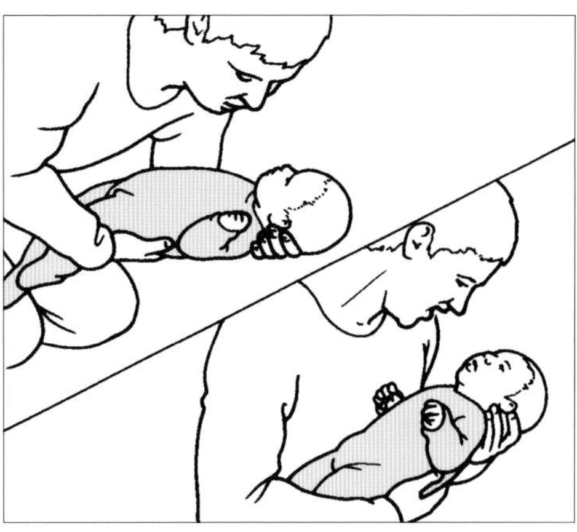

2 Now place your other hand under the lower back and buttocks. Slowly bring the baby towards your chest before you start to sit up (your baby feels more secure held against your body, so limit the amount of time he or she is suspended in mid-air).

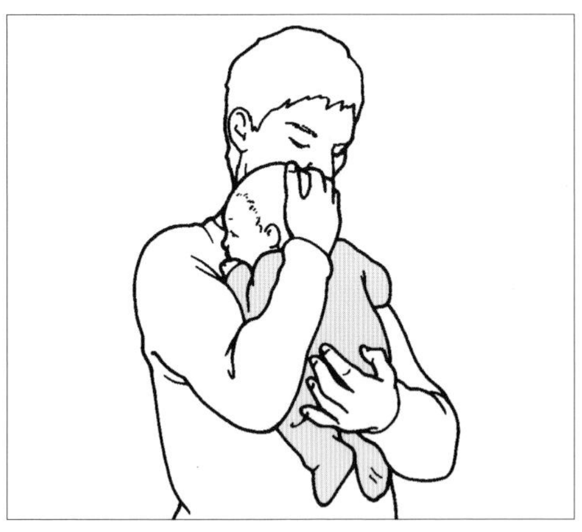

3 Keep your hands in position as you support your baby upright against your chest, with his or her head on your shoulder. Once you get the hang of carrying your baby, you'll be able to use your elbow to support the bottom, while the hand of the same arm keeps the head in position.

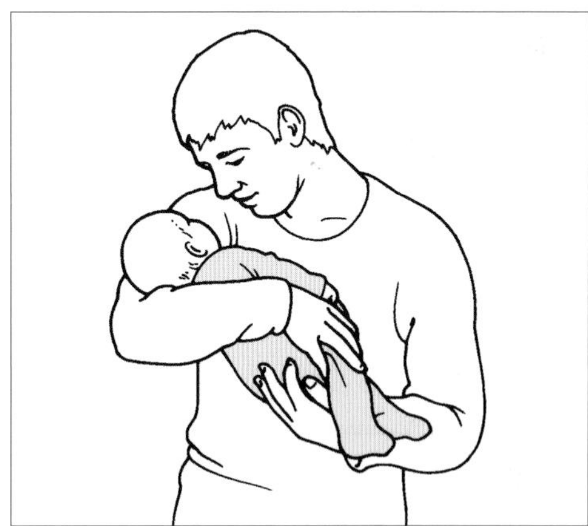

4 Another good position is the cradle hold. Keeping your hand under the baby's bottom and lower back, gently bring the head to rest on the upper part of your forearm. Keep the baby close to your body, and place your spare hand on the baby's hip and thigh.

A PRACTICAL HISTORY OF HOLDING

Many babies born in the first half of the 20th century were raised according to the childcare theories of Truby King. Babies were not comforted when they cried – this 'weakened the character' – and they were fed on a strict four-hourly regime. In the 1960s a more compassionate approach was advocated by Benjamin Spock, who urged parents to follow their instincts above all. 'You know more than you think you do' was his mantra. Jean Liedloff, writing in the 1970s, went further. Having observed the practices of Amazonian peoples, she proposed that mothers hold the baby continuously, day and night, for the first six months.

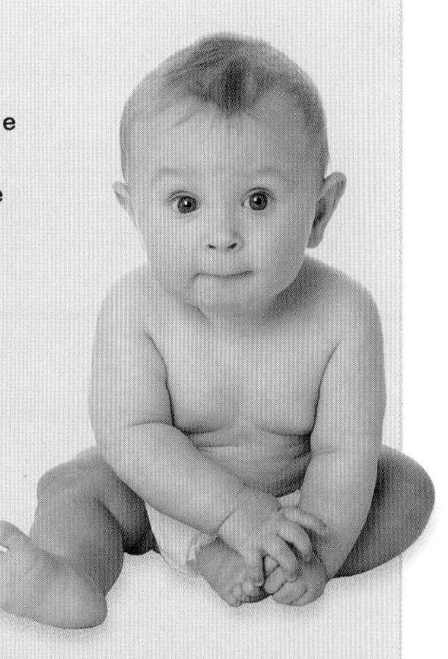

HOW TO CHANGE A NAPPY

A baby has its nappy changed some 4,000 times: every parent is an expert in the end. Babies don't enjoy having their clothes removed – it makes them feel unsafe – so work as swiftly as you can. Have everything to hand, but out of baby's reach. Nappy-changing can be fun, a time when you deepen your bond through singing or chatting, and through the sublime knowledge that you are meeting your child's needs. That's during the day; at night the last thing you want is playtime. Learn to nappy-change in dim light, avoid eye contact – and keep mum.

INDISPENSABLE THINGS

- Clean changing area
- Changing mat or towel
- Flannel or cotton wool
- Warm water
- Nappy rash cream (if needed)
- Clean nappy (plus liner if using a cloth nappy)
- Clean clothes if necessary
- Nappy bag (if using disposable nappies) or lidded nappy bucket (for cloth ones)

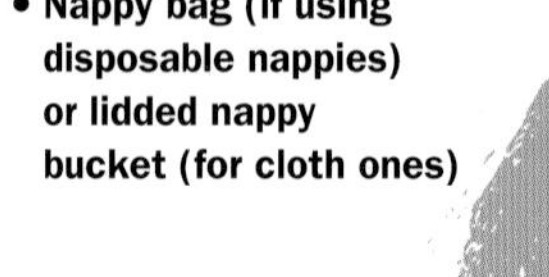

PRACTICAL TIP

It's better for a young baby's skin to clean up with water rather than wipes. If you prefer to use wipes, choose a brand that is free from alcohol or fragrance. Don't use talc since the baby may inhale the powder.

INDISPENSABLE WARNING

Never leave your baby on a raised nappy-changing surface unattended; keep one hand on the baby to prevent him or her from rolling off.

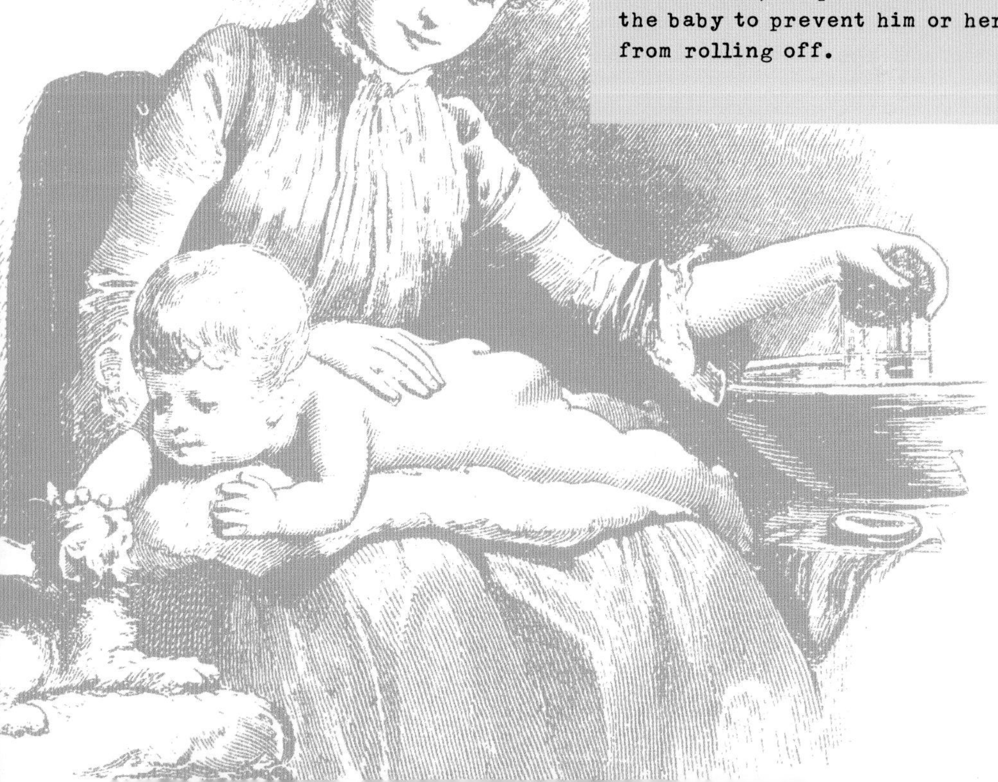

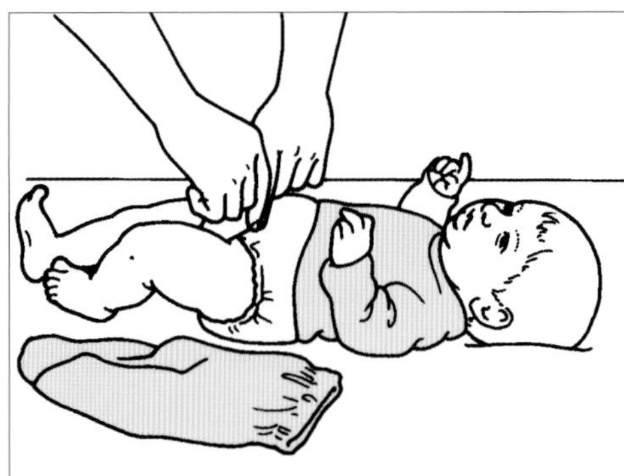

1 Wash your hands, then place your baby on a flat changing surface. Put a towel under the baby to keep him or her warm. Take off the baby's lower clothing, then unfasten the nappy.

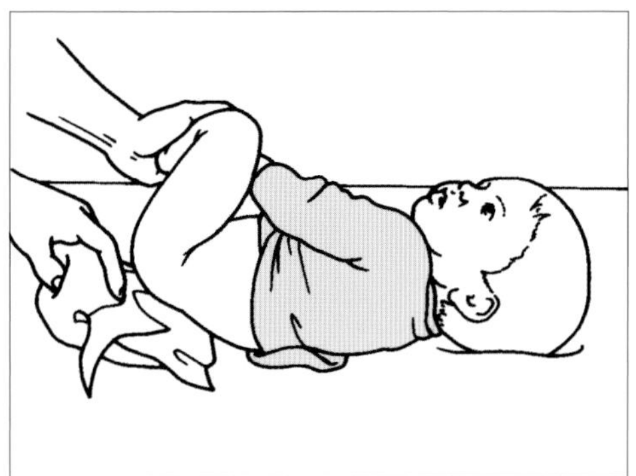

2 Lift up the baby's ankles with one hand. Wipe away as much as possible of any liquid stools, using the front of the nappy. Remove the nappy, folding it in half and place out of reach. If changing a boy, place a dry flannel over his penis: baby wee can travel far.

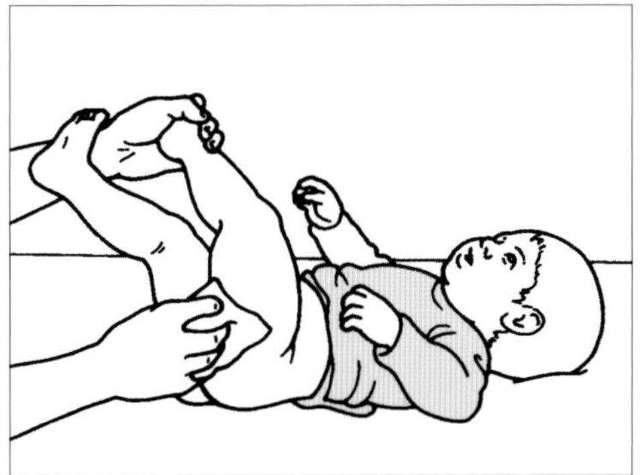

3 Using a flannel or cotton wool dipped in lukewarm water, clean the area thoroughly, including the leg creases. Always wipe a girl from front to back.

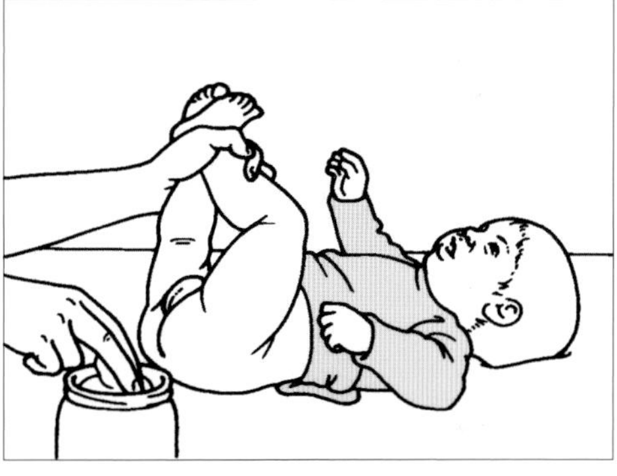

4 Pat the nappy area dry with a clean towel or flannel; this will help to prevent nappy rash. If the skin is sore, apply a thin layer of barrier cream.

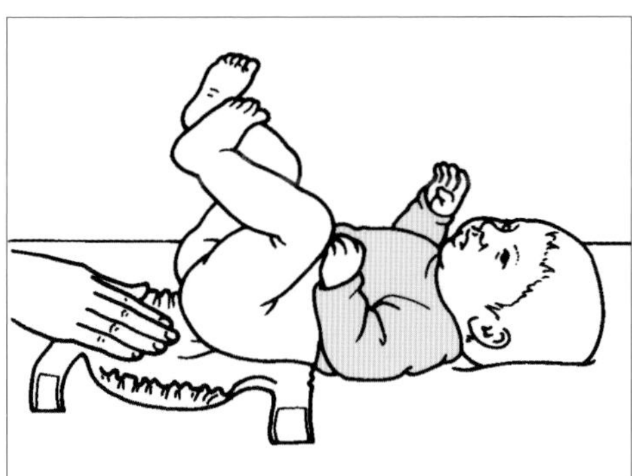

5 Open out a clean nappy, and lay it under your baby's bottom, level with the waist. Fasten (make sure a boy's penis is tucked down first). Fold the front of the nappy clear of the cord, if your baby is newborn.

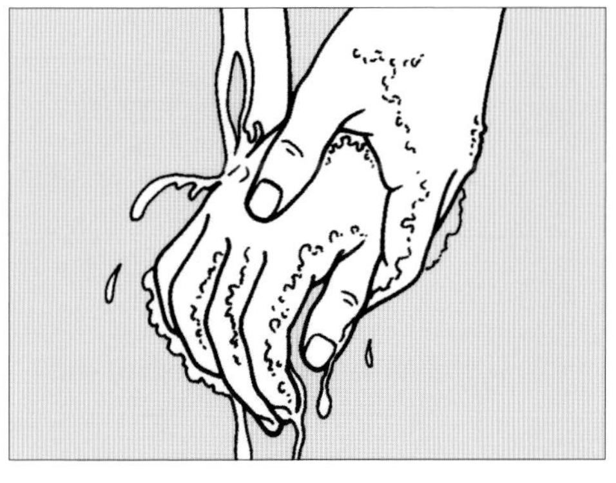

6 Wash your hands, and dress your baby. Clean the area and dispose of the nappy and flannel/cotton wool. Wash your hands one last time.

HOW TO STOP A BABY CRYING

Babies cry – it's what they do. Until they acquire the power of speech, yelling their heads off is their only way of communicating. So the key to stopping a baby crying is to figure out what is bugging the little mite and deliver it as quickly as possible. And don't worry if your baby's crying stresses you out: you are biologically programmed to feel unhappy if your special boy or girl is unhappy. The good news is that most crying has a limited number of causes. If you know what they are, then you are already halfway to having a contented baby.

INDISPENSABLE THINGS

- Love

INDISPENSABLE WARNING

Always seek medical advice if your baby's cry is unusual or persistent, with no clear cause.

CHECKLIST

Babies generally cry for a reason, and it is likely to be one of these: hunger, wind, discomfort (from a wet nappy, feeling too cold or too warm, or from clothing that is too tight), overstimulation or loneliness. Get in the habit of running through a mental list of possible causes. It is amazingly easy to forget the nappy, which is the most obvious cause of all.

BABY-WEARING

Hold your baby as much as possible. Studies have found that babies who are carried often tend to cry less. Limit the time your baby spends in the pram, bouncy chair or car seat, so that he or she gets plenty of human contact.

CHANGING PLACES

Babies often cry when they are in a place that is too busy – such as a shopping centre or a family party. Going somewhere quiet, and holding your baby close (skin to skin if possible) may help him or her calm down. Fresh air sometimes has a soothing effect.

COMFORT

The idea that you spoil a baby by responding to his or her cries is a myth that refuses to die. You are likely to soothe a baby much more quickly if you respond straight away to any sign of distress – and he or she is more likely to grow into a happy, secure child.

STOPPING THE CRYING

To soothe a baby, hold him or her securely. Gently rock or sway your baby, while shushing calmly in the ear (this replicates the motion and sound of being in the womb). If your baby is still distressed, try putting him to the breast for a short comfort feed to settle him, (or offer the crook of your clean little finger if you are not breastfeeding).

HOW TO GET A BABY TO SLEEP THROUGH THE NIGHT

There is no easy way to make a baby sleep through the night, no matter what your granny says. What is more, every baby is different. Some little angels naturally go eight hours from quite a young age, but many others don't: one survey found that less than a quarter of English babes were sleeping through the night at the age of ten months. So, to some extent, your child's sleeping habits are out of your hands (which, when you think about it, is a kind of comfort for stressed-out new parents). Nevertheless, there are ways of promoting good bedtime routines and 'sleep hygiene'.

INDISPENSABLE THINGS

- Patience
- Calm
- Love

INDISPENSABLE WARNING

Always put your baby to sleep on his or her back, with the feet at the foot of the cot; this is known to reduce the risk of Sudden Infant Death Syndrome (SIDS). Make sure that the baby doesn't get too hot, use lightweight covers (not duvets) and keep extraneous objects out of the cot (cot bumpers, toys, pillows, etc.).

SLEEP ENVIRONMENT

Make sure the bedroom is conducive to sleep: dark, quiet and reasonably warm (16–18°C/60–65°F). Blackout blinds can be very useful. It's best if your baby shares your room until the age of six months.

FILL THE TUMMY

A baby sleeps better after a good feed. If giving a bottle, wake your baby to feed at your bedtime. If breastfeeding, 'cluster-feed' in the evening. Many nursing mothers find that the baby feeds almost constantly from late afternoon to bedtime.

LEARNING TO SLEEP

Teaching your baby to drop off alone can take time. Ideally, put him or her in the cot while awake, but sleepy. It can help to provide gentle sound such as a musical mobile, ticking clock or a recording of white noise (vacuum cleaner, washing machine, etc.). Stay close by, and pick your baby up if he or she becomes distressed. Never leave a young baby (under six months) to cry.

SWADDLING

Many babies like the security of swaddling. Use a lightweight sheet or swaddling cloth. Swaddling may not be suitable in hot weather; ask your health visitor for advice.

BEDTIME

When you feel it is time to establish a bedtime, follow a fixed routine each evening. Keep the hour before bedtime calm. Do one or more of the following: warm bath, massage, pyjamas, story, song, rocking or cuddling, feed, cleaning teeth, stroking time in the cot. Stick to the same order of events each night.

HOW TO BABYPROOF A HOME

Babies and toddlers possess irrepressible curiosity. For some reason, they seem instinctively drawn to everyday objects that — in their little hands — are suddenly perilous: the hot cup of tea on the kitchen table, the electric socket with its three fascinating holes, the scissors in the sewing basket... As a parent, you must get in the habit of scanning every room you enter for danger. And don't think babyproofing once is enough. Every day, and every stage of development, gives your baby new opportunities to seek out danger and so scare the daylights out of you.

INDISPENSABLE THINGS

- **Common sense**
- **A small measure of paranoia**

TOYS

Respect age ranges on toys – they are there for safety reasons. In particular, avoid giving under-threes anything with long strings or small parts. Check secondhand toys very carefully; they may not conform to today's stringent safety standards.

GARDENS

Garden ponds are pretty, but highly dangerous. The only really safe option is to fill it in. At the very least, place a secure fence around it, and cover it with mesh. Drain paddling pools and turn them upside down after use. Lock away garden chemicals and tools.

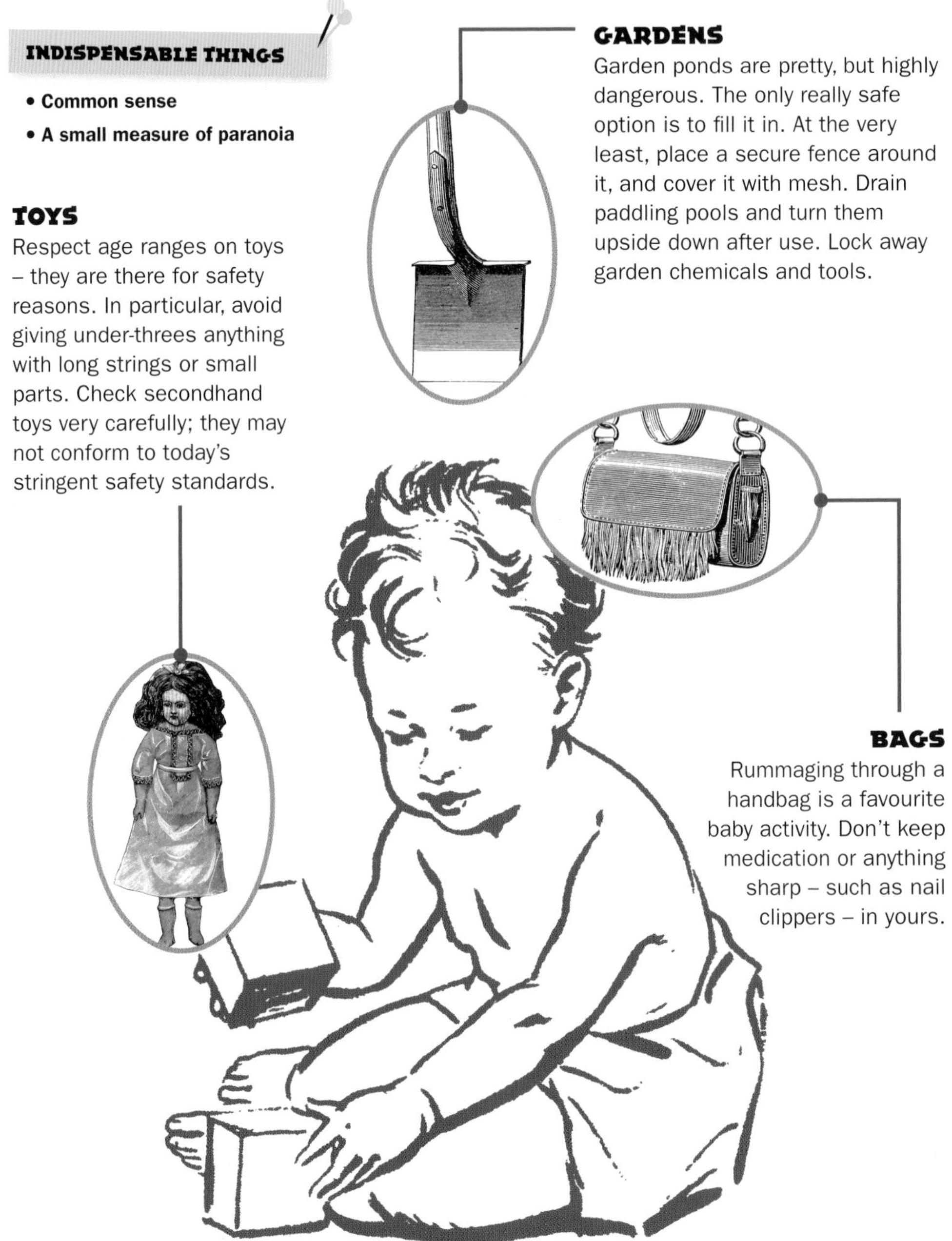

BAGS

Rummaging through a handbag is a favourite baby activity. Don't keep medication or anything sharp – such as nail clippers – in yours.

STAIRS

Fit stairgates as soon as your baby is getting ready to crawl. Don't wait until he or she is up and running. Check the banisters in your home: they should be vertical and spaced no more than 10cm (4in) apart.

FURNITURE

Put away light pieces of furniture that an experimental and adventurous baby could pull over. Fit corner covers on the sharp edges of coffee tables and similar pieces. Secure freestanding bookshelves to the wall.

FIRE

Fit smoke alarms on every floor, and a carbon-monoxide alarm near the boiler. Switch off appliances at the wall when not in use, and use socket guards. If you have an open fire, be sure to use a fixed fireguard when it is in use (and while the ashes are still warm).

GENERAL SAFETY

Fit childproof locks to kitchen drawers and cupboards, and store cleaning products, medication and other dangerous items out of reach. Always cook with the pan handles turned inwards.

WINDOWS

Make sure all windows are locked. Never leave an upstairs window open if your child can reach it, and do not place low items of furniture nearby.

FLEXES

Watch out for trailing flexes of, say, lamps – keep them tucked away. Always keep your iron and the flex well out of reach (it's best to iron when your children are safely tucked up in bed).

HOW TO CLEAN A BABY

Little babies can be as slippery as an oiled fish. Getting one in and out of the bath can be tricky. Fortunately, you don't have to do it every day. The latest thinking holds that it is better for a baby's skin if you wait a few weeks before giving the first bath. Thereafter a couple of baths a week is sufficient. Daily 'topping and tailing' – cleaning the messy ends with cotton wool – is a perfectly adequate way to keep your baby clean between baths.

INDISPENSABLE THINGS

- 2 towels
- Cotton wool
- Bowl of cooled boiled water
- Clean nappy

PRACTICAL TIP

Keep the room warm and your baby covered. If your baby is less than 10 days old, you'll need to wipe around the base of the umbilical cord – check with your midwife how to do this.

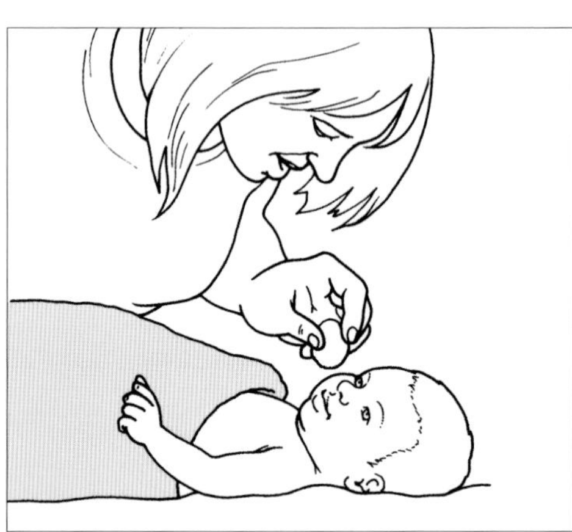

1 Undress your baby to nappy and vest, and cover with a towel. Dampen a piece of cotton wool and wipe one eye from the bridge of the nose outwards. Clean the other eye in the same way, using a fresh piece of cotton wool.

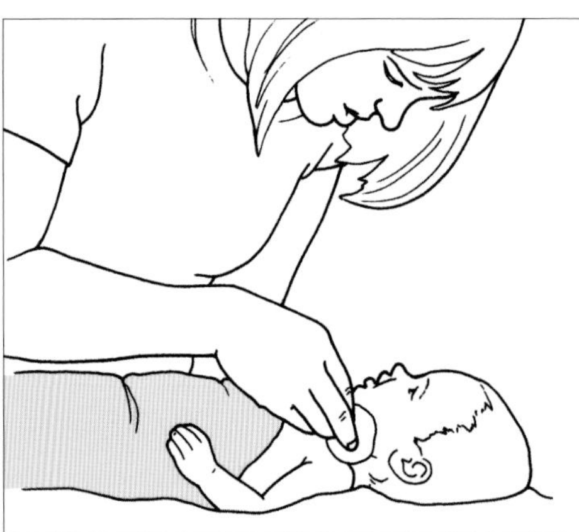

2 Wipe the baby's face using more damp cotton wool. Clean round the ears (but not inside them), and wipe the folds of the neck. Pat dry. Then clean the hands and under the arms in the same way.

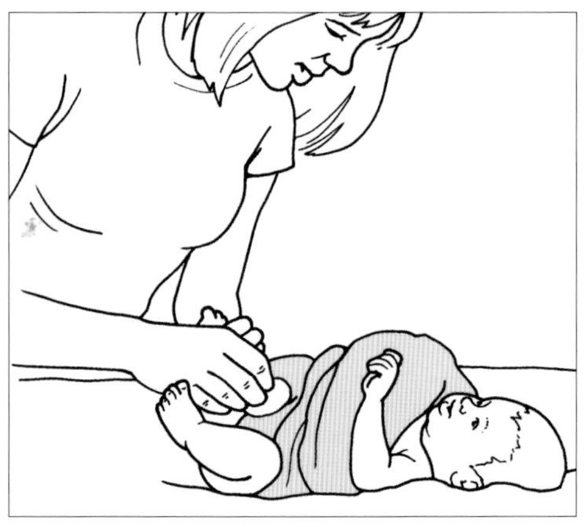

3 Now take off the nappy and wash the nappy area, making sure that you clean all the folds around the groin and legs. Wipe from front to back, and do not pull back the labia or foreskin. Pat dry, then put on a clean nappy and dress your child.

HOW TO BATH A BABY

Don't expect your baby to enjoy a long soak. Young babies are often freaked out by being stripped and placed in water. The key is to hold them securely, talk in a reassuring way, and above all keep bathtime brief. Babies are incapable of regulating their own body temperature, so it's vital that both the room and the bathwater are comfortably warm.

INDISPENSABLE THINGS

- Towel (preferably hooded)
- Cotton wool
- Cooled boiled water (for eyes)
- Baby bath or washing-up bowl
- Warm water
- Clean nappy
- Clean clothes

INDISPENSABLE WARNING

Never leave a baby alone in the bath. Always test the water temperature with a bath thermometer, and with your elbow or wrist (both are more sensitive to heat): it should be comfortably warm, not hot.

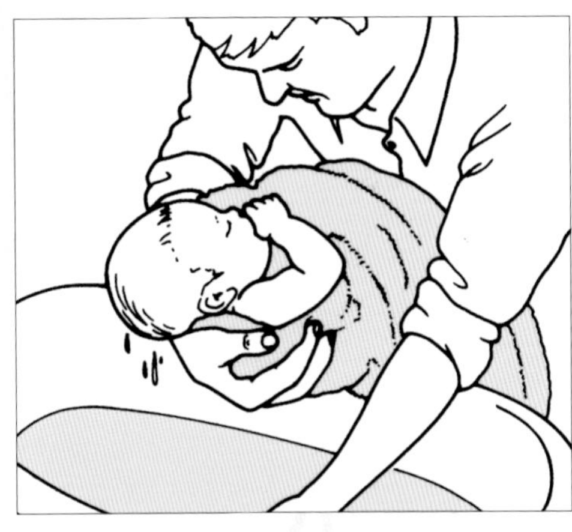

1 Undress your baby to the nappy, wrap in a towel and wash eyes and face as described opposite. Hold over the bath, supporting the back, neck and head with one arm and hand. Use the other to gently rinse the baby's hair with water. Pat it dry.

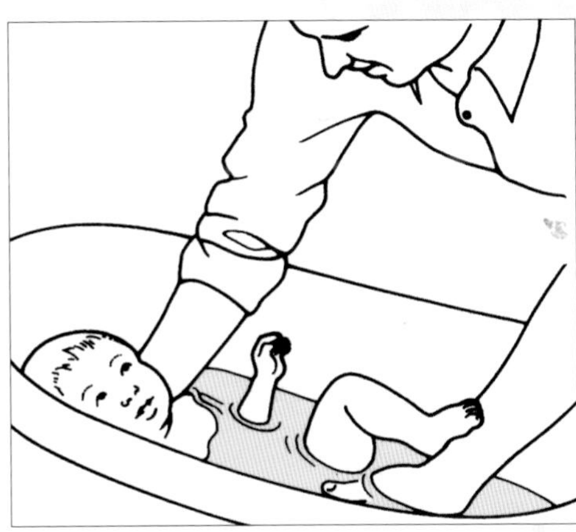

2 Remove the nappy, then place the baby in the bath (clean the nappy area first if soiled). Hold the baby's upper arm with your hand, using your wrist to support the head and neck; use your other hand to support the bottom. Use this hand to splash the baby's body once he or she is safely in the bath (repeating this keeps your baby warm).

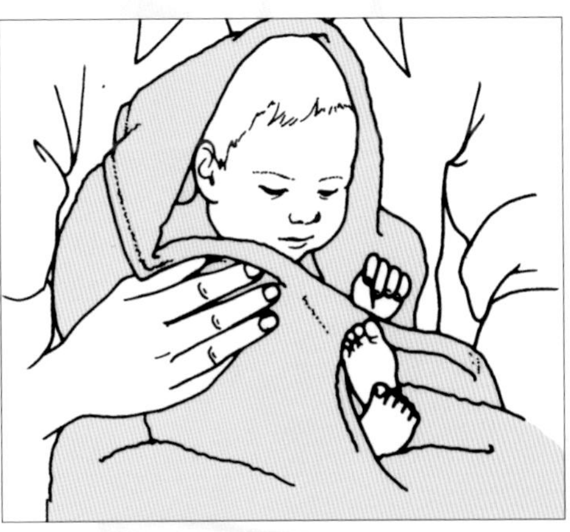

3 Lift the baby out in the same way and wrap in a towel, making sure you cover the head as well as the body. Cuddle, then pat dry, making sure all the creases are dry. Put on a clean nappy and clothing.

HOW TO TAKE A TODDLER ON A PLANE

For an adult, international air travel is a joy and a thrill; for an adult with small children, international air travel is a pain and a nightmare. There is no way in the world to make an aeroplane journey with toddlers or babies a restful, happy experience. The most you can hope for is to get to your destination with your sanity intact. The key to this is to carry with you an armoury of items designed to distract, pacify and otherwise relax your little travelling companions.

INDISPENSABLE THINGS

- Toys, books and DVDs
- More toys
- Edible treats
- Infinite patience
- Spare clothing (you and child)
- Nappies and changing paraphernalia

RESIGN YOURSELF

You are not going to get to read that novel, or watch the film. For you, the entire journey is a cramped and rather long-winded nursery session. You might as well come to terms with that fact while you are still on the tarmac.

BE PREPARED

A selection of toys to keep your child amused is essential hand luggage: crayons, colouring sheets (printed from the internet), sticker books and finger puppets are excellent light options. It's a good idea to wrap toys up and produce them at intervals (say, one an hour). Do pack a special soft toy or comfort object in case your child wants to sleep.

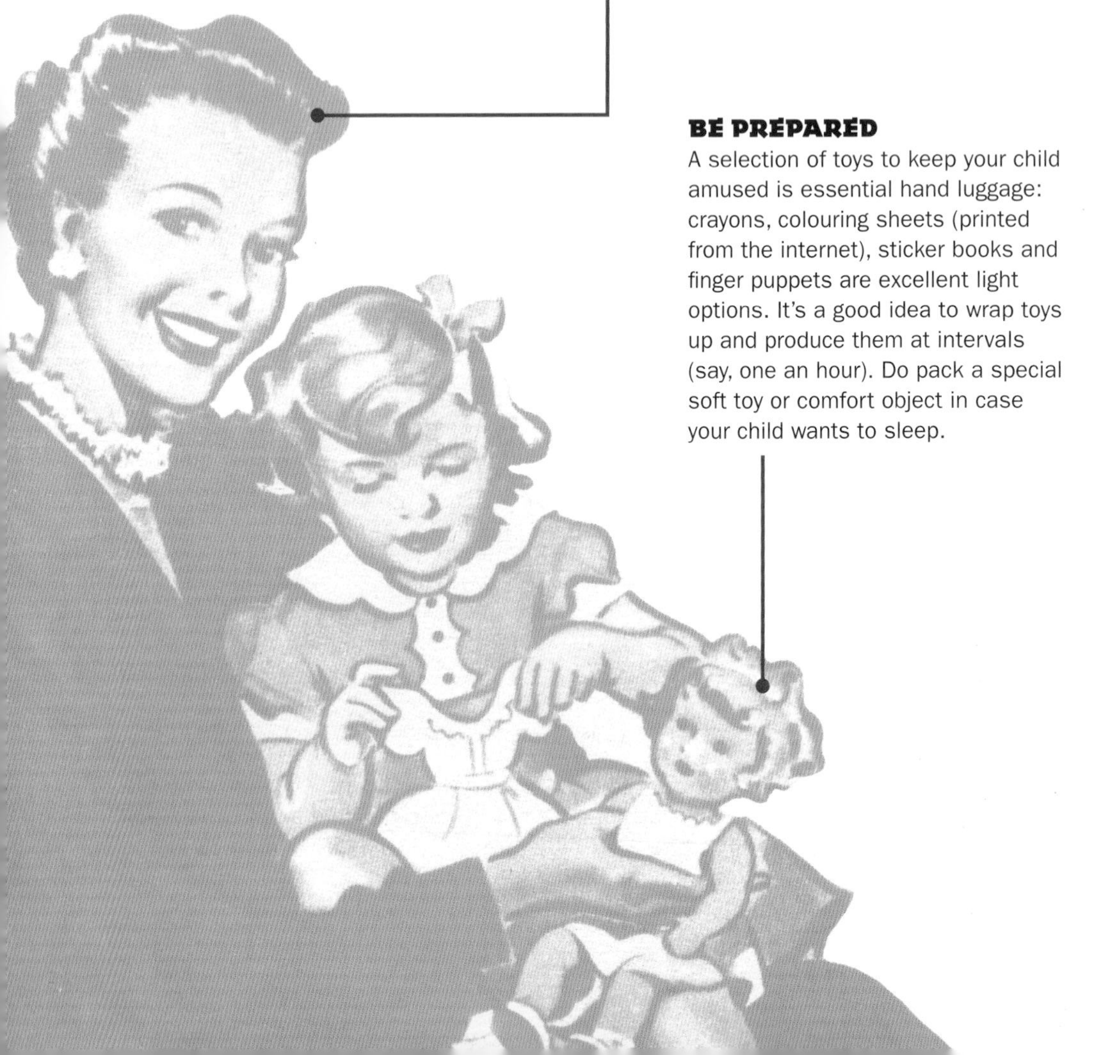

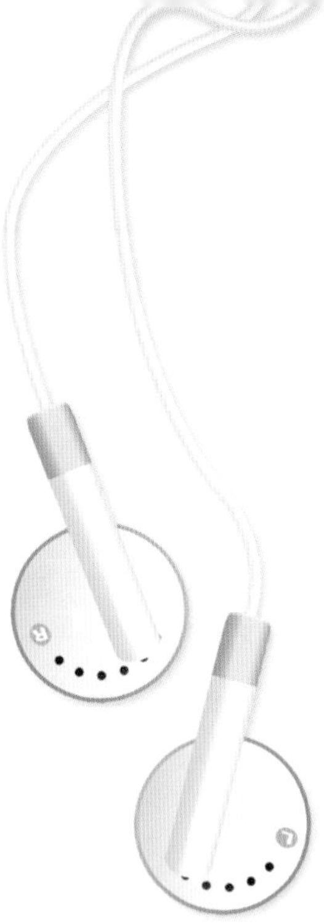

BEFORE THE FLIGHT

Talk to your child about what to expect in the days before the journey. An 'At the airport' book will be invaluable – most children will enjoy the anticipation beforehand and then spotting things featured in the book once they get to the airport. Take the pre-boarding option if you can, so that you can get settled more easily.

SEATING PLAN

Book a window seat; ideally book a seat for your toddler and take along an airline-approved car seat to strap him or her into.

STORY TIME

Take a judicial mix of long-term favourites and exciting new books to read to your children. A good book is worth its weight in gold, because it can buy you half an hour's peace and quiet. Storybooks loaded onto an MP3 player will prove a welcome diversion, while a portable DVD player and selection of DVDs is a godsend for long flights.

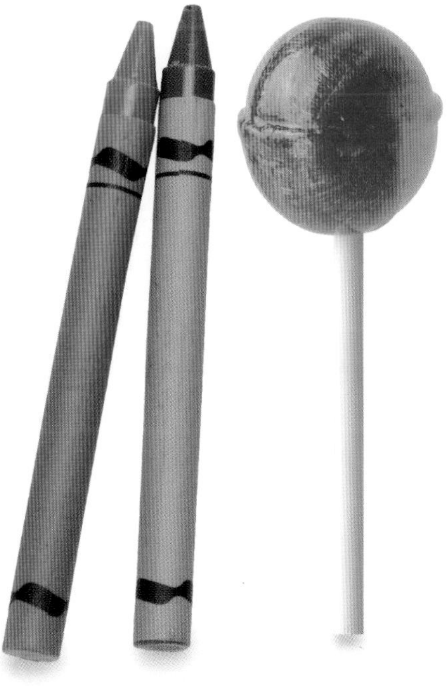

THINK SNACKS

Pack your own food for the children rather than rely on the inflight meal. Give them familiar picnic food, but be prepared to suspend all normal nutritional rules for the duration of the journey. A lolly to suck on is great for take-off and landing.

HOW TO BREASTFEED

Breastfeeding is the best and most natural way to feed your baby, but from a mother's perspective, breastfeeding is also a skill that takes time to get right. Fortunately, you won't want for practice. Tiny babies feed an awful lot (ignore anyone who says, 'Surely he can't be hungry again already?'). The most important thing is to let the baby feed whenever and for as long as he or she wants; some kind of routine will gradually develop after the first six weeks. And remember to drink plenty of water and to eat lots. You need 500 extra calories a day when you are breastfeeding – all nursing mothers should eat cake.

INDISPENSABLE THINGS

- Time
- Patience
- Cushions, pillows or breastfeeding cushion

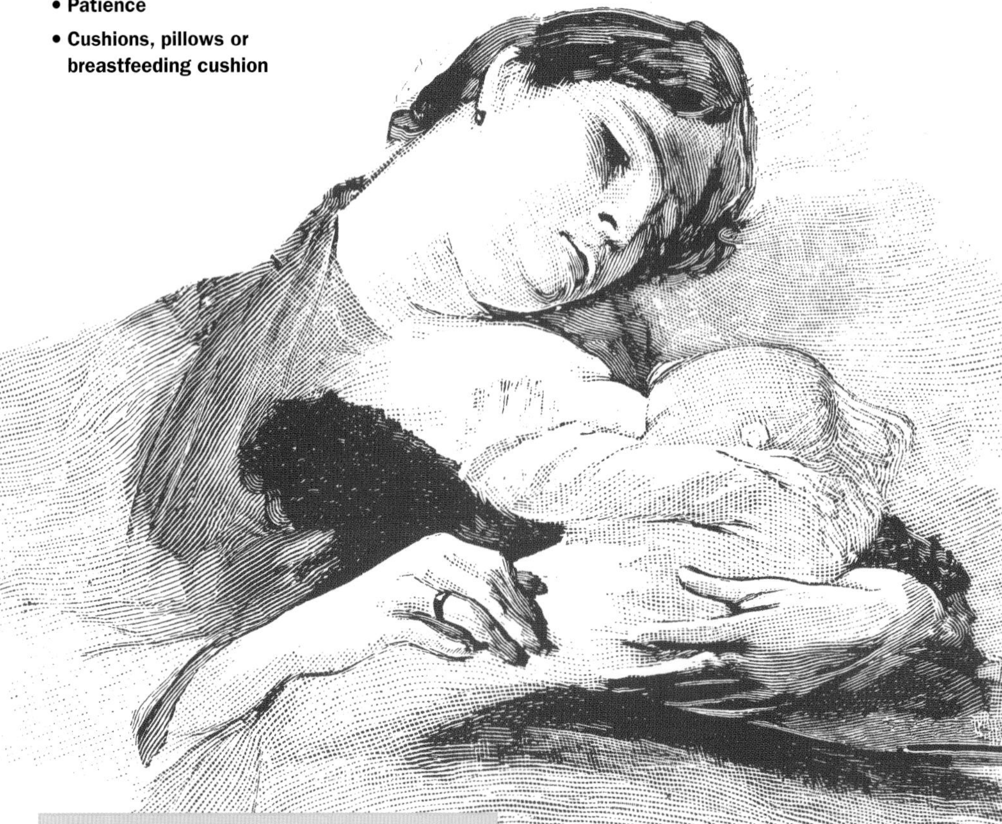

PRACTICAL TIP

Seek help from a breastfeeding counsellor if you feel you are struggling with breastfeeding, or contact a breastfeeding support organization such as La Leche League.

1 First, find a comfortable position to feed your baby; keep your back straight and use cushions to support your back and arm. This is the traditional cradle position, in which the baby lies along your arm, head just below the crook, bottom in your hand.

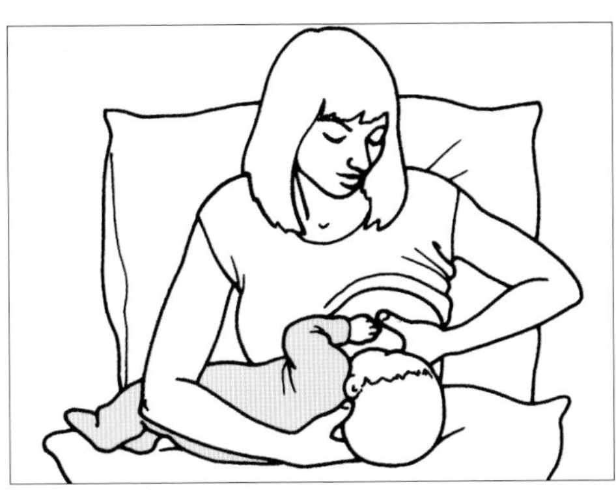

THE CROSS-CRADLE is brilliant for new mothers, since it is easier to manoeuvre the baby into the right position. The baby's head is in your hand, bottom in the crook of your arm; you feed from the opposite side as you hold the baby. Use your spare hand to support the breast.

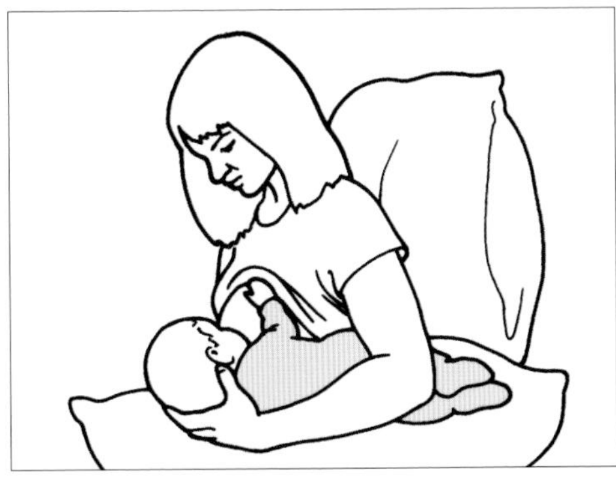

THE RUGBY HOLD is good for newborns, twins, as well as women who have had a C-section. You feed from the same side as you hold the baby (keeping him or her away from any scar). The baby's head is in your hand, back along your arm, legs resting on a pillow.

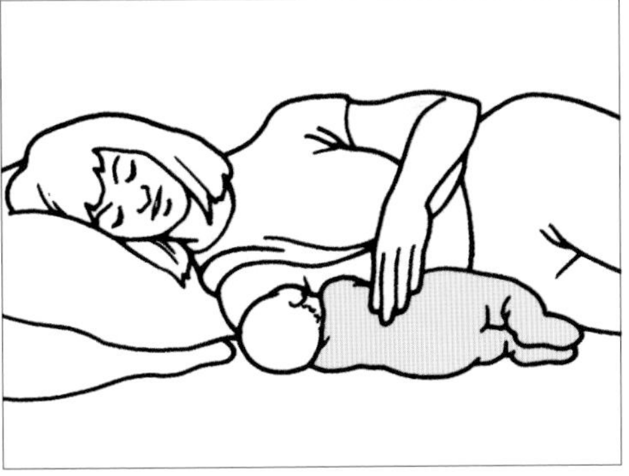

THE LYING-DOWN POSITION is great for night-time feeds. Face the baby and cradle with your lower arm. You'll need pillows to get comfortable: put them behind your back and between your knees, as well as one behind the baby to keep him or her close.

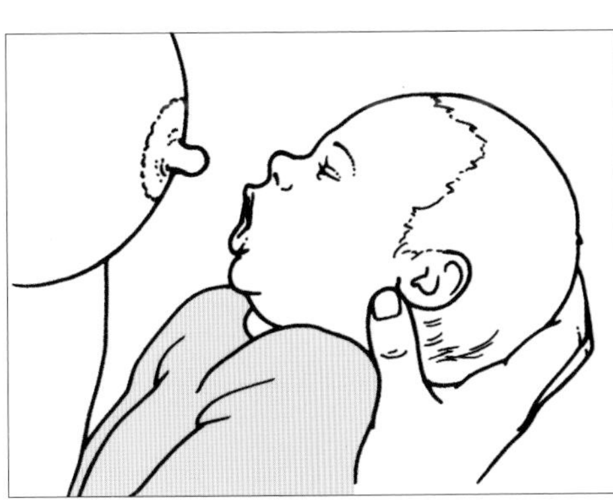

2 Hold the baby on his or her side, so that the head and back form a straight line, the tummy towards you, and the nose opposite your nipple. Brush the baby's top lip with your nipple if he or she doesn't open the mouth. Wait until the mouth opens really wide.

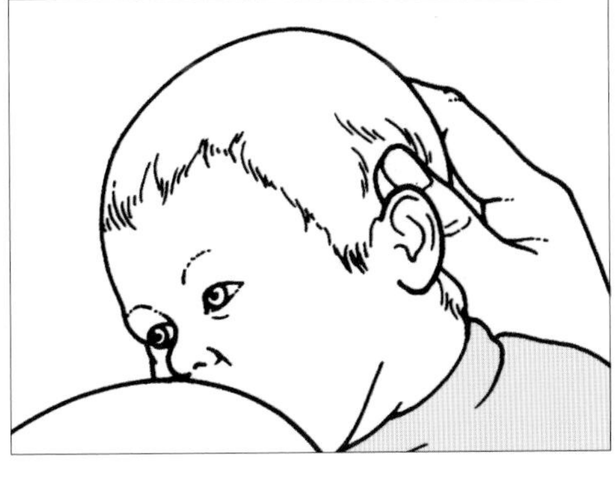

3 Draw the baby's shoulders towards you so that the chin approaches the breast first. Once latched on, the mouth should be wide, nose almost touching your breast. If it hurts for more than a few seconds, slip your little finger into the baby's mouth to release the hold and try again.

HOW TO GIVE A BABY A BOTTLE

The bottle-feeding family has to be super-organized — nobody wants to be holding a screaming baby at 3 a.m. while waiting for the sterilizer to ping. Plan ahead, and you will save yourself a lot of grief. The great convenience of bottles is of course that both parents can share the feeding. A young baby will develop a secure attachment with whoever is meeting his or her needs, so even if Mum is the main provider, Dad can put in occasional guest appearances. Drinking milk and cuddling are a baby's greatest pleasures, so giving the feeds is the best way for you to bond.

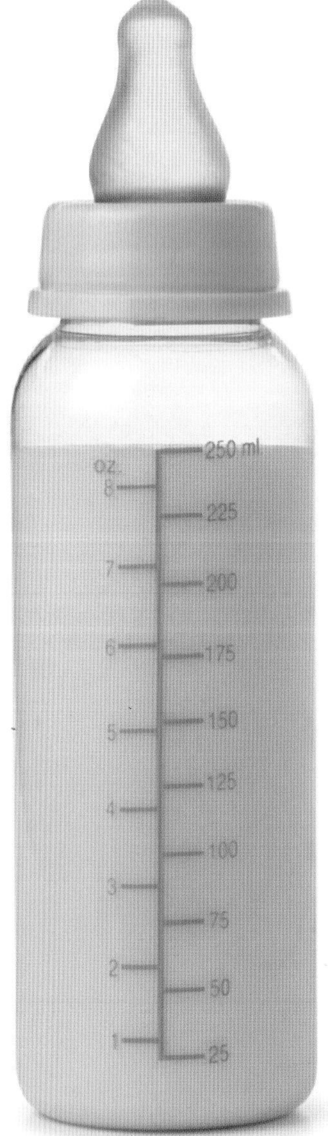

INDISPENSABLE THINGS

- **6 wide-necked bottles**
- **6 teats**
- **Bottle brush**
- **Sterilizing equipment**
- **Infant formula milk**
- **Cooled, freshly boiled water**
- **Bowl of hot water**

GIVING A FEED

Hold your baby so that the upper body and head are upright (a 45-degree angle is comfortable). Sit quietly and make lots of eye contact. If you can, loosen your own clothing and place the baby against your chest for some skin-to-skin contact. Do not prop a bottle up so that your baby can feed himself or herself – there is a risk of choking.

STERILIZING

Your baby's bottles and teats need to be well washed and sterilized before use. Use a bottle brush to clean thoroughly, turn the teat inside-out, then sterilize in a steam unit or by boiling in a large lidded pan for 10 minutes (leave the lid on until you are ready to make up the bottles; they won't stay sterile once you remove it).

HOW MUCH, HOW OFTEN?

Be guided by your baby's appetite rather than a rigid schedule. Feed your baby when he or she seems hungry, and let the baby decide how much milk to take. A feeding pattern will naturally emerge over the weeks – and your baby won't be miserable in the meantime.

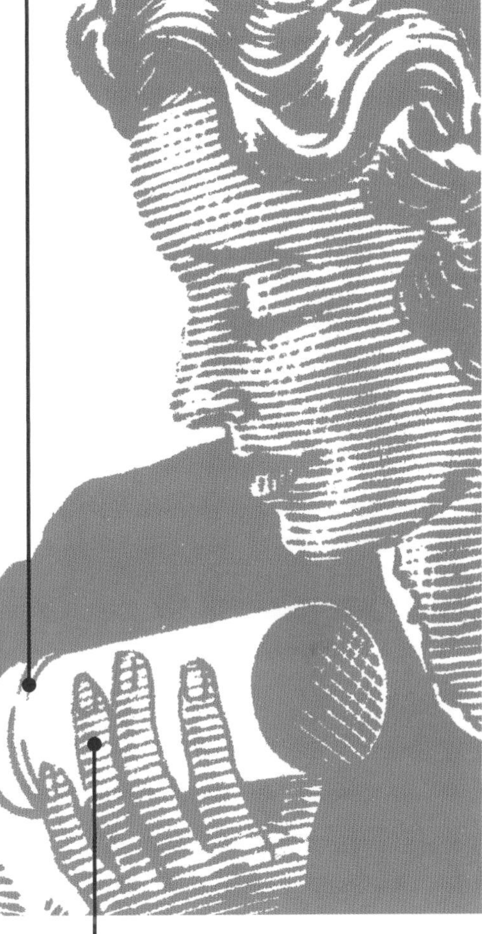

WHICH TEAT?

Choose a teat with an orthodontic shape, to help protect your baby's teeth. Make sure that you get the right flow rate for your baby (newborn, slow, medium or fast). Too fast a flow, for example, will rush your baby. He or she is likely to take in more air, leading to painful wind. Check teats regularly, and discard them at the first sign of damage.

MAKING UP THE FEED

Always measure the water first, then add the powder according to the manufacturer's instructions. You'll need recently boiled water, cooled to room temperature. Mix in the bottle, shake to combine, then keep in the centre of the fridge until needed. Warm by standing the bottle in a bowl of hot water, and shake a few drops on your wrist to check the temperature. Do not heat in a microwave: this can cause 'hot spots' in the milk. Discard undrunk milk after 1 hour.

HOW TO INTRODUCE SOLID FOOD

Giving solids is fun, but many people start too early. The latest scientific thinking suggests that it is better for your baby if you wait until six months, when a baby's digestive system can handle mashed-up versions of many 'adult' foods (so no faffing about with purées). Also the 'tongue thrust reflex' – which makes babies poke food straight out of their mouths – will have disappeared. So waiting that bit extra makes weaning straightforward.

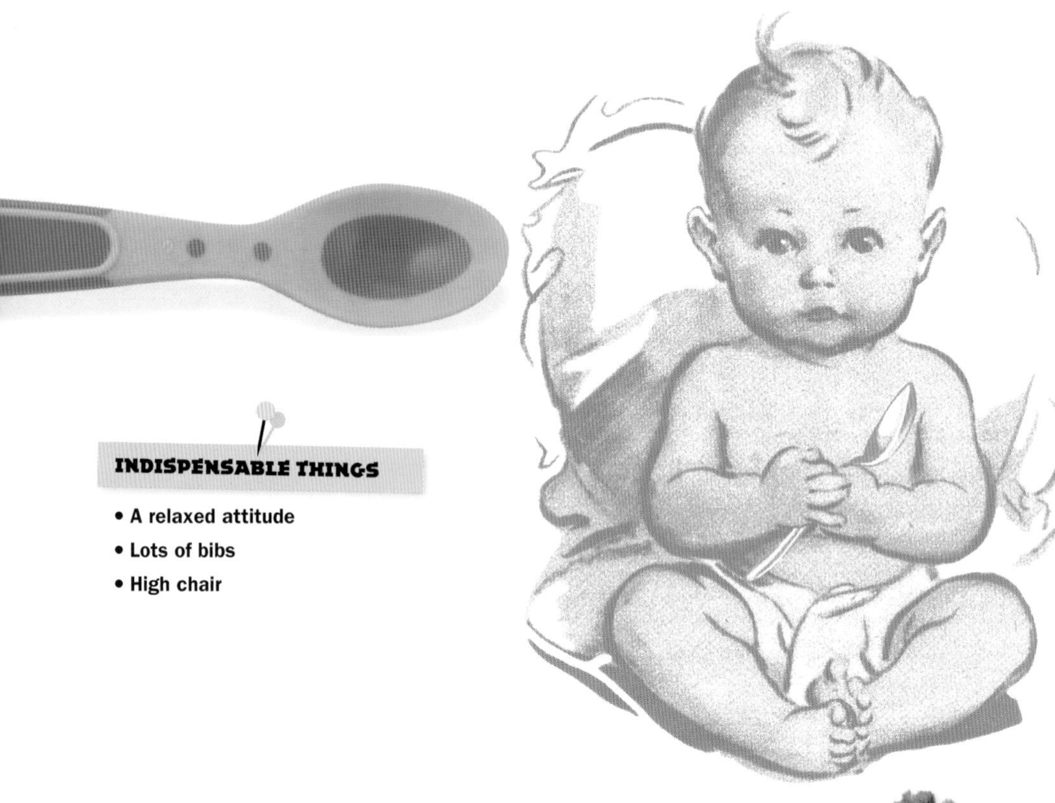

INDISPENSABLE THINGS

- A relaxed attitude
- Lots of bibs
- High chair

INDISPENSABLE WARNINGS

It's advisable to introduce common allergenic foods – eggs (well-cooked yolks only), dairy products, soya, cereals that contain gluten (wheat, rye, barley, oats), fish and so on – one at a time from the age of six months and to start with a small amount. If there is a family history of allergies or allergic conditions (hay fever, eczema, asthma), introduce solids very carefully and do not give your baby peanuts or sesame seeds for the first three years. Always read labels carefully to check for nut content. See your health visitor for individual advice. Do not give honey or shellfish to children under one year of age, or whole or chopped nuts to children under five.

HOW TO DO IT

Start by offering small amounts, and let your baby decide whether to take it. Gradually build up to several meals a day. Never force a baby to eat – he or she gets most of the nutrition necessary from formula or breastmilk.

DON'T RUSH IT

Generally a six-month-old will show great interest in food and may try to grab food out of your hand. But don't worry if your baby isn't interested yet; some babies do not start eating until later in the year.

WHAT TO GIVE

A six-month-old baby can eat most grown-up things – but should not be given very spicy, oily, salty or sweet foods. Start with low-allergen foods such as slivers of ripe pear or cooked carrot mash, and then progress to chicken, pulses, grains and other foods (appropriately prepared and cut). Give fresh homemade foods rather than jars.

FINGER FOODS

Good chewing foods include: cooked carrots cut into sticks; toast soldiers; banana cut into long fingers; cooked green beans; rice cakes; and slices of grilled polenta. Later on, try strips of chicken, sticks of cheese, cooked haricot beans, and so on. Stay close in case of choking.

DRINKS

Don't cut back on milk in order to get your baby to eat more food. Stick to sips of water with mealtimes if your baby seems thirsty, rather than giving diluted juice (which is bad for the emerging teeth).

STARTING EARLY

All the advice here is for healthy babies of six months. If you want to start your baby on solids earlier, talk to your health visitor. Many foods – including bread – should not be given because of the risk of allergies. No baby should be given solid food before the age of four months.

HOW TO READ A BEDTIME STORY

Babies can't read – but they love books and stories long before they can follow what is happening on the page. To a six-month-old, a tale told out loud is like a favourite piece of music, which is why they are happy to have the same story again and again. Daily story times will help your baby come to see books as an inexhaustible source of knowledge and pleasure. The habit of reading is one of the best gifts you can give your child.

INDISPENSABLE THINGS

- Time
- Fun books

HOW TO READ

Get comfortable together. Read slowly and expressively, using different voices for different characters. Point things out in the pictures. Be enthusiastic about the things that grab your child's attention. Give the child plenty of time to look at the images.

GIVE CHOICE

Let your child choose the bedtime story. Don't worry if he or she picks the same one day after day. It may be dull for you, but children enjoy repetition, and learn from it. He or she will eventually want to move on to something new.

BOOKS FOR TODDLERS

Young toddlers enjoy stories featuring familiar objects and activities. Older ones appreciate books about counting, colours and shapes as well as those with simple stories they can learn by heart.

BOOKS FOR BABIES

Small babies like brightly coloured picture books. The best are made from cloth or board, and can be safely chewed.

HOW TO MAKE PLAY DOUGH

All children are natural-born potters and sculptors. Little boys, for example, love fashioning little men out of play dough, smashing them flat with a tiny fist and then rolling out arms and legs and torsos all over again. There is no need to buy commercial modelling clay; making your own play dough is cheaper, and it is more fun for your child. The dough will keep for a month or so in a sealed plastic bag or container (store it in the fridge).

INDISPENSABLE THINGS

- Plain flour
- Cream of tartar
- Table salt
- Cooking oil
- Food colouring
- Saucepan
- Rubber gloves

BASIC RECIPES
Place 125g (4½oz) plain flour, 1 tablespoon cream of tartar and 60g (2¼oz) table salt in an old saucepan, then pour in 125ml (4fl oz) water and 2 teaspoons of oil. Stir over a low heat for a few minutes until the mixture forms a ball of dough that pulls away from the sides of the pan. Cool before using.

ADDING COLOUR
Divide the dough into several large balls. Put a few drops of different food colouring onto each batch – the more you put on, the brighter the hue – then work into the dough. Wear rubber gloves to prevent your hands from getting stained.

GOOD CLEAN FUN
Get your children to play on a wipe-clean mat. A blunt children's knife, biscuit cutters and a toy rolling pin are all good utensils.

INDISPENSABLE WARNING

Homemade play dough is high in salt, so don't let your child eat it. Keep it out of pets' reach.

TRAVEL & SPORTS

ON THE ROAD

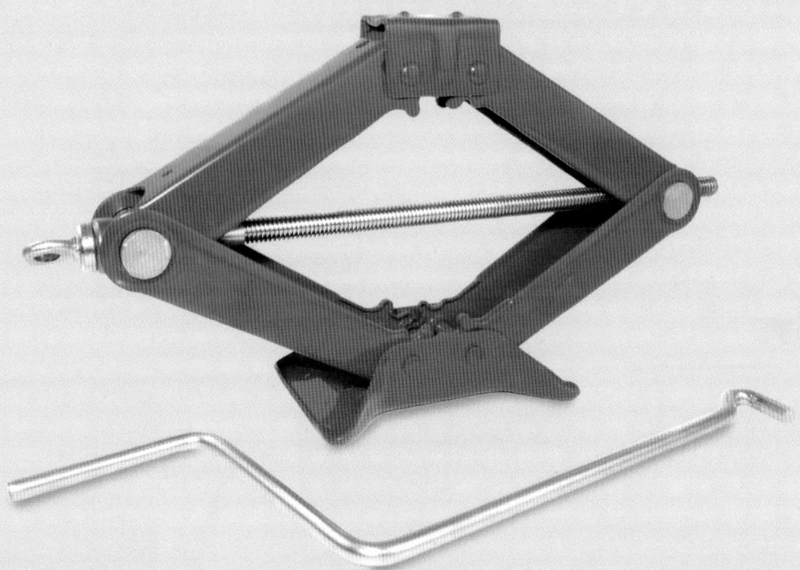

Driving a car is one of the great pleasures of our age — as is riding a bike. But it can also go horribly wrong if you're not well prepared. Here are some essential tips on how to keep your wheels turning smoothly.

HOW TO PARALLEL PARK

Are you one of those annoying people who whizzes up to a parking space and backs into it perfectly, in one neat, flowing move? Well, shoo then — you don't need to read this. Or are you one of those people who always goes into the space at the wrong angle and ends up either driving over innocent pedestrians or needing a gangplank to get from the car to the pavement? In that case, read on. Here are five simple steps to ease the pain.

INDISPENSABLE CHECKS

- Check for oncoming cars
- Check your rearview mirror
- Check for pedestrians

PRACTICAL TIP

Practise first somewhere there aren't any other cars, using bollards if you have them.

1 First thing is to find a suitable parking space. Ideally, it should be about 1.5m (5ft) longer than your car – and certainly no less that 60cm (2ft) longer. Signal and place your car level with the car parked in front of the empty spot and about 60cm (2ft) away from it. Keep your signal lights on.

2 Take your time. Check your mirrors. If there are other cars approaching, let them pass before you start your manoeuvre. When you are ready, put the engine into reverse and start backing into the space. Look over your shoulder and turn the wheel as far as it will go towards the kerb.

3 Straighten the wheel once the rear edge of the driver door is level with the bumper of the other car. You should be 45 degrees to the kerb and about 1m (3ft) away. Your driver door should be about 15cm (6in) from the car in front. If you're too close too soon, try again.

4 Back into the space until your front bumper is clear of the car in front's rear bumper. Then turn the wheel as far as possible away from the kerb and continue reversing until your car is in the space. Imagine the whole manoeuvre as an 'S' – and watch out for the car behind!

5 Straighten the wheel and move your car forward until you are centred in the space. Ideally, you should be 15–20cm (6–8in) away from the kerb. If you don't get it right first time, keep trying; after all, practice makes perfect.

HOW TO CHANGE GEAR

'Gears? What are they?' If you're used to driving an automatic car, that may well be your attitude. But not all cars are automatic and, particularly if you're driving in Europe, you may find yourself having to change gears in the old-fashioned way. The good news is that it's not as difficult as it sounds. In fact, you might find yourself enjoying the human/machine symbiosis so much you won't want to go back to your pig-headed automatic.

INDISPENSABLE CHECKS

- **Use a low gear around corners**
- **Never 'ride' the clutch**

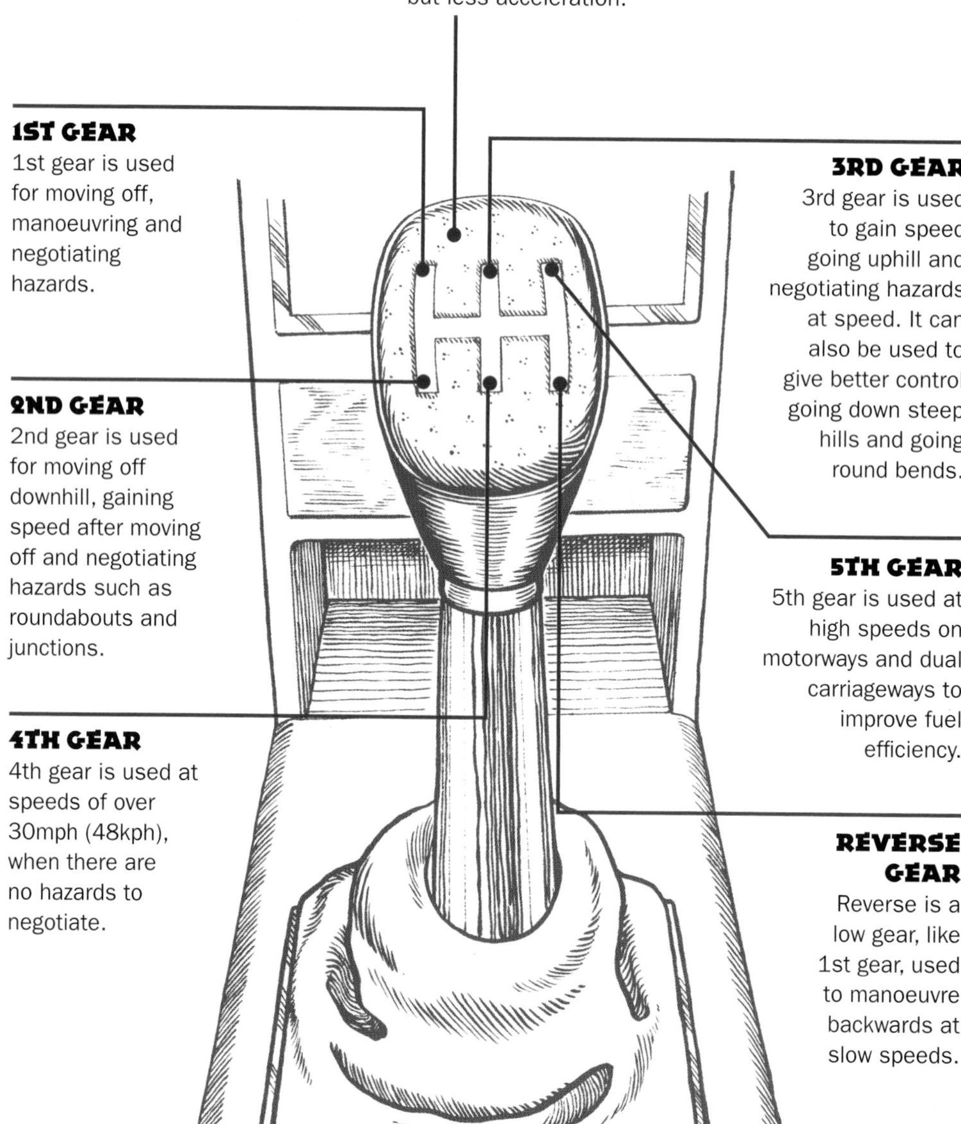

GEAR PATTERNS

It's important to memorize the gear pattern. Most cars have an H-shaped diagram on the gear-stick handle to show the position of the gears. The position of the reverse gear varies from car to car, and you will probably have to either push the gear lever down or lift it up in order to engage in reverse. This is to prevent you accidentally going into reverse while driving.

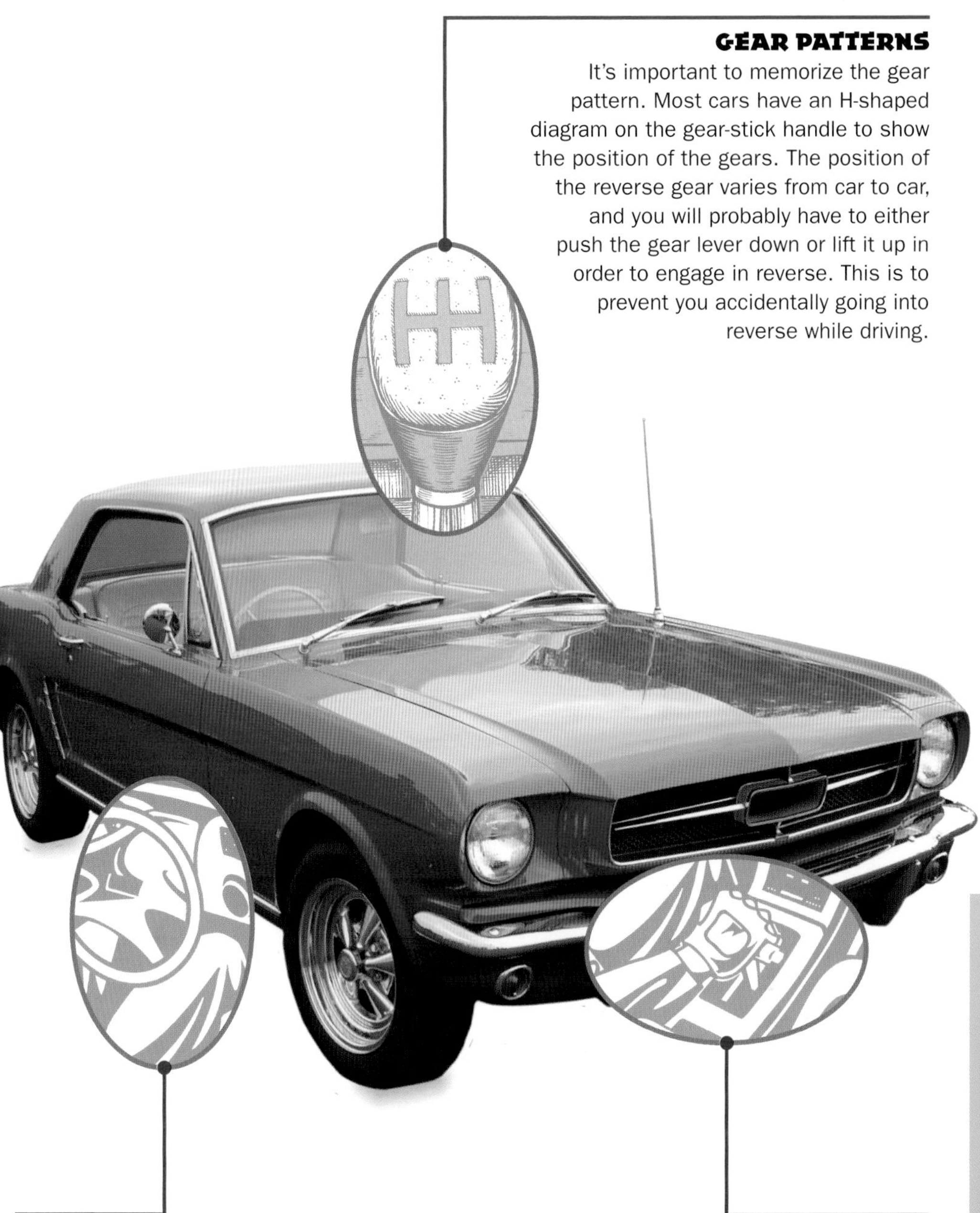

CLUTCH CONTROL

The tricky bit is using the clutch to transfer from one gear to another. Push the clutch pedal all the way down and select the gear you want (1st gear if starting on the level or uphill; 2nd gear if starting downhill). Put your foot on the accelerator and increase the pressure as you release the clutch. Imagine you are transferring the weight from one foot to the other. If you are starting from a standstill, you'll need to release the brake as the clutch engages. Listen to the engine: if it starts to falter, it needs more fuel, so press down on the accelerator (not too much!); if it starts to 'race', it's got too much fuel, so ease off the accelerator (that's better!). Once the gear is properly engaged, release the clutch completely and away you go. Practise in a safe place until you are familiar with the 'biting point' of the clutch – that is, the point at which the engine starts to engage.

WHILE YOU WAIT

Never 'ride' your clutch while stopped at traffic lights. It wastes fuel, pollutes the atmosphere and damages the clutch mechanism. Put the handbrake on and change into neutral.

HOW TO CHECK YOUR OIL & WATER

Just because you have your car serviced every few months doesn't mean you can ignore it the rest of the time. Basic maintenance, such as checking the oil and water levels, should be as routine as hoovering the carpet. Not only could it help you catch a problem before it becomes serious, but it will also familiarize you with the inner workings of your car. And that's a lot more empowering than ending up on the hard shoulder with a steaming engine, waiting for the recovery van to come.

INDISPENSABLE CHECKS

Monthly checks:

- Engine oil level
- Engine water/coolant level
- Transmission oil level (on automatic cars)
- Brake fluid level
- Power steering fluid level
- Tyre pressure and condition
- Windscreen wiper fluid level
- Windscreen wiper condition
- Lights

PRACTICAL TIP

Look closely at the oil on the dipstick. If it's jet black, it's time to change the oil; if it's brown/black, then it's OK. If it's streaked with white, like coffee, then you've got a problem. Take your car to a mechanic to be checked.

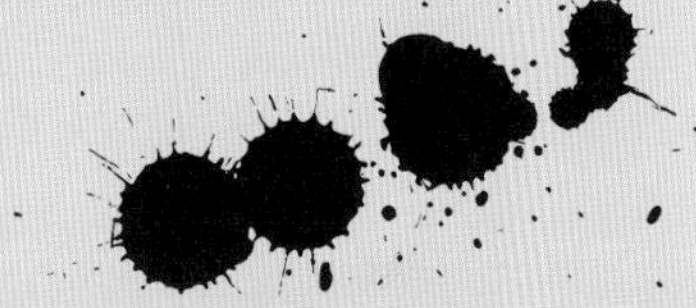

CHECKING THE OIL LEVEL

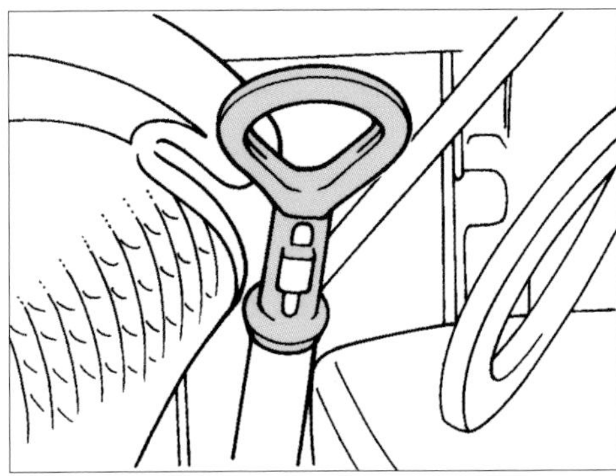

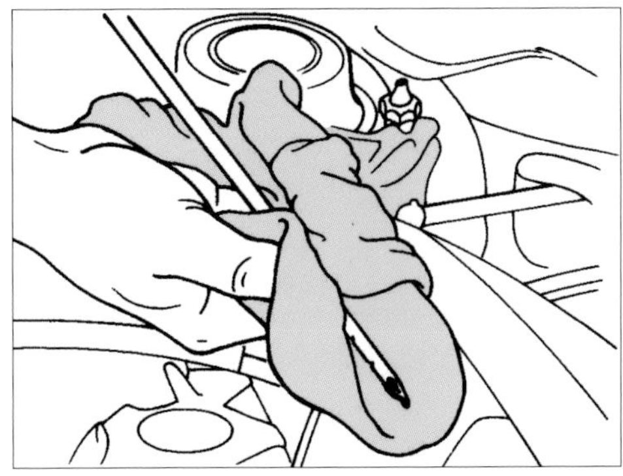

1 Park your car on level ground, and make sure that the engine is warm but not hot. Locate the dipstick. It will stick out the side of the engine and probably have a red handle. If you can't find it, refer to the owner's manual.

2 Pull the dipstick out and wipe it clean on of any oil residue with a dry, lint-free rag. Push it all the way back into place.

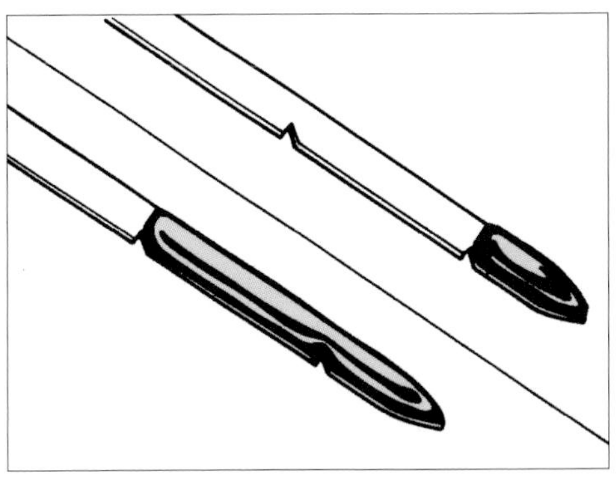

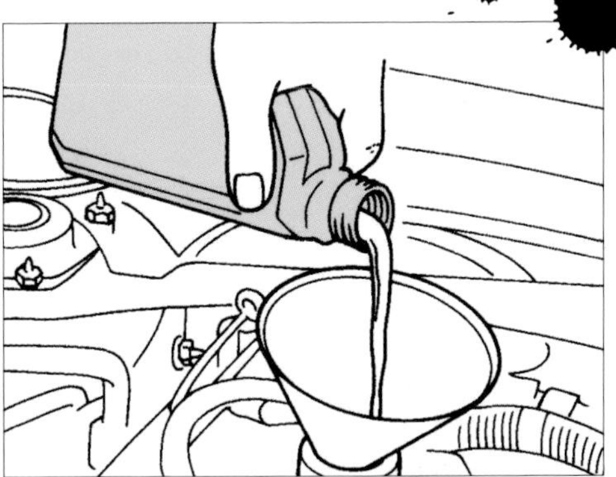

3 Pull the dipstick out again and check that the oil level is in between the 'maximum' and 'minimum' marks. If it's low, you'll need to top up with the recommended grade of oil (refer to your manual or ask at a garage).

4 Locate the oil tank lid and pour in about a litre (2 pints) of oil. Check the level on the dipstick before adding any more. It's better to pour in a little at a time than to overfill the tank. When the level is correct, close the lid and reinsert the dipstick.

CHECKING THE WATER LEVEL

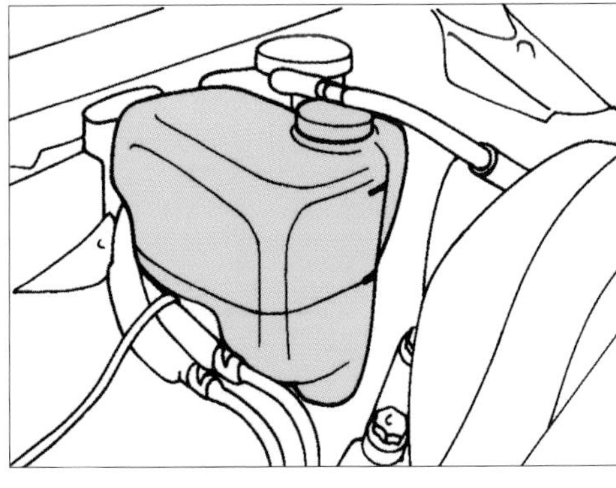

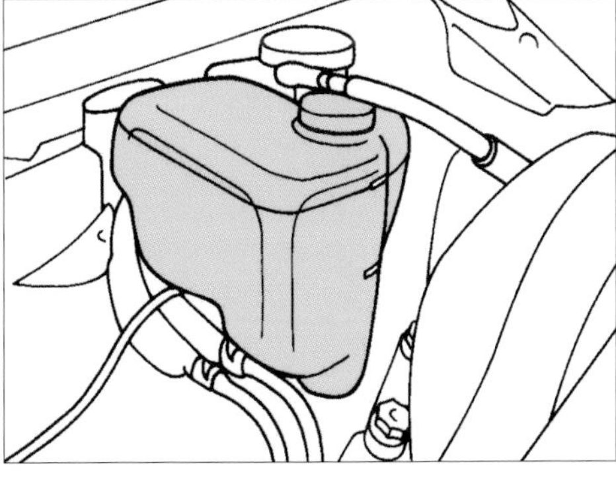

1 Locate the plastic coolant reservoir (not to be confused with the windscreen washer fluid or the brake oil reservoir). Wait for the engine to cool before opening the lid.

2 Check the coolant level is between the 'maximum' and 'minimum' marks. If it's low, top up with the recommended mix of water and antifreeze (usually 1:1, but refer to your manual or ask at a garage).

HOW TO TOW A VEHICLE

Even the best-made car is likely to break down sometimes. If you belong to a car recovery service, it should be able to sort you out. If not, it will work out a lot cheaper to persuade a friend to tow your car home, to a garage or, if all else fails, to the scrap heap!

INDISPENSABLE THINGS

- Strong rope, cable or chain
- Secure tying point

BE VISIBLE

Switch your hazard lights on and make sure you have an 'ON TOW' sign visible behind the car that is being towed.

TOW POINTS

Use a sturdy rope, cable or chain no longer than 4.5m (15ft) to attach the front of the broken-down car to the rear of the tow car. Do not attach the rope to the bumpers! Most cars have inbuilt tow points specially made for the purpose. If your car doesn't, attach the rope to the undercarriage.

NEUTRAL

Make sure the car being towed is in neutral.

STEADY SPEED

Drive the tow car as smoothly as possible to avoid the rope 'snatching'. Keep your speed below 45mph (72kph) as the effective load greatly increases above this speed. Keep the tow rope taut to prevent sudden jerks that might break it.

ROPES

Ready-made tow ropes with hefty metal hooks at either end are sold at most motorists' shops. If you're using plain rope, make sure it's strong enough and that the knots at either end are secure. If the tow rope is more than 1.5m (5ft) long, you must ensure it is clearly visible to other motorists by attaching a rag to the middle of it.

TOWING RULES

Both drivers must be fully qualified and both cars must be legally on the road, with functioning lights and brakes, etc. You are only allowed to tow a car on a motorway for the minimum distance necessary to reach a place of safety.

HOW TO BUMP-START A CAR

Flat battery? Fear not, you can still get going by bump-starting — or 'jump-' starting — your car. The idea is to get a bit of momentum going by pushing the car down a hill and then engaging the engine to get it spinning. Put your foot down on the accelerator and, brrrm, you're away! Don't try this on an automatic, though — it only works on cars fitted with manual transmission.

INDISPENSABLE THINGS

- A willing helper or two (don't try this on your own)
- Flat or downhill road

ENGAGE

When the car is moving at a fair clip (at least 3–5mph/5–8kph), signal to your helper(s) to stand aside, and engage the clutch. As soon as the engine starts, press your foot down on the accelerator to rev it up. You can then either carry on driving as usual or stop and run the engine in neutral for a few moments to make sure everything's working properly.

DOWNHILL

If possible, position the car so that it's pointing down a hill, or at least on the flat. Switch the ignition on, and make sure all electrical accessories are switched off. Put the engine in first or second gear, depress the clutch pedal fully with your foot and then release the brake.

PUSH

Once you've released the brake, signal to your helper(s) to push the back of the car with all their might. Don't try pushing the car on your own and jumping in to bump-start it; people have been run over doing this. Find someone to help. And remember, the faster the car is going, the more likely the engine is to start.

FIND THE SOURCE

Make sure you find the source of the problem. If it's because the lights were left on overnight, you can recharge the battery by driving the car around for about 25 minutes. If the battery goes flat repeatedly, it probably means that it needs replacing or there's a problem with the car's alternator or possibly the fan belt.

HOW TO CHANGE A TYRE

Thump-a-thump-a-thump-a-thump! Believe it or not, many people don't realize right away that they've got a puncture. If you're driving along and the steering becomes erratic and the car starts to bump on the road more than usual, then you've probably got a flat. Slow down immediately, switch your emergency lights on and pull over somewhere safe, like a layby. The sooner you stop, the less damage there'll be. And girls, don't bother asking a fella to help; this is one you can do yourselves. Honest!

INDISPENSABLE THINGS

- Spare wheel
- Jack
- Wrench
- Large screwdriver (optional)

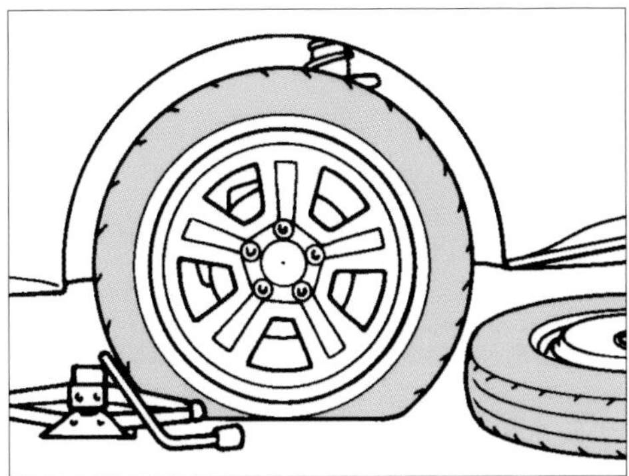

1 Park the car on level, firm ground, preferably with the punctured tyre facing away from the road, and well clear of any traffic. Set your emergency triangle about 30m (100ft) behind the car. Put the handbrake on or, if the car is an automatic, put it in 'Park'. Switch off the engine.

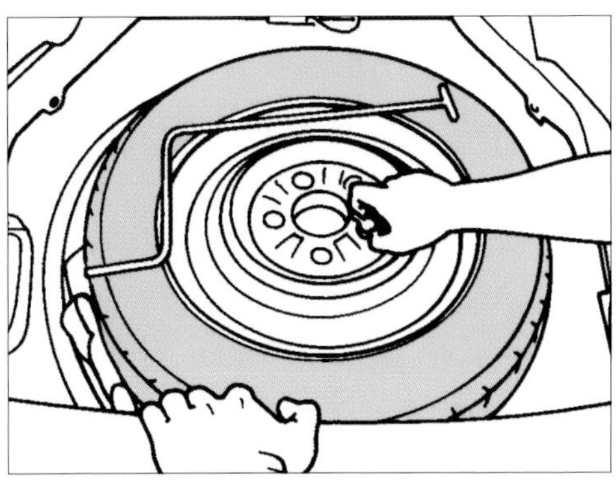

2 Check that you've got all the tools you need (see list on page 186). They'll probably be in the boot with the spare wheel. If you can't find them, refer to the owner's manual. Get down on your knees and find the nearest jacking point. Make sure the jack fits and take a couple of turns with the handle.

3 Before jacking the car up fully, loosen the wheels nuts slightly. If a hubcap or wheel cover is fitted, use the flat end of the wheel wrench or a large screwdriver to lever it off. Fit the wrench to one nut at a time and break it loose by turning it firmly anti-clockwise. If you can't turn it by hand, use your feet.

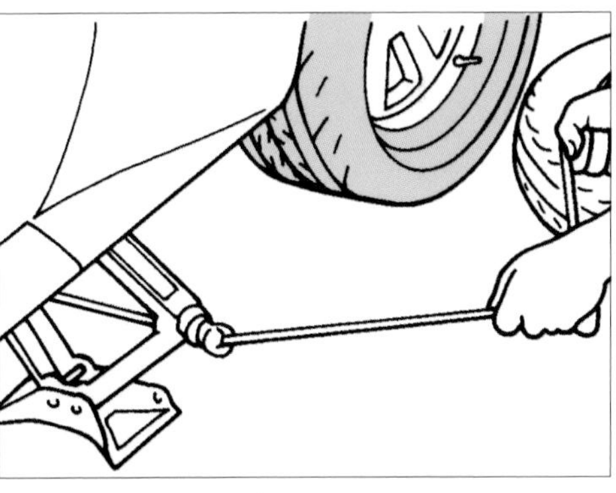

4 Once you've loosened all the wheel nuts (not too much!), use the jack to lift the side of the car until the punctured wheel is raised off the road. Now loosen the nuts completely and put them in a safe place. Remove the faulty wheel and put it in the boot of the car.

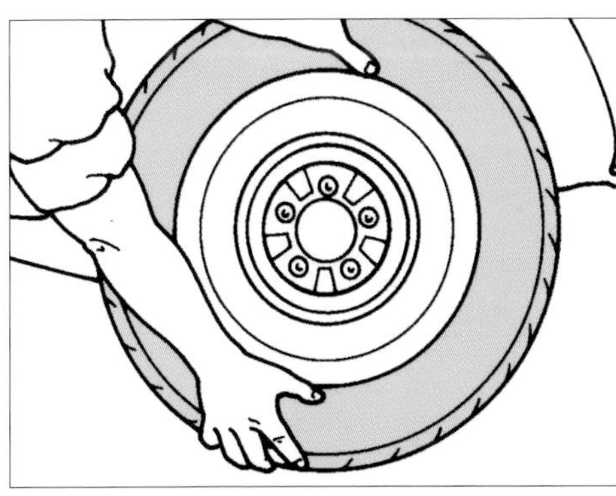

5 Line the spare wheel up with the bolts and lift it into place. You may need to raise the car a little more with the jack to give sufficient clearance. Starting from the bottom, tighten the nuts first by hand, then with the wrench. Don't tighten them fully yet.

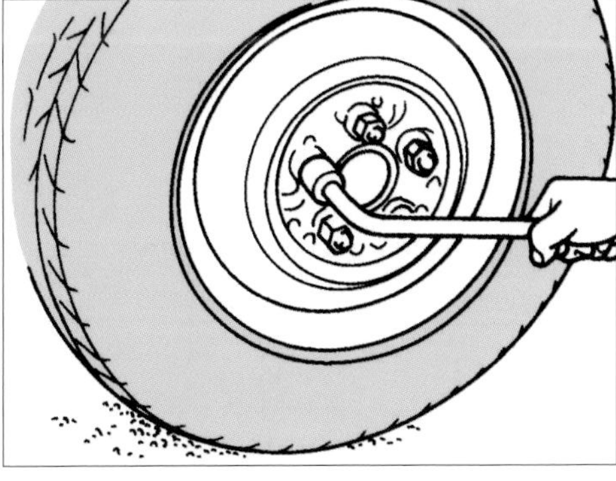

6 Let the car down fully and remove the jack. With the wheel held in place by the weight of the car, tighten the nuts as firmly as possible by hand. Start with any nut, tighten the one opposite and then finish off the rest. Replace the hubcap or wheel cover and put away your tools. Don't forget to get the puncture fixed!

HOW TO HOOK UP JUMP LEADS

A less stressful alternative to bump-starting a car with a flat battery is to connect it to another car. The idea is simply that you use the power from another car's battery to fire your engine. A set of jump leads can be bought from any car spares shop. Finding a friend who will donate their car for a few minutes might be a little harder.

INDISPENSABLE THINGS

- A donor car
- Jump leads

POSITION THE CARS

Position the donor car so that the batteries are close together – but not so close that the cars touch, as this will create sparks.

RED CABLE

With both engines switched off, connect one end of the red cable to the positive terminal (marked with a '+') of the flat battery. Then connect the other end to the positive terminal of the donor battery, making sure you don't let it touch either car on the way.

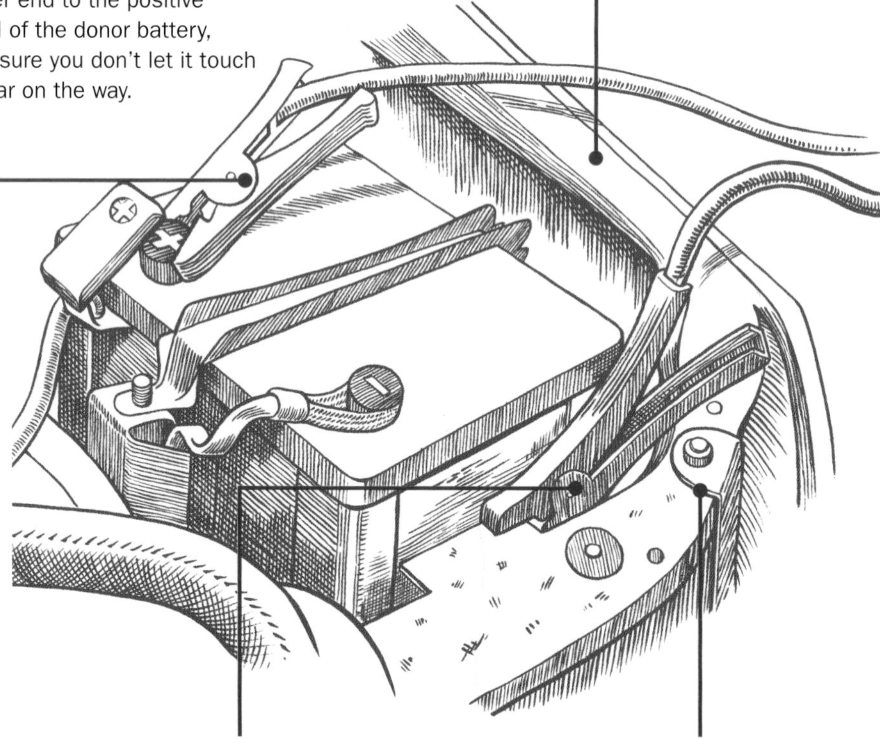

BLACK CABLE

Connect one end of the black cable to the negative terminal (marked with a '–') of the donor battery and the other end to any exposed metal part of the other car (e.g. bolt or metal bracket). This is safer than connecting it directly battery-to-battery.

START THE ENGINE

Once the leads are connected, start the engine of the donor car and run it at a fast idle speed. Allow it to run for a minute or so before starting the engine of the other car. Leave your engine running for a few minutes before switching off the engine of the donor car and disconnecting the cables in reverse order.

HOW TO FIX A SQUEAKY FAN BELT

Does your car sound like it's got a budgie under the bonnet? Sounds cute, doesn't it? Trouble is, it's probably the fan belt squeaking, which could signal problems further down the line. In any case, the novelty is liable to wear off, and pretty soon you'll be thinking of ways to kill that budgie! Here's some tips on how to do it.

INDISPENSABLE THINGS

- Lubricant (talcum powder, wax, soap)
- New fan belt

TOO OLD?

Fan belts also squeak when they're old and the rubber has become hard, cracked or frayed. If that's the case, you'll need a new one. It's easy enough to do yourself, with the help of a car repair manual, or your local mechanic should be able to sort it out in a jiffy.

TOO LOOSE OR TIGHT?

A squeaking fan belt usually means it's either too loose or too tight. Use the owner's manual to locate the fan belt, and press it (with engine switched off!) to check how much 'play' it has. It should have about 2cm (1in) – much more or much less and you should have it adjusted.

LUBRICATE

A temporary solution is to rub some lubricant on the inside edge of the fan belt. What lubricant? Well, suggestions range from talcum powder to candle wax, but most mechanics will tell you to steer clear of oil as this will only encourage the belt to slip. Our advice? A good old-fashioned bar of soap.

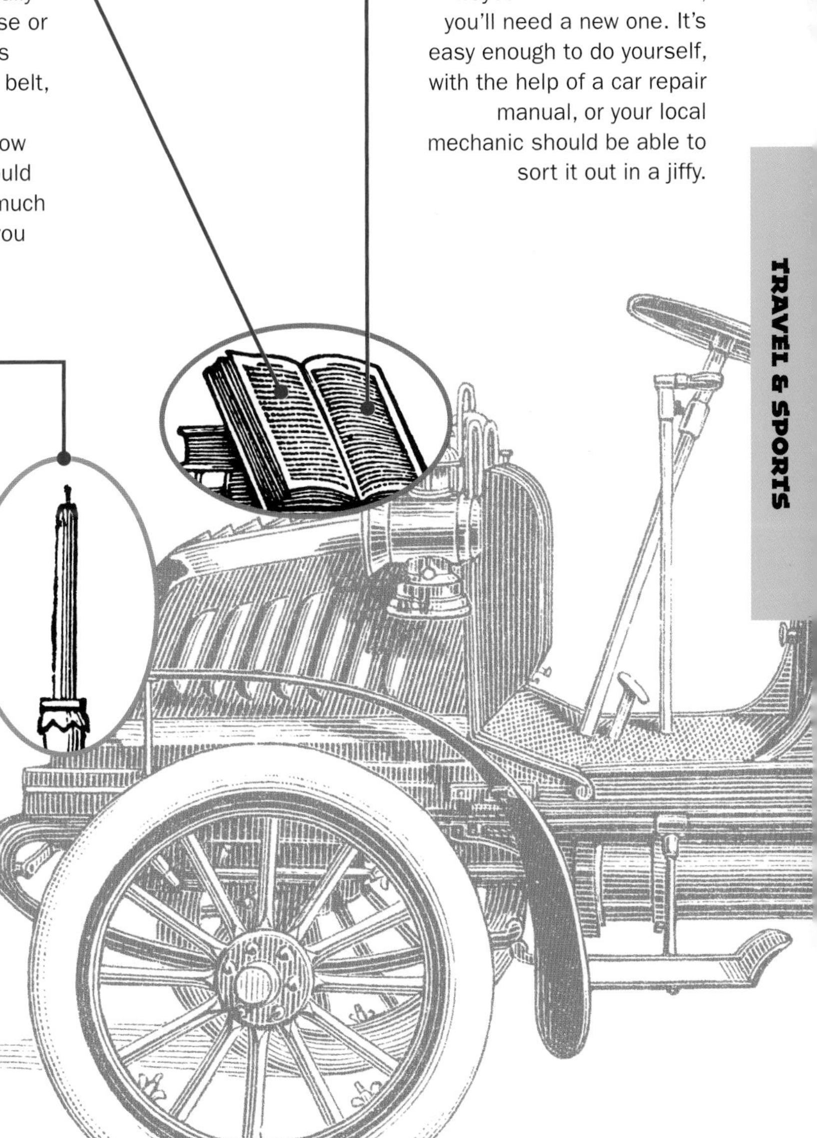

HOW TO SERVICE A BICYCLE

Riding a bike with squeaky brakes, rusty chain and skipping gears is no fun at all. On the other hand, paying for someone to fix it can cost more than the price of a new bike. The solution is to service your bike yourself. Just a few minutes a month washing off the mud and oiling the moving parts could save you hundreds. Even adjusting the brake pads isn't that difficult, once you know how.

PRACTICAL TIPS

Keep your bike running smoothly by washing it whenever it becomes dirty to prevent any build-up; wiping all exposed metal with an oily rag; using bike oil (not WD40); keeping your tyres pumped up to avoid excess wear; and servicing it regularly.

INDISPENSABLE THINGS

- Pump
- Chain lubricant
- Cloth or rag
- Bike oil
- Spray lubricant
- Wrench or Allen key

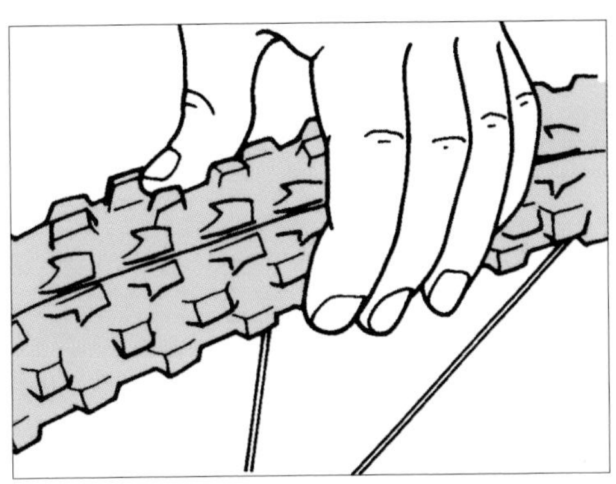

1 Check your tyre pressure once a week. Squeeze the sides of the tyres; if they squeeze together easily, the tyre needs pumping up. Don't squeeze the outer face, as that is more rigid and will disguise low air pressure.

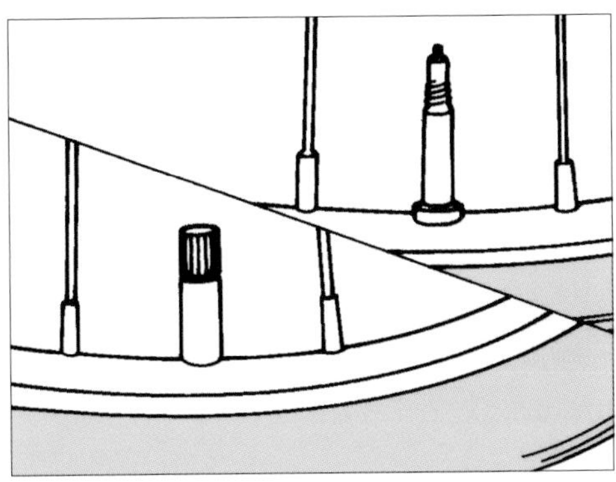

2 Check what sort of valve your bike has. A Presta valve is very slender and has a lock nut, which will need to be undone before you start pumping. A Schrader valve looks like a car tyre valve and doesn't need unlocking. Pump the tyres up until the sides are firm, but not rock hard. If you pump them up too much, they may burst.

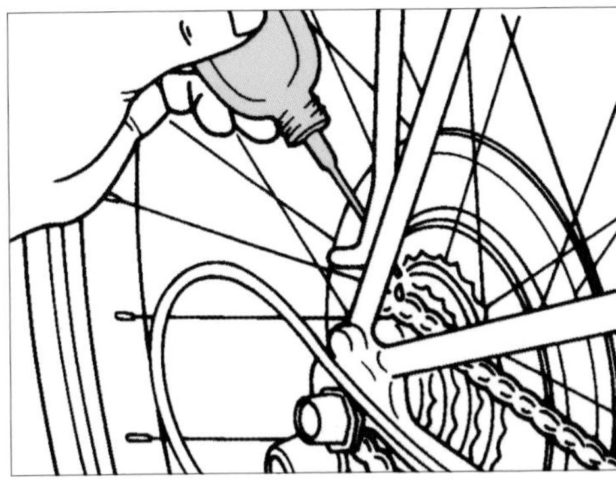

3 You should oil your chain once a month. Most experts advise against using spray oils such as WD40 and recommend specially made chain lubricant. Turn the pedals backwards and apply the lubricant until the chain is covered in a thin layer. Wipe off any excess with a rag.

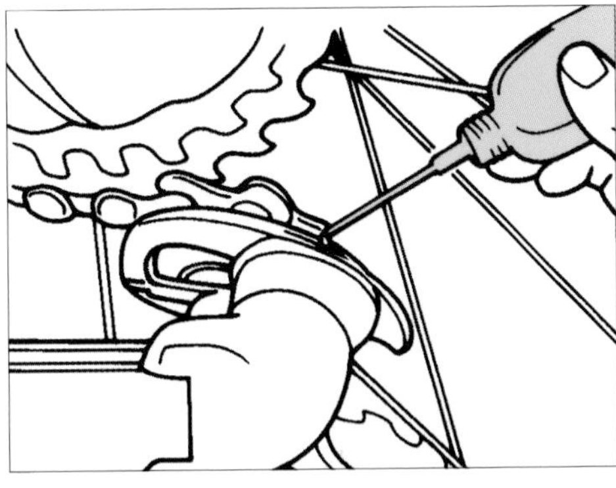

4 Oil the joints of the front and rear gear mechanisms (known as derailleurs). Oil the brake and gear cables, changing gear and applying the brakes to expose more cable. Use a special spray lubricant (not WD40), which can be sprayed into the cable housing. Wipe off any excess with a rag.

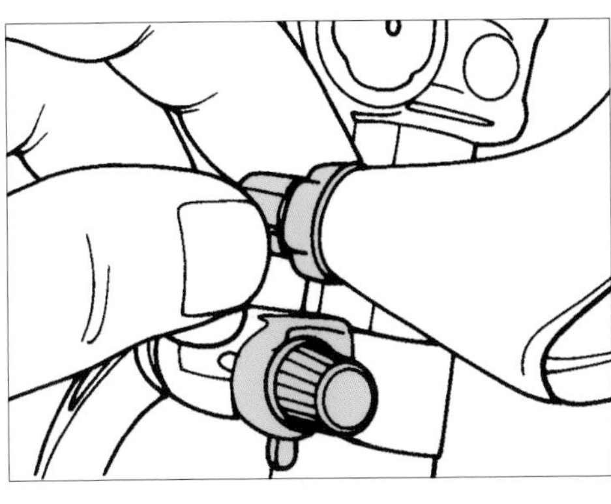

5 Brakes become less effective in time, as cables stretch and brake pads wear down. Most bikes have an adjusting barrel between the brake lever and the cable housing and/or between the brake and the cable housing. Turn either one anti-clockwise to increase brake tension.

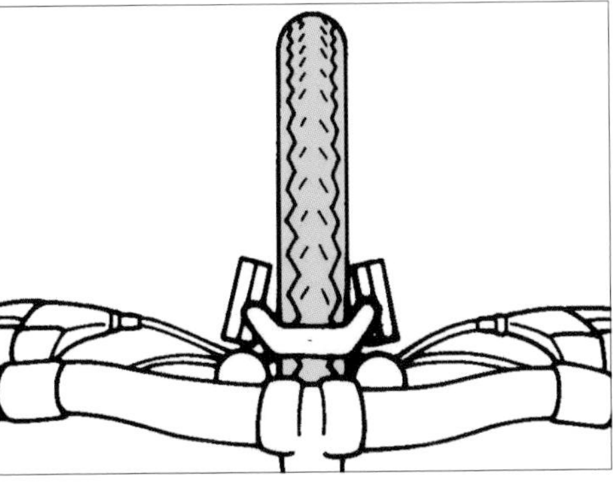

6 Check that the brake pads are at the right height. They should touch the rim of the wheel, not rub on the tyre or hang over the rim. Ideally, the leading edge (nearest the front of the bike) should be 'toed', or angled slightly in, to prevent squeaking. Use a wrench or Allen key to adjust accordingly.

HOW TO FIX A BICYCLE PUNCTURE

You can go for years without a puncture, and then get three in a row. But that's no excuse to park your bike in the shed! With just a few basic tools, you can mend it and be back on the road in no time. It's cheaper than taking it to the bike shop – and so much more satisfying. Mending a puncture is also an excellent way to familiarize yourself with your bike and check that everything is functioning properly – from the brakes to the ball bearings.

INDISPENSABLE THINGS

- Spanner (possibly)
- Pen, lever or wrench
- Pump
- Bucket of water
- Puncture repair kit: rubber patches; rubber vulcanizing solution (glue that sticks rubber together); small piece of sandpaper

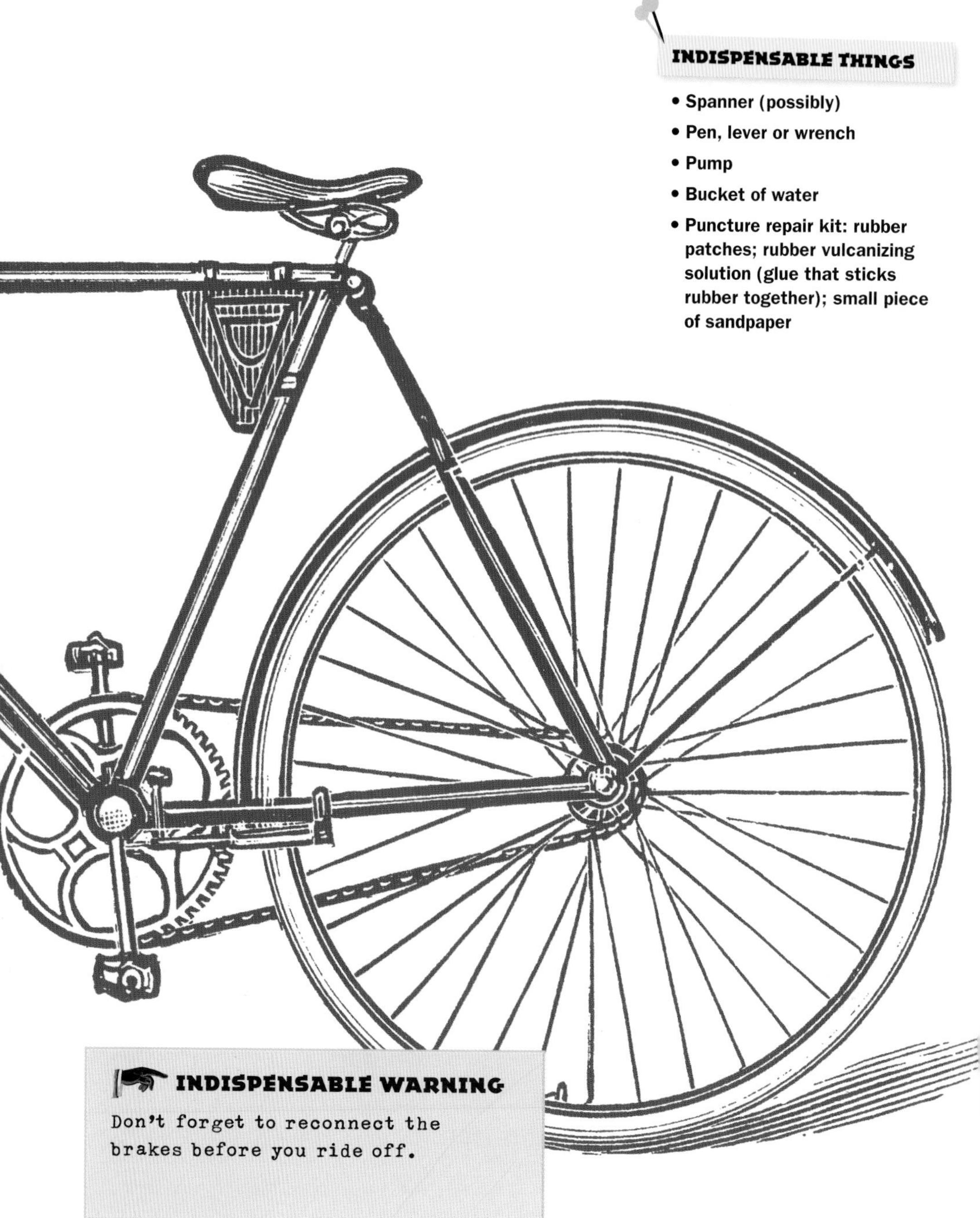

INDISPENSABLE WARNING

Don't forget to reconnect the brakes before you ride off.

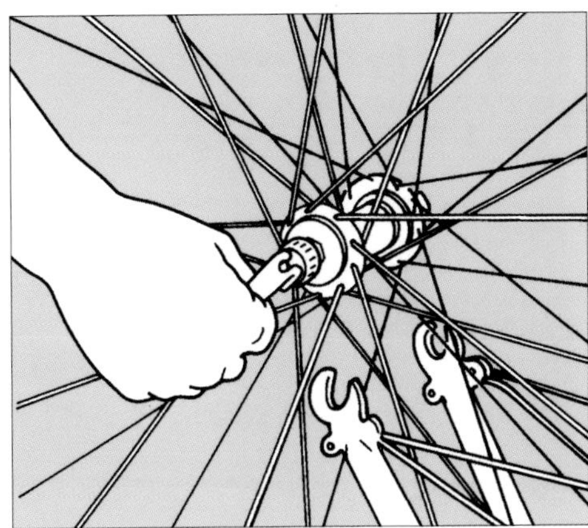

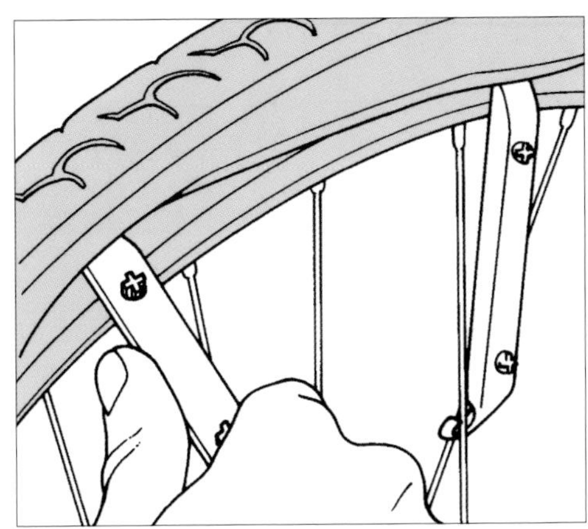

1 Take the wheel off. Release the brakes by squeezing the pads together and unhooking the cable. Then turn the bike upside down. If it is fitted with quick-release wheels, simply open the lever and lift the wheel out. If the bike doesn't have quick release, use a spanner to undo the nuts on either side of the axle.

2 Let all the air out of the tube. Insert a lever between the rim and the tyre, prise the tyre away from the rim and hook the end of the lever onto a spoke. Repeat this process with another lever and keep on going until you can pull the tube out. Be careful not to pinch the tube with the levers.

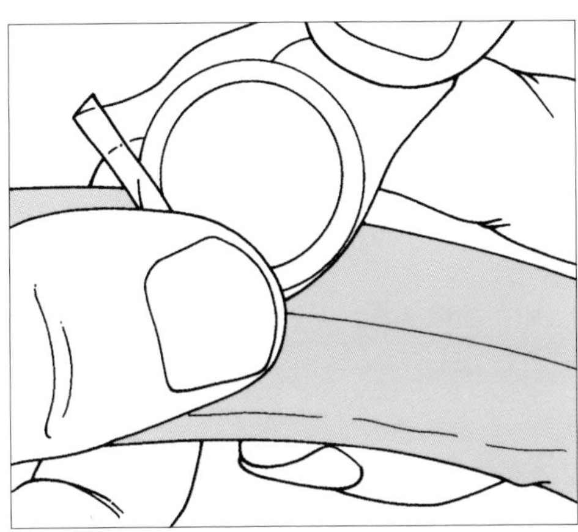

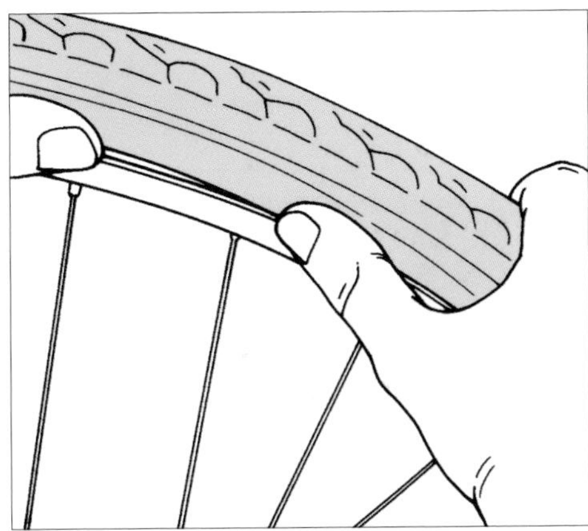

3 Pump the tube up and listen for escaping air. If that doesn't work, feed it into a bucket of water and watch for bubbles. Mark the leak with a pencil and roughen the area with sandpaper. Once the tube's dry, apply a thin layer of glue and wait until it's touch-dry. Peel off the protective film on the patch and press it into place.

4 To reinstall the tube, inflate it slightly to prevent it getting pinched. Insert the valve into its hole and slide the tube into the rim. Push the tyre bead over the edge of the rim with your thumbs, starting at the valve and working your way round. Only use a lever if you have to. Once the tyre is in place, refit the wheel and pump the tyre up to normal pressure.

A PRACTICAL HISTORY OF WHEELS

The earliest depiction of a wheeled vehicle is on a vase dating back to c.3500BC. The oldest wheel in existence was discovered in Slovenia and is thought to be at least 6,000 years old. The first 'modern' bike was the Rover Safety Bicycle created by English inventor John Kemp Starley in 1885. Some 1.4 billion bikes are now in existence. The inventor of the modern automobile was Karl Benz, who patented his first combustion engine in 1879 and his first car six years later. There are currently more than 590 million cars in the world.

HOW TO KEEP THE KIDS ENTERTAINED ON A LONG CAR JOURNEY

Computer games and iPods have taken much of the stress out of long car journeys with the kids. But even those can lose their interest after a while – and, besides, family activities are so much more fun.

INDISPENSABLE THINGS

- Puzzle books
- Plenty of snacks
- Music compilation
- Note pad and pens
- Regular stops
- Patience of a saint

SONGS

You can't beat a good sing-along to lift the spirits. Print out the lyrics of old favourites from the Internet before you leave, or make a CD compilation. Even teenagers can't stop themselves singing along to Abba!

WORD ASSOCIATION

Someone says a word, the next person says the first word it brings to their mind, and so on around the car, e.g., 'White', 'Black', 'Knight', 'Sword', etc. Players can challenge if the association isn't clear.

MAPPING

Before you leave, print out a map of your route and highlight the major towns you'll be passing through for the kids to cross out as you drive past. Better still, write a list of place names for them to tick off.

ALPHABET GAMES

Take turns to compile a list of shopping items using words starting with the letters of the alphabet, for example, one persons says, 'I went to the grocery and bought apples', and the next person says, 'I went to the grocery and bought apples and baguettes', and so on.

LICENCE PLATE GAME

Get your children to write down the letters of a licence plate and to make as many words as possible out of them (for example, 'POR' becomes 'pork', 'export', etc.). For older kids and adults, see who can be the first to think of a word – the sillier the better!

FUN & GAMES

Wouldn't life be boring if we just sat around all day working and watching TV? Learning to have fun is one of the most important life skills. And it's no good saying you don't know how to sail a boat or do an ollie or play roulette — we'll show you how.

HOW TO ROW A BOAT WITH ONE OAR

You've taken your girl/boyfriend for a row on the lake to impress them with your rowing prowess. Halfway across, you lean over to give him/her a romantic kiss. Mmmwaah! When you open your eyes, one of the oars has slipped into the water and is drifting towards the duck pond. Without hesitation, you swing the remaining oar over the back of the boat and save the day by practising your newly acquired art of sculling. He/she is duly impressed, you row back to shore and live together happily ever after.

INDISPENSABLE THINGS

- Oar
- Relaxed wrists

PRACTICAL TIP

Rowing with two oars? Easy! Hold the handles so the blades are a hand's width above the water. Lean forward and dip the blades in the water. Push your body back and pull the oars towards you. Lift the blades out of the water and repeat!

MOVING THE OAR

As you move from left to right, your hand makes a figure-of-eight movement, with the blade of the oar moving like the tail of a fish. It's one of those things that's more complicated to explain than it is to do. Everything will become clear once you have an oar in your hand.

HEAVY & NARROW

The best boat for sculling is heavy and narrow. A light boat (such as an inflatable dinghy) provides too little leverage, and the back gets thrown from side to side.

ADVANTAGE

Sculling has several advantages over rowing with two oars. For a start, the oar never comes out of the water, which means there is less wind resistance when you row into a strong wind. If towing another boat, it also provides a steady pull and prevents 'snatching'.

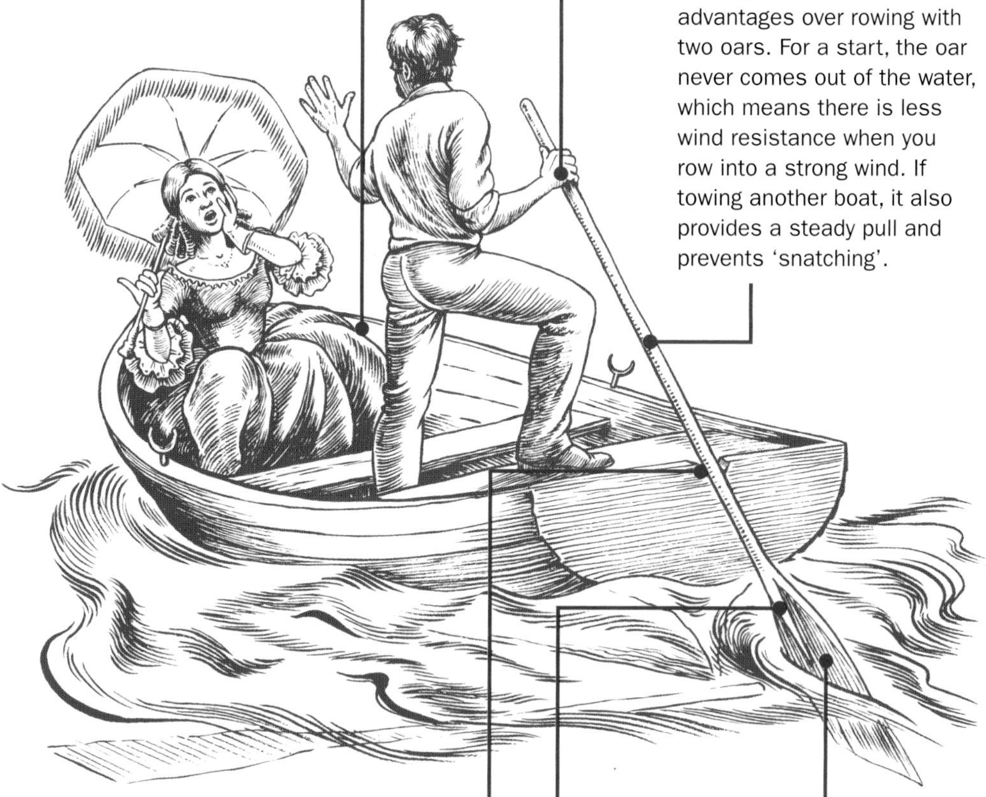

NOTCH

With luck, the boat will already have a notch cut into the back, which the oar will fit into. If not, hopefully you planned in advance and have fitted an extra rowlock (the metal crutches that hold the oars) where the notch should be. It will need to be offset if you use an outboard engine.

SWEEP & PIVOT

Note how the depressed, or deepest, edge of the blade cuts a path in the water. As you reach the end of that sweep, push your wrist downwards and your knuckles up, and push the oar to your left. Again, note how the deepest edge of the blade cuts the water. When you reach the end of that sweep, pivot the oar back to its original position and repeat the process.

ANGLING

Run the oar over the back of the boat and into the water at an angle of about 45 degrees, resting it in the notch. Facing the back of the boat, grip the handle with your right hand, wrist raised, knuckles down, elbow slightly lowered. Lever the oar against the notch by pulling it firmly to your right.

HOW TO SAIL A BOAT

Oh no! The captain's fallen over the side, the mate's in bed with dysentery and the deckhand fell in love with a *señorita* and jumped ship. There's only you left to sail the boat safely back to port. Plucking up all your courage, you lick your finger and stick it up in the air. The air cooling one side of your finger instantly tells you which way the wind is blowing, and you're ready to take command. 'Splice the mainbrace!' you shout, as you grab the helm.

PRACTICAL TIP

Check that you know the direction of the wind ... it's usually at right angles to the waves.

INDISPENSABLE THING

- A steady wind

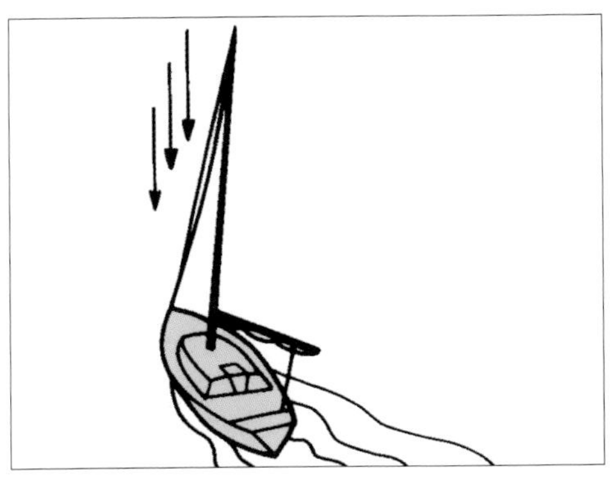

1 Make sure the boat is pointing into the wind – that is, the 'pointy' front end of the boat should point in the direction the wind is coming from. This is like being in 'neutral' and means that when the sails are raised, the boat won't go charging off.

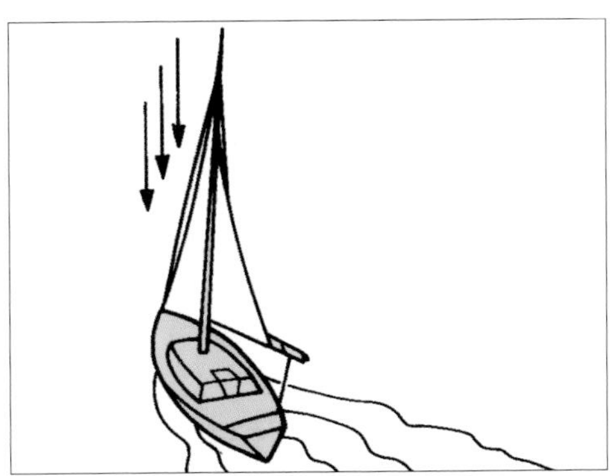

2 Uncover the mainsail and find the halyard. The mainsail is the big sail attached to the back of the mast, and the halyard is the rope that hoists the mainsail to the top of the mast. Check the sail is unhindered and pull it up as far as it will go.

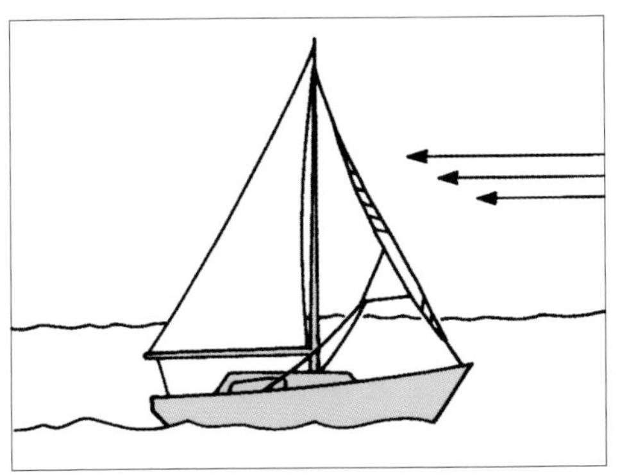

3 On most modern boats, there is a sail attached to a roller at the front of the boat. This is called the genoa, and it's controlled by two ropes on either side of the boat called genoa sheets. Unfurl the genoa by releasing the roller and pulling on one of the genoa sheets.

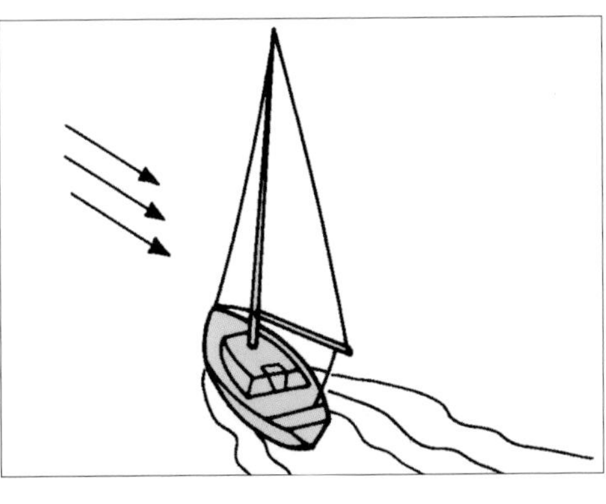

4 Check the wind direction. In order to move, the boat must be at an angle of about 45 degrees or more to the wind. Once you've decided which direction you're going, make sure the genoa is on the opposite side of the boat from which the wind is blowing.

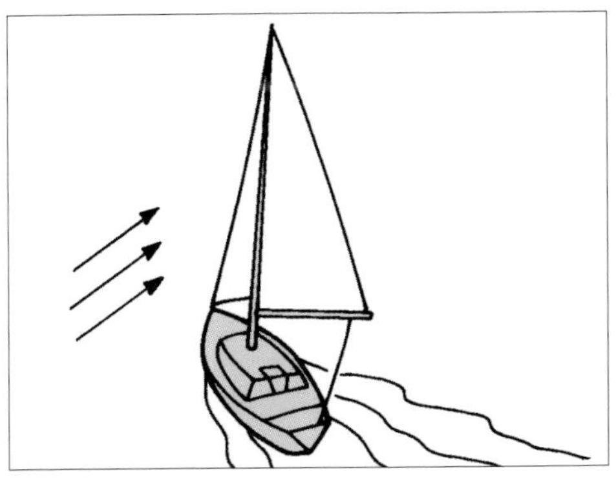

5 Set a course at 45 degrees to the wind and adjust the genoa sheets until the sail stops flapping. The angle of the mainsail is controlled by a rope at the back of the boat called the mainsail sheet. Adjust this until the front edge of the sail stops flapping. Keep a steady course!

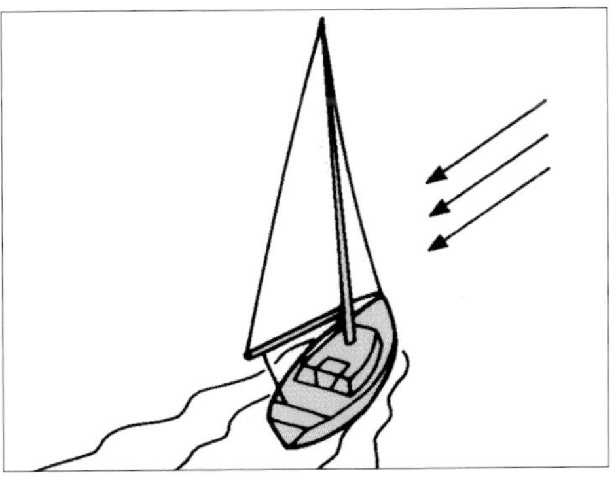

6 To change direction, ease out the sails as you head away from the wind. If you need to go the other way, let go of the genoa sheet and turn the boat until the wind is on the other side and the boat is again pointing at least 45 degrees to the wind. Make sure the genoa is on the other side of the mast, and adjust the sheets again.

HOW TO DO THE FRONT CRAWL

It's all very well being able to do the breast stroke, but you can only really swim once you can do the front crawl. It's not only faster and more efficient than any other swimming stroke, it also looks more impressive. Practise it in a quiet corner of the pool, when no one's watching. Start with just the arms and, once you've established a rhythm, the legs will follow. Pretty soon you'll be swimming in the lanes with the best of them.

INDISPENSABLE THINGS

- A straight body line
- Measured breathing
- Swimsuit
- Goggles

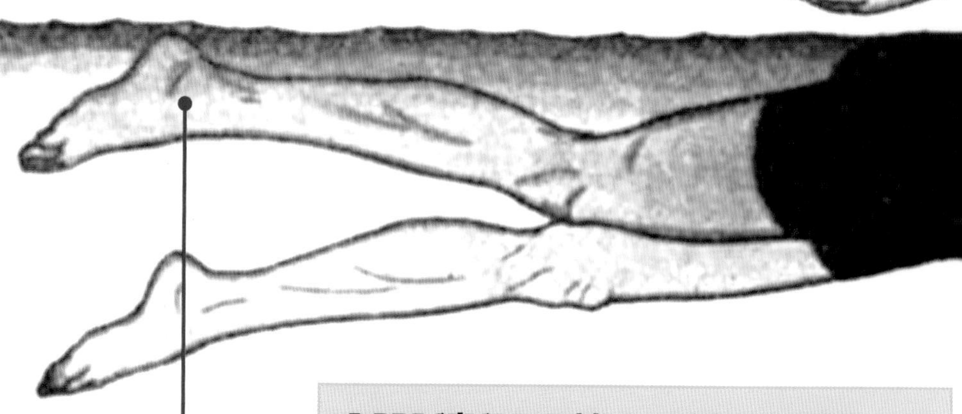

LEGS

Use the 'flutter' kick, keeping your legs close to the surface of the water. Kick from the hips, bending your knee slightly going down and straightening for the up kick. Keep your ankles loose and your toes pointed. Use short, fast kicks.

A PRACTICAL HISTORY OF THE CRAWL

The superiority of the front crawl was proven beyond doubt when a group of native Americans took part in a swimming competition in London in 1844. Although the stroke had been used for centuries in the Americas, it was unknown in Britain, where the breast stroke still prevailed. The native American swimmers duly thrashed their European competitors. Because the front crawl entailed a considerable amount of splashing, however, the British considered it barbaric and stuck with their breast stroke until the 1870s.

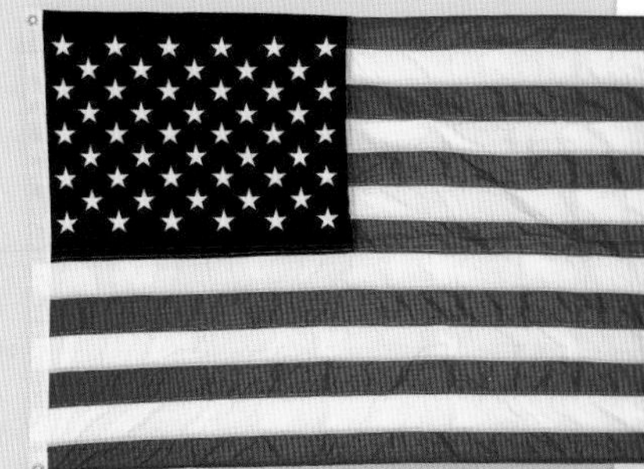

ENTRY
Plunge your hand into the water directly in front of your shoulder, with the elbow slightly flexed and palm facing outwards. Turn your palm down, as you stretch your arm forward.

DOWNSWEEP
Flex your arm at the elbow and sweep down until the hand is facing directly backwards. As the arm sweeps up, extend the arm slightly (not completely) and move your hand backwards, outwards and upwards. Think about your thumb touching your thigh as it exits the water. As your hand comes out of the water, move your hand forward, keeping your elbow high and your hand close to your body.

BODY
Swim with your body close to the surface of the water and keep your movements long and narrow. Imagine you are swimming through a tube and are not allowed to touch the sides. Do your best not to splash.

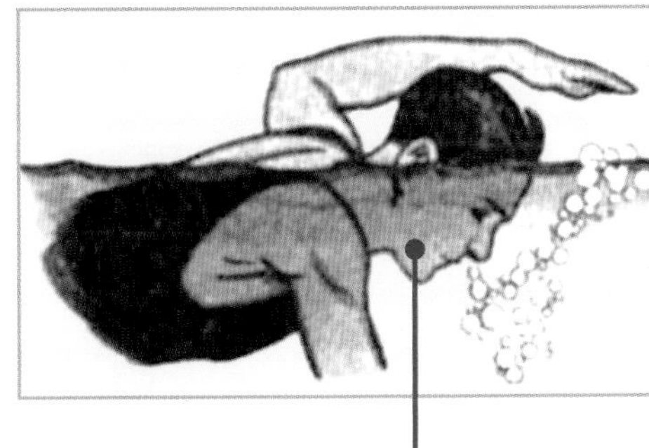

BREATHING
Turn your face down and forwards. Your line of vision should be like the headlights on a car. When your arm is in recovery mode, turn your head into the triangle of your arm and the water, and take a breath. The 'hollow' created by your bow wave will create a space for you to breathe. Raise your head as little as possible.

HOW TO DO THE BUTTERFLY STROKE

It might look like a lot of effort for not very much gain, but the butterfly stroke is undeniably cool. It also has the fastest peak speed of any swimming style – although, because of the long recovery time in between strokes, its average speed is slightly slower than the front crawl. Still, 2.177 metres per second (7.8kph/4.87mph) isn't to be sneezed at. Unless you breathe in at the wrong moment and get a lungful of water. Try it next time you're in an empty swimming pool. It's easier than it looks.

INDISPENSABLE THINGS

- Undulating body
- Swimsuit
- Goggles

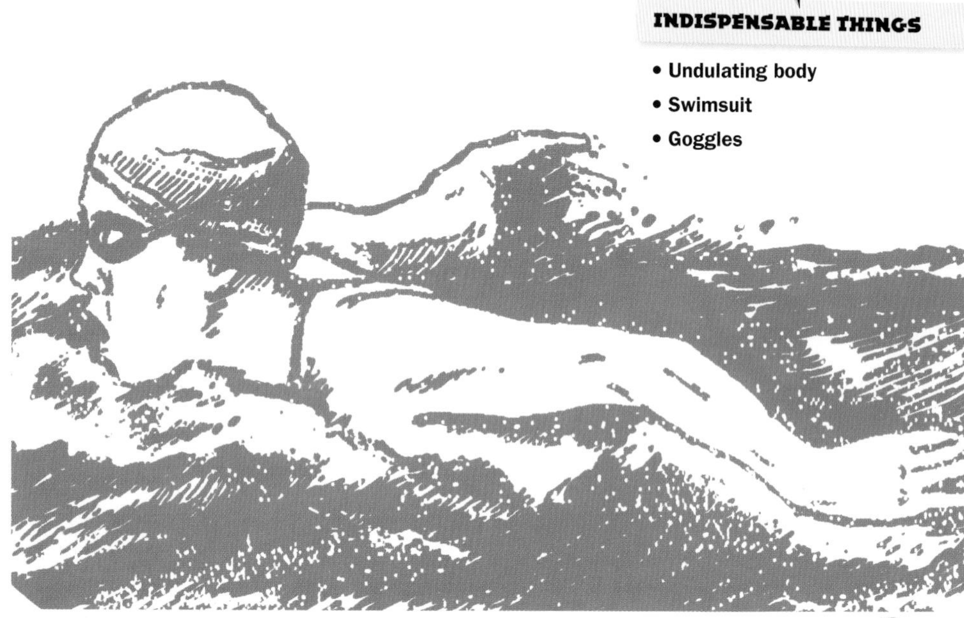

A PRACTICAL HISTORY OF THE BUTTERFLY STROKE

The origins of the butterfly stroke are disputed. According to one version of the story, David Armbruster and Jack Seig, both from the University of Iowa, developed the butterfly breast stroke and the dolphin kick independently in the 1930s. They then combined their discoveries to create what we now know as the butterfly stroke. Another version of the story suggests that Jack Stephens, of Belfast, invented the elements of the stroke some 30 years before Armbruster and Seig. Either way, it was regarded as a variant of the breast stroke until 1952, when it was finally recognized as a style in its own right. It achieved Olympic recognition in 1956, when separate categories were created for the male and female 100m butterfly.

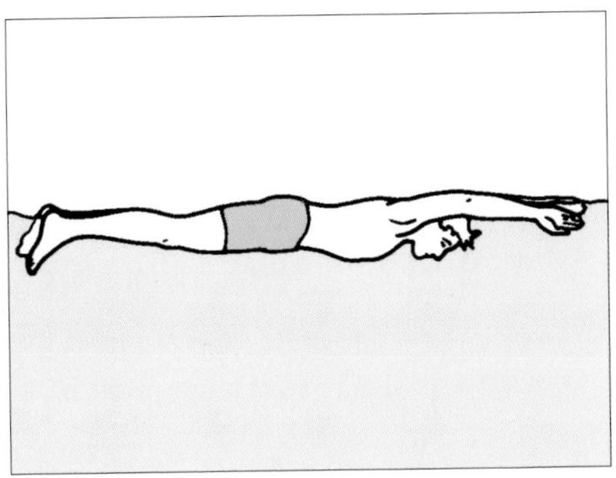

1 Extend the arms forward, thumbs down, shoulder-width apart. Your feet should be close together, like a fish's tail, legs straight. Kick your legs to get started.

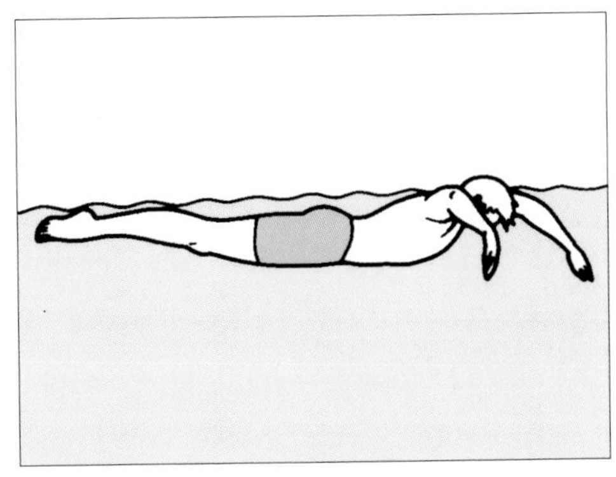

2 Sweep your hands down and out, to create a 'Y' shape, scooping the water with your palms. Keep your head down.

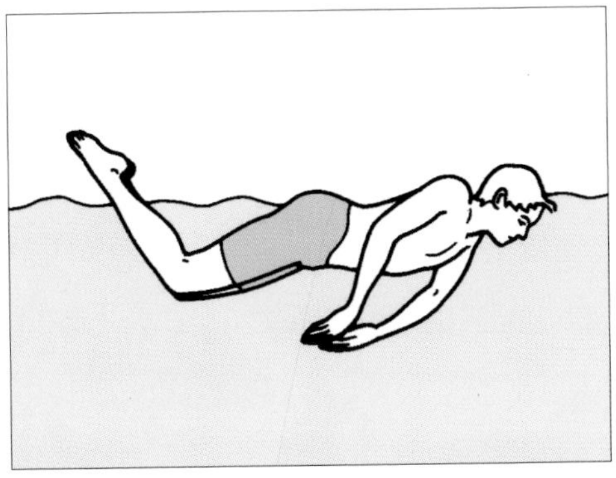

3 Brings your hands together under your belly to complete a keyhole shape. Bend your legs to prepare for the big kick.

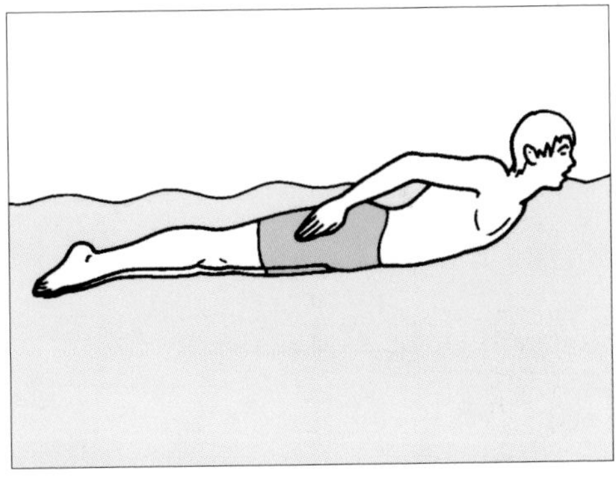

4 Kick back strongly and point your feet down. As your body surges forward, streamline your arms by the side of your body, ready to fling them forward. Raise your head and breathe!

5 While your body still has forward momentum, throw your arms forward over the water in a wide arc. Kick your legs and repeat the process, undulating your body in time with your arms and legs.

TOP SWIMMING SPEEDS

- FRONT CRAWL 2.349m/s (8.4kph/5.254mph)
- BUTTERFLY 2.177m/s (7.8kph/4.87mph)
- BACK STROKE 2.0433m/s (7.35kph/4.57mph)
- BREAST STROKE 1.839m/s (6.6kph/4.115mph)

HOW TO MAKE A RAFT

It must be every child's dream to build a raft and paddle across the local pond/river/ocean. Trouble is, you'll probably upset the neighbours if you start chopping down trees to make your dream raft. Besides, have you ever tried lifting half a tonne of unseasoned timber onto a roofrack? Here's an ingenious idea that saves the trees, uses up those plastic bottles that you keep forgetting to recycle, and creates a raft that is genuinely unsinkable. Eat your heart out, Noah!

INDISPENSABLE RAFTS

In 2006 two MIT students built a raft using 129 empty bottles of Gatorade energy drink. It took them a year to collect the bottles, during which they drank 340 litres (598 pints) of Gatorade. The finished raft used 244 litres (430 pints) worth of bottles and carried their combined weight of 118kg (260lb) across Lake Charles, Massachusetts.

INDISPENSABLE THINGS

- Empty plastic bottles and lids
- Duct tape
- Broom handle
- A snack in case you get lost!

BOTTLE SIZE

You can use almost any size of bottle, but the smaller they are, the more you'll need and the more taping you'll have to do. Those 5-litre (9-pint) water bottles are ideal, or those sturdy 2-litre (3½ pint) bottles that certain brands of fizzy drinks come in. If you're mixing different-size bottles, make sure the bigger bottles are at the centre, with the smaller bottles attached to them in decreasing order of size. Save some sturdy bottles for the outermost layer, which will take the most knocks.

HOW MANY?

The number of bottles you need will depend on the number of people you're going to carry. If you allow about 1 litre (1¾ pints) of buoyancy per 450g (1lb) of weight, you should have ample buoyancy. Alternatively, a simple 10 x 10 grid of 1.5-litre water bottles (i.e. 100 bottles) will comfortably carry one adult.

MAKING THE RAFT

Tape the bottles together to create 'cells' that you then join together to create bigger cells, until they are all taped together to make the raft. Start by taping two bottles together to make the first cell; then tape two pairs of bottles together to make a four-bottle cell; then tape two sets of four together to make an eight-bottle cell, and so forth. Make sure the bottles are upright, with lids firmly secured. Reject any bottles without lids. Use duct tape – don't settle for anything less.

MAKING THE PADDLE

A paddle can be made from a 3-litre (5¼-pint) plastic bottle cut in half down its length and taped to the end of a broom handle.

HOW TO DO AN OLLIE

Skateboard culture has been sweeping the world since the mid-1970s. The latest estimate puts the total number of users at 18.5 million, mostly under the age of 18. But why let the kids have all the fun? Practise on your offspring's skateboard while they are at school and – once you've worked out how to stay on it – try doing an ollie. It's the basic trick that every skateboarder has to master, and it will impress the kids no end.

INDISPENSABLE THINGS

- Skateboard
- Trainers or flat, rubber-soled shoes
- Padded clothing and gloves

A PRACTICAL HISTORY OF THE OLLIE

The ollie was invented in 1979 by Alan 'Ollie' Gelfand, a Florida skateboarder, as a skatepark trick and later adapted from freestyling. The official record for the highest ollie is held by Danny Wainwright from England, who jumped 113cm (44in) – although an unofficial video shows Peruvian skateboarder Jose Marabotto reaching an estimated 127cm (50in).

1 This is your starting position. The front foot is placed about two-thirds of the way along the board, in between the middle of the board and the front truck, or wheels. The ball of the rear foot is resting on the tail.

2 Crouch down as low as you can. Basically, the lower you crouch, the higher (and therefore more impressive) your ollie will be. If you're worried about doing this on the move, practise first on grass – you'll have a softer landing anyway!

3 Strike the tail of the board on the ground as hard as you can, at the same time jumping up from your rear foot. Getting the timing of this move right is crucial, so you might want to practise it a little before moving on to the next step.

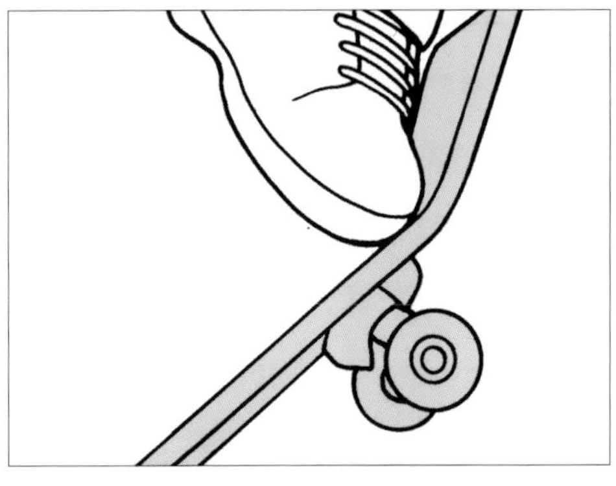

4 As you push off with your rear foot, roll your front foot and slide it up the board, raising your knee right up to your chest. The friction of the shoe against the griptape (the gritty layer on top of a skateboard) lifts the board higher and allows you to guide it into position.

5 Raise your rear foot and, as you reach the top of your ollie, level the board under both feet. Once you start to get the timing right, it will all turn into one continuous move, with the board hovering under your feet as if it's being held by a magnet.

6 You can't defy gravity forever. As you come down, make sure your knees are bent. This will absorb the shock of landing and help you keep the board under control. Injuring yourself while trying to impress your kids is not cool.

HOW TO DIVE

Diving is easy, right? So why is it that, instead of the beautiful, elegant dive we imagine we're going to perform, we usually end up doing an ungainly belly flop? According to the experts, it's all down to that first push. Here are some step-by-step instructions that will ensure that, next time you dive, you'll cut the water like a knife – instead of bombing it like an elephant.

INDISPENSABLE THINGS

- Deep water
- Streamlined body

PRACTICAL TIP

Guys, if you really want to make an impressive dive, you'll have to sacrifice fashion. Those baggy swimming shorts act like a drogue underwater. Buy a natty pair of Speedos or other tight-fitting swimming trunks. They're all the rage in Brazil.

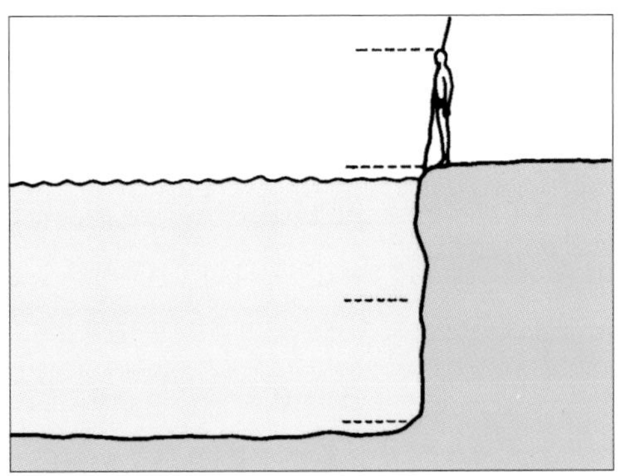

1 Think. Check that you've got enough water before you dive. A general rule of thumb is that the water should be at least twice the height of the person diving. The higher you start from, the deeper the water should be. About 1,000 people a year in the US alone suffer from spinal cord injuries from diving into shallow water* – don't be one of them.

2 Stretch your arms in the air, palms facing downwards, so that your biceps squeeze your ears. Bend your legs slightly – but don't bend your head.

* ThinkFirst National Injury Prevention Foundation & the North American Spine Society, quoted by the Mayfield Clinic of Cincinnati.

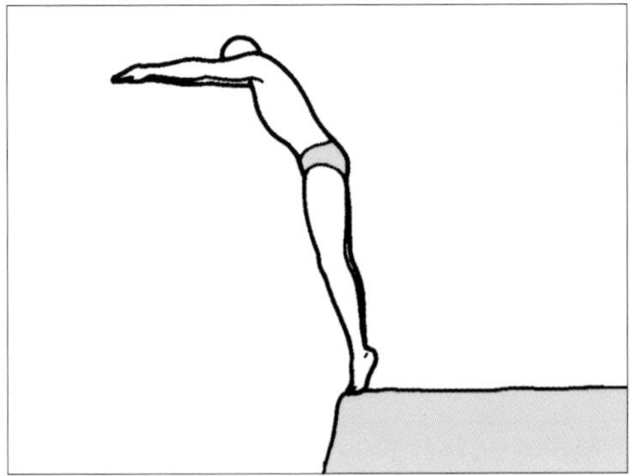

3 Lean forward. Just before you start falling, push off with your feet. Judging when to push is crucial as it will determine the angle of your trajectory: push too soon, and you could dive straight down and hurt yourself on the bottom; push too late and you'll end up doing a belly flop.

4 A good push off at the right angle will raise your feet and legs and ensure that the top half of your body leads the dive. Follow an imaginary arc with your body, keeping your legs and hands together.

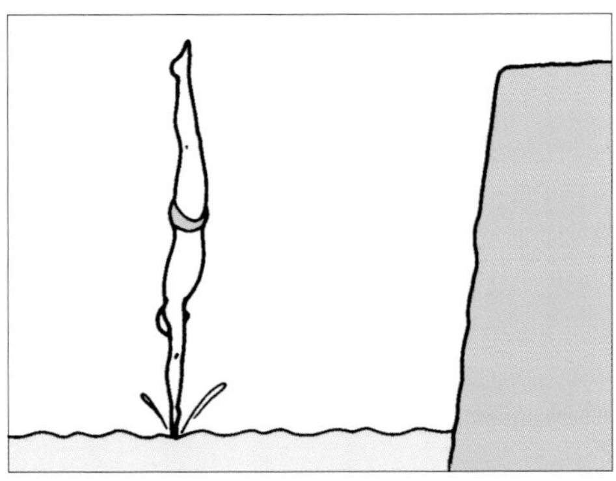

5 Make sure that your hands hit the water first to reduce the impact of the water on your head. It can be surprisingly painful if you misjudge it! Keep your body as straight and as streamlined as possible to avoid making a splash.

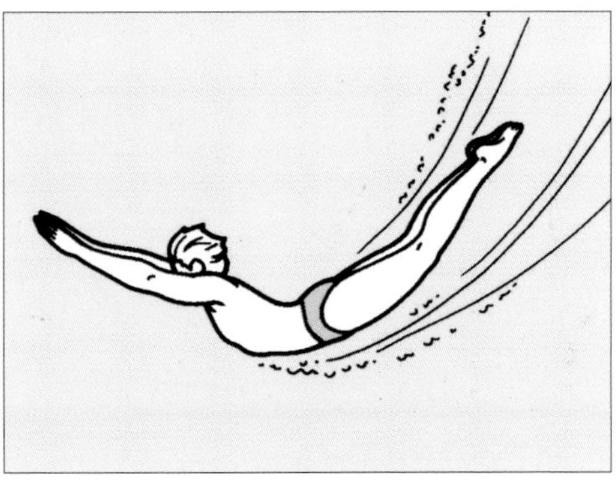

6 Once you're in the water, keep your body stretched out and arch your back backwards to steer towards the surface. If you've gone too deep, don't panic; open your eyes and swim up towards the light.

HOW TO MAKE A KITE

Kites originated in China, where they were first flown some 2,800 years ago. Nowadays, stunt kites can easily cost more than £200 apiece, but you can have as much fun with a cheap kite made from bamboo skewers and plastic bags. You can get the kids to decorate it, and you won't worry so much when it (inevitably) gets tangled up in a tree.

INDISPENSABLE THINGS

- 2 bamboo skewers
- Electrical tape or cotton thread
- 1 balloon stick
- Bin liner/refuse sack
- Felt-tip pen
- Insulation tape
- Scissors
- Plastic carrier bags
- Fish netting line

JOINING THE SKEWERS

To join the bamboo skewers together, overlap them by about 8–10cm (3–4in) and secure them with electrical tape or cotton thread. The crosspiece skewers should be joined with a 5cm (2in) length of balloon stick or similar to allow you to bend the joint slightly and create a 'dihedral' (i.e. curved wing) effect. Very sophisticated!

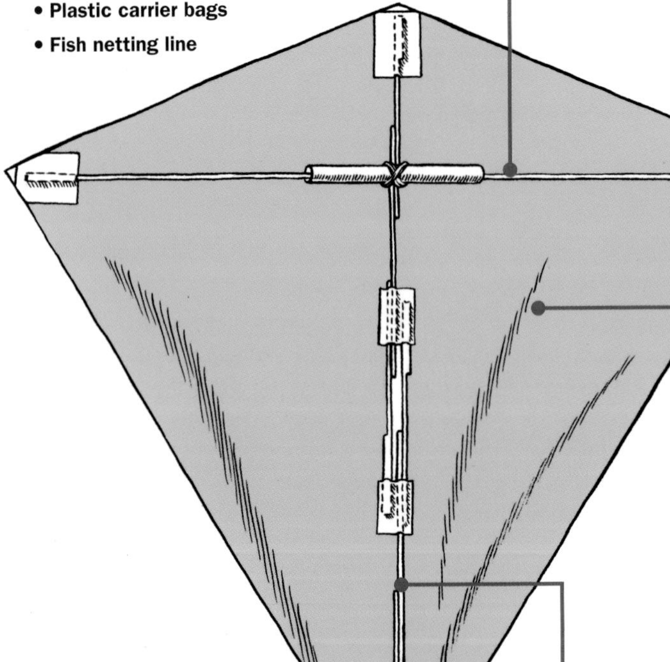

MAKING THE SAIL

To turn a bin liner into a sail, first cut it open and spread it out on the work surface. Lay the frame on top of it and mark out its extremities using a felt-tip pen. Join the points together with a straight edge and cut out the sail. Lay the frame over the plastic and secure the extremities with strips of insulation tape folded over each corner. Make sure the sail is stretched tightly over the frame.

MAKING THE TAIL

You can make a tail out of old shopping bags by cutting the bags in horizontal strips to create plastic rings. Loop the rings together until you have a tail four times the length of the kite.

MAKING THE FLYING LINE

Fish netting line makes ideal kite flying line. Make a harness by tying one length of string from top to bottom and another from side to side, leaving a little slack. Attach the flying line where the two cross. You'll need about 30m (100ft).

HOW TO SKIP STONES

Stone skipping (or skimming) is a serious business, as the many competitors who travelled to Scotland for the 2008 World Stone Skimming Championships will testify. Finding the right stone is crucial, but after that it's all about technique. Here's how to beat the current Guinness World Record of 51 skips.

ANGLE

The optimum angle for skipping is 20 degrees. The faster the stone hits the water and the more spin it has, the further it will go. Technique is more important than brute force; don't let your enthusiasm compromise the correct angle.

SMOOTH & CALM

The stone should be smooth and flat with well-rounded edges, and should fit comfortably in the palm of your hand. What's more, the water should be calm, if you can arrange it.

SKIPS

After extensive research, French scientist Lydéric Bocquet concluded that the maximum number of skips can be achieved by throwing a stone at an angle of 20 degrees, a speed of 12m (39ft) per second and a spin of 14 revolutions per second.

THROWING THE STONE

Hold the stone between your index finger and your thumb, with your other fingers loosely curled under it. Stand sideways to the water and curl your hand in towards your body. Snap your wrist and arm out at the same time, releasing the stone when your arm is fully extended. It's a bit like throwing a Frisbee.

INDISPENSABLE THINGS

- Smooth, flat stone
- Calm water

HOW TO JUGGLE THREE BALLS

If you can't wriggle your ears or make your eyes look in opposite directions, then juggling is a good substitute as a party trick. Anyone can do it. It's just a matter of persistence. Start with one ball, then add another, and another, and pretty soon you'll be juggling a whole crate of oranges. And if you can already wriggle your ears and make your eyes look in opposite directions, then juggling at the same time will impress your friends even more.

PRACTICAL TIP

If you don't have bean bags, you can try juggling tennis balls – although they are liable to bounce away when they're dropped. Some fruit works well, and if you practise in the garden it's less likely to get bashed when/if you drop it.

INDISPENSABLE THINGS

- Juggling balls
- Bean bags or fruit if you don't have juggling balls

A PRACTICAL HISTORY OF JUGGLING

The earliest evidence of juggling is on an ancient Egyptian tomb painting dating from c.1994-1781BC, which shows a line of dancers throwing balls. The past-time is still commonly practised in many Pacific islands, especially Tonga, where most schoolgirls learn to juggle at least four tui-tui nuts at a time. The record for beanbag juggling, as recognized by the International Jugglers' Association's Numbers Competition, is 10 beanbags for 23 catches, performed by Bruce Sarafian in 2001.

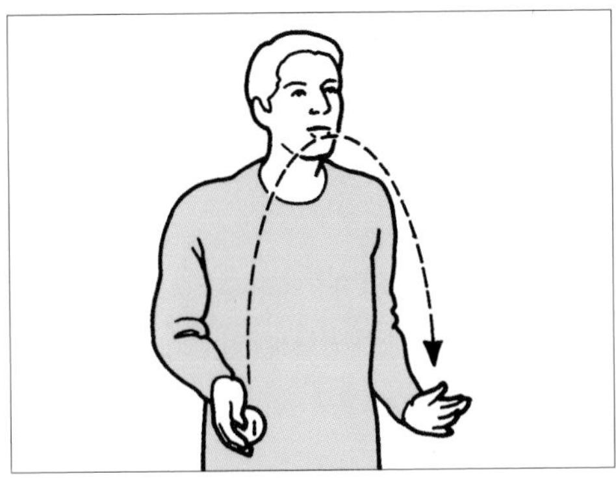

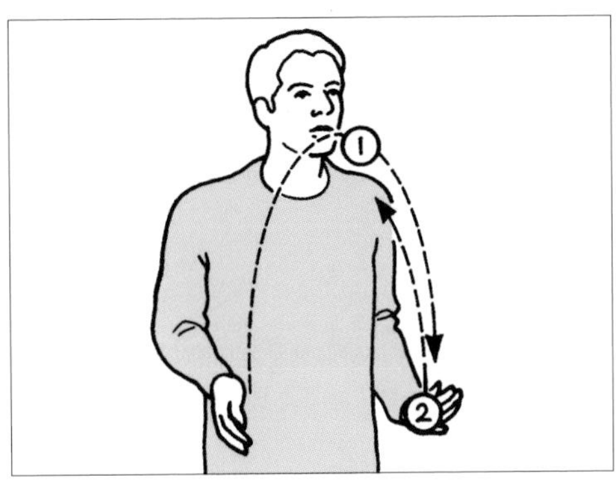

1 Practise first with one ball. Bean bags are ideal for beginners because they don't roll away when dropped, but try also tennis balls, fruit and chainsaws (just kidding!). Start with the dominant hand, throw the ball in an arc to eye height and keep your elbows tucked in.

2 Try it with two balls now. Start with one ball in each hand, and throw the ball in your dominant hand (ball 1) in an arc. When it reaches eye height, toss the ball in the subordinate hand (ball 2) *under* ball 1. Catch the balls and stop. Repeat the exercise, starting with the opposite hand.

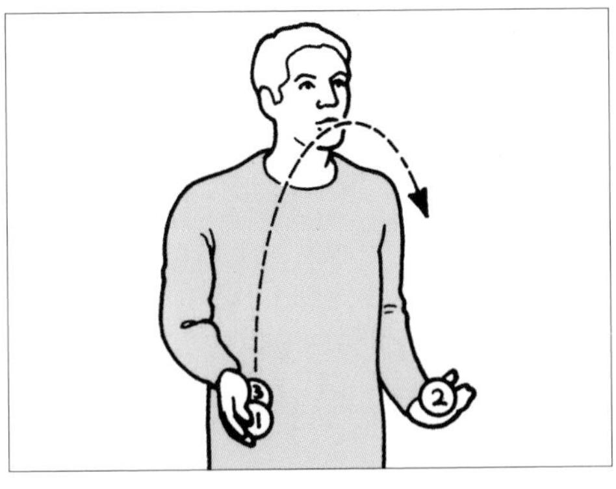

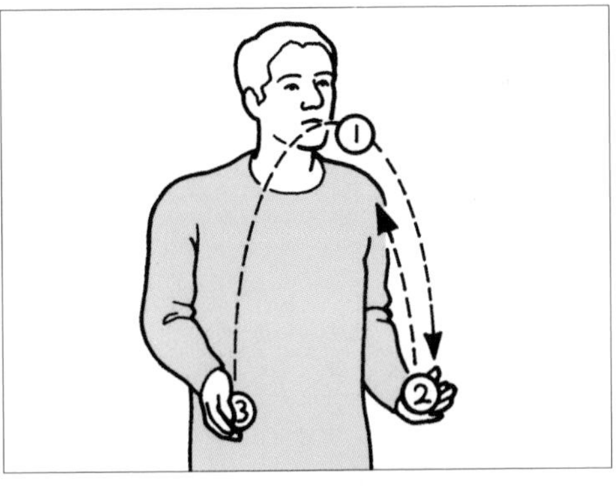

3 Now for the real thing: juggling three balls. Hold two balls (balls 1 and 3) in your dominant hand and one (ball 2) in the subordinate hand. Throw the front ball in your dominant hand (ball 1) in an arc.

4 When ball 1 reaches the top of its arc (i.e. eye height), you need to throw ball 2 *under* ball 1, and then catch ball 1 with your subordinate hand.

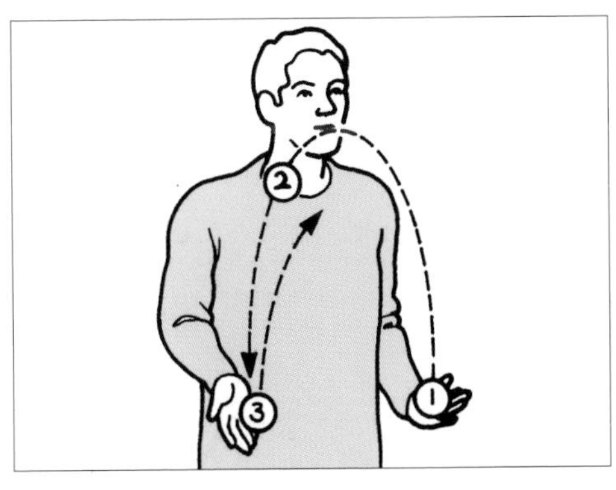

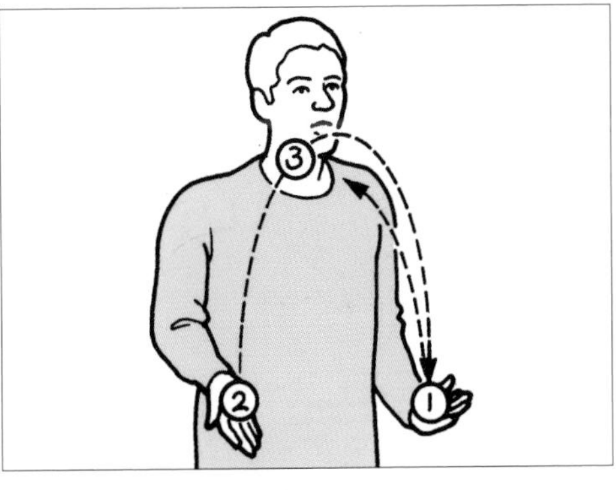

5 When ball 2 reaches the top of its arc, throw the remaining ball in the dominant hand (ball 3) *under* ball 2. You can make things easier by rolling ball 3 down onto your fingers before throwing it. Catch ball 2 with your dominant hand.

6 When ball 3 is at the top of its arc, toss ball 1, which is now in your subordinate hand. Keep going! Don't be discouraged if you drop the balls. Even Marcel Marceau dropped his balls to start with.

HOW TO SHUFFLE A PACK OF CARDS

Can you do the Hindu shuffle? Or even the Corgi, Faro or Mongean shuffles? Nor can most people. There are dozens of ways of shuffling cards, all of which have the same objective: to rearrange the pack in a random order. But if there's one shuffle you should learn it's the riffle shuffle. Not only does it look good, it's surprisingly easy.

INDISPENSABLE THINGS

- Pack of cards
- Table (or lap)

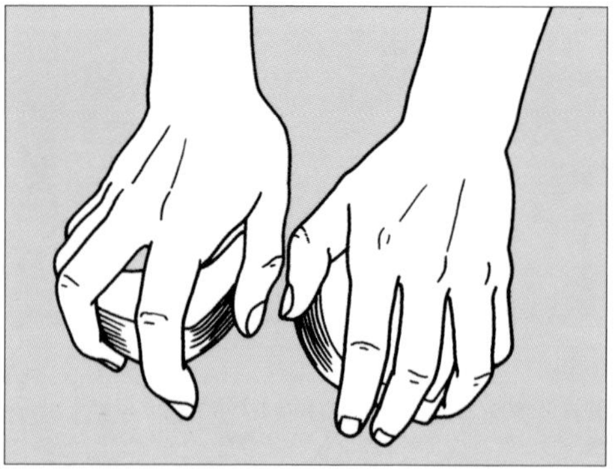

1 Divide the pack into two roughly even piles. Hold one pile in each hand, facing downwards, with the thumbs gripping the ends. Lever the ends up with your thumbs and line them up so that your thumbs are nearly touching.

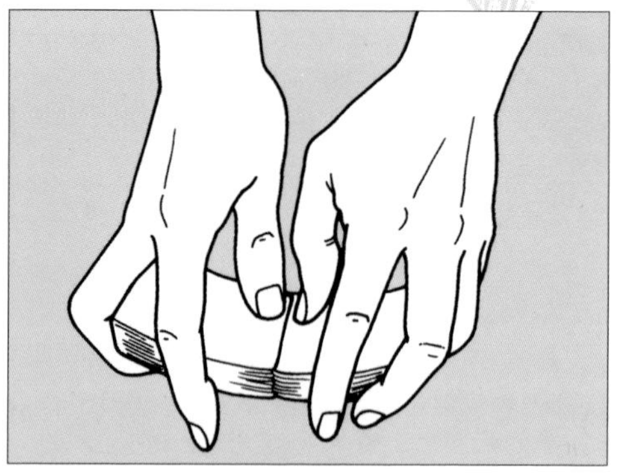

2 Riffle the cards together by slowly sliding your thumbs up the edge of each pile, alternating between piles if possible (in practice, this will happen without you even trying). This can be done on a table or, with practice, on your knee.

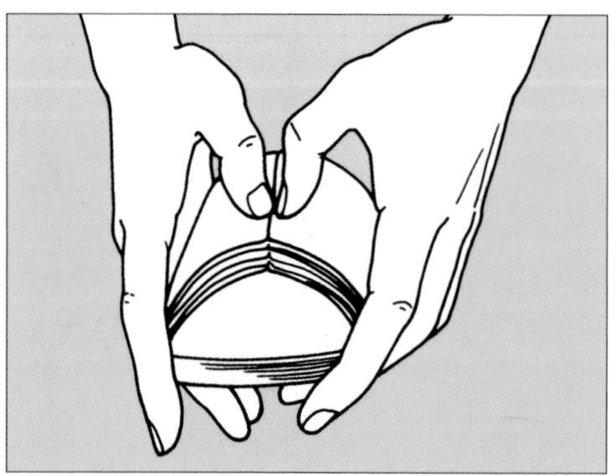

3 Make sure the piles interlock enough to be secure. Now perform the cascade finish. Bend the cards together, pushing upwards slightly with your fingers and using your thumbs to prevent them spilling.

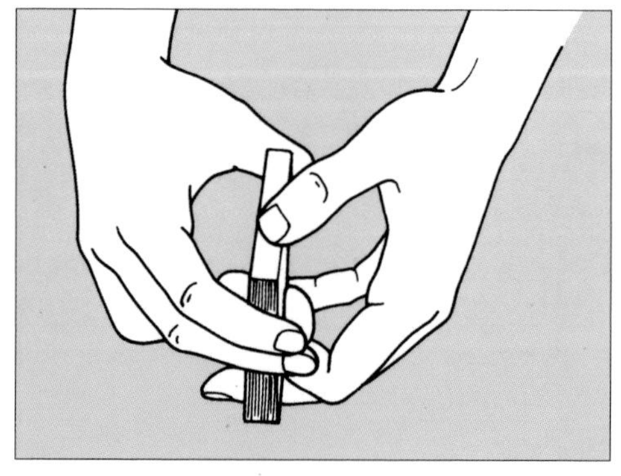

4 Square up the deck by tapping it gently on a hard surface. Shuffle again if necessary. You'll need to shuffle seven times to completely randomize the pack – although two or three times is usually sufficient for most purposes.

HOW TO SCORE TENNIS

'You have got to be kidding!' This famous exclamation by three-times Wimbledon champion John McEnroe sums up how many non-tennis people feel when someone tries to explain how to score the game. Yet, once you've accepted the concept of 'love' being a valid score (i.e. zero), it's all just strawberries and cream.

INDISPENSABLE THINGS

- Notebook
- Good memory

SETS

A match is made up of several 'sets' of games: up to five sets for men and three sets for women. The winner is the first person to win more than half the sets, i.e. the first man to win three sets or the first woman to win two sets.

POINTS

Each game is made up of a number of points. The first player to win four points and be at least two points ahead of his/her opponent wins the game. The scoring sequence is as follows: 0 points = love; 1 point = 15; 2 points = 30; 3 points = 40. If both players reach 40, this is described as 'deuce'. The next player to win a point is said to have the 'advantage'. If this player wins the next point, he/she wins the game. If the other player wins the next point, the score returns to deuce, and they play on until one player has two clear points.

GAMES

Each set is made up of a number of games. The winner of each set is the first to win at least six games and be two games ahead of his or her opponent. If the score reaches 6–5, then a further game is played. If the leading player wins this game, he/she wins the set by 7–5; if the trailing player wins this game, the score goes to 6–6 and a tie-break is played. The winner of the tie-break wins the set. In the UK, no tie-break is played in the final set of a match.

HOW TO PLAY ROULETTE

Roulette has been around since the 17th century and is a lot more sophisticated than playing the one-arm bandits down the arcade. True, the pace is slower than craps or blackjack, which means you're likely to win less. On the other hand – and perhaps more realistically – it also means you'll have less time to lose all your money.

INDISPENSABLE THINGS

- Roulette wheel and layout
- Chips
- Roulette ball
- Dolly (winning number marker)

CHIPS

Special chips are used for roulette, with different colours for each player. At the end of the game, the chips are exchanged for regular casino chips, which can be exchanged for cash at the cage. Each table has a maximum and minimum bet.

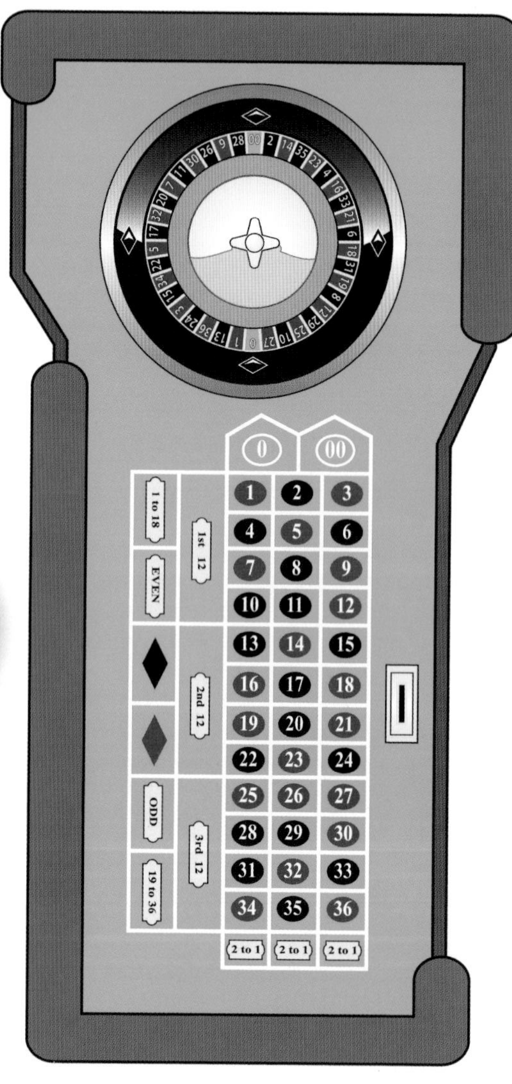

INDISPENSABLE ROULETTE TABLE

Roulette is played at a long table with a wheel at one end, and a layout where the bets are placed. The wheel has 37 numbered slots (38 in the US), which correspond to numbers on the layout. The layout itself is made up of two parts: the 'inside' area (usually red and black) and the 'outside' area (usually green).

CROUPIER

A croupier (in Europe) or a dealer (in the US) spins the ball around the wheel. Once the ball has settled in a slot, the dealer places a marker (known as a 'dolly') on top on the corresponding number on the layout and proceeds to collect the losing bets and pay out the winners.

INSIDE BETS

Straight up: a bet on one number. Place your chip directly on the number. Pays 35:1.
Split: a bet on two numbers. Place your chip on the line between the two numbers. Pays 17:1.
Street: a bet on a row of numbers. Place your chip on the line at the end of a short horizontal row. Pays 11:1.
Corner: a bet on four numbers. Place your chip at the interjunction of the four numbers. Pays 8:1.
Double street: a bet on two rows of numbers (i.e. six in total). Place your chip on the line at the end of the short horizontal row, straddling two rows. Pays 5:1.

ZERO

In some casinos, if the ball stops at '0', the 'house' collects. American roulette has an additional '00', which increases the odds in favour of the house.

OUTSIDE BETS

Red or black: a bet on the ball landing on either red or black. Pays 1:1.
Odd or even: a bet on the ball landing on either odd or even numbers. Pays 1:1.
1 to 18 and 19 to 36: bets on the ball stopping at either set of numbers. Pays 1:1.
Dozens: bets on the ball stopping at 1 to 12, 13 to 24 or 25 to 36. Pays 2:1.
Columns: bets on the ball stopping at a number in one of the three long vertical columns. Pays 2:1.

HOW TO PLAY BLACKJACK

Blackjack has been around for at least 400 years and has become massively popular in recent years thanks to the explosion in online gambling. So what is a blackjack, and do you need to get one to win the game? And why are you allowed to hit in the game, but you're not allowed to tap the table by mistake?

INDISPENSABLE THINGS

- Pack of cards
- 6–7 players
- Chips

THE CARDS

At start of play, each player receives two cards, face down if played with one pack, face up if played with two packs or more (i.e. most casinos). The dealer also deals him- or herself two cards; one face up, the other face down. The 2–10 cards are valued at their face value, irrespective of suit or colour. Face cards (jack, queen, king) are worth 10 points. Aces are worth 1 or 11 points, at the player's discretion.

BLACKJACK

Blackjack (also called 21) is played at a semi-circular table, with a dealer and 6–7 players. Bets are placed before play begins, by putting chips in the designated spot in front of each player.

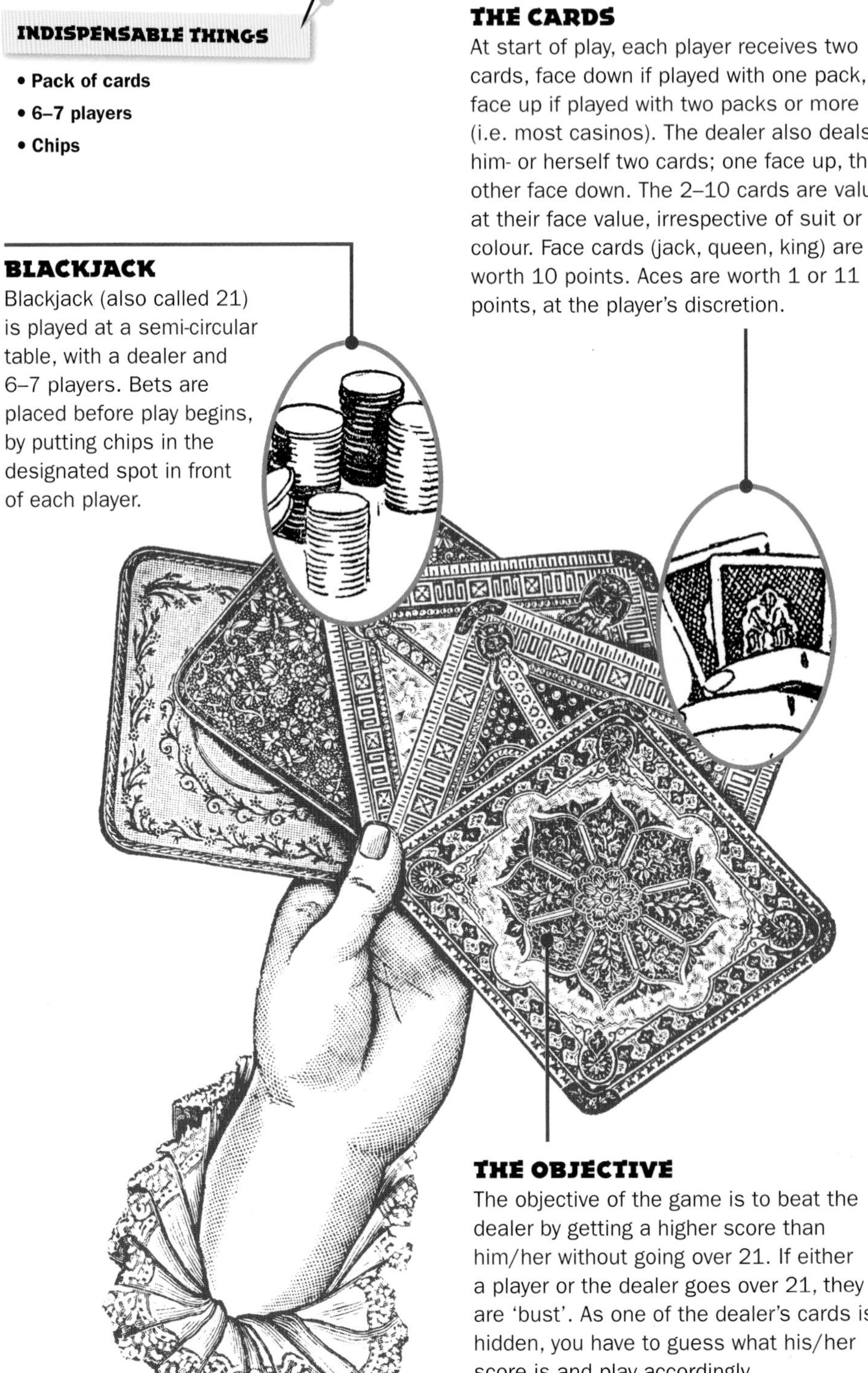

THE OBJECTIVE

The objective of the game is to beat the dealer by getting a higher score than him/her without going over 21. If either a player or the dealer goes over 21, they are 'bust'. As one of the dealer's cards is hidden, you have to guess what his/her score is and play accordingly.

INDISPENSABLE OPTIONS

Once the first two cards are dealt, players have several options:

- BLACKJACK You receive an ace and a 10-point card, giving you 21 points – that is, a blackjack or a 'natural' – and win. If the dealer also has a blackjack, it's a 'push', and no one wins. If only the dealer has a blackjack, all the players lose.
- HITTING You want another card. Signal to the dealer by tapping the table with a card (or, if cards are face up, tapping the table).
- STANDING You are content with your hand and wish to 'stand'. Signal to the dealer by sliding your cards under your bet (or, if cards are face up, by waving one hand horizontally).
- SURRENDER You give up your hand and lose half your bet.
- DOUBLING DOWN You double your bet by placing extra chips next to your original bet. You must now 'hit', but you can only do so once.
- SPLIT HAND You have two identical cards, so you split them and play them as two hands. Place a second bet, equal to the first, next to the new hand.
- INSURANCE If the dealer's 'up' card is an ace, you can make an additional bet, using half the chips you've already placed, that the 'down' card is a ten. That way, if the dealer does get a blackjack, you have a consolation prize.

HOW TO CALCULATE ODDS

It's one thing to pretend you're James Bond in the casino, but if you don't understand odds, then you'll never outwit the baddies. It's the same if you go to the races or gamble on your favourite football team. Thanks to our indispensable payouts table, you don't need to be a mathematician.

INDISPENSABLE ODDS

- **Killed in car crash: 1 in 5,000**
- **Struck by lightning: 1 in 700,000**
- **Killed in plane crash: 1 in 11 million**
- **Winning the lottery: 1 in 14 million**

INDISPENSABLE PAYOUTS

Payouts based on £10 (including original stake):

Odds	Payout	Odds	Payout	Odds	Payout
50/1	£510	5/1	£60	3/2	£25
35/1	£360	9/2	£55	7/5	£24
30/1	£310	4/1	£50	6/5	£22
20/1	£210	7/2	£45	1/1	£20
17/1	£180	3/1	£40	4/5	£18
15/1	£160	5/2	£35	3/5	£16
11/1	£120	2/1	£30	1/2	£15
10/1	£110	9/5	£28	2/5	£14
8/1	£90	8/5	£26	1/5	£12
6/1	£70				

The basic formula to calculate the payoff is as follows:

$$\frac{(\text{stake x first number in the odds}) + (\text{stake x second number in the odds})}{\text{second number in the odds}}$$

ODDS AGAINST

Most odds are 'odds against'. That means the bookmaker is gambling on the probability of the event not happening. The number on the left is therefore bigger than the number on the right, e.g. 5/2.

ODDS ON

'Odds on' means the bookie thinks the event is more likely to happen than not and is effectively challenging you to bet that it won't happen. The number on the right is bigger than the number on the left, e.g. 2/5.

EVEN ODDS

'Even odds' means that the bookie will pay out the same amount as the person bet. The numbers are the same on both sides, i.e. 1/1.

HOW TO WIN AT MONOPOLY

No one really takes Monopoly seriously, do they? Wrong! As anyone who's spent rainy Sunday afternoons in with their family knows, it is a vicious game played (if that's the right word) to the death. Learn the odds and never again be the one storming out of the room in a temper.

INDISPENSABLE ODDS

- **Monopoly board game**

HOT PROPERTIES

Collect orange and red properties. Because of their position on the board, they receive the most visitors and provide the best return on your investment. Don't bother with blue, yellow and green – unless it prevents your opponents from completing a set. Buy stations; avoid utilities.

GET OUT OF JAIL

Pay to get out of jail during the first part of the game, when you need to collect properties; stay in jail later when moving around is riskier.

POPULAR SQUARES

The most visited squares on the board are: Trafalgar Square, Vine Street, Fenchurch Street Station and King's Cross Station. The least visited are: Old Kent Road and Whitechapel.

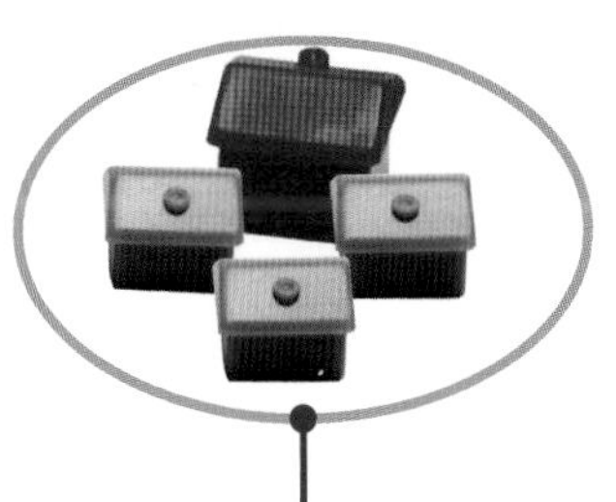

HOUSES

The optimum number of houses to have is three. Create a housing shortage by building three or four houses on each property, instead of building hotels.

ODDS

Remember the odds. You are most likely to throw 7 and least likely to throw 2 or 12. The order of probability, with the most likely outcome first, is: 7, 6 and 8 (equally probable), 5 and 9, 4 and 10, 3 and 11, and 2 and 12. On average it takes around five turns to get back to 'Go'.

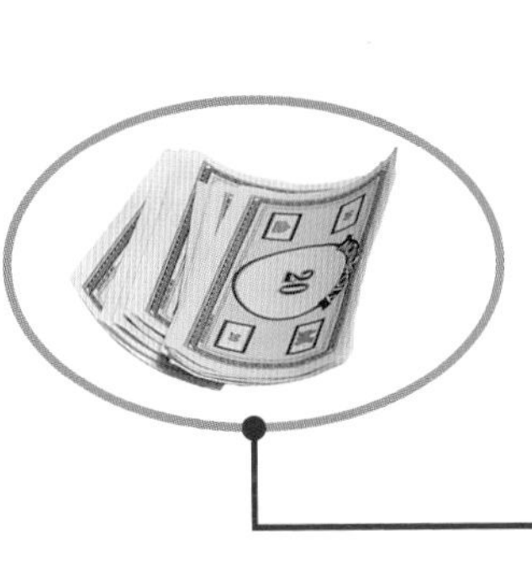

BUY

Buy as much as you can early in the game to build up your earning power quickly. Aim to complete as many sets as possible.

HOW TO ROLL A JOINT

According to Bill Clinton, it's not necessary to inhale to enjoy marijuana, but how is a joint rolled? Just in case you find yourself in the company of a former US president and he asks for a demo, this is how it's done.

INDISPENSABLE THINGS

- Cigarette papers
- Herb of choice
- Card

INDISPENSABLE WARNING

The publisher does not condone illegal activity of any kind. Cannabis consumption is illegal in most countries, including the UK. Some studies have found that excessive use of cannabis, particularly by young people, can increase the chances of mental illness.

1 Take a lump of your herb of choice and break it up into small fragments. Remove any bits of twig as they are not potent and create lumps. Put seeds aside for future gardening projects.

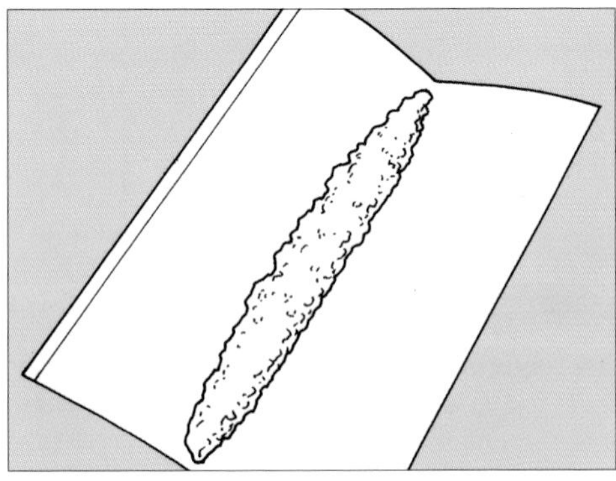

2 Sprinkle the herb down the centre of the paper. If it's that stronger European herb, you'll need to thin it down with some tobacco – a 60:40 tobacco:herb ratio is recommended.

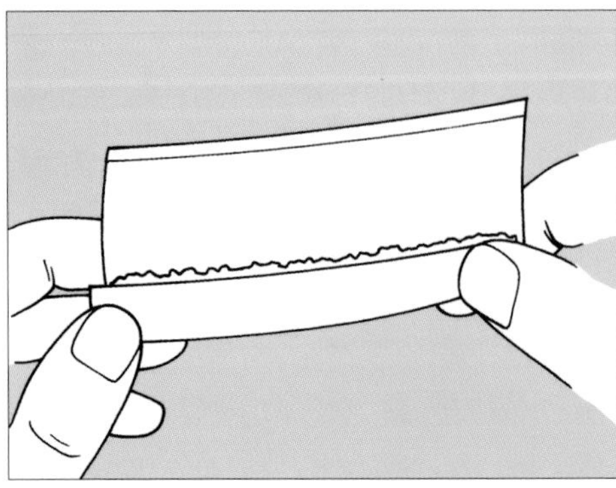

3 Roll a short length of card into a cylinder to create a 'roach' about 2cm (¾in) long. The roach doesn't work as a filter, but it does prevent the end of the joint dissolving – saving every last bit of herb.

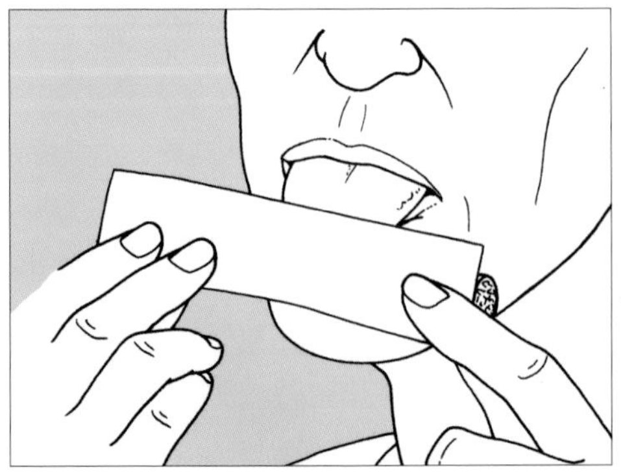

4 With the gum strip facing you, pick the joint up and roll it between your thumb and index finger. Once the contents feel firm, tuck the side nearest you under and roll the other side over it. Lick the gum strip and seal the joint. Enjoy!

IN THE WILD

There's no better way to put life back in perspective than to spend a few days living in the great outdoors. Leave behind your camping gear and you'll learn survival skills that will bring you even closer to nature. And you never know when you might need that.

HOW TO TIE A ROUND TURN & TWO HALF HITCHES

Pick up a book of knots and you'll find so many knots on offer you might not know where to start. But, if you only ever learn one knot, learn this one. It's easy to tie, it can be used in a multitude of situations, and it's much stronger than might at first appear. Lash the loose, 'working' end to the 'standing' part and it'll never come loose. Good for ocean liners, tow ropes and tree swings alike.

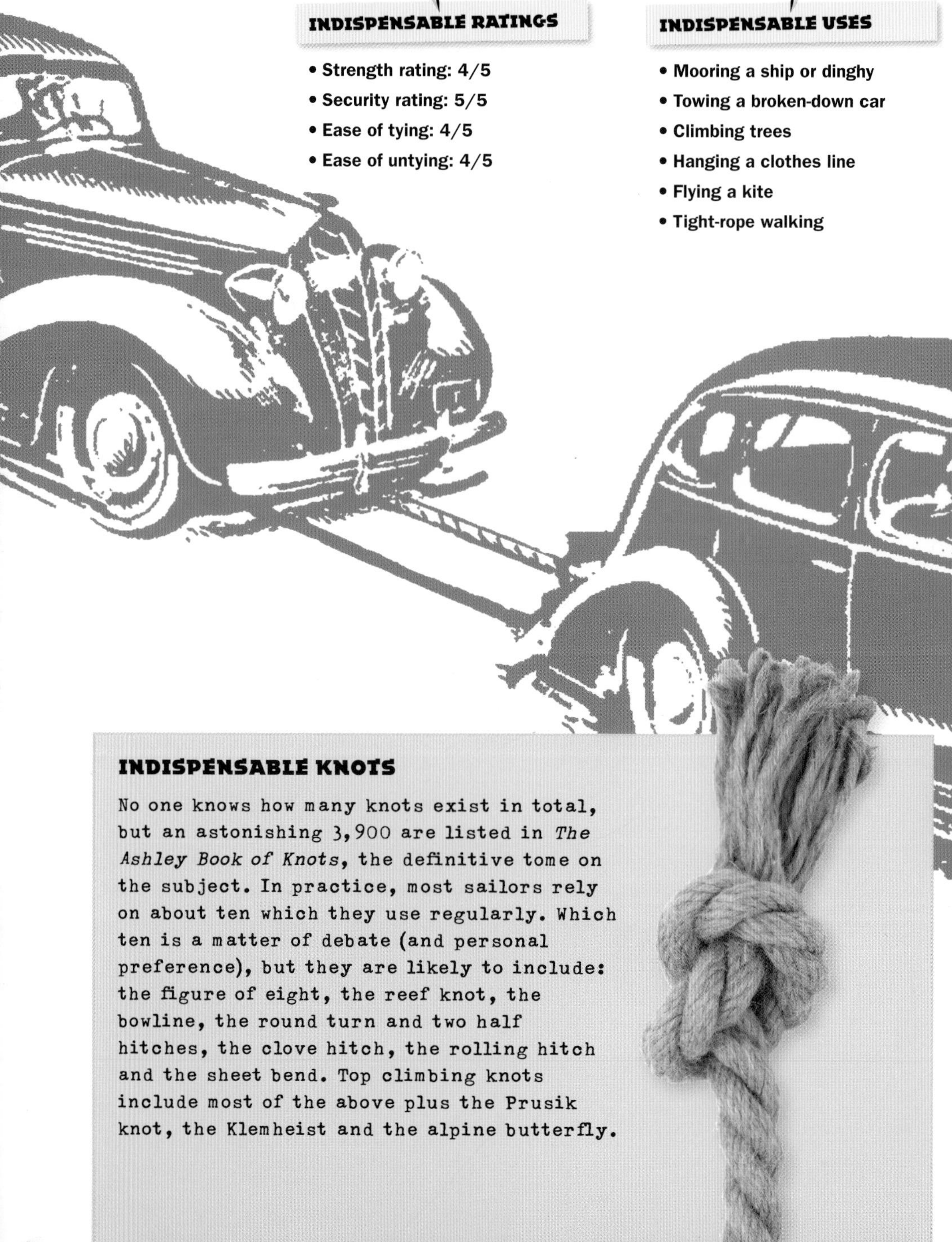

INDISPENSABLE RATINGS

- Strength rating: 4/5
- Security rating: 5/5
- Ease of tying: 4/5
- Ease of untying: 4/5

INDISPENSABLE USES

- Mooring a ship or dinghy
- Towing a broken-down car
- Climbing trees
- Hanging a clothes line
- Flying a kite
- Tight-rope walking

INDISPENSABLE KNOTS

No one knows how many knots exist in total, but an astonishing 3,900 are listed in *The Ashley Book of Knots*, the definitive tome on the subject. In practice, most sailors rely on about ten which they use regularly. Which ten is a matter of debate (and personal preference), but they are likely to include: the figure of eight, the reef knot, the bowline, the round turn and two half hitches, the clove hitch, the rolling hitch and the sheet bend. Top climbing knots include most of the above plus the Prusik knot, the Klemheist and the alpine butterfly.

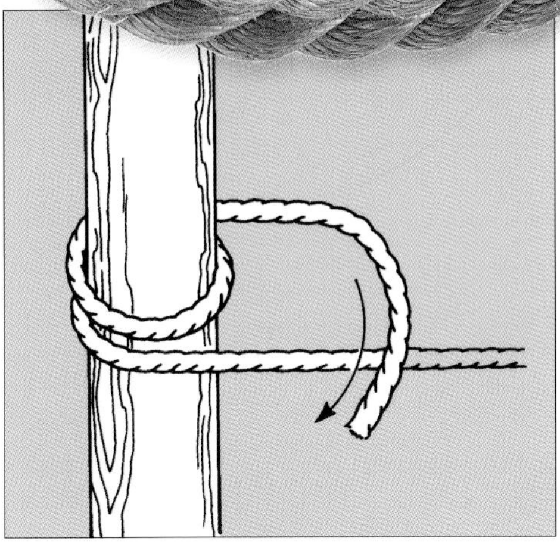

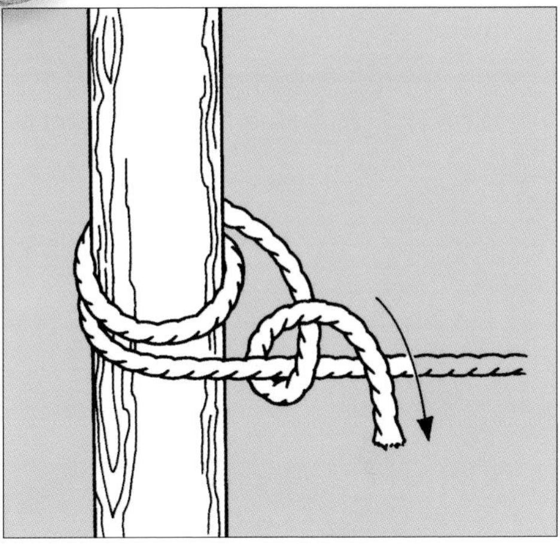

1 Take a turn around the post, rail or whatever it is that will provide the anchorage for the rope. Note that the end of the rope actively involved in tying the knot is called the 'working end', while the other extremity is the 'standing end' and the bit in between is the 'standing part'.

2 Pass the working end over and around the standing part, and tuck it under itself to form the first hitch. The number of turns and hitches you use depends on how great a load is being secured. Generally, more turns help spread the load, while more hitches prevent the knot loosening.

3 Keep going in the same direction to create the second hitch. It's important that the working end goes around the standing part in the same direction (clockwise or anti-clockwise) for every hitch.

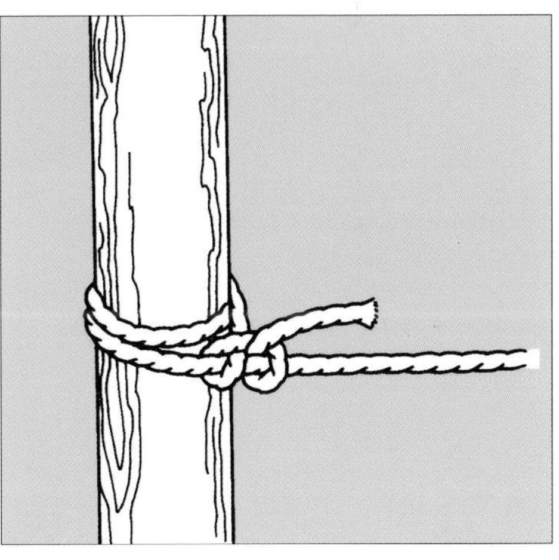

4 Once both hitches have been tied, tighten the knot by pulling the working end and the standing part in opposite directions. Any slack in the knot can be taken up either by pulling the standing part or feeding the slack through the hitches before final tightening.

HOW TO TIE A BOWLINE

There's something beautifully ingenious about a bowline. Of course there are simpler ways to tie a loop, but the bowline is one of those clever knots that uses the strain on the rope to increase its strength – so the greater the load, the tighter the knot. And yet, no matter how tight it gets, it can always be undone. What's more, there's a simple trick for remembering how to tie it, which involves a rabbit, a tree and a hole.

INDISPENSABLE USES

- Mooring any size of craft
- Rescue operations
- Start point for lashing a parcel
- Preventing a sail being 'taken aback' (see below)
- Tying a leash to a collar

INDISPENSABLE RATINGS

- Strength rating: 3/5
- Security rating: 3/5
- Ease of tying: 3/5
- Ease of untying: 4/5

A PRACTICAL HISTORY OF THE BOWLINE

The bowline takes its name from its usage on the great square-riggers during the age of sail. A line was attached from the top of a square sail to the front, or 'bow', of the boat to prevent the sail being blown inside out – or, in nautical terms, being 'taken aback'. The earliest mention of the knot is in *A Seaman's Grammar* written by John Smith in 1627, which refers to a bowline being found in the rigging of the ancient Egyptian Pharaoh Cheops' 'solar ship' during its excavation. The real age of the knot is therefore likely to be several thousand years.

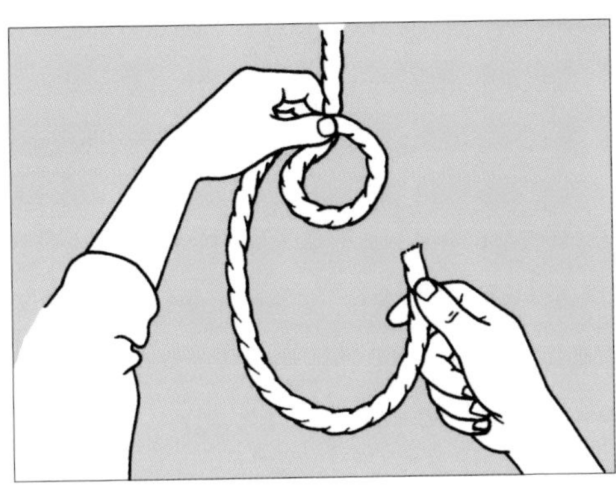

1 Create a loop in the rope, making sure that the line nearest the 'working end' (i.e. the active end of the rope) is on top of the loop. This is the rabbit hole, and the inactive, or 'standing', part of the rope (at the top of the illustration) is the tree.

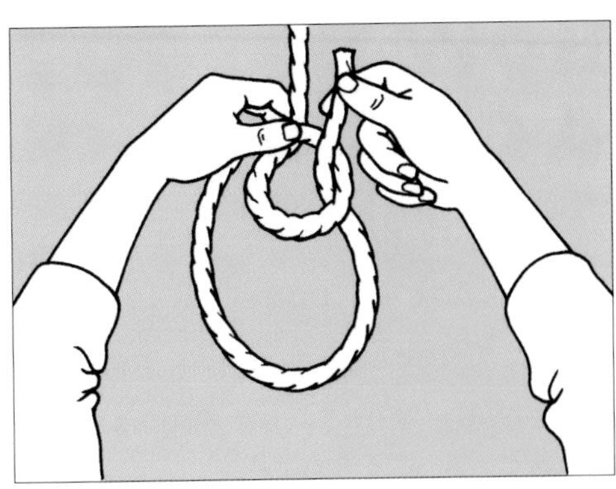

2 Pass the 'working end' up through the loop. This is our rabbit popping up out of its hole to say hello.

3 Pass the 'working end' around behind the 'standing part'. This is our rabbit running around the back of the tree.

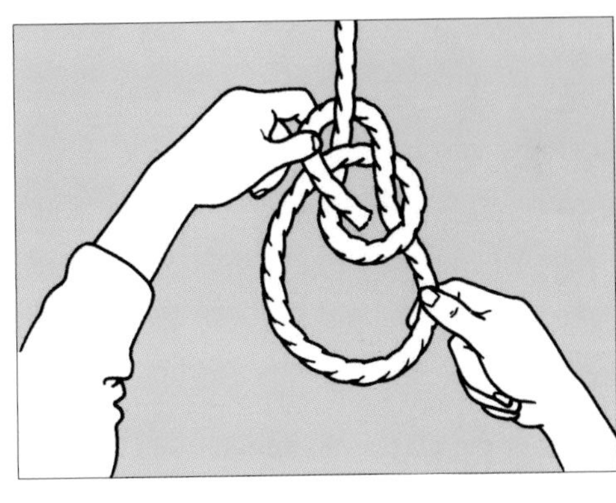

4 Insert the 'working end' back into the initial loop. This is our rabbit diving back down its hole – perhaps having spotted an approaching fox.

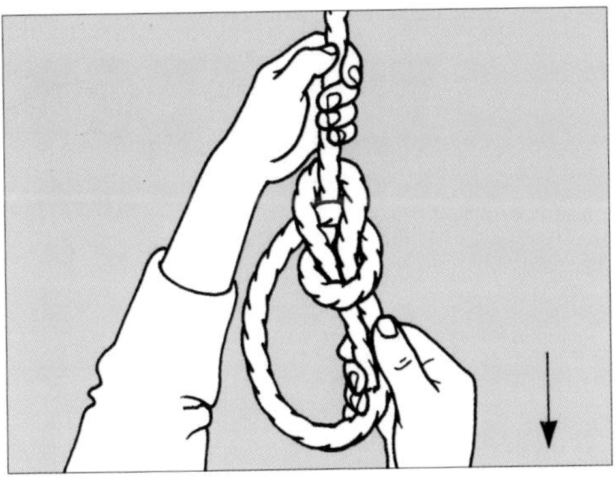

5 To tighten the knot, pull the 'working end' and the rope adjacent to it in the hole with one hand, while pulling on the standing part with the other hand. This is our rabbit snuggling down in its hole. To untie the knot, 'break' it open by feeding the 'standing' part through the top loop.

HOW NOT TO TIE A GRANNY KNOT

We've got nothing against grannies, but if you don't want your knot to come undone, then please don't use a granny knot. There's almost no difference between a granny and a proper reef, or 'square', knot – except that one holds and one doesn't! Learn the difference and forever keep your shoelaces tied up and your mainsail reefed.

1 The simple rule to remember when you're tying this is: left over right followed by right over left (or vice versa, if you like – it will end up the same). Then pull the ends in opposite directions to tighten the knot. The key is that the working ends should come out snugly next to their adjacent 'standing' parts, with a loop resting over both of them.

2 This is how NOT to do it. The granny knot is made by going left over right followed by left over right (or right over left followed by right over left). This results in the working ends coming out next to the opposite standing parts, which can lead to all manner of trouble: from shoelaces coming undone to parcels opening in the post and sails shaking loose. Heaven forbid!

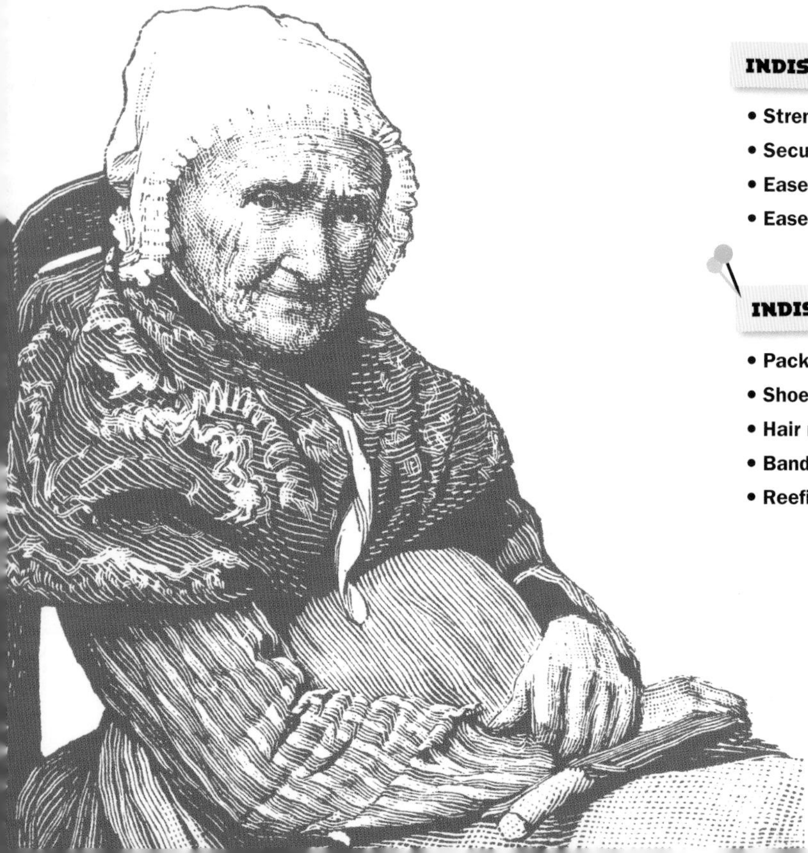

INDISPENSABLE RATINGS

- **Strength rating: 3/5**
- **Security rating: 3/5**
- **Ease of tying: 5/5**
- **Ease of untying: 5/5**

INDISPENSABLE USES

- **Packages**
- **Shoelaces**
- **Hair ribbon**
- **Bandages**
- **Reefing pennants on sails**

HOW TO TIE A ROPE HARNESS

Not everyone is happy to climb hand-over-hand down a rope – never mind up one. Lowering (or lifting) someone on a loop such as a bowline is one answer. An even better solution is a double-loop knot, such as the bowline in the bight, where one loop can be used to support the person's bottom and the other to support their chest.

INDISPENSABLE RATINGS

- Strength rating: 4/5
- Security rating: 5/5
- Ease of tying: 3/5
- Ease of untying: 3/5

INDISPENSABLE USES

- Rescue
- Climbing
- Child's swing
- Bosun's chair
- Hanging shelves

1 First off, make sure the rope is strong enough – test it by hanging off a tree, where there's less chance of getting seriously hurt if it breaks. Start the knot by doubling it – either just at one end or the whole thing. Then make a loop in the rope, allowing plenty of slack to make the 'chair', and pass the doubled-up end of the rope up through the loop.

2 So far, so much just like an ordinary bowline, but this knot is even easier to tie than that. Simply open the doubled-up end and pass the large loop through it.

3 Once the doubled-up end has passed right around the loop, pull it down tight over the 'standing' part to secure the knot. Before you finally tighten it, adjust the size of the two loops so that they pass around the thighs and chest.

HOW TO SPLICE ROPE

There are many ways to join two lengths of rope — nearly all of them much quicker and easier than splicing. But if you want a permanent join that won't snag on things when the rope is in use and will be almost invisible, then a splice is the way to go. You'll also have the satisfaction of continuing a tradition which goes back to Lord Nelson and beyond. Please note this only applies to three-strand rope, and not to modern multi-strand cordage.

INDISPENSABLE USES

- Sailing
- Climbing
- Tree swings
- Mooring lines
- Escape lines

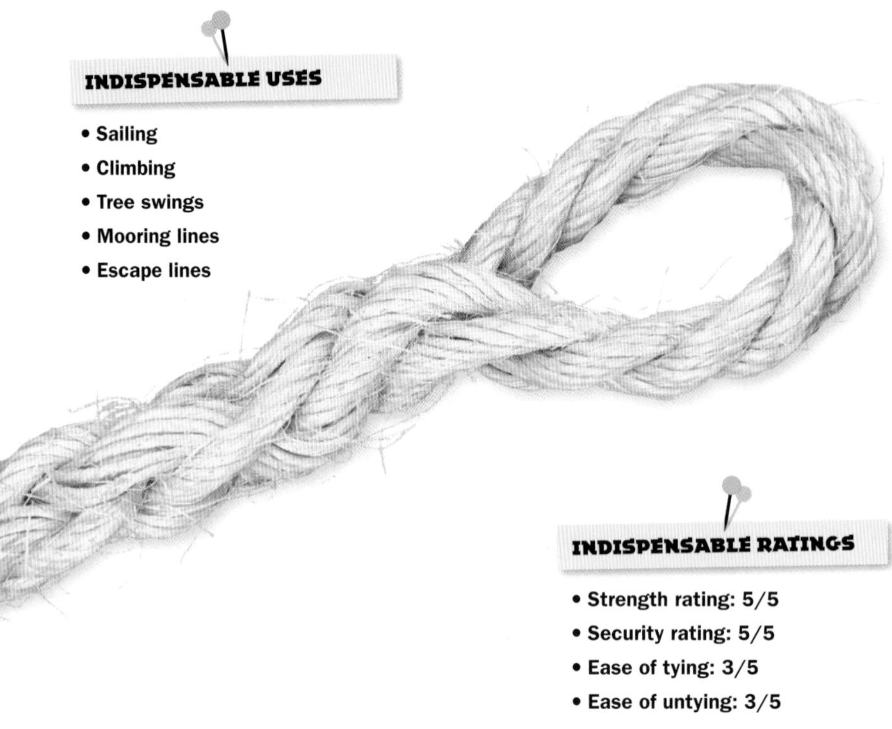

INDISPENSABLE RATINGS

- Strength rating: 5/5
- Security rating: 5/5
- Ease of tying: 3/5
- Ease of untying: 3/5

A PRACTICAL HISTORY OF THE MAINBRACE

The braces are hefty ropes that were used to control the angle of the sails on a square-rigged sailing ship. The main brace is the heftiest of them all and, if damaged in battle, required considerable skill and effort to repair with a splice.

A successful splice was often rewarded with an extra ration of rum and, in time, the expression 'splice the mainbrace' became a euphemism for issuing a round of drinks. Bottoms up!

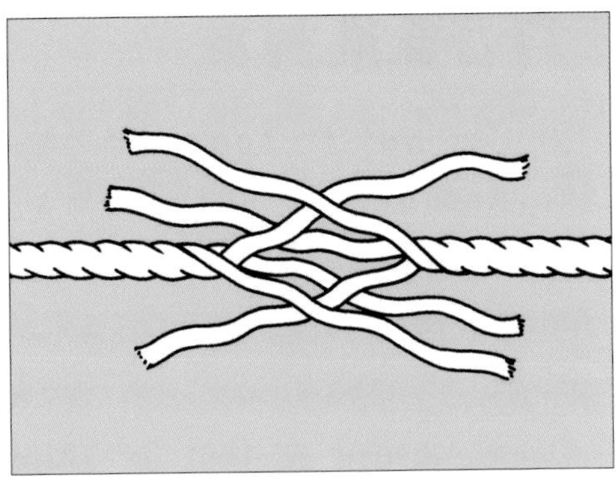

1 First, unlay the ends of both ropes by a few centimetres. Bring them together, so that the strands of one alternate with the strands of the other. If the ends continue to unravel, seize (bind) them with a short length of electric tape or twine.

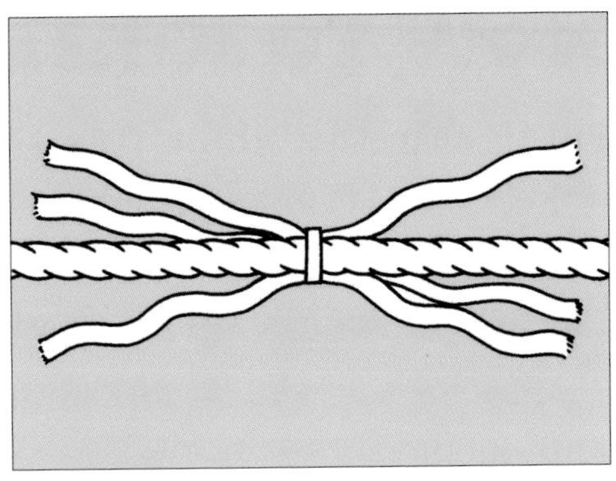

2 When the two ropes are snugly entwined, seize the joint with a short length of electric tape or twine to prevent it working loose while you are splicing. This seizing can be removed once the splice is completed.

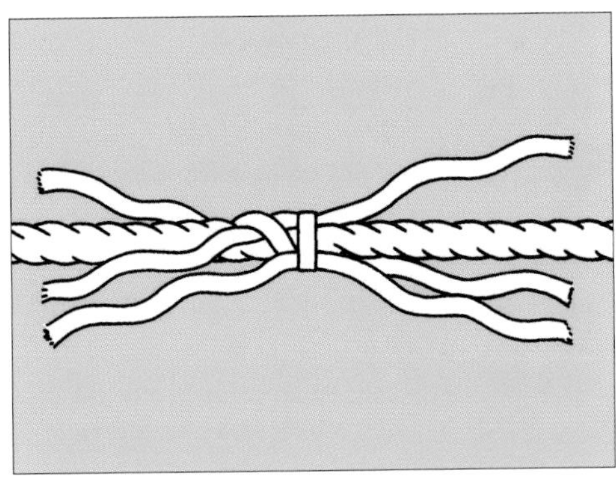

3 Pick any strand, pass it over the adjoining strand of the opposite rope and tuck it under the next strand. Work against the twist of the rope so that the strands are almost at right angles to one another.

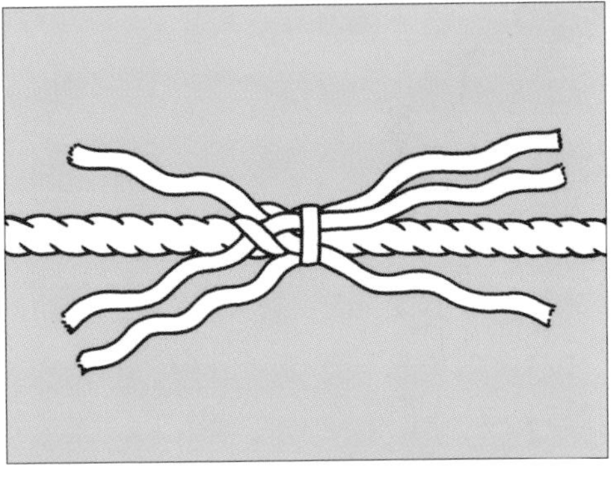

4 Take the next untucked strand and pass it over and under the adjoining strand of the opposite rope, as before. Use a letter opener or similar (e.g. a marlin spike, if you've got one!) to tease the strands apart.

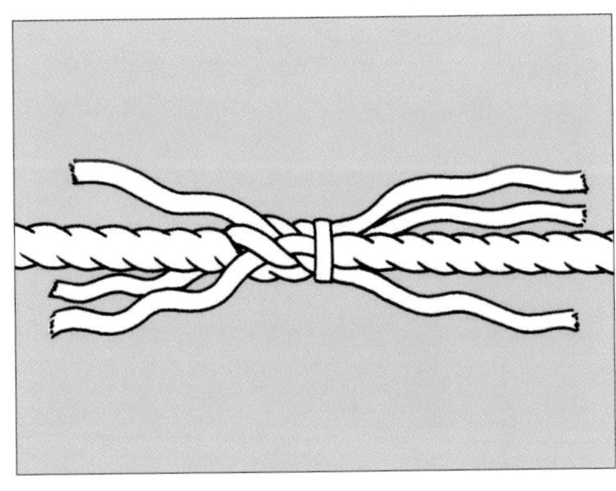

5 Take the remaining untucked strand and pass it over and under, as before. You should end up with three strands of one rope emerging between three strands of the opposite rope.

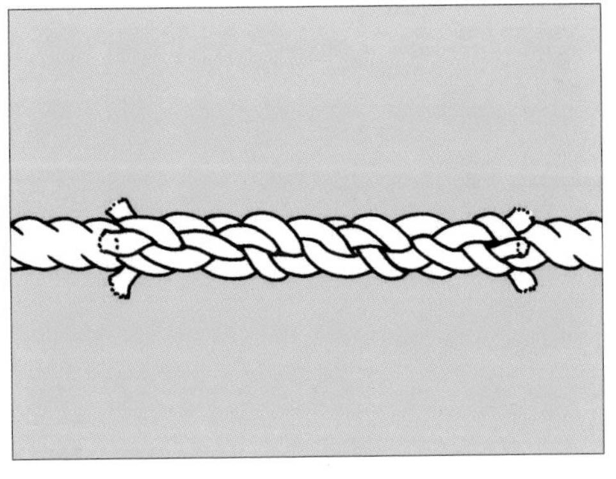

6 Take another tuck with each strand, before starting work on the untucked strands of the other rope. Keep going until each strand is tucked at least three times (four times for synthetic rope). Roll the splice underneath your foot, and trim the ends of the strands.

HOW TO IGNITE A FLAME

Being able to light a fire when you're out in the wild can make the difference between life and death. But what to do if your lighter has run out of gas and your matches have gone soggy? Rubbing wire wool against the terminals of a torch battery should produce a spark or two, and gunpowder from a bullet will quickly get a fire going. Alternatively, you can try more traditional methods.

INDISPENSABLE THINGS

- Length of wood
- Knife or rock for cutting
- Wooden spindle
- String
- Cane/wood for bow
- Wood, stone or bone for socket
- Tinder/bark (*see page 234*)
- Wooden shaft
- Flint
- Penknife (or other steel tool)
- Lens (from camera, binoculars, magnifying glass, spectacles)

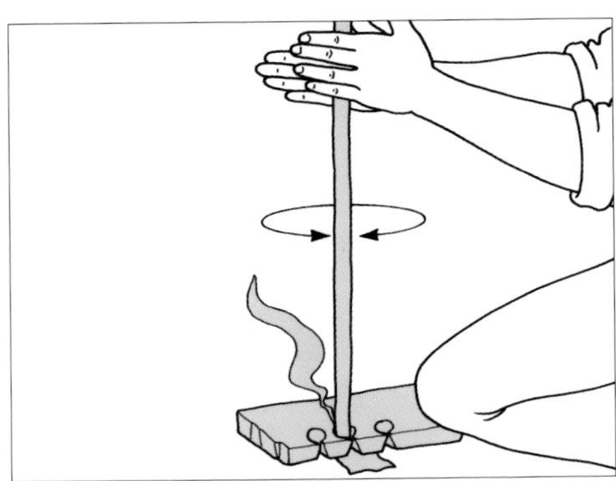

1 A hand drill works best with dry, soft wood. Cut a V-shaped notch in a board using a knife or rock. Stand a 60cm (2ft) long spindle over the notch. Spin it between your hands, pressing down to increase the friction. Keep going until a red ember shows.

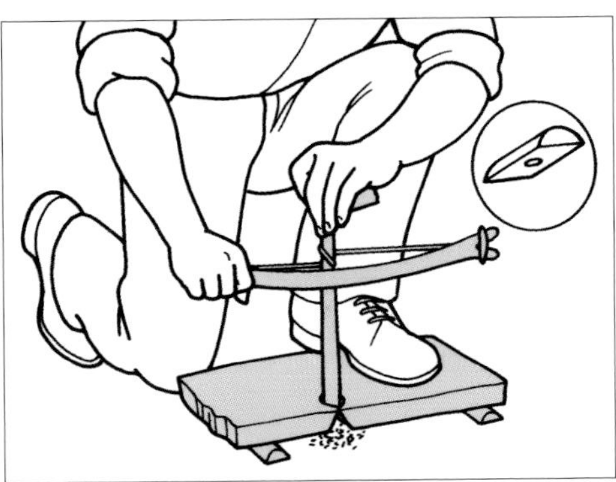

2 To speed up the process, string a bow and turn once around the spindle. Devise a socket in wood, stone or bone to hold the top of the spindle. Once you've got a rhythm, speed up and apply more pressure until an ember forms. Tap the ember into a bit of bark and transfer to the tinder. Blow into a flame.

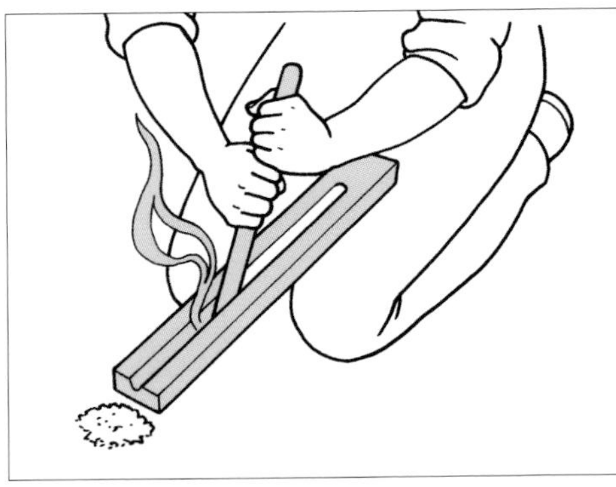

THE FIRE PLOUGH is a neat alternative to the hand drill. This has the advantage of creating the tinder it then ignites. Cut a groove down a length of wood, and drag a wooden shaft up and down the groove, using the blunt tip to make wood shavings and create an ember. Blow to ignite the shavings.

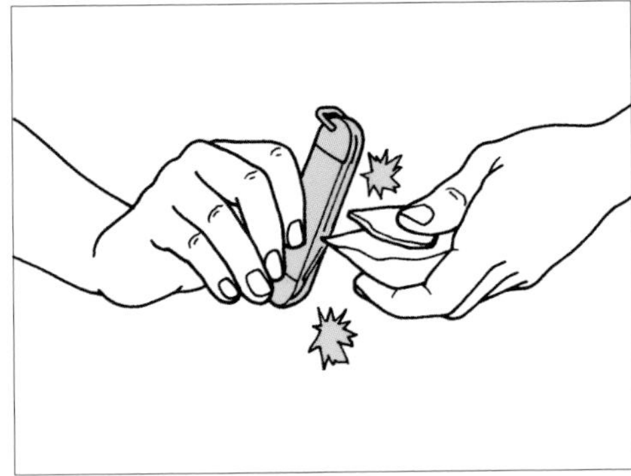

FLINT AND METAL are hard to beat. Hold a piece of flint firmly in one hand, with a scrap of your favourite tinder placed on top of it. Strike it with a mild steel tool, such as a (closed) penknife, file or axe, until the tinder catches. It's possible to do this using stainless steel, but it's much harder going.

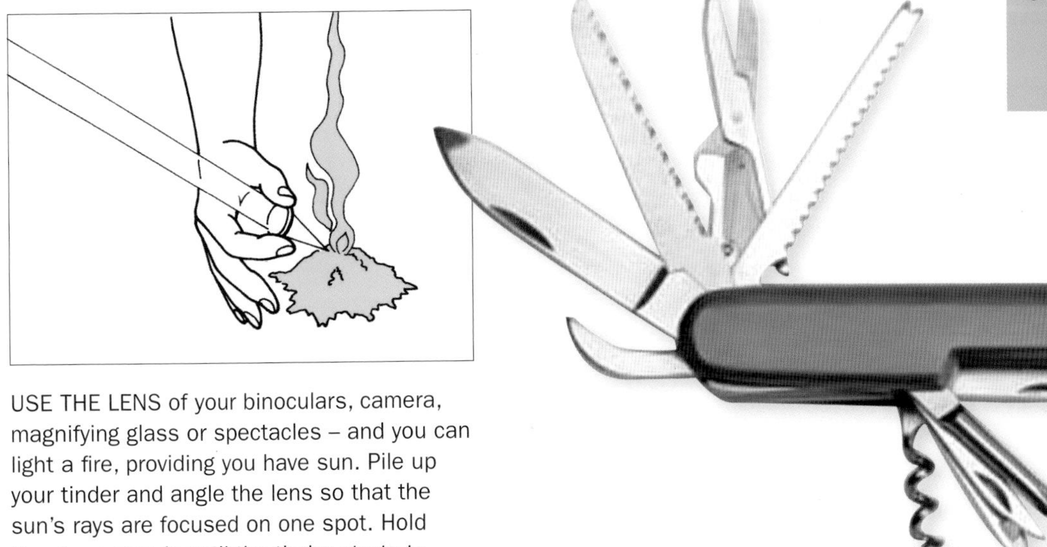

USE THE LENS of your binoculars, camera, magnifying glass or spectacles – and you can light a fire, providing you have sun. Pile up your tinder and angle the lens so that the sun's rays are focused on one spot. Hold the glass steady until the tinder starts to smoulder. Blow into a flame.

HOW TO MAKE A CAMPFIRE

Lighting a fire outdoors without the benefit of fire lighters and a fireplace can be tricky — especially if it's raining. Here's a foolproof method that should give you a hearty fire on which to roast your freshly caught rabbit.

INDISPENSABLE THINGS

- Tinder
- Fuel

INDISPENSABLE MATERIALS

You'll need three types of material to light your fire — all should be as dry as possible. Avoid rotten or 'green' wood.

- TINDER: This is the foundation of the fire and can be composed of twigs, wood shavings, leaves, bark, paper and pine needles.
- KINDLING: This is mostly small branches of softwood (e.g. pine) about 3–5cm (1-2in) in diameter, which should be broken up to fit inside the fire.
- FUEL: These are the large pieces of hardwood (e.g. oak) that keep the fire going. They should be about 1m (3ft) long and as dry as possible.

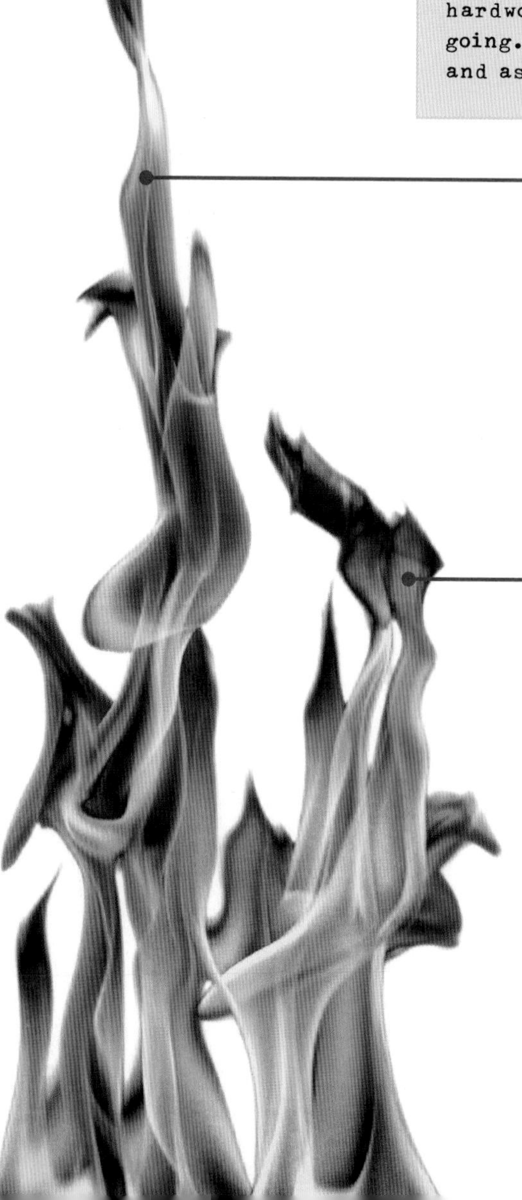

CLEARING A SPACE

Clear a space at least 3m (10ft) away from trees, tents and anything combustible, and ring it with stones to provide a barrier. Have a source of water to hand to put out the fire if it gets out of control.

LIGHTING THE FIRE

Place a handful of tinder in the middle of the fireplace, using the twigs to make a pyramid around it. Use the kindling to build a box around the tinder, overlapping the ends and making sure there are plenty of gaps to allow the oxygen to circulate. Place the fuel logs on either side of the box, and light the tinder (from the upwind side). The flame should spread from the tinder to the kindling to the fuel, creating a hot core of ashes as it goes.

HOW TO BUILD A BIVOUAC SHELTER

You don't have to have a fancy tent to camp outdoors. In summer especially, a simple bivouac will give you shade and protect you from rain, without blocking the view. All you need is a couple of tarpaulins, a length of rope, a saw, a knife – and a warm sleeping bag.

INDISPENSABLE THINGS

- **2 sheets of tarpaulin**
- **Rope**
- **Saw**
- **4–6 wooden stakes**
- **Knife**
- **Sleeping bag**

TREES

If you can, find a pair of trees about 2.5m (9ft) apart, with clear, flat ground between them. Tie a line between them at chest height to make a ridge pole. If you can't find any suitable trees, cut two stakes, each with a Y at one end, and drive them into the ground. Use a branch stretched between them as a ridge pole.

CREATING THE SHELTER

Cut four stakes about 25cm (10in) long. Whittle one end into a point, so they can be driven into the ground more easily, and cut a notch at the other end to attach the tarpaulin string. Stretch the tarpaulin over the ridge pole, and drive a stake into the ground at each corner. Tie off the corners, lay a second tarpaulin on the ground, and you've got a snug shelter.

LOCATION

Think about the location. If you camp too near the top of a hill, you'll be exposed to the elements; too far down a valley, you'll be cold and damp. Don't forget: heat rises.

HOW TO MAKE A LATRINE

The call of nature is something no one can avoid, especially when camping. There are many ways of dealing with it, but probably the most hygienic is to build a latrine. At least that will save any nasty surprises. A latrine can be as fancy as you like: from a simple hole in the ground to a fully fledged shelter with washing area. If you're staying in one place for some time, remember that you'll need to move the latrine periodically when it becomes full.

INDISPENSABLE THINGS

- Hessian screen
- Spade
- Ash from the fire
- Wood shavings

CAT-HOLING

Some people believe that so-called 'cat-holing' has less impact on the environment than building a latrine, as it spreads the faeces over a wide area rather than concentrating it in one place. Dig a hole about 15cm (6in) square by 15cm (6in) deep and squat over it. When you are done, stir in a little soil with a stick and fill the hole. However, this method is not recommended for large numbers of people camping in the same area.

CLEANING UP

Toilet paper is generally acceptable, providing it is well buried after use. Alternatively, you can use nature's own toilet paper: leaves, sticks (smooth ones!), stones or, if you're camping in cold climes, snow. If you have toilet paper, keep it in a sealed container or plastic bag to prevent it going soggy.

WET PIT
A properly kitted-out latrine should have a 'wet pit' for urinating and a 'squat pit' for defecating.

SCREEN
Screen off an area at least 60m (200ft) away from your camp, your water source and any path or trail. A hessian screen is ideal, or get creative with some branches.

SQUAT PIT
The squat pit should be a rectangular trench about 1m (3ft) long, 30cm (1ft) wide and 60cm (2ft) deep.

SOIL COVER
The dug-up soil is left next to the trench and used to cover the faeces. When the pit has filled to within 10cm (4in) from the top, it should be filled completely and camouflaged. A new trench can then be dug elsewhere.

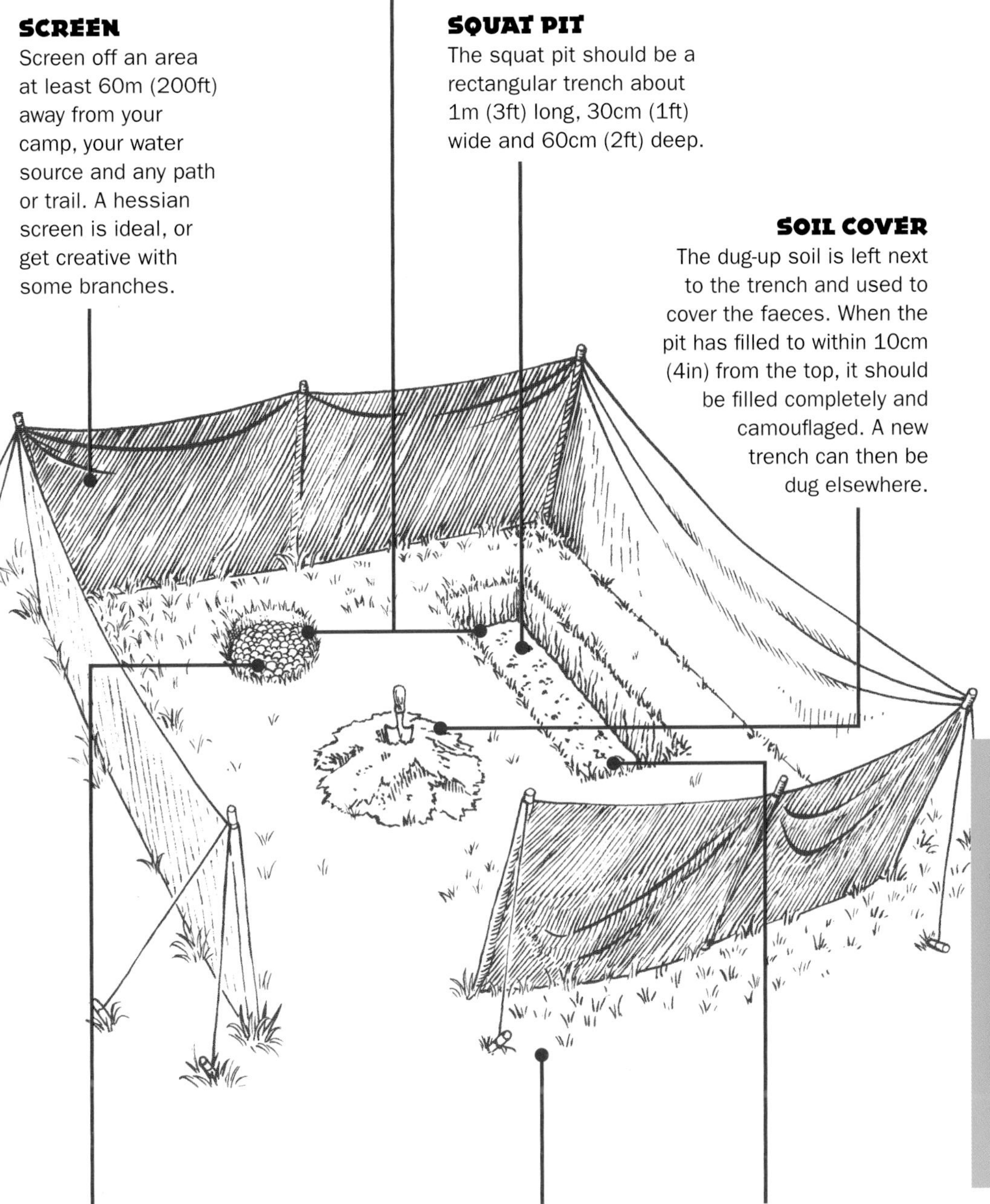

LINING
The wet pit should be a shallow hole lined with stones or pebbles, to help with drainage.

SURFACE DISPOSAL
Another method is surface disposal. This involves simply spreading the faeces with a stick to speed up the process of decomposition. This should only be used in remote areas far away from human habitation, and at least 60m (200ft) away from your camp, water sources and trails.

ASH
Use ash from the campfire to cover the faeces, and top it with a sprinkle of wood shavings to get rid of the smell.

HOW TO FIND WATER

The human body is made up of 60–75 per cent water, depending on age and gender. We lose about 3.5 litres (8 pints) of that a day through sweating and urination – more in the desert or if physically active – so finding water to replenish it is a priority in the wilderness. As for whether you should ever drink salt water, the jury's still out on that one, but you're probably safest avoiding it if you possibly can. They say it makes you go mad...

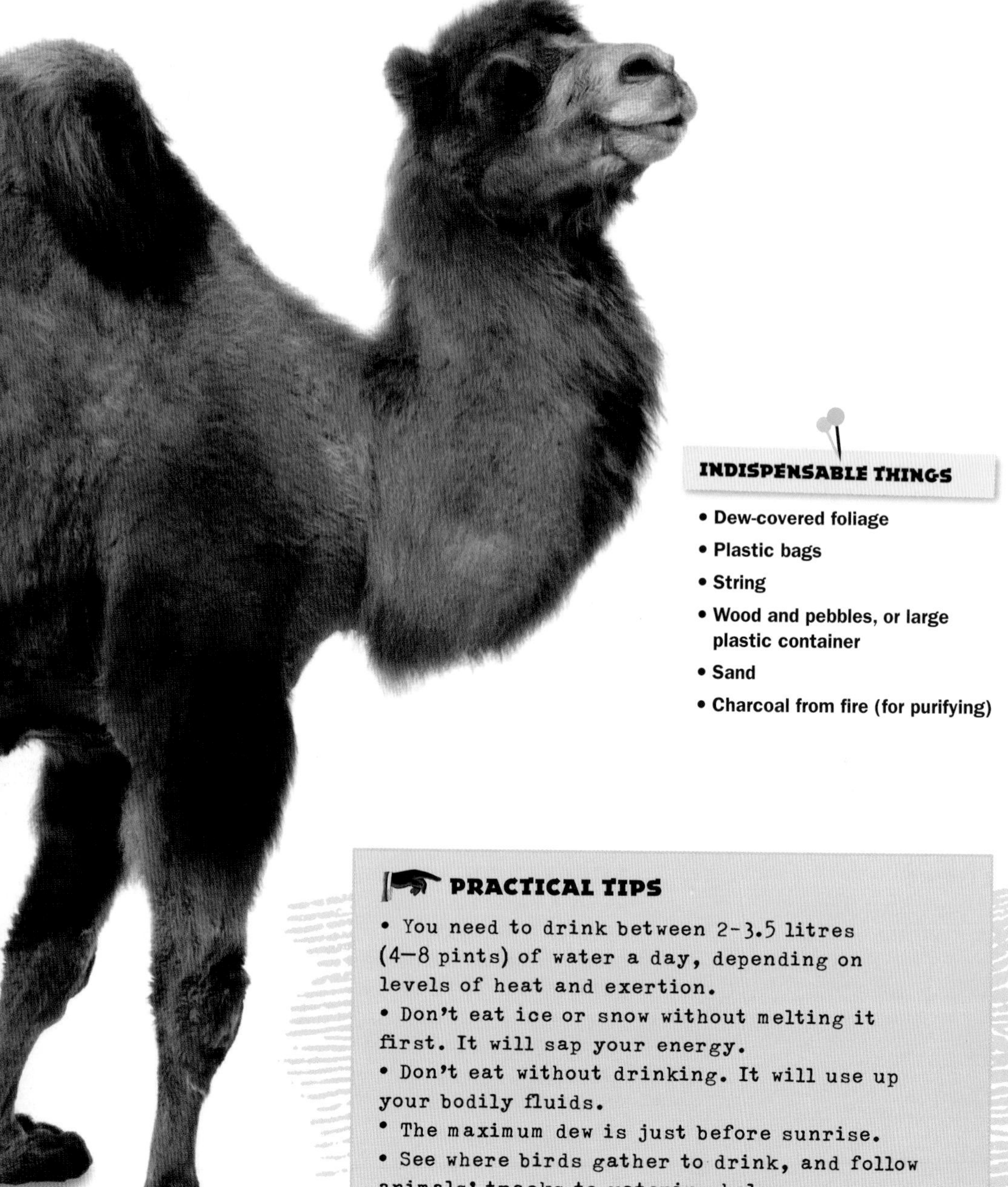

INDISPENSABLE THINGS

- Dew-covered foliage
- Plastic bags
- String
- Wood and pebbles, or large plastic container
- Sand
- Charcoal from fire (for purifying)

PRACTICAL TIPS

- You need to drink between 2–3.5 litres (4–8 pints) of water a day, depending on levels of heat and exertion.
- Don't eat ice or snow without melting it first. It will sap your energy.
- Don't eat without drinking. It will use up your bodily fluids.
- The maximum dew is just before sunrise.
- See where birds gather to drink, and follow animals' tracks to watering holes.

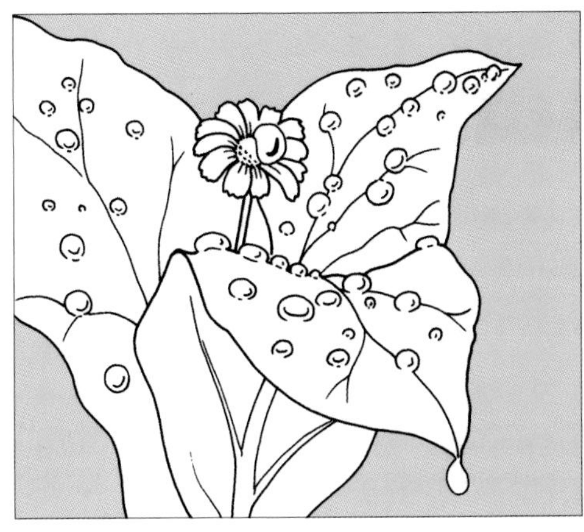

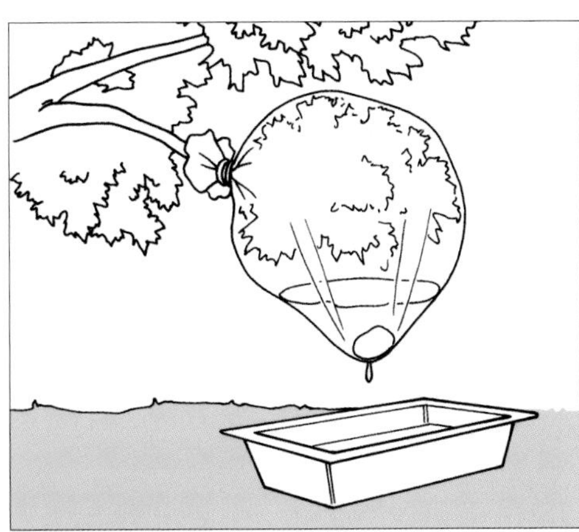

1 Look for obvious sources, such as rivers and streams. Check your map, and look at the landscape for clues. A crooked line of trees indicates there is probably a stream beneath. Get up early and collect the dew off (non-poisonous) flowers and leaves. If it tastes funny, it's just that it doesn't contain the same minerals as stream water does.

2 Make a sun still (*see page 333*), or use the transpiration method. Put a clean rock in a plastic bag and, in the morning, tie it around the leafy branch of a tree (non-poisonous). By evening, the perspiration of the tree will have collected in the lowest point of the bag, created by the rock. Prick a hole in the bag and collect the water.

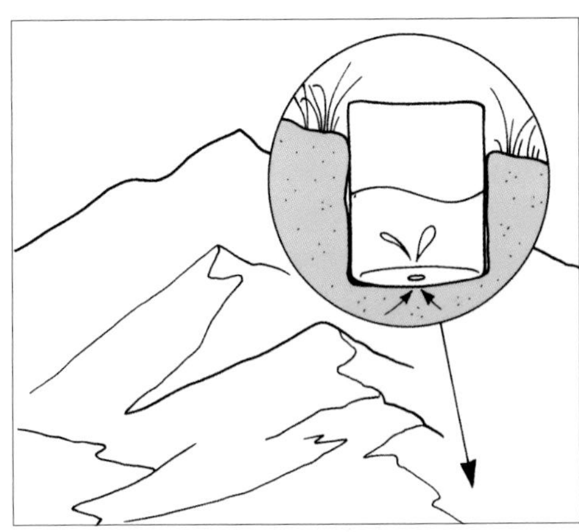

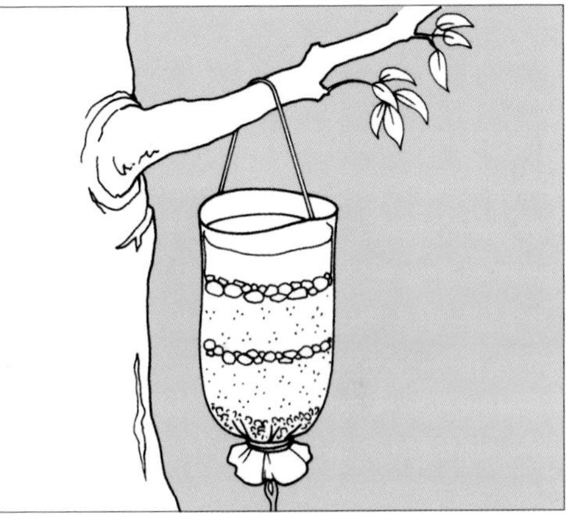

3 If you're on a beach, dig a hole about 1.2m (4ft) deep behind the first set of sand dunes – or about 30m (100ft) from the sea. Put pebbles in the bottom of the hole and line the sides with wood – or insert a large plastic container with a hole in the bottom, if you have one. After a few hours, the cavity should fill with filtered water. If not, find a lower stretch of sand.

4 Filtering the water will remove sediment and improve the taste. Cut a hole in the bottom of a plastic bag, and fill it with alternate layers of rock and sand. Hang the bag from a tree, pour in the water and collect it in a container placed under the hole. Charcoal from the fire, if thoroughly washed, will help remove undesirable smells. Purify the water by boiling it for 10 minutes.

HOW TO COOK WITHOUT UTENSILS

If you really want to commune with nature, leave the cooking utensils at home and cook straight over the fire. With a little imagination, most things can be skewered, baked or fried using organic utensils. Not only does it save you carrying cooking equipment around, but it also does away with any washing up!

INDISPENSABLE THINGS

- 2 Y-shaped stakes
- Sticks for skewering
- Large, flat stones
- Clay
- Fresh grass or leaves
- Half an onion
- Scooped-out orange peel

HOT COALS

Make sure the fire has burned down to hot coals without any large flames before you start cooking.

UTENSILS

Cut two stakes with Y shapes in one end and drive them into the ground on either side of the fire. Skewer anything you like: vegetables, chicken, wild boar – even eggs. Just prick a hole in either end of the egg, thread a thin skewer or string through it and hang over the fire for 20 minutes.

ORGANIC EQUIPMENT

Place large, flat, non-porous stones in the middle of the fire and allow them to heat. Use them like a frying pan to cook meat, fish and eggs. Try covering vegetables in a thick layer of clay before placing them directly on the coals to cook. You can do the same with meat and fish, but wrap them first in (edible) fresh grass or leaves.

HOLE BAKING

Clear a space in the fire and dig a shallow hole in the ground. Place potatoes or washed corn (with leaves and silk) in the hole and bury. Relay the fire and leave to bake for 20 minutes for corn, 45 minutes for potatoes.

ORGANIC PAN

Cut an onion in half and scoop out all but the last two layers. Crack an egg into it and place directly on the coals to cook. You can do the same with a scooped-out orange, either using an egg or bread/cake mixture.

HOW TO DIG A CLAY OVEN

It's a method that's been used for thousands of years and, if judged right, produces delicious results with minimal wastage and maximum nutrition. Earth ovens, also known as pit ovens, are holes in the ground into which you place hot coals and a large lump of meat or fish and leave to cook. Here's how it's done.

INDISPENSABLE THINGS

- Spade
- Hardwood for fire
- Flat, non-porous stones
- Edible leaves/grass to protect food
- Layer of soil
- Aluminium foil (optional)

DIG A HOLE
Dig a hole about three times the size of the item to be cooked.

LINING
Line the hole with flat, non-porous stones. Use the big ones to line the sides and spread the rest over the bottom.

LIGHT A FIRE
Light a fire inside the hole, using hardwood (such as oak or elm) if possible. Allow the fire to burn for 45 minutes or so, until it's reduced to coals.

WRAPPING
Wrap the food in edible leaves or aluminium. If you're using aluminium, you can lay the item straight on the coals. If not, clear the coals to the sides, put a layer of leaves on the hot stones and lay the wrapped item on the leaves.

LAYER OF LEAVES
Cover the food with another layer of leaves, sprinkle it with water to assist the steaming process, and then place an animal hide, bark or carpeting over the food to protect it. Fill the hole with at least 10cm (4in) of soil and leave to cook. About 1½ hours should suffice for a large fish, or 3–4 hours for a whole lamb.

HOW TO CATCH A RABBIT

You've set up camp, built a latrine and found a supply of water. What you need now is a steady supply of fresh food. Rabbit meat is high in protein, as well as essential vitamins and minerals such as B12 and iron. What's more, the little critters breed like, er, rabbits, so it's highly likely there will be a few hopping around nearby.

INDISPENSABLE THINGS

- 2 large empty cans
- Sharp knife
- Duct tape
- Length of string
- Gloves
- Length of wire
- Hinged wooden box
- Stick

PRACTICAL TIP

Bear in mind that the laws relating to trapping wild animals vary from country to country. Check before you trap.

SETTING A TRAP

Get two large empty tin cans and cut the bottom off one of them. Join them end-to-end with duct tape and place some enticing rabbit food in the bottom. Balance the trap on a stone so that, when the rabbit hops in for a nibble, it tips up and traps the bunny inside. Use a length of string to secure the trap to a high branch to stop it rolling over once the rabbit is inside.

LOCATION
Place your trap in an area regularly used by rabbits. Check for trails and droppings to find their favourite spots. Keep your scent hidden by locating the trap elsewhere and wearing gloves while you are handling it. Mask your scent with wood smoke. Rabbits are crepuscular, which means they are most active around dawn and dusk.

MAKING A SNARE
Make a snare by bending a length of wire into a running loop (like a noose), and tie a length of string to the 'standing' end of the loop. Find a place where the rabbit trail narrows, and secure the string to a nearby tree or bush. Place the snare about 8cm (3in) off the ground and conceal it with twigs. When the rabbit pokes its head through the snare, the wire will tighten around its neck and trap it.

HUMANE TRAP
A more humane trap can be made from a simple box with a hinged lid. Place the box on its side and prop the lid open with a stick. Tie a piece of string to the stick, about 5cm (2in) off the ground, and attach a carrot or other favourite rabbit food to the other end. Put the carrot in the box and wait for the rabbit to hop along for a nibble.

KILLING THE RABBIT
Kill the rabbit humanely. Drowning is considered one of the most humane methods and/or a sharp blow to the head with a heavy object. Your aim should be to kill it quickly and to cause as little suffering as possible.

HOW TO SKIN A RABBIT

Catching a rabbit is just the beginning of the process: next, you've got to skin and gut it. It's not a job for the faint-hearted, but if you're going to survive in the wilderness, it's got to be done. And at the end of it you'll have the satisfaction of knowing that you were involved in the food-gathering process from start to finish, as nature intended, rather than handing over all the messy jobs to someone else.

INDISPENSABLE THINGS

- Chopping board
- Sharp knife
- Axe
- Strong stomach

PRACTICAL TIPS

- A quarter of a cup of animal blood contains as much nutritional value as 10 eggs.
- Bone marrow is also rich in nutrients. Crush the bones, boil them and sieve the liquid for a rich, nourishing stock.
- Intestines and sinews are surprisingly strong and can be twisted and used as rope. Wash them thoroughly first. Expect flies.
- The human body can't survive on meat alone. Balance your diet by foraging for berries and vegetables.

1 Lay the rabbit on a chopping board and pinch the loose skin in the lower part of the belly. Cut a neat incision, being careful not to puncture the stomach lining. Be careful to avoid piercing the animal's organs in the process, as this may contaminate the meat with urine or faeces.

2 Extend the cut all the way around the rabbit's torso, either by tearing or cutting the skin with a knife. The fur will pull away from the trunk quite easily.

3 Turning the skin inside out, pull the rear end over the hind legs and the front end over the head, until both ends tear off completely. It feels similar to pulling a rubber glove off your hand.

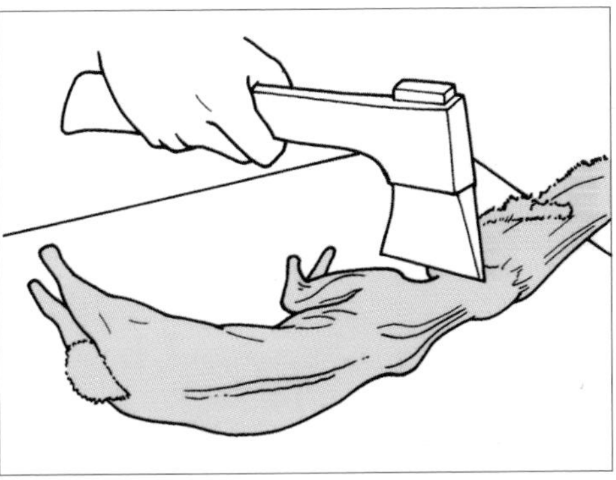

4 Use an axe or a knife to sever the head, paws and tail. Save the blood to add to a soup or stew – it contains iron and other essential nutrients.

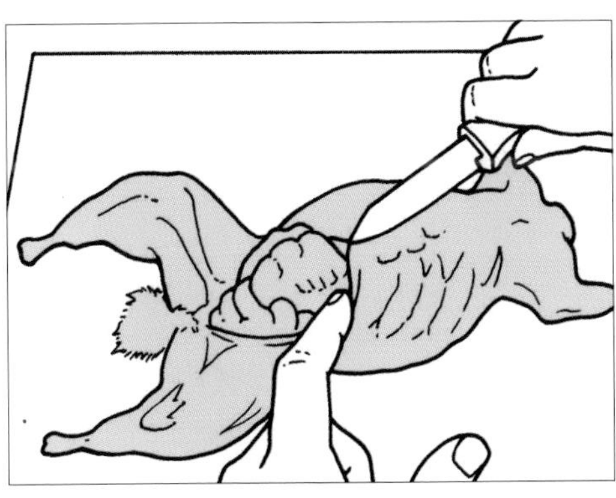

5 Cut the stomach lining open, taking care not to pierce any organs. Remove the guts. If you see any blotches or growths on the organs, discard the rabbit as it may be diseased and therefore unfit to eat.

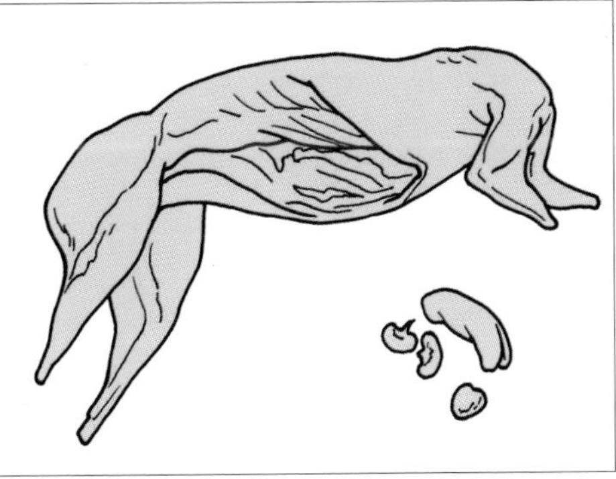

6 If the organs look healthy, keep the heart, liver and kidneys to eat, but discard the rest. Wash the carcass and soak overnight in salted water, prior to roasting over a campfire.

HOW TO CATCH A FISH

Fish is a fantastic source of nutrition and probably the single most valuable food if you are stuck in the wilderness, far away from your favourite sushi bar. Tasty and easy to cook, it contains essential protein, iron, vitamin D and Omega 3 fatty acids. But first you've got to catch the slippery blighters. There are many ways of catching fish; try out several different approaches and find out which works best in your particular environment.

INDISPENSABLE THINGS

- Wooden stakes
- Stones
- Paper clips, safety pins, pins, needles, nails, wire or metal strips for hooks
- Sliver of wood, bone or metal
- Sharp knife
- Shoelaces, dental floss, wire, thread or twisted bark for line
- Tree branch
- Worms, insects, berries or meat for bait, or a strip of red cloth
- Shirt or trousers for a net

FISH TRAPS

Fish traps are very effective. Drive stakes into the bottom of shallow water to create a three-sided rectangle, with the open side facing the current. Upstream, make a V-shaped wall to funnel the fish into the trap. In tidal areas, use stones to create rock pools to trap fish when the tide goes out.

A PRACTICAL HISTORY OF FLY-FISHING

There are references to anglers in ancient Greece and Rome tying red feathers and wool to their hooks. But the first detailed descriptions of artificial flies being used for fishing comes in *The Treatyse of Fysshynge Wyth an Angle*, published in 1496 at St Albans, England. This popular work describes 12 artificial flies made from silk, wool, and feathers in many colours. The most famous work on fly-fishing is *The Compleat Angler*, by Izaak Walton and Charles Cotton, which was first published in 1653 and is still in print today – some 400 editions later.

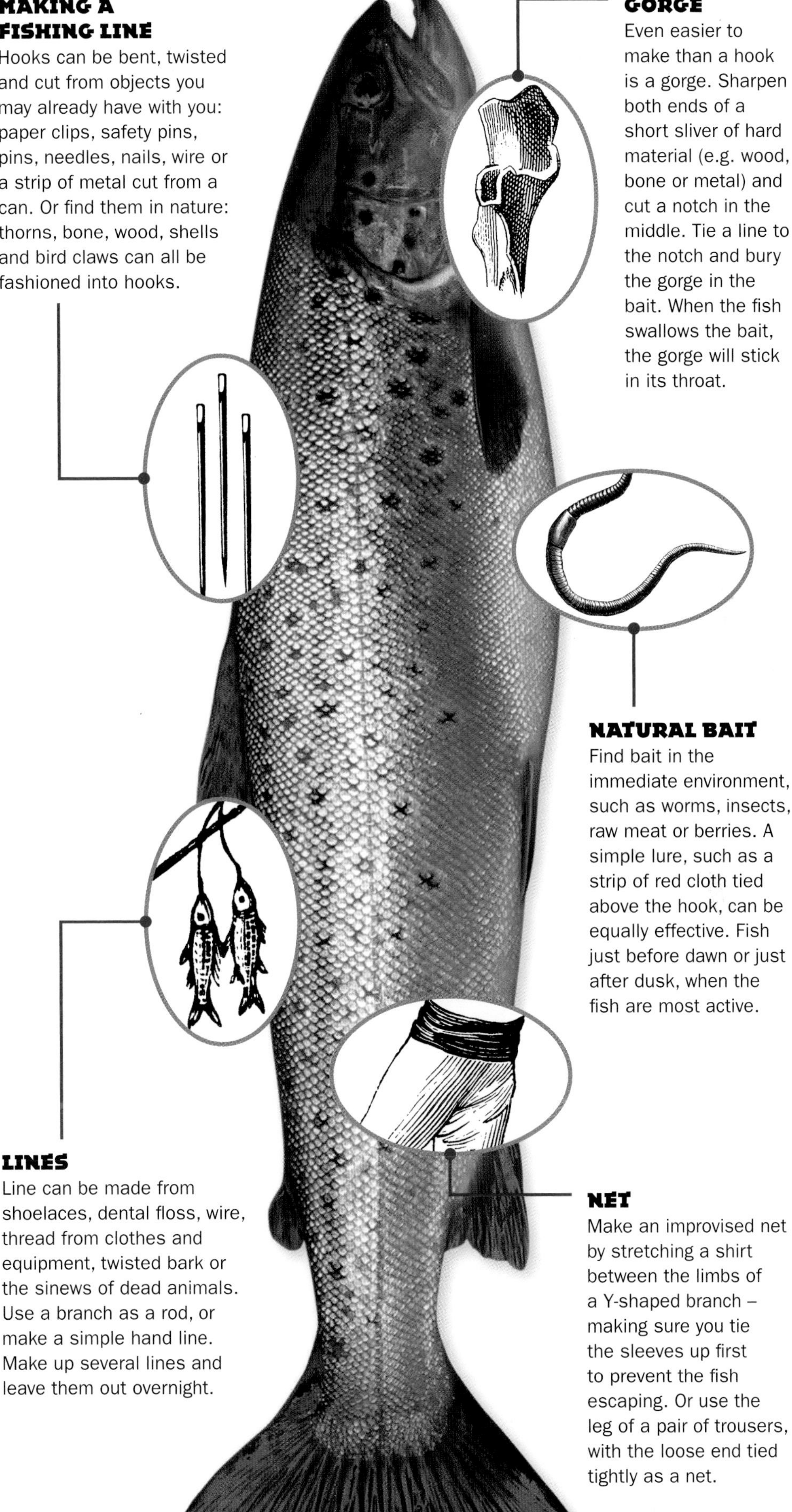

MAKING A FISHING LINE
Hooks can be bent, twisted and cut from objects you may already have with you: paper clips, safety pins, pins, needles, nails, wire or a strip of metal cut from a can. Or find them in nature: thorns, bone, wood, shells and bird claws can all be fashioned into hooks.

GORGE
Even easier to make than a hook is a gorge. Sharpen both ends of a short sliver of hard material (e.g. wood, bone or metal) and cut a notch in the middle. Tie a line to the notch and bury the gorge in the bait. When the fish swallows the bait, the gorge will stick in its throat.

NATURAL BAIT
Find bait in the immediate environment, such as worms, insects, raw meat or berries. A simple lure, such as a strip of red cloth tied above the hook, can be equally effective. Fish just before dawn or just after dusk, when the fish are most active.

LINES
Line can be made from shoelaces, dental floss, wire, thread from clothes and equipment, twisted bark or the sinews of dead animals. Use a branch as a rod, or make a simple hand line. Make up several lines and leave them out overnight.

NET
Make an improvised net by stretching a shirt between the limbs of a Y-shaped branch – making sure you tie the sleeves up first to prevent the fish escaping. Or use the leg of a pair of trousers, with the loose end tied tightly as a net.

HOW TO GUT A FISH

Contrary to what most children think, nature doesn't supply fish in neatly breadcrumbed fingers ready to pop under the grill. That's Captain Birds Eye's job. But it's really not that difficult to scale and gut a fish yourself, and then you've got a bundle of goodness all ready to grill over the fire. If you're feeling squeamish, go and find some wild berries to eat instead.

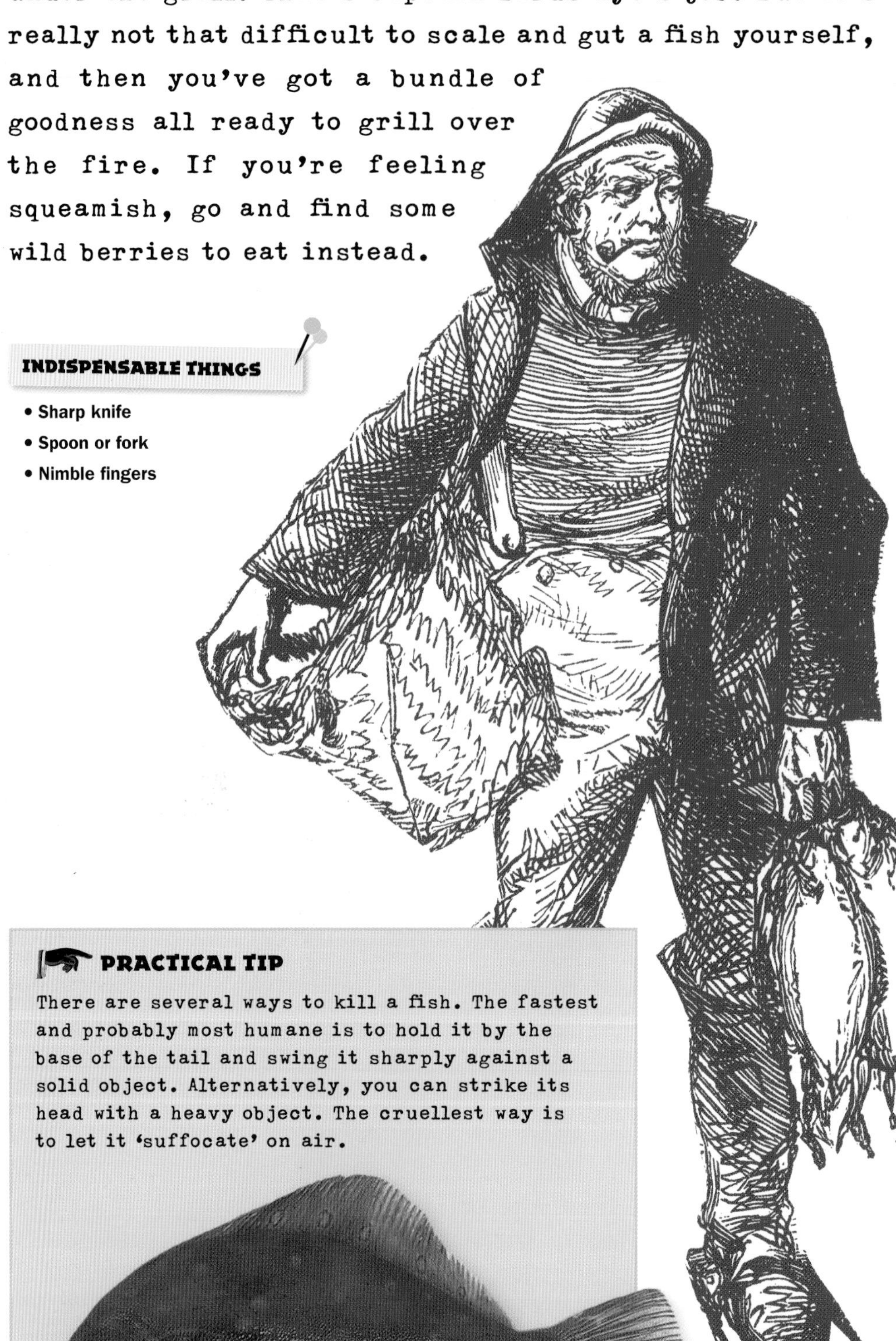

INDISPENSABLE THINGS

- Sharp knife
- Spoon or fork
- Nimble fingers

PRACTICAL TIP

There are several ways to kill a fish. The fastest and probably most humane is to hold it by the base of the tail and swing it sharply against a solid object. Alternatively, you can strike its head with a heavy object. The cruellest way is to let it 'suffocate' on air.

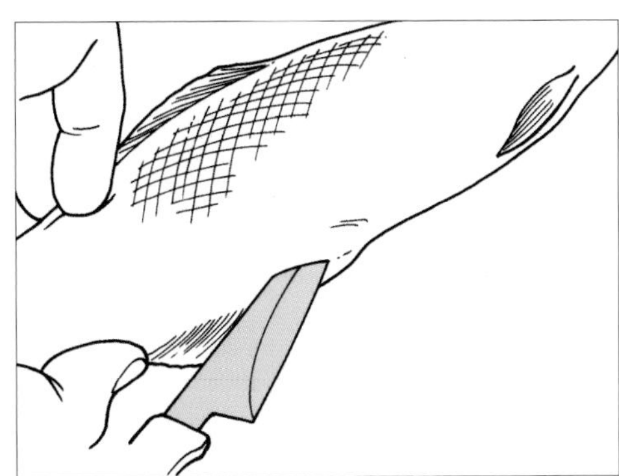

1 Decide if your fish needs descaling by scraping from tail to head with a knife: if the scales lift up, descale the fish, otherwise just wash it. To descale, hold it firmly by the tail and scrape up both sides with a knife held at right angles to the body. Now do the smaller scales around the fins, tail and collar.

2 To gut the fish, hold it firmly by the tail and push a sharp knife into its anus. Draw the knife towards the head, cutting its belly open right up to the base of the gills. Don't cut too deeply because this will pierce the digestive system and contaminate the meat with faeces.

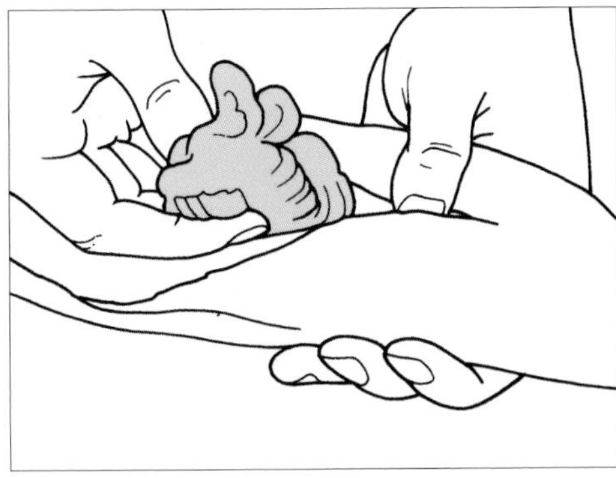

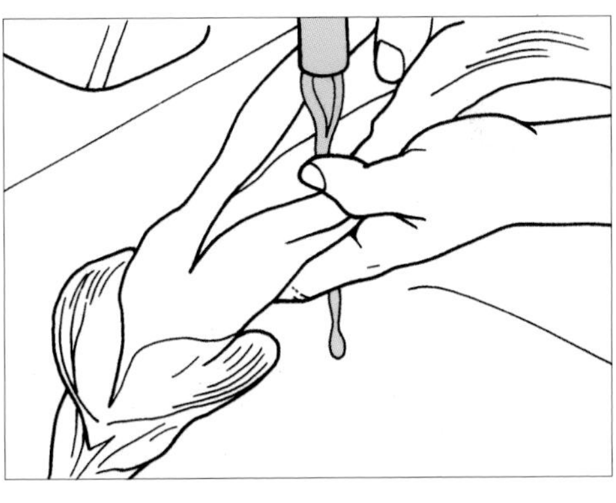

3 If it's a small fish, simply reach inside with your hand or fingers and scoop the organs out. If it's a bigger fish, you'll need to cut the organs off directly behind its head and at the anus, before pulling them out. Remove the black vein from the backbone by scraping it off with a spoon or fork.

4 Clean the abdominal cavity thoroughly in cold water. Don't use river water unless you are absolutely sure it's clean.

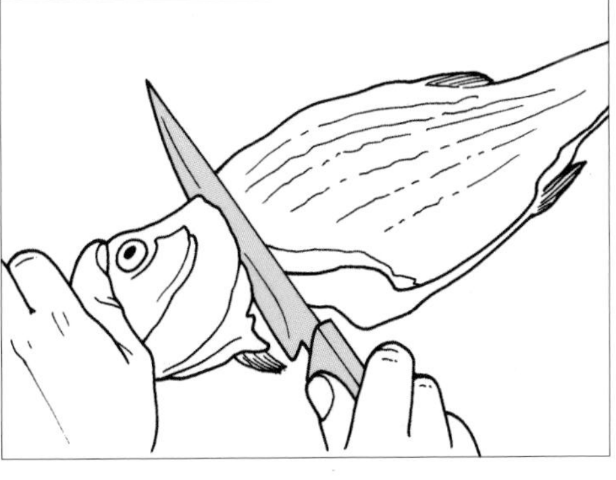

5 The fish is now ready to cook, but there are other steps if you want to make it more palatable. You can cut fillets off the bone by inserting a sharp knife into the flesh directly behind the gills until you feel the vertebra. Slide the knife along the bone, pulling the flesh away with your other hand.

6 Some people don't like being looked at while they are eating – particularly not by the creature they are eating. Using a sharp knife, cut the fish's head off directly behind the gills, pushing hard to cut through the vertebra. The head is full of goodness – save it to make nutritious fish soup.

HOW TO READ A MAP

GoogleEarth may give us the illusion of seeing the Earth in three dimensions, but even the most modern map technology still relies on grid references and contours to show the way. So, how do you represent three-dimensional mountains and valleys on flat paper or a screen? How do you find where you are on a map? And how do you know whether your map is large or small scale?

INDISPENSABLE THINGS

- Map
- Sense of direction

PRACTICAL TIP

Most maps are drawn with north at the top. That means that west is to the left, east to the right, and south is pointing downwards. To make life easier, turn the map until it matches the real lie of the land.

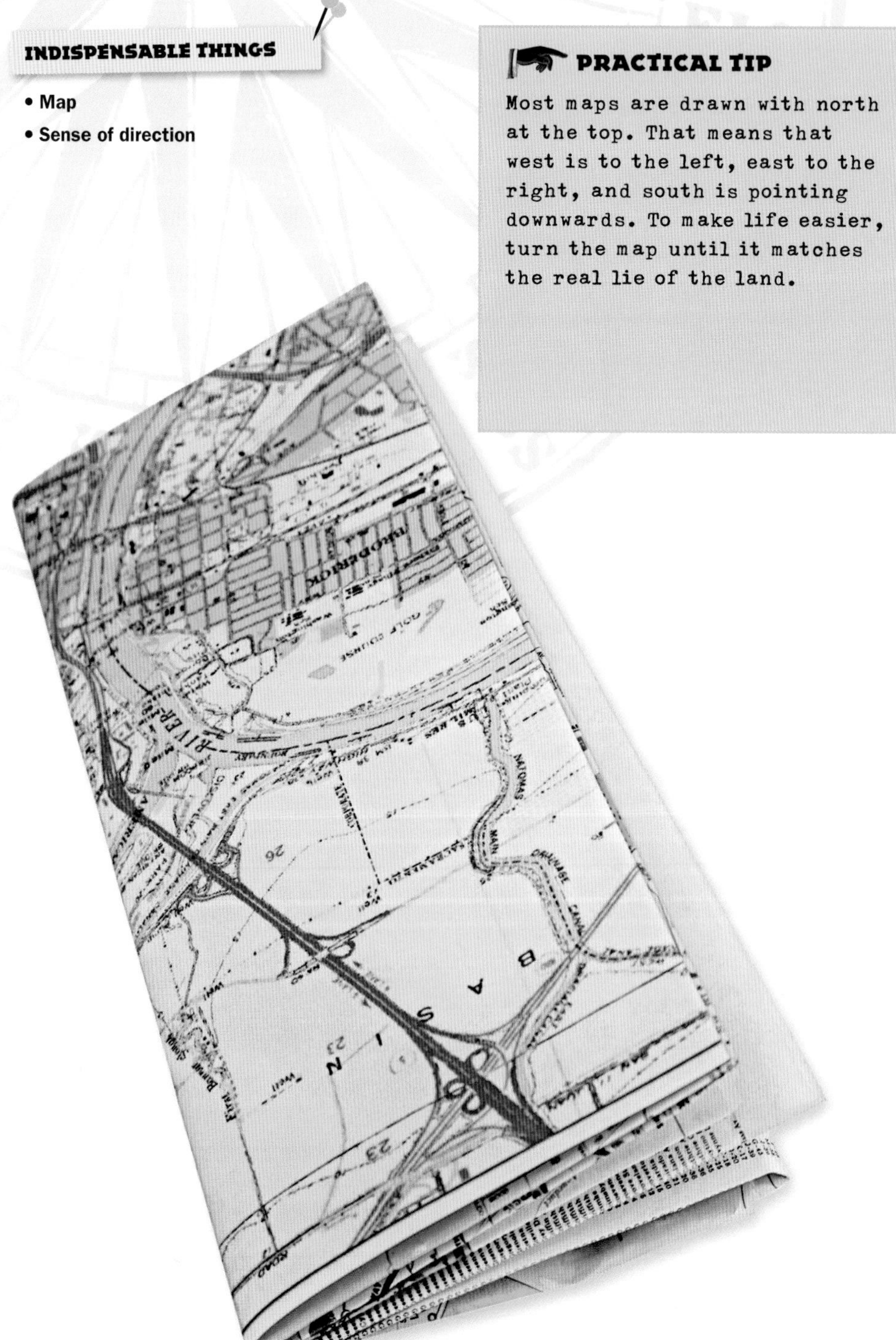

CONTOUR LINES

The height of the land is represented by contour lines. Each line represents a standard height above sea level. Imagine the tide is coming in and, at regular intervals, a line is drawn around the sea's edge; that's what contour lines are like. The closer the contour lines are, the steeper the gradient; the further apart the lines are, the flatter the gradient.

ROADS & RIVERS

Roads are shown in a variety of colours, depending on their size. Buildings are usually shown as grey or black, woods as green and mountains as brown or white, depending on height, but this varies from country to country. Rivers and the sea are always shown in blue. A key will explain what the symbols on the map mean.

SCALE

A 'large scale' map shows features close-up (i.e. big!), but doesn't have space to show very much (e.g. 1:25,000). A 'small scale' map shows features from afar (i.e. small), but can fit more on the page (e.g. 1:24,000,000).

WORKING OUT THE SCALE

Maps come in different scales, depending on their intended purpose. The scale is indicated at the bottom or side of the map in the form of a ratio, e.g. 1:100,000. This means that 1 unit on the map is the equivalent of 100,000 units in real life. A 1:25,000 map has enough detail for walking, a 1:190,000 map is good for driving, while a 1:24,000,000 map shows the whole world.

LATITUDE & LONGITUDE

The numbers on the sides of the map represent latitude, i.e. the distance in degrees north or south of the equator. The numbers at the top and bottom represent longitude, i.e. the distance in degrees east or west of the Greenwich Meridian Line. Each degree is divided into 60 minutes. Each minute represents one nautical mile (or 1.15 land miles/ 1.85 km), so one degree equals 60 nautical miles (or 69 land miles/111km).

HOW TO USE A COMPASS

Did you know that the Earth is a giant magnet? Well, there is a magnetic field running north to south, which is why the needle of a compass always points north. The Chinese invented the first compass at least 2,000 years ago, and the same concept has been used by voyagers ever since – from Christopher Columbus to every Scout in the land. Clever stuff, hey? But what happens when you don't want to travel north? Well, let's see...

INDISPENSABLE THINGS

- Compass
- Steady hand

PRACTICAL TIP

To use a compass, stand in a clear space and check the compass is level. Make sure there are no large metal objects nearby, which may create a magnetic attraction and affect the reading. Once the needle has settled down, turn the compass until the coloured end of the needle lines up with North on the dial.

NEEDLE & DIAL

Most compasses are made of a needle balanced on a pivot. The end of the needle that points to North is usually painted either red or fluorescent green. A dial around the compass shows North and the other cardinal points (South, East and West).

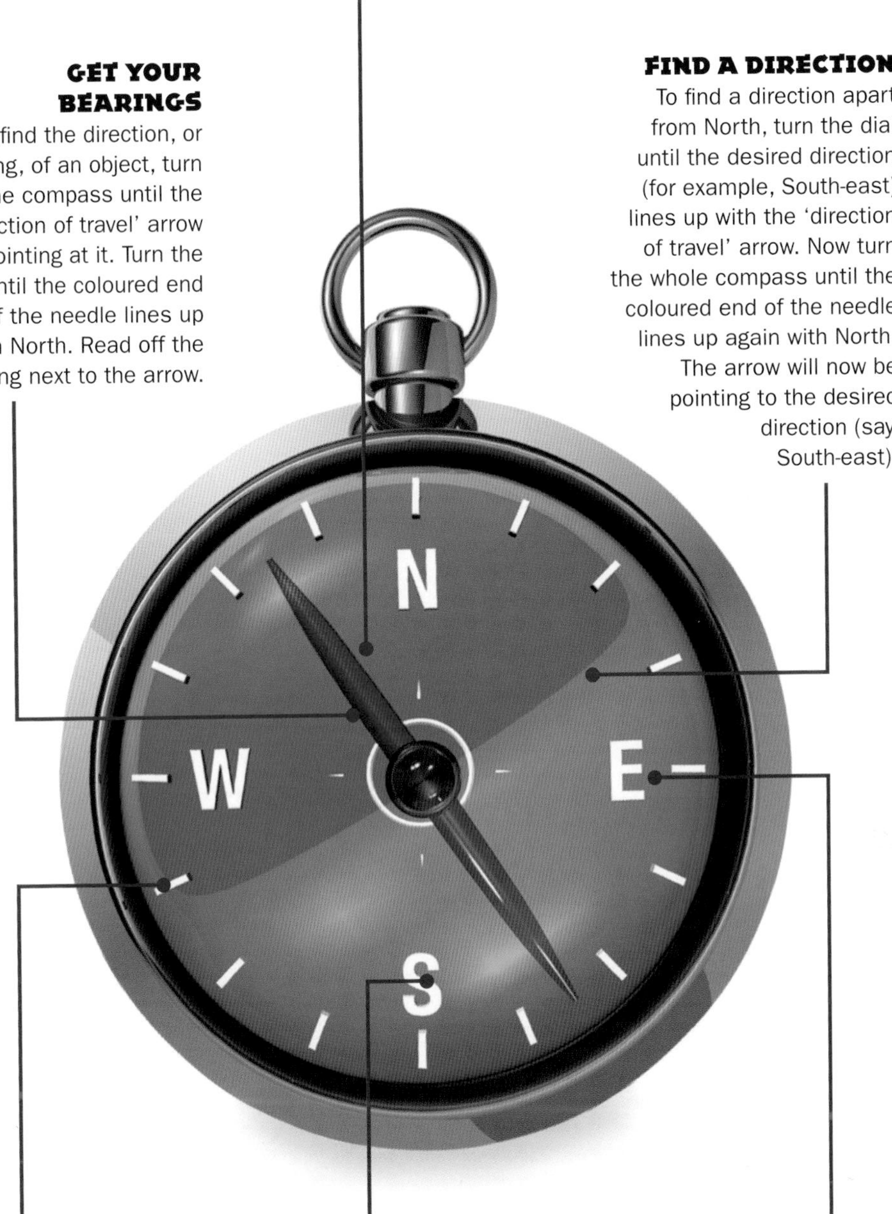

GET YOUR BEARINGS

To find the direction, or bearing, of an object, turn the compass until the 'direction of travel' arrow is pointing at it. Turn the dial until the coloured end of the needle lines up with North. Read off the bearing next to the arrow.

FIND A DIRECTION

To find a direction apart from North, turn the dial until the desired direction (for example, South-east) lines up with the 'direction of travel' arrow. Now turn the whole compass until the coloured end of the needle lines up again with North. The arrow will now be pointing to the desired direction (say, South-east).

CARDINAL POINTS

The four cardinal points of the compass are: North, South, East and West.
In between these are the intercardinal points, such as North-west, South-east, etc. These can be divided again, to give North-north-west, East-south-east, etc, although for orienteering the intercardinal points are usually accurate enough.

CHECK

Use your common sense.
If you are walking towards the sun in the northern hemisphere, you are heading south (north if you are in the southern hemisphere).
If you are supposed to be travelling the other way, check your compass again. It's a common mistake to line up the wrong end of the needle.

DEGREES

The compass dial can also be divided into 360 degrees, with 000° standing for North, 090° for East, 180° for South and 270° for West. Courses can be set to the nearest degree, allowing for more accurate navigation, suitable for a ship or a plane.

HOW TO MEASURE THE DISTANCE WALKED

Knowing how far you've travelled is key to knowing where you are now. It also enables you to work out how far you've still got to go and, crucially, whether you'll reach your destination before the bar closes. A GPS (Global Positioning System) will give you an exact fix and a pedometer will measure precisely how far you've walked, but there are simpler ways to work out these things, using just your eyes, arms and legs – plus a little mental arithmetic.

INDISPENSABLE THINGS

- Strong legs
- Stopwatch
- String or pebbles

PRACTICAL TIPS

To work out how far away an object is – for example, a barn on the other side of a valley, approximately 30m (100ft) wide – extend one arm and stick your index finger in the air. Close one eye and line up your finger with one end of the object. Without moving your finger, open just the other eye and observe how far your finger appears to have moved. Estimate the distance between the two apparent positions (for example, three times the length of the barn). Times that distance by ten; that is how far away the object is ... very approximately.

PACE YOURSELF

Measure your pace. A double pace is easier to count than a single pace. Walk two paces, starting with your dominant foot (e.g. left foot/right foot/left foot) and measure how far you've walked. Better still, count how many double paces it takes to walk a set distance. Divide the distance by the number of double paces and you've got an average measure of your pace, e.g. 30m (100ft)/ 20 double paces = 1.5m (5ft) per double pace.

PREVAILING CONDITIONS

Your pace will vary according to the terrain and the prevailing conditions. It will be shorter walking uphill than downhill; it will be shorter walking into a head wind than with a tail wind. Gravel and sand will also shorten your pace, as will snow and ice. Fatigue will affect your pace. Measure your pace in different conditions and over different types of terrain and adjust your calculations accordingly.

TALLY

Use the 'tally and pace' system, where 100 paces = 1 tally. Keep track of the number of tallies by tying a knot in a piece of string or by putting pebbles in your pocket. Get several people to count and work out the average result. An average pace is 0.8m (2½ft), or 1.5m (5ft) for a double pace. It therefore takes 528 double paces to walk half a mile (0.8km).

USE TIME

With experience, you can use time to measure the distance you have travelled. Use a stopwatch to time how long it takes you to walk a mile. To work out your hourly rate, divide 60 by the number of minutes it takes you to walk a mile, e.g. 60/20 minutes = 3 miles per hour. The average person walks at 2–3 miles per hour, depending on terrain, any load carried and fitness.

HOW TO ESTIMATE REMAINING DAYLIGHT HOURS

It's late afternoon and the sun will be setting soon. But how soon? Should you set up camp now, or keep going to the next valley? Should you eat the last bit of chocolate, or save it for later? With access to an almanac or the internet you can find out the time of sunset to the nearest second, but here's an ingenious method, using just your fingers, that will give you an approximation.

- Sunlight
- Steady hands

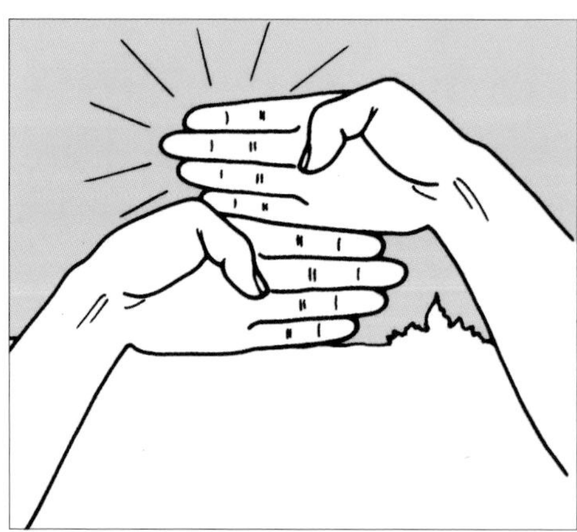

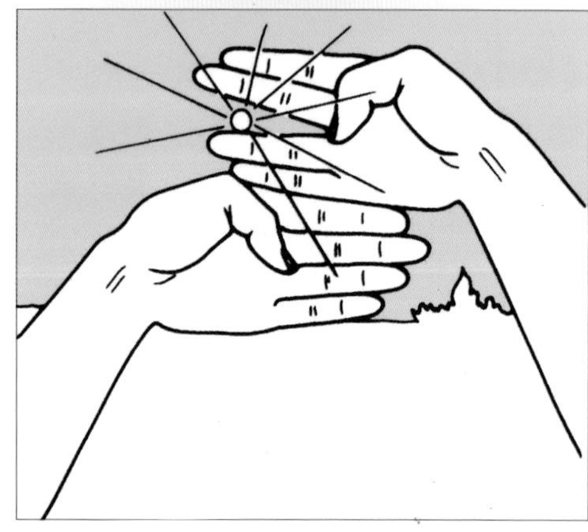

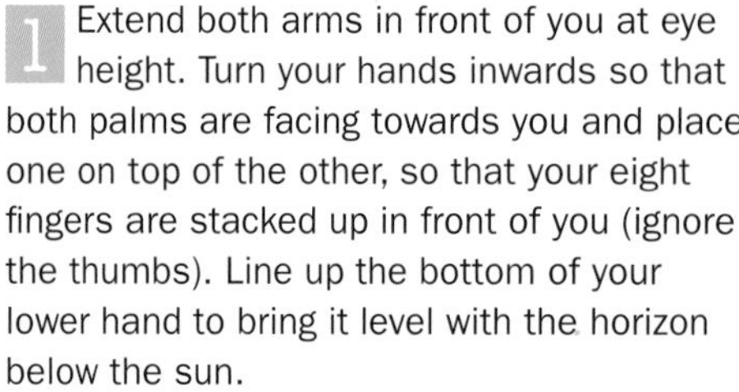

1 Extend both arms in front of you at eye height. Turn your hands inwards so that both palms are facing towards you and place one on top of the other, so that your eight fingers are stacked up in front of you (ignore the thumbs). Line up the bottom of your lower hand to bring it level with the horizon below the sun.

2 Starting from the top, lift your fingers until the sun is peeping over the top of the uppermost finger. Count how many fingers there are left between the sun and the horizon and times that number by 15. That's how many minutes it will be before the sun sets, e.g. 6 fingers x 15 = 90 minutes. Size of fingers varies of course, so experiment to work out what each of your fingers is worth – they might only be 10 minutes or they might be a whacking 20 minutes thick.

HOW TO FIND YOUR BEARINGS USING A WATCH

Did you know you can find North and South using an ordinary analogue watch? OK, it's not quite as accurate as a compass and you do need some assistance from the sun, but it will give you an approximate bearing, which will get you out of trouble in an emergency. Or try it just for fun.

INDISPENSABLE THINGS

- Watch
- Sunlight

INDISPENSABLE BEARINGS

- In the northern hemisphere, the sun is in the South
- In the southern hemisphere, the sun is in the North
- Facing the sun (in the north), East is to your left
- In the southern hemisphere, East is to your right

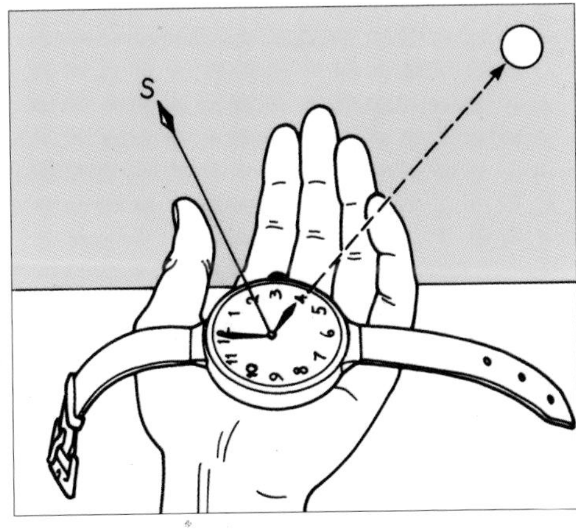

IN THE NORTHERN HEMISPHERE, place the watch horizontally and line up the hour hand with the sun. The line that lies halfway between the hour hand and midday points to South. Use standard time; if the watch is set to daylight saving time, the South–North line lies between the hour hand and 1300 hours (i.e. 1 p.m.). If in doubt, bear in mind that the sun rises in the East, sets in the West and is due South at noon.

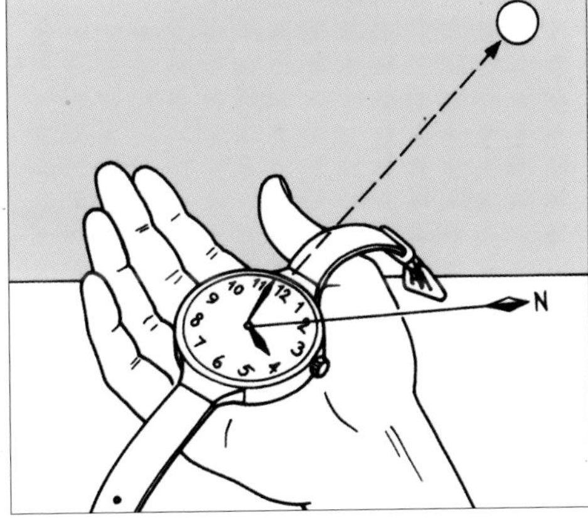

IN THE SOUTHERN HEMISPHERE, place the watch horizontally and line up the 12 o'clock mark with the sun. The line that lies halfway between 12 o'clock and the hour hand points to North. If the watch is set to daylight saving time, line 1300 hours (1.p.m.) with the sun; the North–South line will lie between it and the hour hand. If in doubt, bear in mind that the sun rises in the East, sets in the West and is due North at noon.

HOW TO FIND NORTH USING A STICK

Who needs a compass when you can find North using just a stick? Unfortunately the stick method is less portable than a compass and considerably less accurate. What's more, it's not much use on overcast days or at night or if you're in a hurry... Apart from that, it works great. Just don't try to use it at sea.

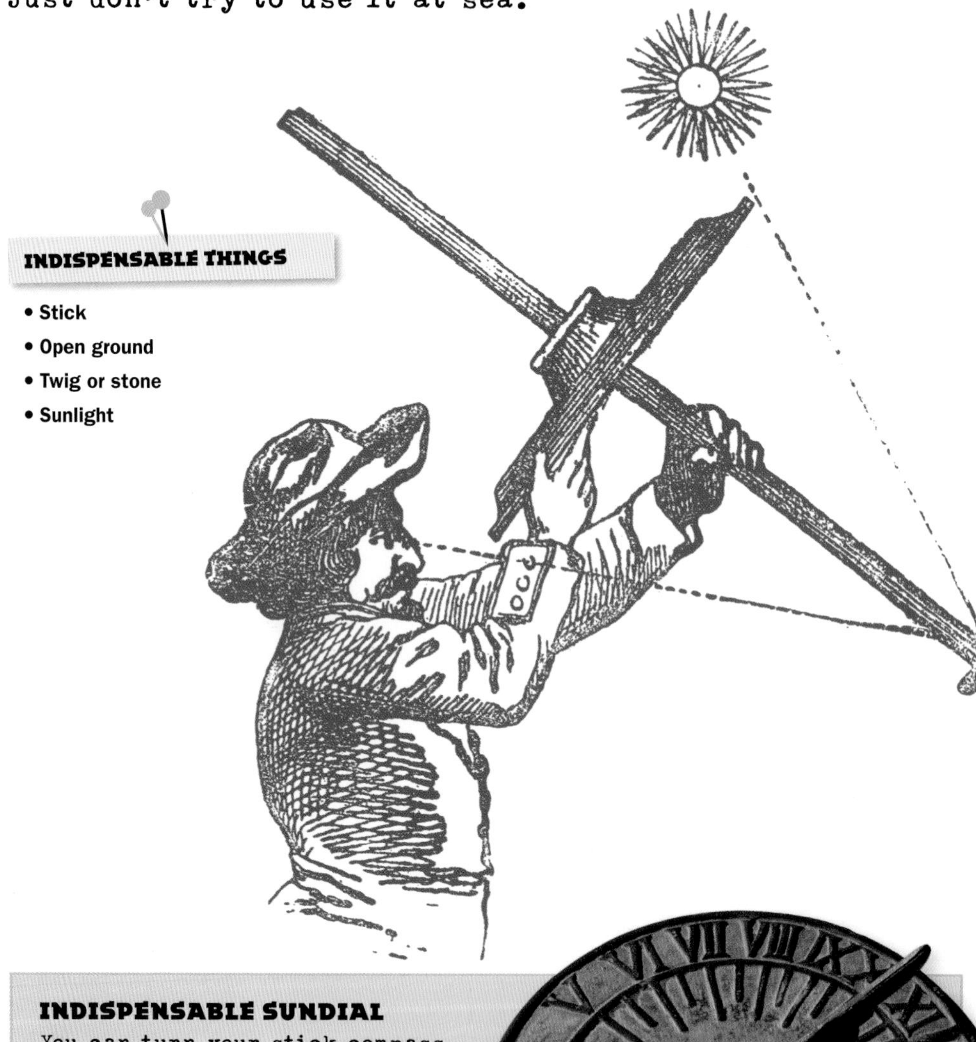

INDISPENSABLE THINGS

- Stick
- Open ground
- Twig or stone
- Sunlight

INDISPENSABLE SUNDIAL

You can turn your stick compass into a basic sundial by driving the stick vertically into the ground at the intersection of the East-West and North-South lines. The west side of the East-West line represents 0600 hours (6 a.m.), while the east side represents 1800 hours (6 p.m.). The North-South line represents midday. The path of the shadow through the arc will vary depending on location and time of year, but, with a little attention, can make an acceptable substitute for a clock.

1 Find some open ground which is reasonably level and free of undergrowth. Drive a stick about 1m (3ft) long into the ground – it doesn't matter how straight or upright the stick is, providing it casts a distinct shadow on the ground.

2 Mark the tip of the shadow with a twig or stone, or a mark in the ground. This is the West mark, irrespective of whether you are in the northern or southern hemisphere.

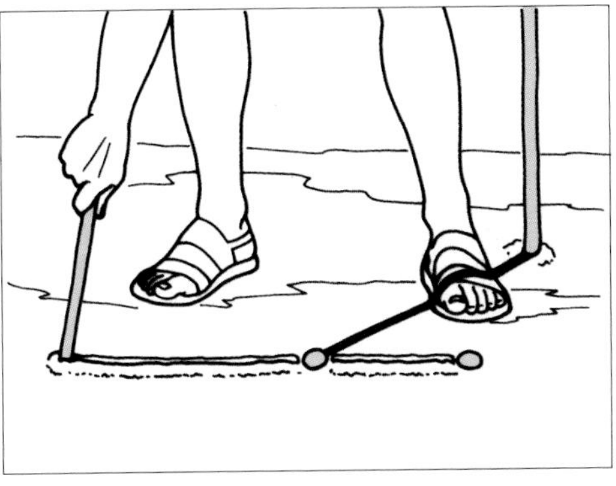

3 Wait for 10–15 minutes, until the shadow has moved a short distance. Mark the new position of the shadow tip as before. This is the East mark.

4 Draw a straight line between the two marks, extending the line slightly past the second mark. This gives you an approximate East–West line.

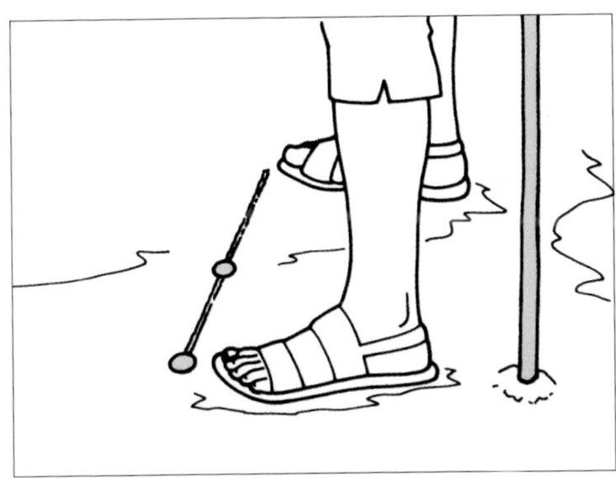

5 Stand on the line with the West mark to your left. You will now be facing North, irrespective of whether you are in the northern or southern hemisphere. Draw a line perpendicular to the first line to give you a North–South line.

6 For a more accurate reading, mark the first shadow 15–20 minutes before noon and, using the mark as your radius, draw an arc around the base of the stick. Wait for 15–20 minutes after noon and the tip of the shadow will touch the other side of the arc. Mark that point and join the two marks to create an East–West line as before.

HOW TO FIND THE NORTH STAR

No need to stop walking just because the sun's gone down. Travelling by night can be a magical experience and, even without a compass, you can navigate with reasonable accuracy using the stars. There are 5,000 stars visible to the naked eye but, in the northern hemisphere at least, you only need one to find your way: the North Star.

INDISPENSABLE THINGS

- **Night sky**
- **Sharp eyes**

THE NORTH STAR

The constellations in the sky vary from season to season because of the journey of the Earth around the Sun. They change their position from hour to hour because of the rotation of the Earth on its axis. The one star that remains virtually constant every night, all night, is the North Star. That's because it's located above the Earth's axis, just 1 degree off true North.

URSA MAJOR

The North Star is the last star in the 'handle' of Ursa Minor, also known as the Little Dipper. Two constellations rotate anticlockwise around the North Star: Ursa Major and Cassiopeia. Ursa Major (also known as the Big Dipper or the Plough) is a group of seven stars shaped like a saucepan. To locate the North Star, follow the line of the two stars which form the outer edge of the 'saucepan'. These are called the 'pointers', and they point towards the North Star.

CASSIOPEIA

If the Big Dipper isn't visible, locate Cassiopeia, which is a group of five stars in the shape of an 'M' or 'W', depending on the time of night. The middle star of Cassiopeia points straight to the North Star.

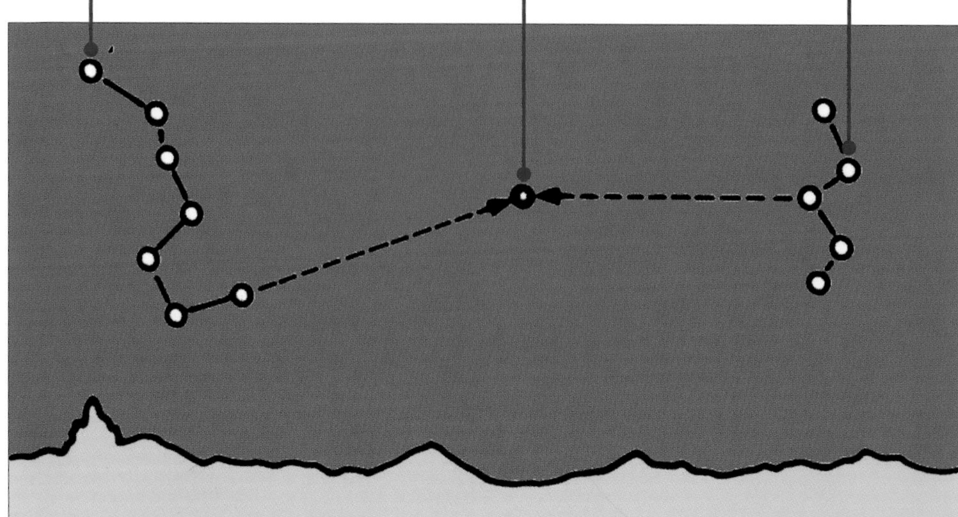

HOW TO FIND THE SOUTHERN CROSS

The North Star isn't visible in the southern hemisphere, and there's no other star conveniently parked under the South Pole to use in its place. Instead, the voyagers of the South have devised an ingenious alternative for night-time navigation without a compass. And this time it's got nothing to do with ploughs or dippers.

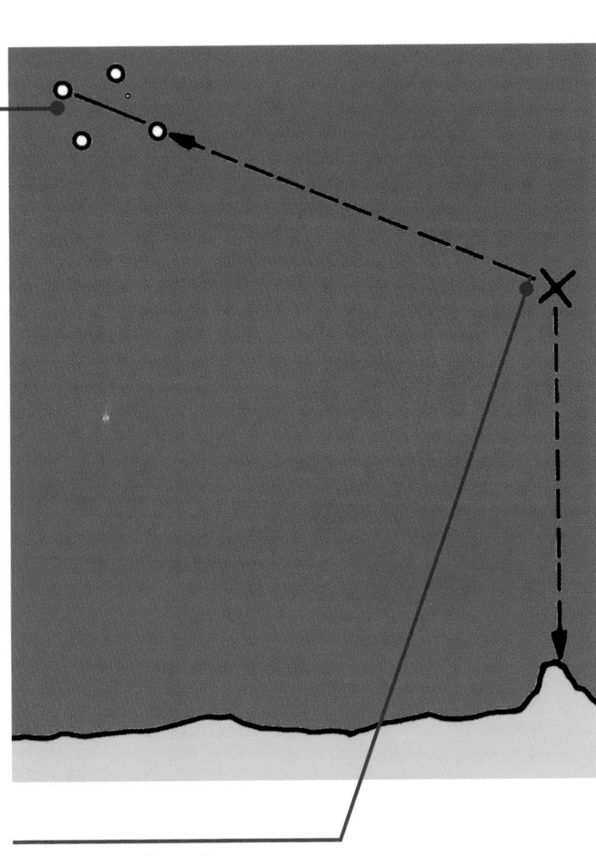

FINDING THE CROSS
The Southern Cross is a constellation of five stars, visible only in the southern hemisphere. The four brightest stars form a cross, tilting to one side. The two stars furthest apart in the group are the pointer stars.

INDISPENSABLE THINGS

- Night sky
- Even sharper eyes

FINDING SOUTH
To find South in the southern hemisphere, draw an imaginary line from the pointer stars in the Southern Cross. Extend the line so that it is 4.5 times the distance between the two stars. Where the line ends is the point above the South Pole. To avoid having to repeat this process, find a landmark on the horizon below this imaginary point and use that to navigate by.

PRACTICAL TIPS
Don't confuse the Southern Cross with the Diamond Cross and False Cross, both of which are located in the southern sky. The Southern Cross is distinguished by its two pointer stars, which stand out from the rest. It's also more kite-shaped than the others, which are more diamond-shaped.

HOW TO CLIMB A TREE

Climbing a tree gives you a different perspective on life. It frees you from your usual attachment to the ground and makes you look at familiar things with new eyes. It also makes you feel like the king/queen of the world – it should be on everyone's list of things to do to stay young.

INDISPENSABLE THINGS

- **Tree with evenly spread branches**
- **Good balance**

CHOOSING YOUR TREE

Choose your tree carefully. Find one that has evenly spread branches, not so close that you might get stuck and not so far apart that you won't be able to move from branch to branch easily.

TESTING THE BRANCHES

As a rule of thumb, if a healthy branch is as thick as your bicep, it should be strong enough to take your weight. Test the branches before you put your full weight on them.

TREES TO AVOID

Some trees, such as sycamore, are prone to splitting suddenly. Avoid them and choose something more trusty, such as an oak. Never climb a dead tree. It might look all right at first sight, but is probably rotten on the inside.

CLIMBING TIPS

Keep your weight as close to the main trunk as possible, where the branches are strongest. Use your legs more than your arms; it's less tiring. Keep a firm grip with your hands at all times, in case your feet slip.

HOW TO CLIMB A CLIFF

There are times when climbing up (or down) a cliff is the only sensible option. There are other times when it's simply the most fun and/or daring option. Either way, there are some precautions you can take that will prevent it from becoming the most dangerous option.

INDISPENSABLE THINGS

- Even balance
- Small steps

POSITION

Unlike the chap in this illustration, you should face the cliff, with the inside of your feet facing in towards the rock. Keep your hands low, preferably between waist and shoulders. Avoid overstretching and becoming spread-eagled. Use several short steps, rather than one long one.

BALANCE

Don't hug the cliff. Keep your body away from the rock face, with your centre of gravity over your feet. Use your feet to power you and your arms for balance. Only move one limb at a time, and keep three points in contact with the rocks – that is, two hands and one foot, or one hand and two feet. Don't use elbows, knees or buttocks.

TEST & REST

Test the rock before putting your weight on it. A crack in the rock face can be used as a hold by placing a hand flat in the crevice and clenching it into a fist to jam it. Rest regularly, keeping your hands low to maintain circulation.

PRACTICAL TIPS

Plan your route carefully. You can minimize the risks by avoiding obvious hazards. The direct route is rarely the safest. Gullies often provide the easiest route, but beware of rockfalls. Don't climb when it's wet.

ACCIDENT & EMERGENCY

GOING TO THE RESCUE

You don't feel like Superwoman or Superman; heck, you don't look anything like them, yet there may come a time when you have to act like them — or, better still, a trained paramedic. You can't become one of these in an instant, but here are some very practical guidelines that could help you help someone in distress.

HOW TO SAVE SOMEONE'S LIFE

As implausible as it may seem, at some point during your lifetime you may find yourself in an emergency situation during which your actions could determine whether someone lives or dies. Certainly an unappealing thought for most of us, but every day, around the world, members of the general public are faced with this scenario. Fortunately, if you follow the advice here you'll dramatically improve somebody's chances of living – it's as easy as ABC.

INDISPENSABLE THINGS

- Mobile phone
- Calm manner
- Safe approach

A PRACTICAL HISTORY OF ABC

The mnemonic or *aide-memoire* ABC was devised in the early 1960s by three doctors, Peter Safar, James Jude and Guy Knickerbocker. Together, along with others, the three developed the ABC protocol along with the closely associated CPR technique (*see pages 268–9*). They presented the procedures during a far-ranging lecture tour and also through the training video 'A Pulse of Life'. Since its inception, ABC has undoubtedly helped to save many thousands of lives.

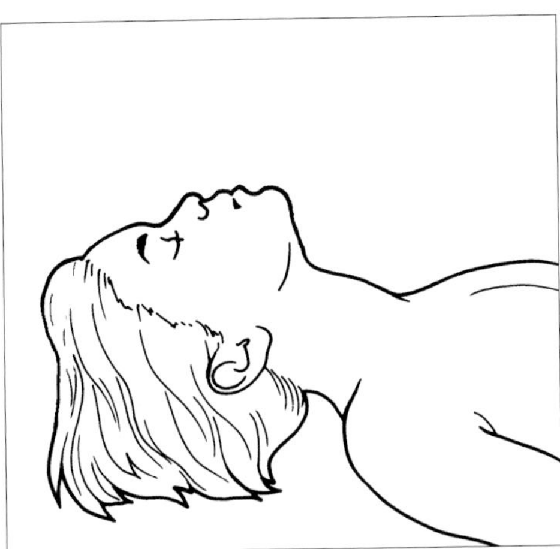

ABC Accepted by the vast majority of first-aid organizations, ABC stands for Airway, Breathing and Circulation – after you've alerted the emergency services, ABC are the first three essential checks that should be undertaken before proceeding with any subsequent first-aid treatment. The checks should be made in that order because without a clear airway, breathing cannot take place, and unless the casualty is breathing, the blood cannot circulate around the body.

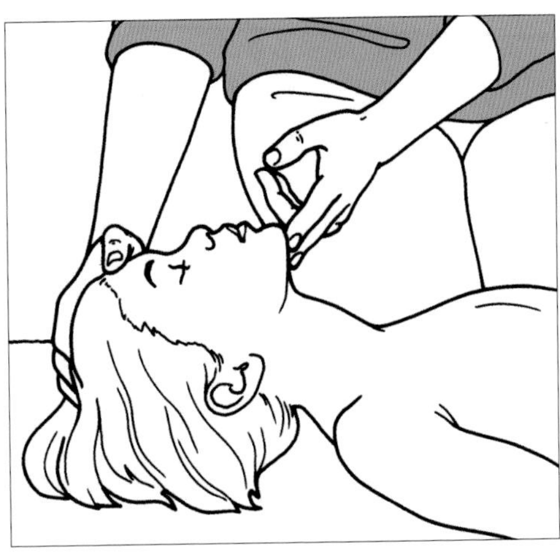

AIRWAY The airway is the passage running from the nose and mouth to the lungs, down which air travels nourishing the blood with vital oxygen. The most common blockages found at the scene of an emergency are caused by food, vomit or the casualty's own tongue. It is vital to remove any blockage (to prevent it falling further into the airway) before effecting a 'head tilt – chin lift' position so that the person can breathe. Lift the casualty's chin with two fingers while at the same time placing your other hand on the casualty's head and tilting it well back.

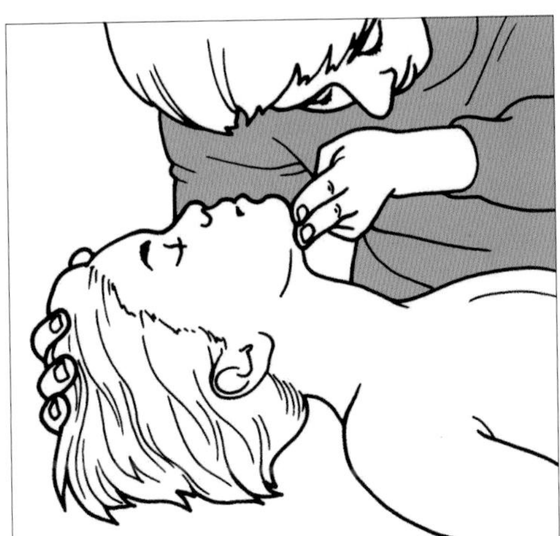

BREATHING With the airway clear, the casualty should be able to breathe. To check this, place your head close to the casualty's mouth and nose – you should be able to feel the person's breath on your cheek and determine how regular the breathing is. If the casualty is not breathing, you'll need to begin CPR (*see pages 268–9*).

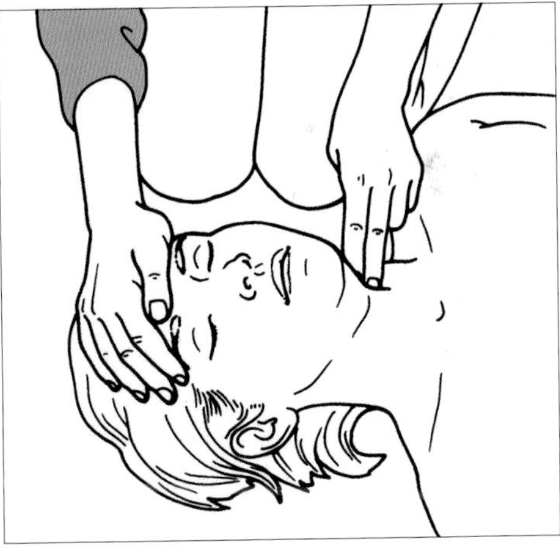

CIRCULATION With a clear airway and the casualty breathing, the heart should be able to pump blood around the body, enabling the exchange of the gases oxygen and carbon dioxide. If the heart is pumping you should be able to feel a pulse. To check for a pulse, place two fingers on the side of the neck in the space between the large neck muscle and the windpipe. If you cannot detect a pulse, begin CPR (*see pages 268–9*).

HOW TO PERFORM CPR

CPR stands for 'cardiopulmonary resuscitation', so we're going to stick with CPR – or you could also think of 'ComPRessions'. Learning how to perform CPR is something that everybody should do; and while the steps shown here provide a good introduction to CPR, they're no substitute for going on a first-aid course and learning the procedure from a qualified first-aid instructor. However, these instructions should help you keep someone alive if they've stopped breathing and the heart's no longer beating until paramedics arrive at the scene and take control – and all the glory (they deserve it).

INDISPENSABLE THINGS

- Mobile phone
- Clear head

PRACTICAL TIP

Before you begin performing CPR, call the emergency services. That way they can get an ambulance on its way and give you reassuring instructions over the phone while you're attending to the casualty.

INDISPENSABLE WARNING

If the casualty is an infant, don't do this because it's too heavy. Hold the back of the neck and press with just two fingers on the midline of the sternum, a finger's breadth below the nipple line.

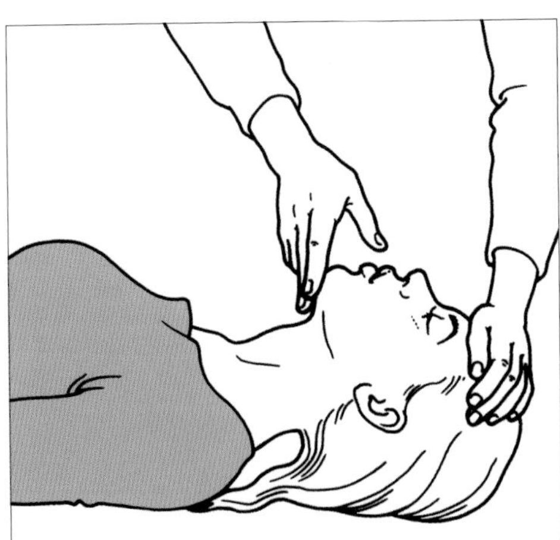

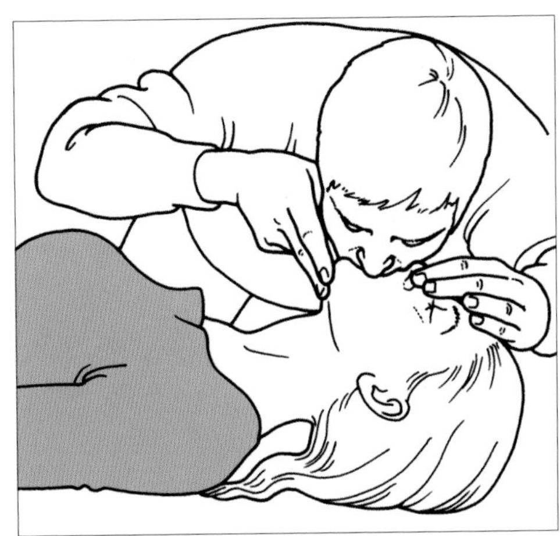

1 First ensure the airway is clear before tilting the casualty's head back. With the casualty lying flat on his or her back, tilt the head back by gently pushing on the chin while at the same time using your other hand to push the person's forehead back. This is the same procedure used for checking the airway in ABC (*see pages 266–7*). Listen for signs of breathing.

2 If the casualty is breathing, check for circulation (*see pages 266–7*) – DO NOT PERFORM CPR. If, however, the casualty is not breathing, close the nose by pinching with your fingers, open the mouth and cover with your own mouth. Take a normal breath and slowly breathe into the casualty's mouth for about a second. The chest should rise as you breathe for him or her. Repeat a second time. This is referred to as rescue breathing.

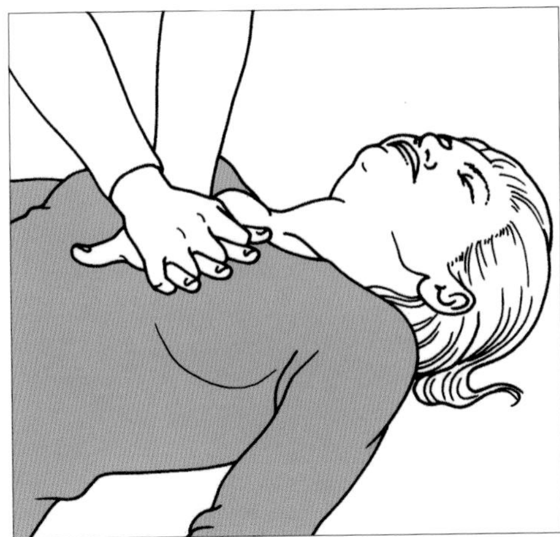

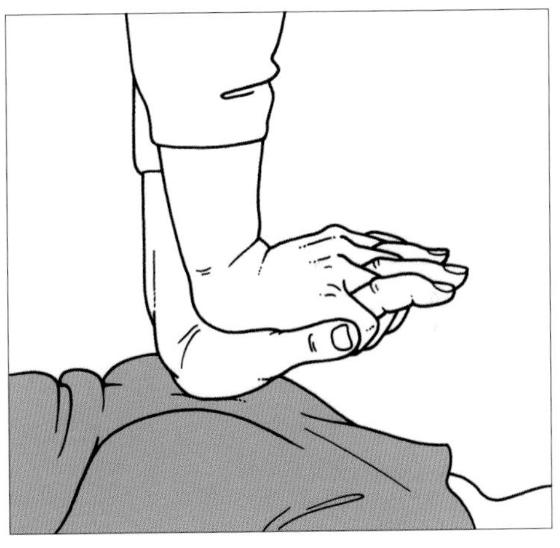

3 Begin chest compressions as soon as you have performed two rescue breaths. Place one hand on the person's chest between the nipples. Place your second hand on top of the first and interlace your fingers. Move your body directly over the patient's, lock your elbows and, using your weight, push down with the heel of the bottom hand. Compress the chest by 4–5cm (1½–2 in). Push hard and fast while counting up to 30.

4 After 30 chest compressions, provide two more rescue breaths and repeat the chest compressions. Perform this cycle five times and then check for a pulse (*see pages 266–7*). If there's no pulse, repeat the cycle until paramedics arrive. If you do detect a pulse, check the casualty's airway and circulation and keep monitoring the pulse to ensure it doesn't fade.

PRACTICAL TIP

Remember you're trying to pump blood round the body from outside the chest wall, so don't be too hesitant. Push hard and fast while counting up to 30.

HOW TO STOP A NOSEBLEED

Although often visually quite spectacular and capable of setting off minor panic in young children, most nosebleeds are perfectly harmless – the sufferer being likely to sustain less damage than any fabric caught within the vicinity of the incident. Caused by ruptured blood vessels, usually due to a strike on the nose, or from picking, sneezing or blowing the nose, most nosebleeds should come under control within around 20–30 minutes.

INDISPENSABLE THINGS

- Chair
- Handkerchief/box of tissues
- Bowl (optional)
- Clean cloth and warm water
- Sympathetic ear

PRACTICAL TIPS

- Encourage the casualty to relax and lie down for 30–60 minutes to avoid the bleeding restarting.
- If the nosebleed persists after 30 minutes, consult a doctor or take the casualty to the hospital, particularly if bleeding has followed a blow to the head and the blood appears thin and watery.
- If a child suffers from repeated nosebleeds, it may be that he or she is picking his or her nose. Keep fingernails trimmed and advise the child against doing it.

KEEP CALM
Keep the casualty calm and reassure the person that there's nothing to worry about. Ask them to sit down on the chair and to lean slightly forwards. This will enable the blood to flow from the nostrils and into a bowl. Offer a handkerchief to mop up any blood on the casualty's hands or face.

KEEP THE HEAD UPRIGHT
Ensure the casualty doesn't tip his or her head back in an attempt to stop the flow of blood. By tipping the head back, blood may flow down the throat and induce vomiting.

PINCH THE NOSE
Ask the casualty to pinch the soft part of the nose (just below the hard cartilage) for about 10 minutes. As well as slowing the blood flow and so encouraging the blood to clot, this will force him or her to breathe through the mouth, which will have a calming effect. After 10 minutes the casualty can release his or her fingers. If the bleeding continues, pinch the nose for a further 10 minutes. Usually the bleeding will stop after this time, after which you can gently clean around the nose with a clean cloth and some warm water.

PRACTICAL TIP
Ask the casualty not to sniff, blow their nose or attempt to clean the nostrils for about 4 hours, if possible, otherwise the bleeding may start again.

HOW TO PERFORM THE HEIMLICH MANOEUVRE

The Heimlich Manoeuvre is a medical procedure used to stop someone from choking. The Manoeuvre comprises a series of abdominal thrusts that are intended to expel the choking object out of the casualty's mouth. First described by Henry Heimlich in 1974, the Heimlich Manoeuvre is estimated to have saved around 100,000 lives in the US alone, including those of Ronald Reagan, Elizabeth Taylor and Goldie Hawn, to name just three.

INDISPENSABLE THINGS

- Strong arms
- Sturdy back

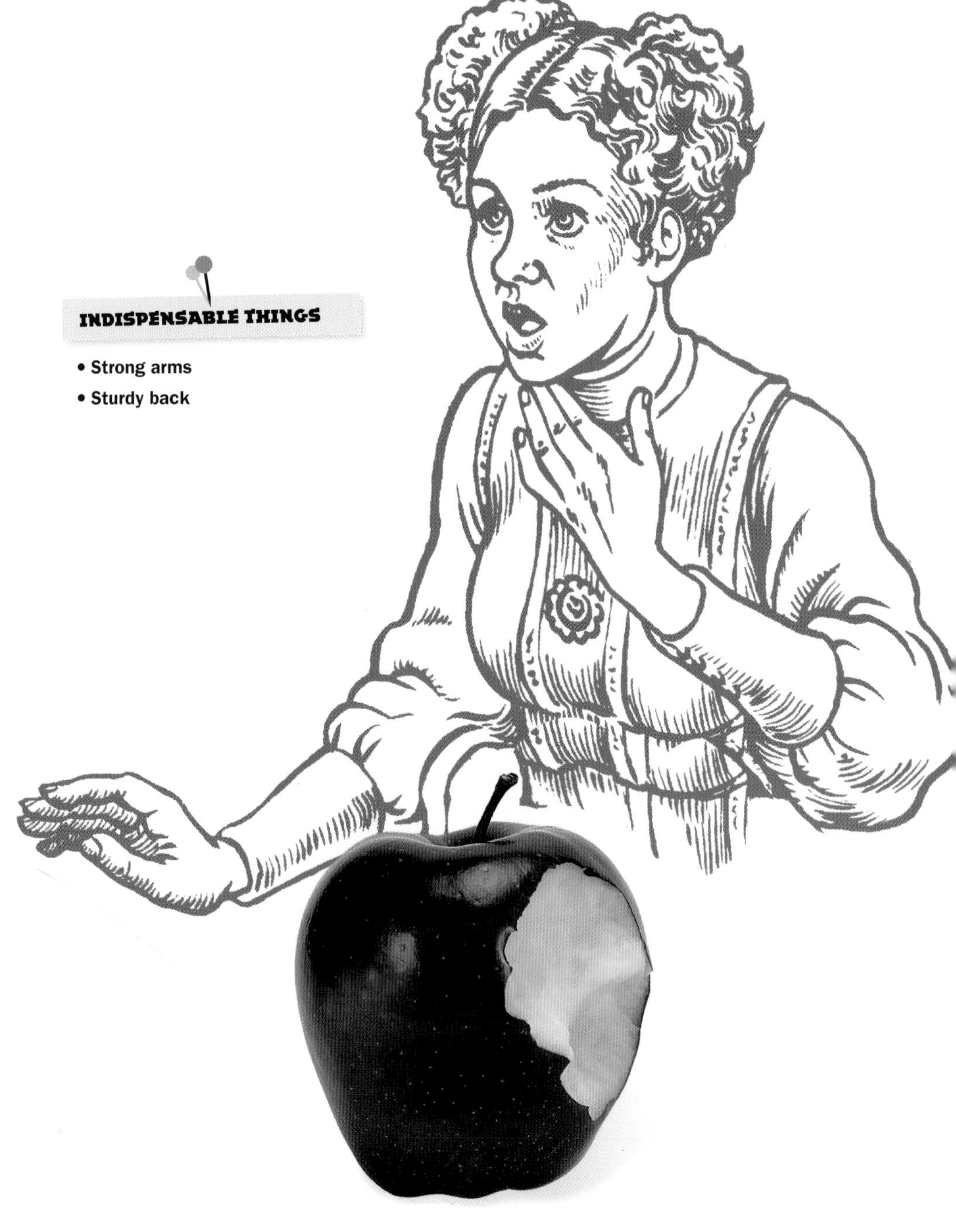

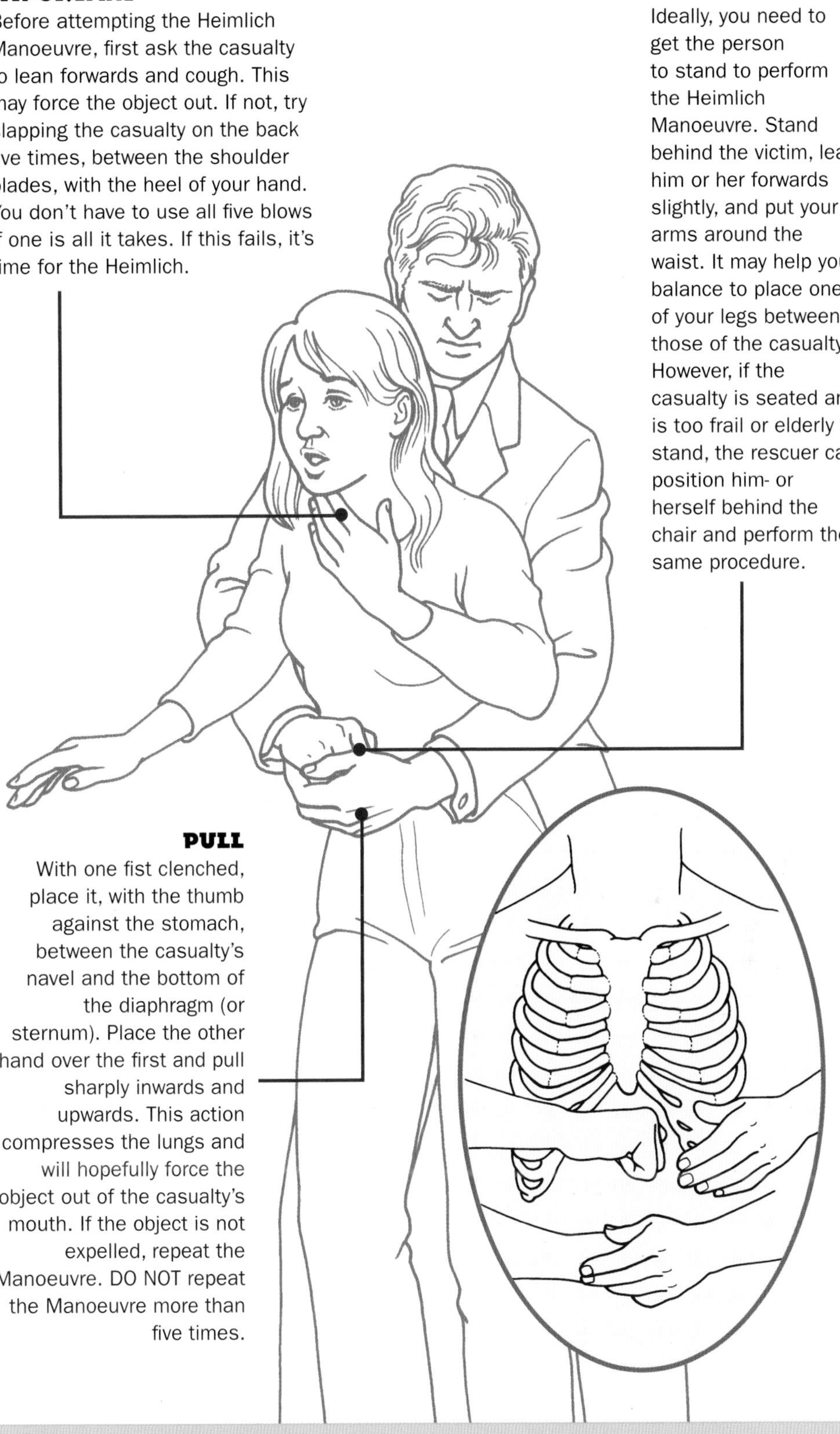

IMPORTANT

Before attempting the Heimlich Manoeuvre, first ask the casualty to lean forwards and cough. This may force the object out. If not, try slapping the casualty on the back five times, between the shoulder blades, with the heel of your hand. You don't have to use all five blows if one is all it takes. If this fails, it's time for the Heimlich.

POSITION

Ideally, you need to get the person to stand to perform the Heimlich Manoeuvre. Stand behind the victim, lean him or her forwards slightly, and put your arms around the waist. It may help your balance to place one of your legs between those of the casualty. However, if the casualty is seated and is too frail or elderly to stand, the rescuer can position him- or herself behind the chair and perform the same procedure.

PULL

With one fist clenched, place it, with the thumb against the stomach, between the casualty's navel and the bottom of the diaphragm (or sternum). Place the other hand over the first and pull sharply inwards and upwards. This action compresses the lungs and will hopefully force the object out of the casualty's mouth. If the object is not expelled, repeat the Manoeuvre. DO NOT repeat the Manoeuvre more than five times.

INDISPENSABLE WARNING

While the arm action of the manoeuvre needs to be short and sharp, it mustn't be too strong. There have been a number of cases of overzealous administrators damaging the casualty's sternum, liver or stomach. Even when performed with an appropriate amount of pressure, the abdomen is likely to suffer some bruising as a result.

HOW TO MAKE A SLING

One of the more unpleasant side-effects of gravity is that it can make little boys and girls fall out of trees and big boys and girls fall off ladders. In fact, gravity is responsible for all sorts of accidents that can often result in broken arms, dislocated collar bones and sprained wrists. Ouch! If you have family members who like trying to cheat gravity, you may find making a sling a useful skill. A sling will keep the injured arm still, preventing further injury, and elevated, which stops swelling.

INDISPENSABLE THINGS

- Piece of cloth about 1m (40in) square or a pillowcase cut open
- Soft material for padding
- Large safety-pin or tape
- Second bandage or piece of cloth or a belt

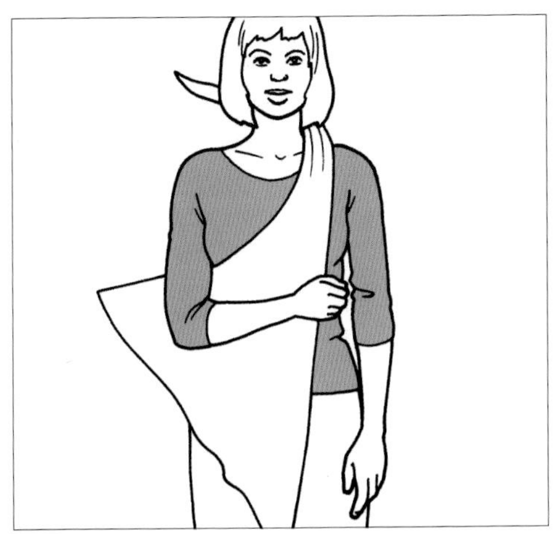

1 Take the cloth or pillowcase and fold or cut it in half to make a triangle. Ask the casualty to support the injured arm across his or her chest so that it is as comfortable as possible; ideally the hand should be slightly higher than the elbow. Gently place the cloth under the injured arm so that half is above the elbow and half below.

2 Bring the top end of the sling around the neck and lift the bottom end up to form a cradle for the injured arm. Make soothing noises while performing this operation as it will help you assume the role of nurse.

3 Tie the top and bottom ends of the bandage together at the neck. Use the knot to adjust the height of the sling, ensuring that the arm remains in the most comfortable position. Place a pad underneath the knot as it can be very uncomfortable for the patient. Make sure that you leave the hand of the injured arm exposed and accessible so that you can check for circulation and sensation. Next bring the third end around the elbow and attach it to the front of the sling using a safety-pin. Be aware, particularly in the elderly, of any neck problems that could be exacerbated.

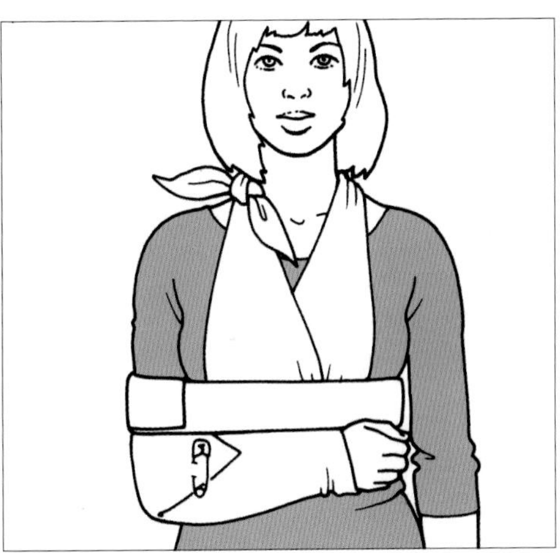

4 Finally, to prevent the sling moving backwards and forwards as the casualty walks or moves about, take a second bandage and fold it into a long strip. Place it under the uninjured arm, around the casualty's back and around the front of the sling. Tie the ends together or attach them using a safety-pin. If you don't have a second bandage, a loosely buckled belt will suffice.

INDISPENSABLE WARNINGS

Remove all rings and any tight jewellery from the patient's injured side, particularly if the arm or wrist is damaged, as swelling can occur.

HOW TO MAKE A SPLINT

If your little one comes dashing to you gingerly holding an arm that appears swollen and/or bruised, and has difficulty moving his or her fingers, the arm may well be fractured – and if the broken end of a bone is poking through the skin, then you have a strong indication that things aren't as they should be. If you can't get medical attention quickly, you'll need to make a splint so that the sharp ends of broken bones don't inflict further damage to veins, arteries or nerves.

INDISPENSABLE THINGS

- Soft material for padding
- Rigid but lightweight lengths of material
- Lengths of flexible material for ties

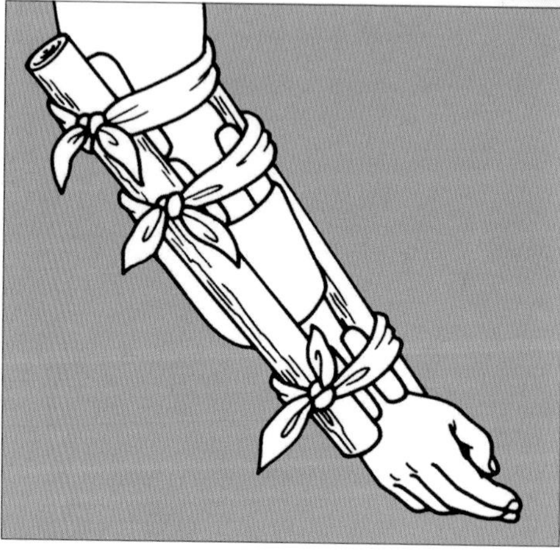

ARM WOUND If you are dealing with an injury to the arm, clean any visible wound as thoroughly as possible before attaching the splint to prevent infection. Do not attempt to straighten the injured arm, simply surround it with soft padding, attach the rigid lengths along the length of the arm and secure them with the ties. Get the casualty to hospital as quickly as possible.

LEG WOUND If you are dealing with a leg wound, ask the casualty to sit or lie, thus taking any weight off the injured leg. Clean any wound and stem the flow of any bleeding. Get the casualty to hospital as quickly as possible. Wrap the leg in blankets or other padding. Apply the rigid lengths to the back of the leg and the bottom of the foot. Add additional rigid lengths to the sides of the leg if necessary, and use the ties to keep the splint together.

HOW TO MEASURE A PULSE

The pulse is an indication of the body's heart rate. There are any number of reasons why you might want to measure and record a person's, or even your own, pulse – whether to assess how well a casualty is responding to treatment, to monitor the effectiveness of your aerobic exercise routine or just to check how fast your heart's beating, although you're unlikely to be checking that yourself.

INDISPENSABLE THINGS

- Sensitive fingers
- Watch

WRIST

The wrist is the most effective location for measuring the pulse. Place your first and second fingers on the casualty's wrist, just below the base of the hand between the tendons and the bone (in line with the thumb is about right). Apply gentle pressure until you can feel the pulse.

COUNT

Count the number of beats you feel in your fingers for 15 seconds. Multiply this by four and you have the casualty's pulse, which is traditionally measured as beats per minute (bpm).

HOW TO RESPOND TO AN EPILEPTIC SEIZURE

Epilepsy was first described some 3,000 years ago, and although doctors know a great deal about the condition today, the specific causes are often hard to pinpoint. The good news is that epileptic seizures are usually successfully managed with a variety of drugs — around 80 per cent of sufferers lead perfectly normal lives. However, the risk of seizure cannot be ignored — here's how to respond.

INDISPENSABLE THINGS

- Anything soft to place under the sufferer's head
- Ability to remain calm

INDISPENSABLE WARNING

Call the emergency services if you think that this is the person's first seizure; if the seizure lasts longer than 5 minutes; if a second seizure begins before the person has regained consciousness; or, the sufferer is pregnant.

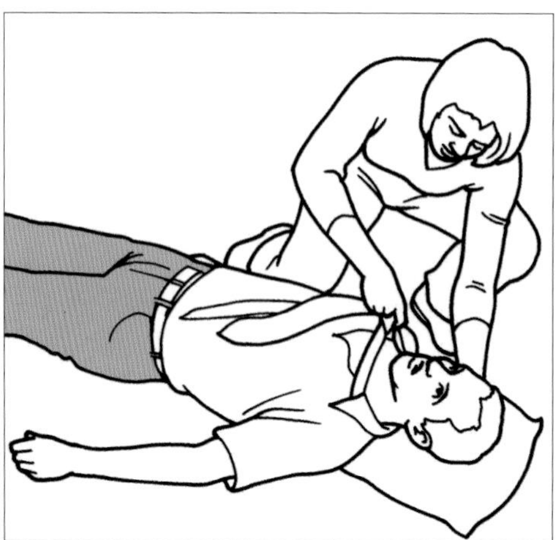

1 In the case of a severe seizure, do not attempt to hold or control the sufferer or administer any medication. Do not check to see if the person has swallowed his or her tongue – this cannot happen during a seizure. Move all objects, such as furniture, well away to prevent injury. Place something soft under the sufferer's head to prevent accidental injury and loosen any restrictive clothing, such as a tie or collar.

2 As the seizure begins to pass, gently roll the sufferer into the recovery position because this will help to keep the airways clear. Do not be alarmed if the person's lips become blue; they should return to normal colour after the seizure. When the person regains consciousness, be calm and reassuring – he or she will soon make a full recovery.

INDISPENSABLE FACTS

Seizures vary in severity. In some cases the sufferer may simply appear dazed, in which case all you need to do is stay with him or her and be reassuring when the seizure has passed. If the person suffers from epilepsy they are likely to be wearing a special medic-alert necklet or bracelet.

HOW TO TREAT A SNAKEBITE

Most poisonous snakes are shy creatures that rarely come into contact with humans. So while the risk of being bitten by a venomous snake is small, that's stark consolation for the 2.7 million people who are bitten on average around the world each year, of whom some 125,000 don't survive. Venomous snakes live on all continents, so all of us need to be aware of the risk — however slight it may be.

INDISPENSABLE THINGS

- Bandage or length of cloth
- Soap and water

KEEP CALM

If you or someone with you is bitten by a snake and you're in a region where venomous snakes are found, stay calm, but assume it's poisonous.

PROCEDURE

Now follow these generally agreed procedures:

- If possible, wash the bite with soap and water.
- Keep the bitten area immobile and below the level of the heart to reduce blood flow.
- Call the emergency services and get the victim to hospital as quickly as possible; try to provide a description of the snake.
- DO NOT give the victim anything to eat or drink, especially alcohol – this will cause the circulation to accelerate and spread the poison more quickly.

REASSURANCE

It is vital that the victim should be calmed as much as possible and their breathing slowed and to keep the entire body (not just the affected limb) immobile in order to reduce the speed with which the poison circulates in the bloodstream.

INDISPENSABLE WARNING

A venomous bite is more likely to be fatal in the young and the old. Do not hesitate to call an ambulance to get the victim to hospital.

HOW TO TREAT A BEE STING

It is almost comical that something the size of a bee can ruin many a relaxed picnic and cause such displays of panic in humans, creatures who are comparatively huge – mice and elephants spring to mind. And for the great majority of us it is comical, aside from the risk of a minor sting; it's far less amusing, however, if you know you suffer from anaphylaxis, or severe allergic reaction.

INDISPENSABLE THINGS

- Knife or piece of card
- Clean dressing
- Soap and water
- Ice/cold compress

STAY STILL

The first thing to do if anyone around you is stung is to ask them to stay still and identify exactly where the sting is. If it's a bee sting, there may well still be a venom sac and sting visible. Brush this off with the back of a knife or a piece of card. Don't attempt to pull it out using your finger tips or tweezers, as you might inadvertently squeeze the venom sac, so releasing more venom into the victim.

DRESS THE WOUND

Wash the sting with soap and water and apply a dressing to the wound. Placing some ice against the dressing may reduce any pain and swelling.

INDISPENSABLE WARNING

Watch the casualty carefully for any signs of an anaphylactic reaction, such as breathing difficulties or a swollen face or neck. If such symptoms arise, call the emergency services immediately and explain what has happened.

HOW TO TREAT A DOG BITE

No doubt most of us at some point have enjoyed the cartoon of a dog chasing a postman – what cheeky little chappies our canine friends are, eh? Well, no, actually. In real life it isn't something to snigger about. Around 6,000 people are hospitalized in the UK each year due to dog attacks, and a whopping 4.7 million people are bitten each year in the US – the majority of them children.

INDISPENSABLE THINGS

- Soap and water
- Gauze swabs
- Clean plaster or dressing

INDISPENSABLE WARNING

In some countries there is a risk that dogs, particularly wild dogs, carry rabies. If you are bitten abroad, always seek medical advice – it may be necessary to have anti-rabies injections.

CHECK FOR TETANUS
Always ask the victim if he or she has had a tetanus injection in the last 10 years. Even if the wound is small, without immunization it's best to seek medical advice.

KEEP IT CLEAN
Not only are dog bites painful, but they also carry a real risk of infection. First wash your own hands (or put on disposable latex gloves if they're available) and then clean the wounded area thoroughly with soap and warm water.

DRESS THE WOUND
Dry the area with clean gauze swabs and apply a plaster or dressing. If the bite is deep, take the victim to casualty or call the emergency services.

HOW TO TREAT A BURN

Although we occasionally laugh at comedy bee stings and long-legged postmen in flight from an excitable pup, cartoonists rarely get much humour mileage from burn victims — and that's because they really aren't funny. As most of us know, even the smallest burn, such as those sustained through careless cooking, can be incredibly painful and the thought of anything more severe really doesn't bear thinking about. Unfortunately, burns are pretty common, so we'd best know how to deal with them.

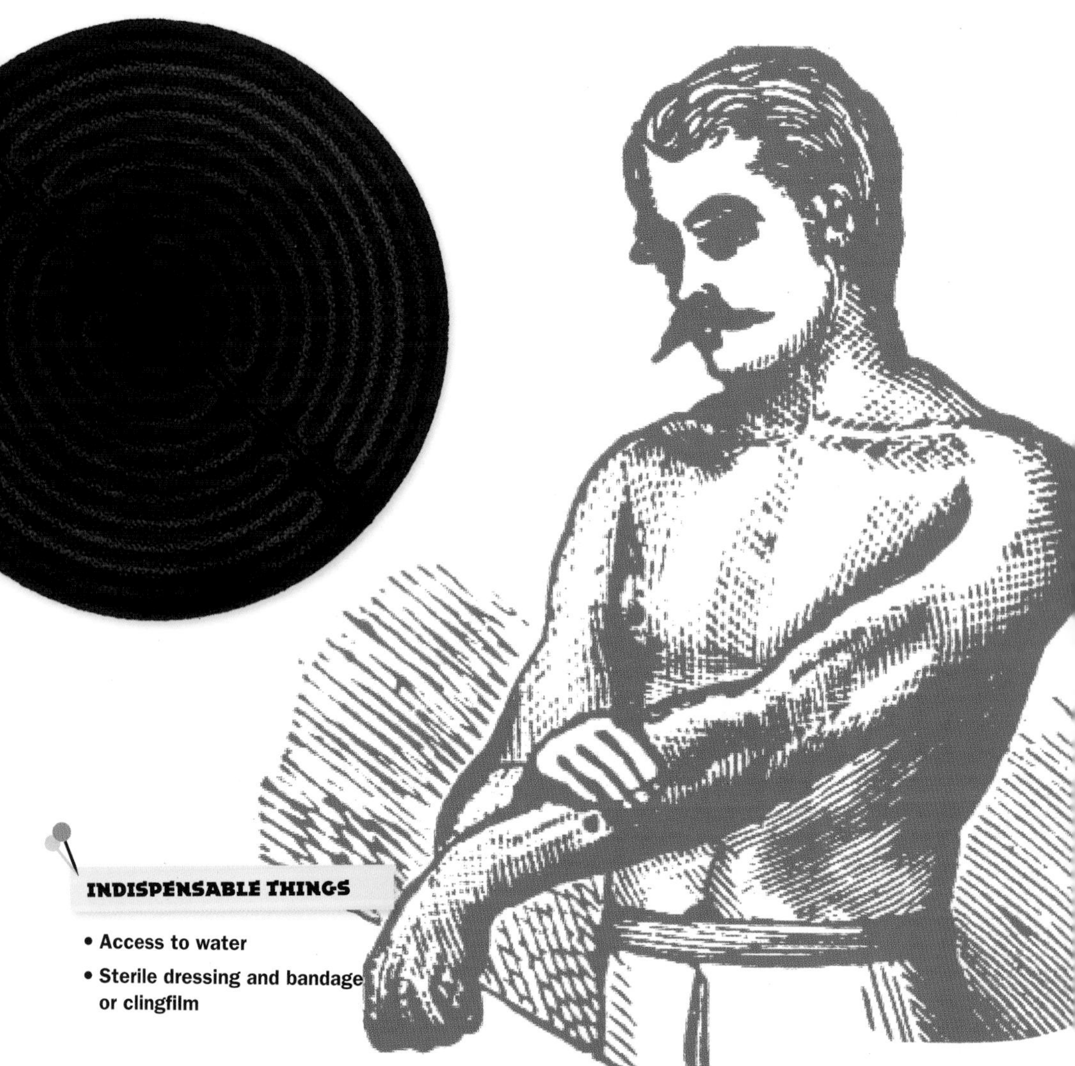

INDISPENSABLE THINGS

- Access to water
- Sterile dressing and bandage or clingfilm

CATEGORIES OF BURNS

• First degree — topmost layer of skin only affected. Skin turns red and, when pressed, white. Blisters don't form and risk of infection is slight.
• Second degree — more layers of the skin are affected, including the wetter tissue layers and those layers containing the nerves. Blisters will form and the area will swell up. Risk of infection.
• Third degree — skin potentially charred or missing altogether. Extremely high overall health risk to victim.

INDISPENSABLE WARNINGS

- Do not apply creams or ointments – they will have to be scrubbed off, which can be extremely painful for the patient. And they may introduce infections to the wound.
- NEVER burst blisters: they help to keep the burn moist and clean.

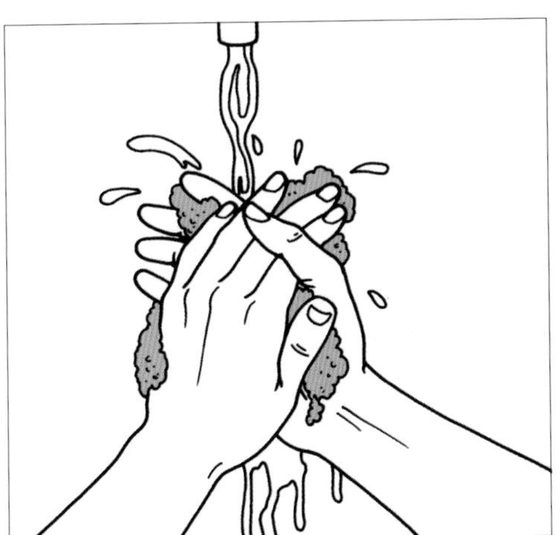

1 The risk of infection with a burn, particularly one in which the skin is broken or actually burned away or has caused bleeding, is very high. Before you attempt any first aid, quickly but thoroughly wash your hands. Alternatively, use disposable latex gloves if they're available.

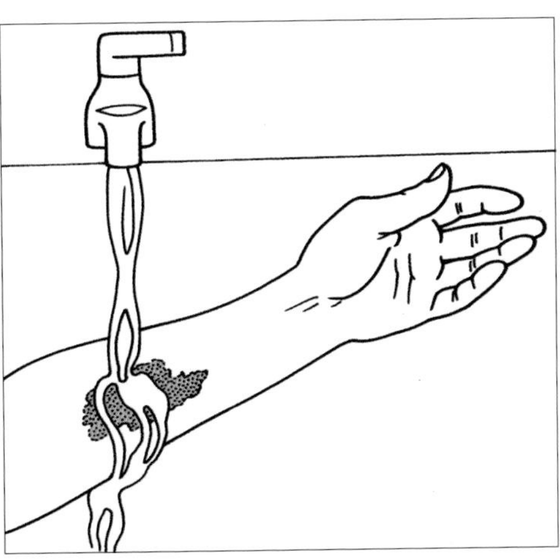

2 After you've made the casualty as comfortable as possible, pour cool (not cold) water over the injured area for at least 15 minutes (depending on the severity of the burn). Preferably immerse the injured part in a bowl or bath to keep it under water. It's essential to lower the skin temperature to minimize damage and to keep loss of body fluids to a minimum.

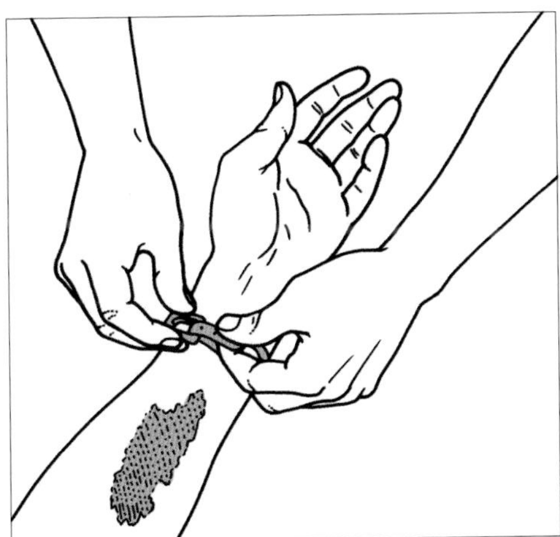

3 Once you've lowered the temperature of the burn, remove any items of jewellery or clothing located near the burn. Depending on the severity of the burn the area is likely to swell up and items such as these may well restrict blood flow and cause additional pain. Do not, however, attempt to remove any clothing or any other item caught in the burn area as this will aggravate the injury.

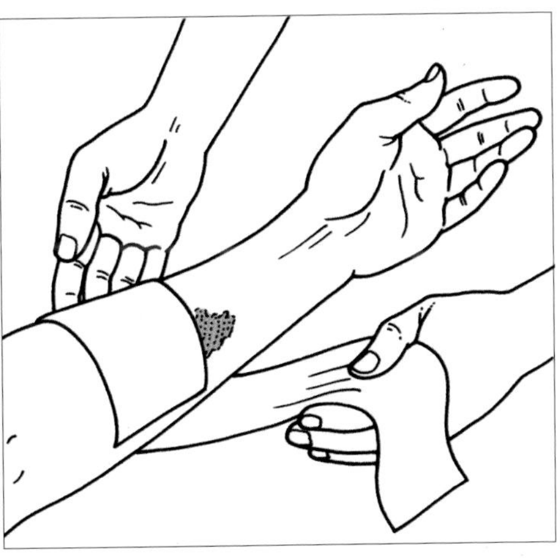

4 Cover the burned area with a sterile dressing and wrap a loose bandage around it to keep it in place. If you don't have a dressing, cover the area with anything that won't introduce fluff or other particles into the wound, such as clingfilm. If more than redness persists after this time, take the patient to A&E for a proper burns dressing to be applied. Ideally travel by car to minimize exposure to the air and any germs.

HOW TO TREAT A GUNSHOT WOUND

In view of the high-profile reporting that gun crime attracts, you'd be forgiven for thinking that the Wild West was constantly being replayed in many of our large towns and cities; in fact, gun crime accounts for no more than 1 per cent of violent crime in the UK, and even in the US, where gun laws are more relaxed, the figure is only around 9 per cent. But we can't be complacent – every day firearms are used to perpetrate a variety of crimes, and on each occasion someone could end up being shot.

INDISPENSABLE THINGS

- Blanket
- Mobile phone
- Clean dressings/towels

INDISPENSABLE WARNINGS

- Do not touch any protruding internal organs. Cover them with clingfilm or a clean plastic bag to prevent them drying out and to reduce the risk of infection. If you have a sterile dressing, use that.
- Do not raise the victim's legs above the wound in an attempt to treat for shock, as this will only exacerbate the bleeding. For a chest injury, secure any dressing on three sides only – you must leave one side open for air to escape from the pleural cavity.

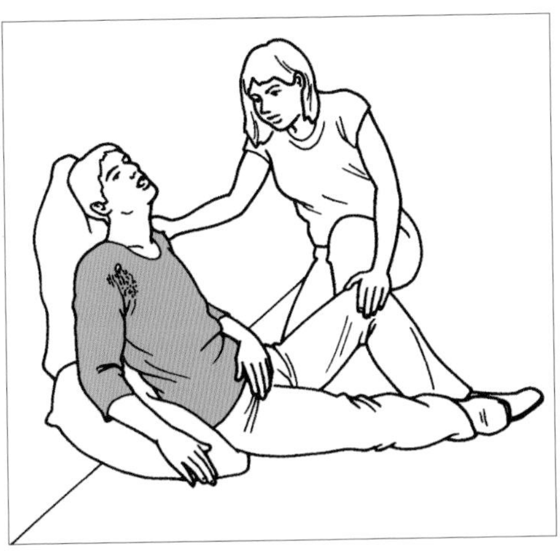

1 Before going to the aid of someone who has been shot, be certain that you are safe to do so. You can't help the victim if you become one yourself. If the casualty is still conscious, try to make him or her as comfortable as possible, put a blanket around the victim, and get him or her to stay as still as possible – unnecessary movement will only aggravate the injury. Call the emergency services.

2 If the victim is unconscious but breathing, place him or her in the recovery position (as illustrated above). Call the emergency services. First check the airway for blood (*see* ABC, *pages 266–7*), especially if the injury is to the chest. Make regular checks to ensure that the victim is still breathing. If breathing stops, you may need to begin CPR (see step 4 below).

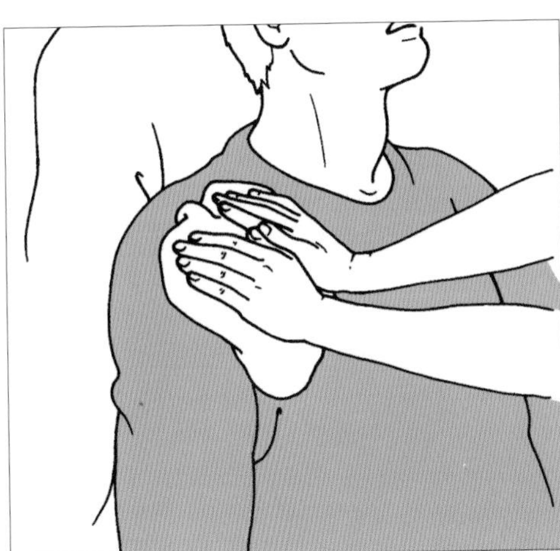

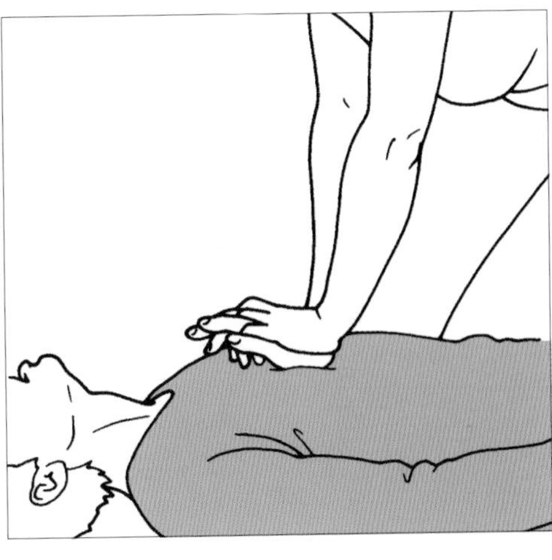

3 With the casualty as comfortable as possible, try to identify the source of any bleeding – you may need to remove clothing to be sure of the exact locations. This is important as next you need to use pressure to stop the bleeding. Ideally, press on the wound with clean dressings; if these aren't available, use towels or anything that will help to soak up the blood.

4 If the victim falls unconscious and stops breathing, check to ensure the airways are clear and proceed with CPR (for full instructions, *see pages 268–9*). If the victim has been shot in the chest, take extra care when performing the chest compressions.

HOW TO TREAT A STAB WOUND

Recent years have seen a sharp rise in the incidents of knife attacks, particularly in the UK. Much of this is due to inter-gang rivalry amongst teenage boys, made worse by the fact that an increasing number of youngsters feel the need to carry a knife as a form of protection. Add to this that, unlike guns, knives are readily available and fairly cheap and you have a bleak outlook.

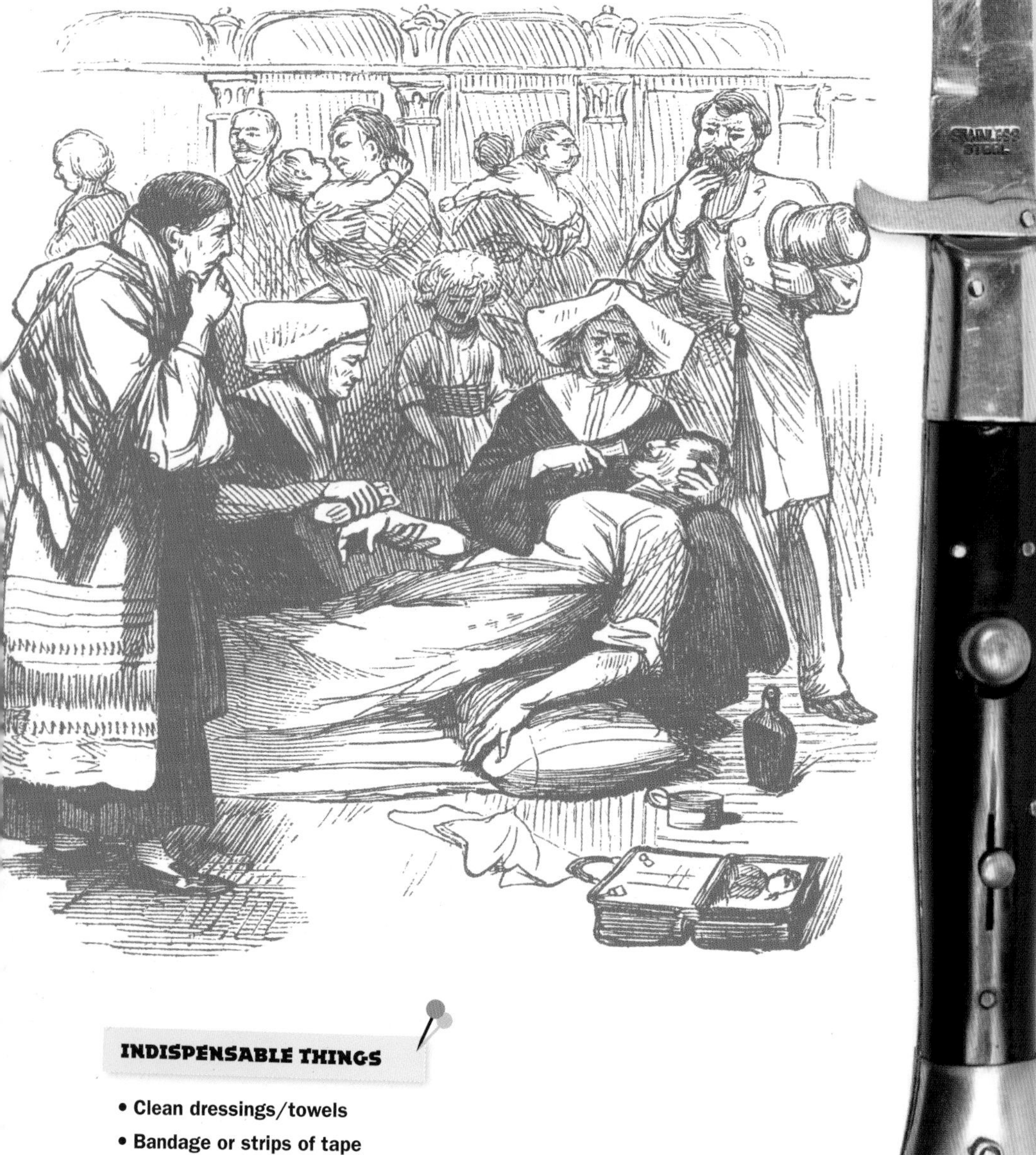

INDISPENSABLE THINGS

- Clean dressings/towels
- Bandage or strips of tape
- Mobile phone
- Blanket

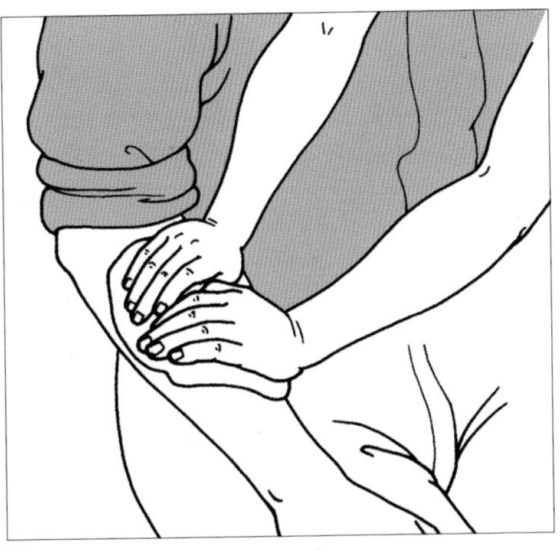

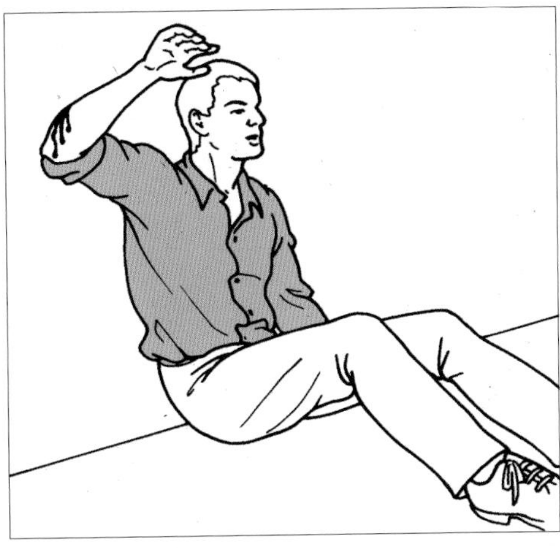

1 As in any violent crime scenario, do not go to the victim's aid until you know it is safe to do so. First check the airway for blood (*see* ABC, *pages 266–7*), especially if the injury is to the chest. Carefully remove any clothing to help you pinpoint its exact location. Use any clean absorbent material, ideally a clean dressing, and press it to the wound to slow the rate of bleeding.

2 Now cover the dressing with a bandage or strips of tape to hold it in place. For a chest injury, secure on three sides only (see box below). Reassure the victim and make him or her as comfortable as possible. Get him or her to sit up and to try to keep the wounded area above the level of the heart to help reduce further blood loss. Phone the emergency services.

3 Continue to monitor airway, breathing and circulation. Use a blanket or coat to keep the victim warm. Loss of blood and suffering from shock can lower the body temperature. Ensure that the casualty is comfortable and is lying as still as possible. Keep reassuring the casualty and let him or her know that medical help is on its way.

INDISPENSABLE WARNINGS

- To avoid the risk of infection, use disposable latex gloves if they're available; alternatively ensure your hands are as clean as possible before undertaking first aid.
- If the victim has suffered a stab wound to the chest, use kitchen foil, clingfilm or a clean plastic bag over the dressing – it's vital to leave one side open for air to escape, and prevent it from entering the pleural cavity, which would cause the lungs to collapse (when the victim inhales, the patch adheres to the skin).
- If the knife has remained in the victim, do not attempt to remove it if this is likely to cause additional bleeding. Dress the wound around the knife as best you can.
- If the victim falls unconscious but is still breathing, place him in the recovery position (*see page 285*) and monitor his breathing.
- If the victim is not breathing, begin CPR (*see pages 268–9*).

HOW TO DELIVER A BABY

It's the scenario that strikes fear into every expectant father (and mother, no doubt). The car won't start, you've called for an ambulance, but there's a fallen tree on the road and the paramedics can't get through – and now mum-to-be's waters have broken! So what next? Well, the first and most important thing is to stay calm; remember women have been giving birth in all sorts of environments for hundreds of thousands of years and the vast majority of them coped without sterile maternity wards and banks of monitoring equipment – it'll be fine...

INDISPENSABLE THINGS

- Pillows
- Plastic sheeting (or newspapers)
- Clean towels
- Disposable latex gloves (if available)
- Blankets
- Plenty of warm water
- Sanitary towels

INDISPENSABLE WARNINGS

- Do not cut the umbilical cord.
- Do not throw away the placenta; medical staff will need to check this is complete.
- Do not smack the baby.

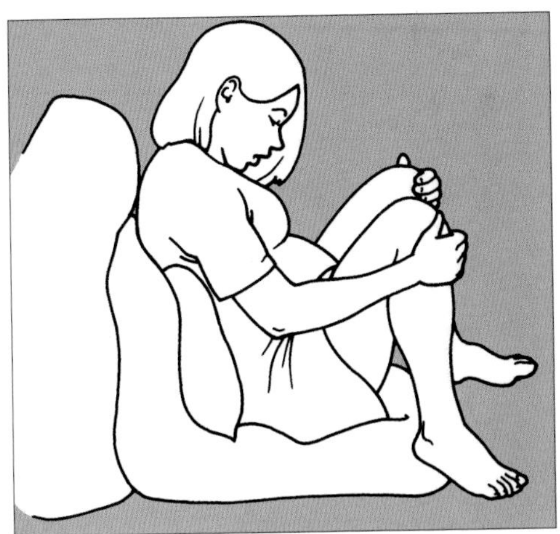

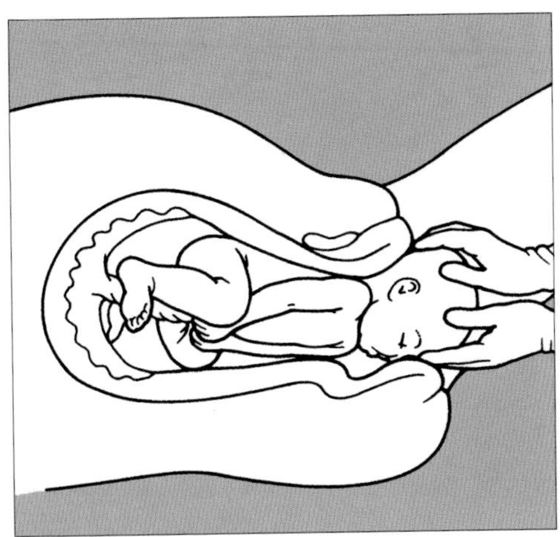

1 Offer plenty of support and reassurance. Start timing the contractions and let the mother assume whichever position she feels most comfortable in, and provide her with pillows. Try to get the mother to take deep, slow breaths during and after the contractions. This will help her to remain calm and ease the pain. In the meantime quickly prepare a clean delivery area. Place the plastic sheeting (or newspapers) on a bed and cover with towels. When the time between contractions is less than two minutes, the baby is ready.

2 Ask the mother to lie down on the area you've prepared. Thoroughly wash your hands and arms or put on latex gloves if available. When the baby's head is visible, tell the mother to push when she feels a contraction starting. Ask her to take a deep breath, hold it and push. Get her to relax and breathe deeply between contractions. As the baby's head emerges, gently support it with your hands – DO NOT pull.

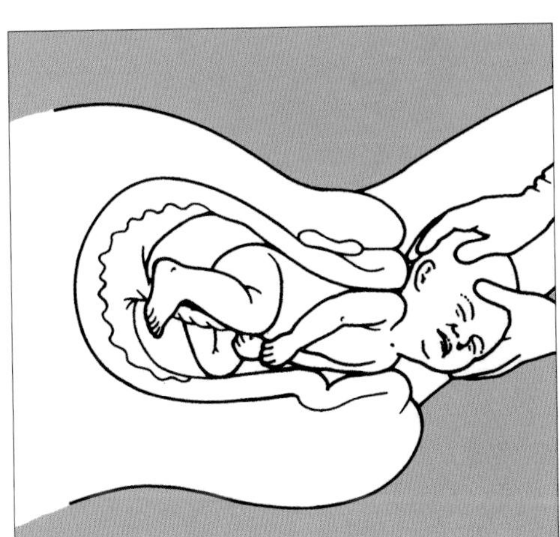

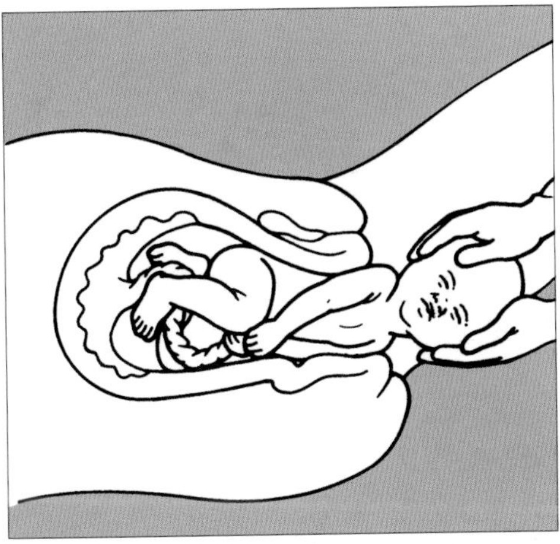

3 As the head continues to emerge it will naturally turn to one side. Gently move to one side and wipe away any membrane that may be covering the baby's face so that he or she can breathe easily. Ensure the umbilical cord is not going to wrap itself around the baby's neck as he or she emerges. If the cord is wrapped around the baby's neck, ensure that it is loose before carefully pulling it over the baby's head.

4 While the mother continues to push, guide the head downwards to allow the top shoulder to emerge first. The rest of the body will follow with the next contraction. Guide and support the baby using a towel so that he or she doesn't slip in your hands. When the baby is fully born, hold him or her so the feet are higher than the head, cover fully in blankets with just the face exposed and lay the baby on the mother's stomach. Encourage her to feed the baby, as this will help to bring about contractions that will expel the placenta. Clean the mother with warm water and provide sanitary towels to absorb any final bleeding.

HOW TO TREAT FOR ELECTRIC SHOCK

The improved design of electrical appliances and more sophisticated electrical circuitry have resulted in fewer cases of electrocution over the years, particularly around the home. Yet it's important to remain mindful when handling any form of electrical appliance – particularly those that use a powerful motor and are used out of doors, such as lawn mowers and hedge cutters. Always check the condition of any appliance and its lead for signs of exposed wires and use a circuit-breaker when recommended.

INDISPENSABLE THINGS

- Broom handle
- Towel

INDISPENSABLE WARNING

Don't attempt DIY fixes on any electrical appliance by removing protective covers – certainly not while it's plugged in.

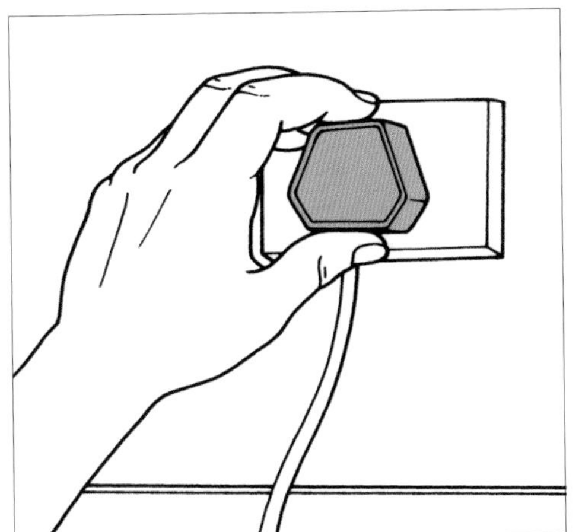

1 If someone has suffered an electric shock and is still in contact with the appliance, the priority is to turn off the appliance. You can do this either by switching off and unplugging the appliance at its local socket or by turning off the mains switch at the consumer unit.

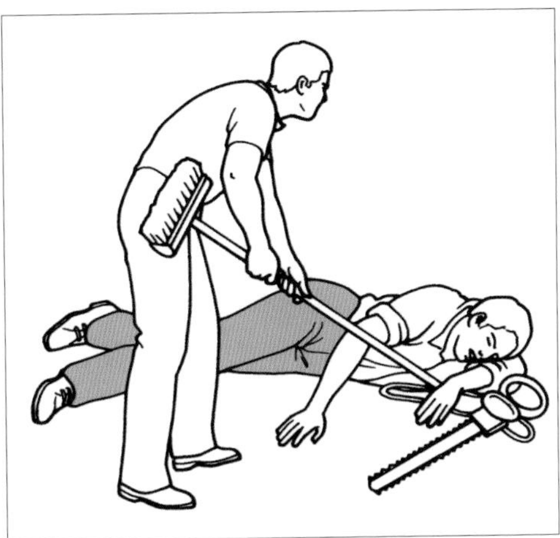

2 If either of the above steps is not possible, knock the appliance away from the casualty's hands using a wooden broom handle. Don't attempt this with a metal pole or the current may pass through you. Nor should you attempt to drag the person away as, again, the current may pass through you.

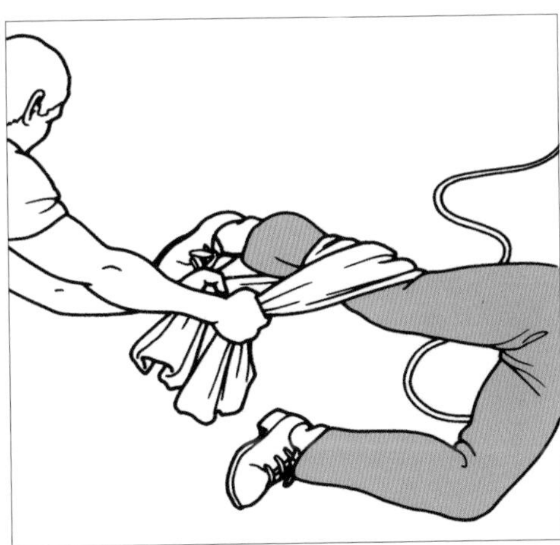

3 If the appliance cannot be easily moved, it may be necessary to drag the person away. Use a towel wrapped around the casualty's leg to pull him or her away. Alternatively, if a towel or similar piece of material is not available, pull on any loose article of clothing that is not in direct contact with the victim.

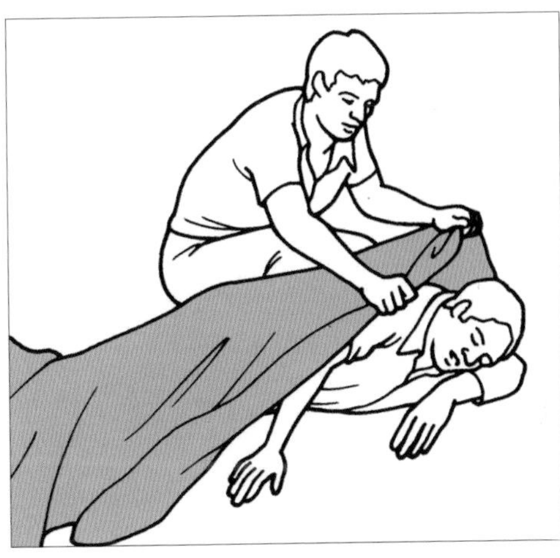

4 Once the casualty has been removed from the appliance and is conscious, cover him or her in a blanket and, depending on the severity of the shock, call the emergency services. If the casualty has sustained burns, try to take the heat out of the burns by running cool water over them and await the emergency services.

If, once freed, the casualty is breathing but unconscious, place him or her in the recovery position (*see page 285*) and periodically check that he or she is still breathing while waiting for the emergency services. If the victim is not breathing, begin CPR (*see pages 268–9*) and continue until paramedics have arrived on the scene.

HOW TO RESCUE SOMEONE FROM DROWNING

Statistics indicate that the risk of drowning in most developed countries is somewhere in the region of 1 in 100,000, or 0.001 per cent – also, when you factor in that a good proportion of those who do perish in inland waterways, swimming pools, rivers, lakes and seas are, unfortunately, young men who have had too much to drink, then the risk to a responsible, sober adult like yourself is pretty small. However, although you might not be the one in the water, one day you may find yourself having to fish someone out.

INDISPENSABLE THINGS

- Buoyancy aid
- Long, sturdy stick
- Length of rope
- PRE (Public Rescue Equipment), if available

INDISPENSABLE WARNING

If you see someone in difficulty in the water, suppress any thought of simply diving in and 'pulling' them out. It just doesn't happen like that. Someone drowning will acquire immense strength and in their panic will do anything to get out of the water, and that includes climbing all over you and pushing you underwater.

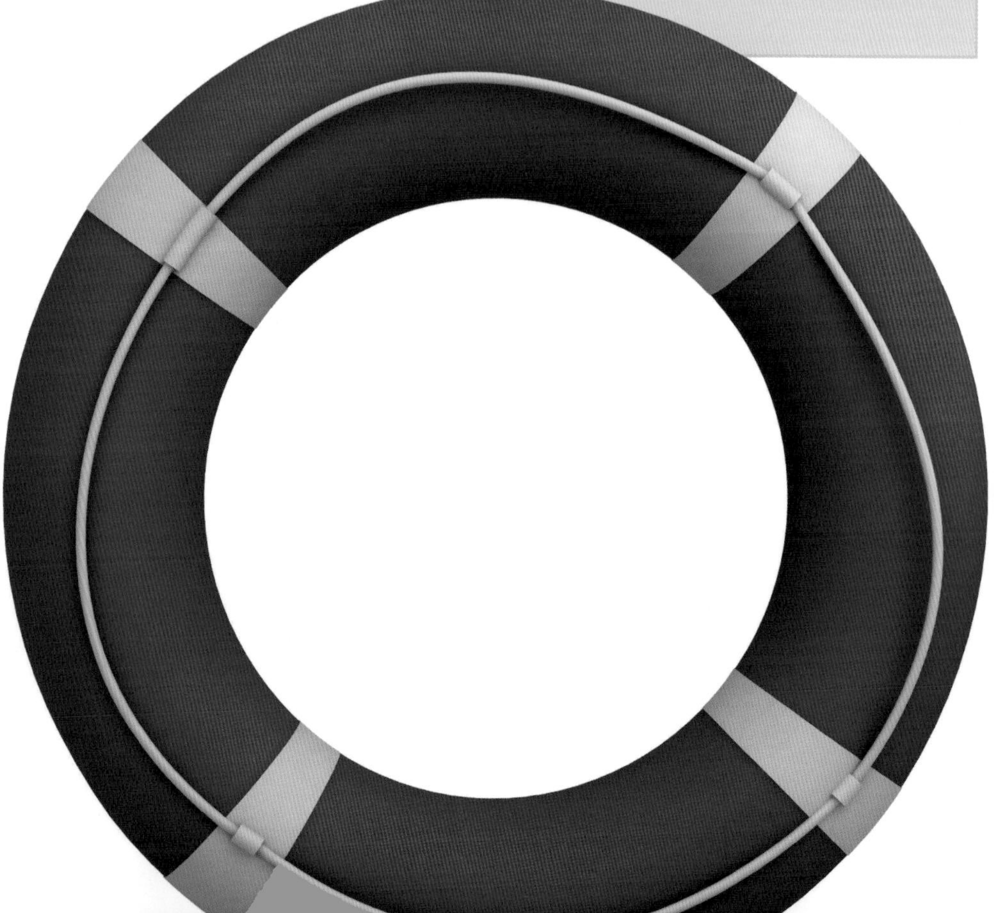

1 After you've called the emergency services, look around for some form of buoyancy aid or flotation device. If you're at a swimming pool, a popular coastal resort or on a boat, there should be one to hand. Ideally the device should have a rope tied to it. Throw it to the person in the water; when he or she has a firm hold, pull him or her gently to the edge.

2 In areas of water less well known for swimming there may not be a buoyancy aid to hand, in which case you will have to improvise. Again, don't be tempted to jump in yourself. Many lakes and river banks are near to stands of large trees. Find a long, sturdy branch to hold out to the person in the water. Alternatively, a piece of rope will do the job.

3 If there is nothing at hand to throw out or offer, lie on the side on your stomach. Ideally there'll be someone there to hold your legs. Now reach out to the person in the water and try to get them to grasp your wrist.

4 Of course learning to swim is one of the best ways to prevent drowning. Most professional swimming instructors begin by getting people to feel comfortable with the idea of just floating. Go to a part of the pool where you can touch the bottom. Pull your feet up and push forward, and try lying on your back in the water with your face above the surface. Take deep but measured breaths and the air in your lungs, together with gentle leg and arm movements, will keep you afloat.

HOW TO PERFORM AN ICE RESCUE

Perhaps it's the fault of the *Omen II* (you remember the man trapped under the ice looking pleadingly up at his would-be rescuers) that icy lakes create such universal dread – or perhaps it's because they're just plain dangerous. Yet every year thousands of people seem to think it's fine to go tearing off onto the ice with little more concern for health and safety than getting the largest guy to jump up and down on the ice a few times.

INDISPENSABLE THINGS

- **Rope**
- **Long, sturdy stick**
- **Mobile phone**
- **Blanket**

LAST RESORT ONLY

If there is nothing with which to reach the victim or throw to him or her, and no way to call the emergency services, as a very last resort crawl out on your stomach. If he or she is a fair way from the bank, form a chain. Lying on your stomach will spread your weight.

USE A STICK OR ROPE

Don't attempt to approach the victim on the ice; if it hasn't supported the casualty's weight there's no reason why it will support yours. Try reaching them with a long stick or pole, or throw them a rope. Naturally, the victim will be struggling against the cold, so get him or her to tie a rope around his or her body so you can pull him or her in. If his or her hands are too cold to do this, the victim should wrap coils of rope around his or her arm, which should hold for long enough to pull the victim out.

DEALING WITH EMERGENCIES

When you sit down to think about it, you're risking your life every time you go out the front door. So don't sit down and think about it. Sure, some people endure bad things all the time, but they're a drop in the ocean compared with the billions of us who go about our emergency-free existence blissfully unaware. But just suppose...

HOW TO PUT OUT A FIRE

According to government sources there is a domestic fire in the UK every 8 minutes, while in the US, fire crews respond to domestic fires every 17 seconds – sobering stats. And while most domestic fires start in the kitchen, it is the careless disposal of smoking materials – in other words, people falling asleep in bed or in a chair while smoking – that causes the greatest fatalities.

INDISPENSABLE THINGS

- ABC-rated fire extinguisher
- Fire blanket
- Bicarbonate of soda
- Mobile phone

PRACTICAL TIP

ABC-rated fire extinguishers are so called because they can be used on all three types of fire: A = wood, paper, etc.; B = fat, oil, etc.; C = electrical. Individual types of extinguisher (i.e. A, B or C) are available, but should only be used on the relevant type of fire.

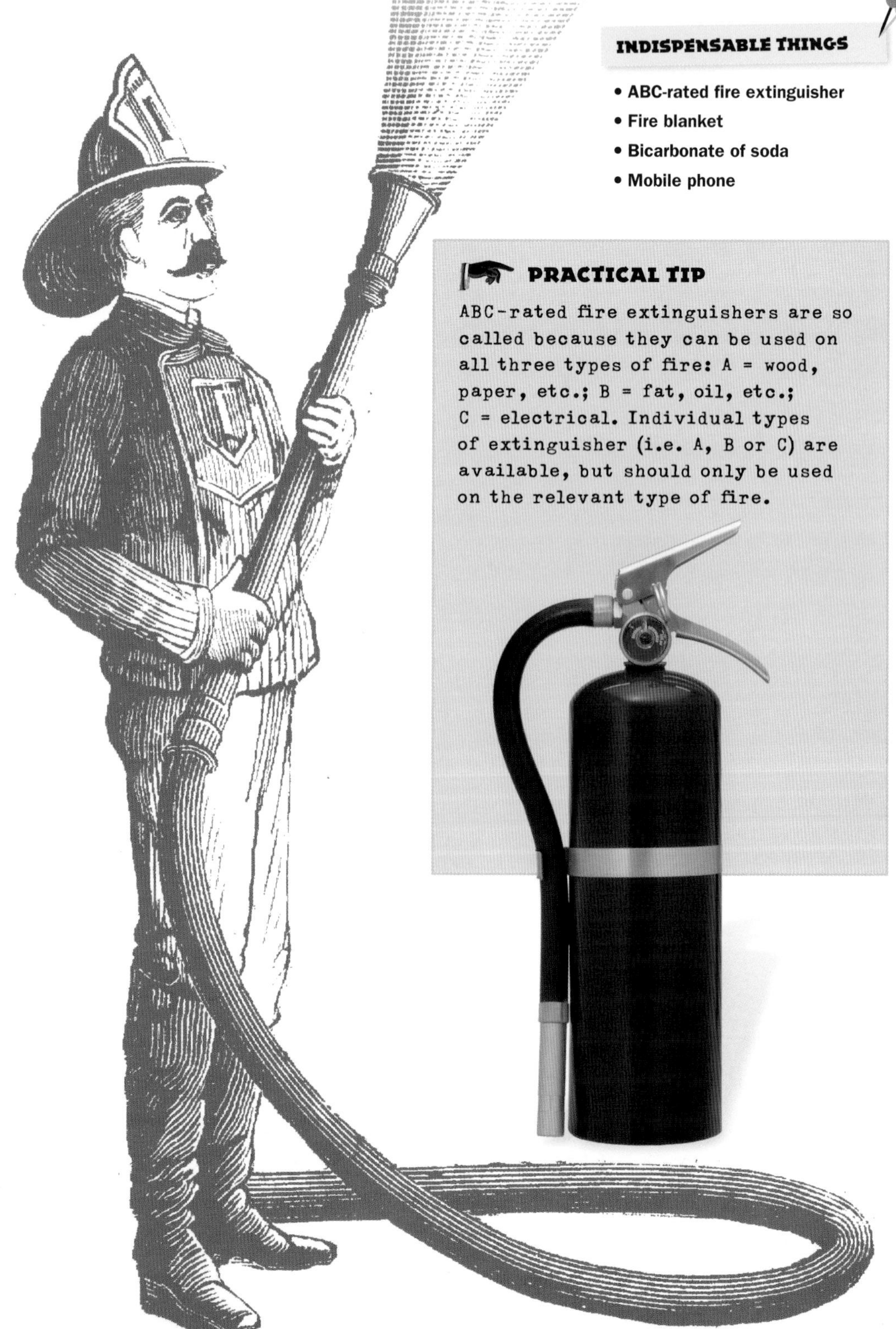

DISCOVERING A FIRE

On discovering a fire in the home, assess its severity and, if in any doubt as to whether or not you can get it under control, evacuate the building. Remember, fire develops quickly – don't lose valuable time trying to gather up important possessions, just leave via the safest route and contact the emergency services.

If you're absolutely certain that you can tackle the small blaze, assess the type of fire it is and act accordingly. There are three types of fire, as shown here:

TYPE A For any fire that involves paper, wood, cardboard, clothing and other material, it is safe to douse the fire with water. If the object on fire is sufficiently small and you are able to hold it safely in some way, take it to the bath or sink. This will contain the fire and prevent it spreading.

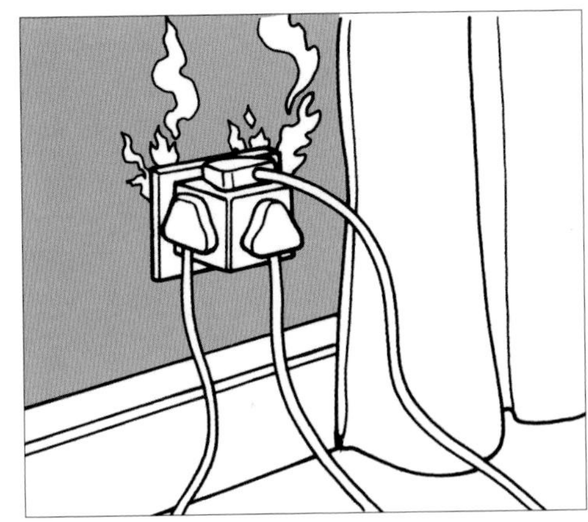

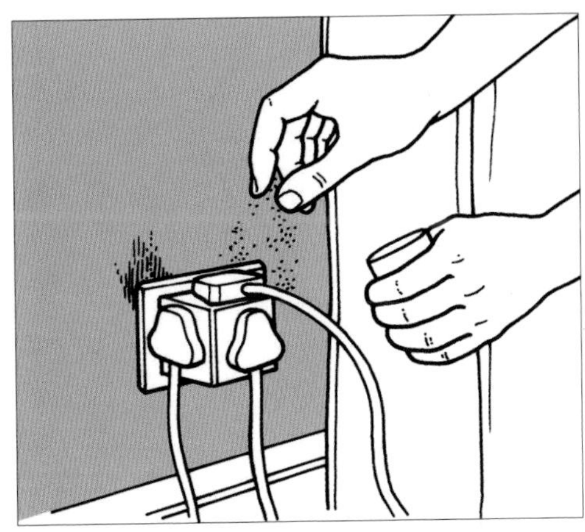

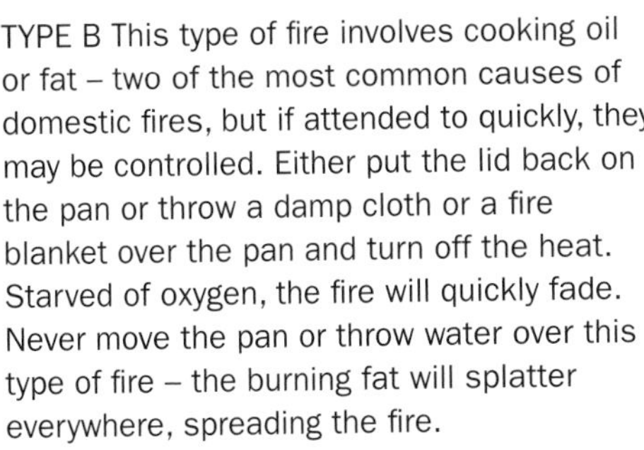

TYPE B This type of fire involves cooking oil or fat – two of the most common causes of domestic fires, but if attended to quickly, they may be controlled. Either put the lid back on the pan or throw a damp cloth or a fire blanket over the pan and turn off the heat. Starved of oxygen, the fire will quickly fade. Never move the pan or throw water over this type of fire – the burning fat will splatter everywhere, spreading the fire.

TYPE C The third type of fire is electrical, usually caused by overloaded sockets, poorly wired electrical appliances or frayed electrical cables. First of all, go to the mains switch and turn off the electricity supply. The best way to tackle electrical fires is by covering them in bicarbonate of soda. Again, do not throw water on an electrical fire, or you may get a powerful electric shock.

HOW TO OPERATE A LIFE RAFT

There you are enjoying a gin and tonic astern before dinner, when a loud crunching and grinding sound followed by shouts and exclamations indicates that you're about to have your own mini *Titanic* episode. Fortunately, unlike the *Titanic*, the ship you're on is fully equipped and has sufficient life rafts for everyone; unfortunately, the small crew are behaving in a most un-*Titanic* fashion and have already abandoned ship with one of the life rafts, leaving you and your companions to fend for yourselves.

PRACTICAL TIP

Give everyone a task such as opening and assessing the emergency kit, looking out for other passengers in the water, attending to first aid and operating any signalling equipment that might be available. Ensuring that everyone has a job to do will help them work together as a team.

INDISPENSABLE THINGS

- Life raft
- Survival kit
- Mobile phone

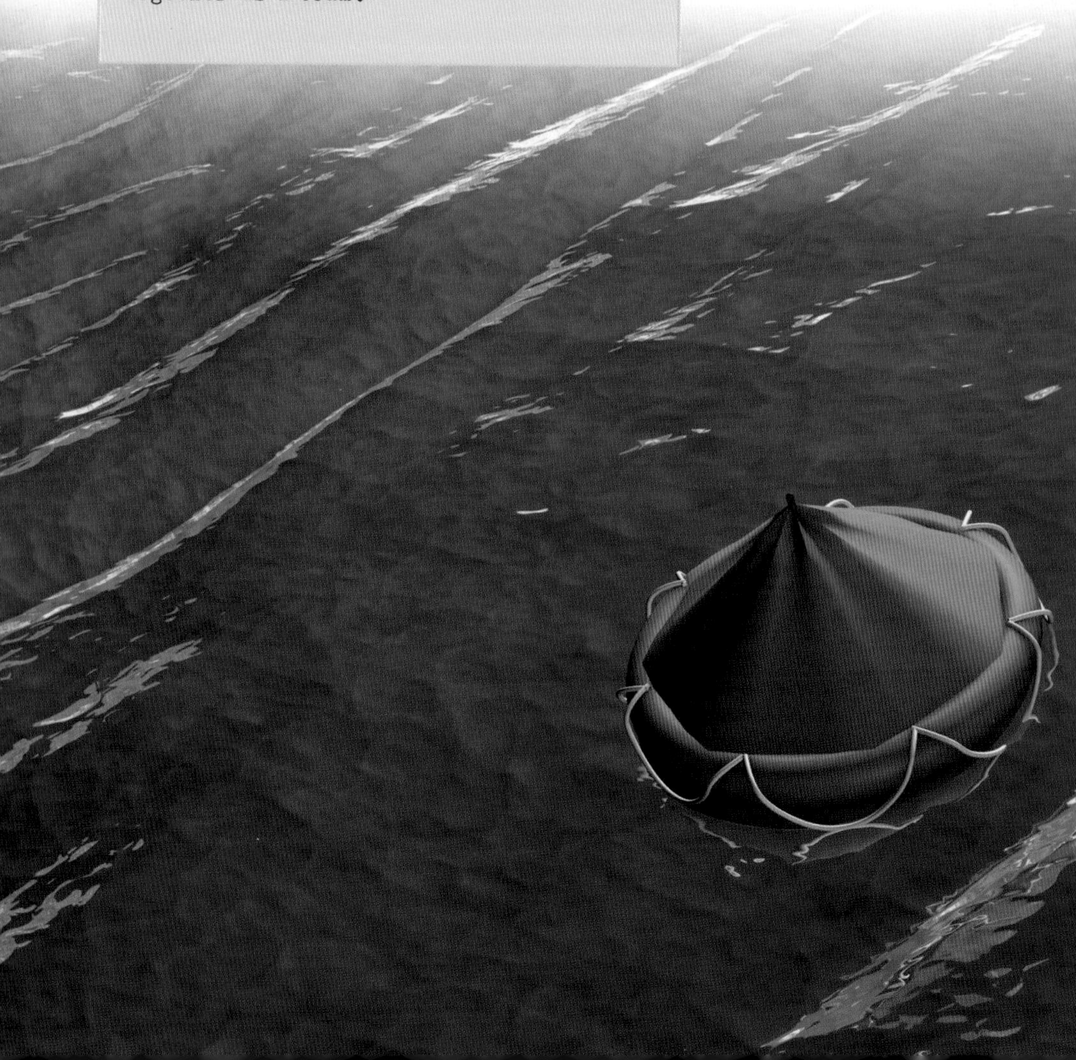

A PRACTICAL HISTORY OF HYDROSTATIC RELEASE

The best life rafts are those fitted with a hydrostatic release device. This device will instigate the automatic inflation of the raft if it hasn't been manually inflated. As the ship sinks, pressure builds in the hydrostatic release until a cutting blade is activated, which cuts the raft free. The activation line itself, however, remains attached to the release and, as the boat continues to sink, the line is stretched tight by the floating raft container on the surface. Eventually the activation line will pull on the gas canister and the raft will inflate. The activation line will then break free from its weak link.

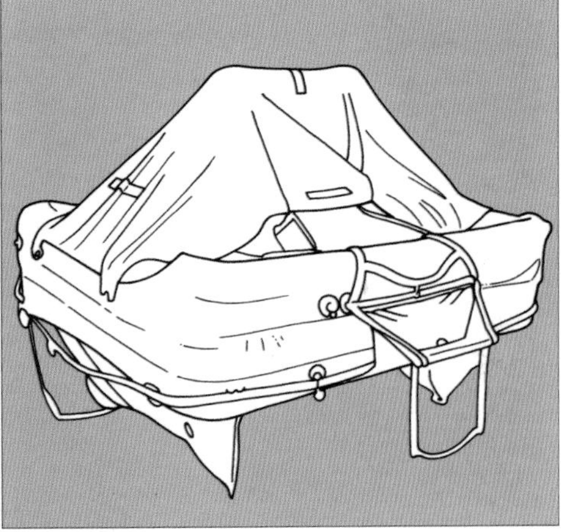

1 If the ship is relatively small, you may have to launch the raft yourself. Ask someone to help you. They don't have to be Superman, but two is definitely better than one. Free the raft from its cradle while still in its container and lift it to the ship's rails. Don't undo the retaining/activation length of rope, which will be attached to a device (hydrostatic release) on the cradle. Ensuring there is nothing sharp in the water to puncture the raft, throw the raft container over the side. Pull the activation line until it is taut, then give it a sharp tug. The raft will automatically inflate. Using the retaining/activation line, pull the raft closer to the ship.

2 Choose the strongest-looking person to get in the raft first. Hand him or her the retaining line to stop the raft from floating away. Ask individuals to then climb into the raft. They should all help to ensure the raft doesn't float away and help the next individual in. Once everyone is in the raft, cut the retaining line at the hydrostatic release end using the knife in the raft, so that you have a length of line attached to the raft. Ask your fellow survivors to spread themselves around the life raft so that it is evenly balanced and not to stand up.

HOW TO OPERATE A LIFE JACKET

Frequent fliers, you might think you're exempt from this section, but you're not — so listen up. And while we're at it, this section applies just as much to the boating fraternity as it does to our fliers — so you need to pay attention, too. In fact, whenever you go out in a boat, no matter how small it is, or how near to the shore you intend to remain, always wear a life jacket — modern designs aren't overly bulky and allow for free movement.

INDISPENSABLE THINGS

- Life jacket

1 As soon as you are informed by the captain or the steward to put on your life jacket, reach under the seat and retrieve the package containing the folded jacket.

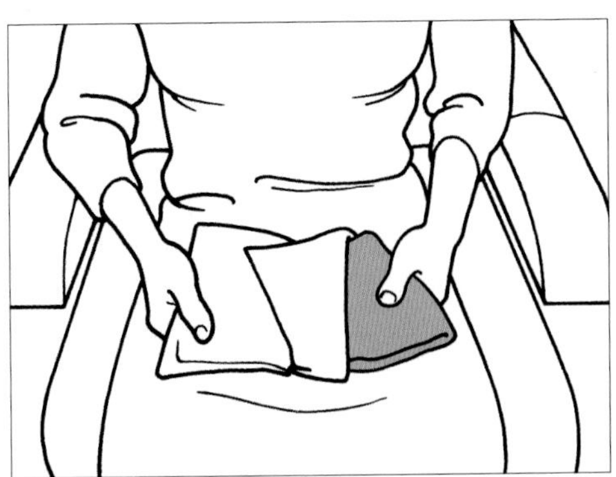

2 Remove the life jacket from the package and unfold it so that the front is facing away from you.

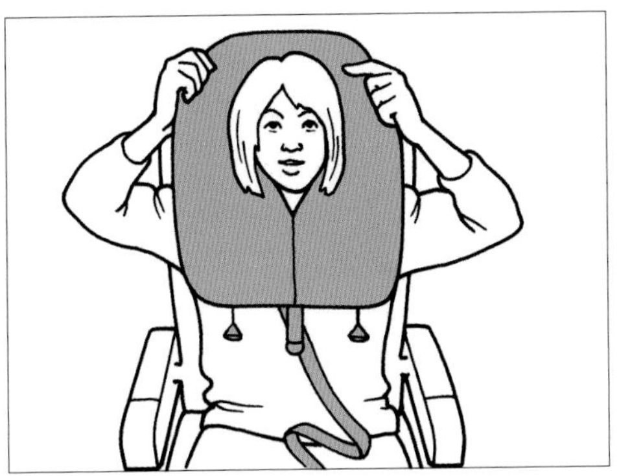

3 Place the life jacket over your head and pull it down so that it sits firmly on your shoulders.

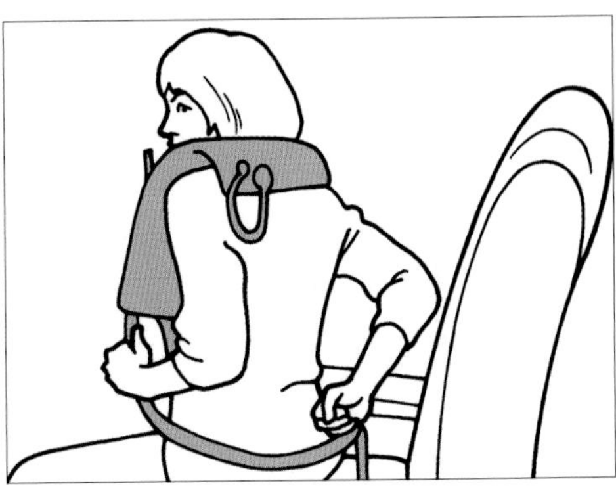

4 Pass the drawstrings around behind you and back to the front. Some models of life jacket are then secured by tying a double knot in the drawstring.

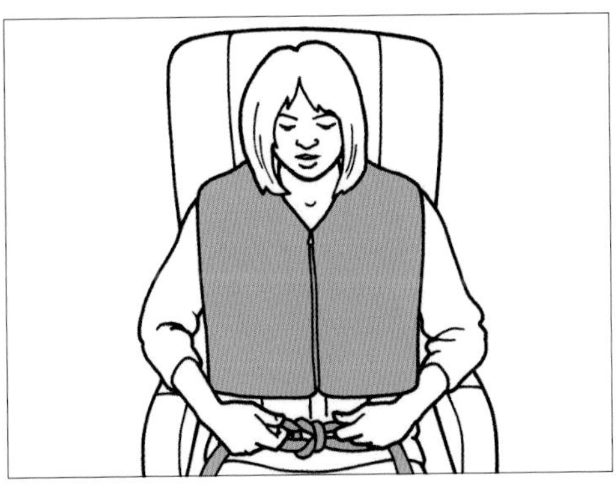

5 Other models, particularly Type III marine life jackets, are fastened by pushing together two plastic clips. The fit of the jacket can then be adjusted by pulling on the adjustment straps attached to the clips. There are other types of marine life jacket, however, so always refer to the specific instructions that come with your jacket to ensure it fits and will work efficiently.

PRACTICAL TIPS

- If you're travelling with a young child, it's important that you put your life jacket on first before helping the child. It may sound counter-intuitive, but if you're flailing around in the water trying to put your life jacket on, you won't be in a position to offer further assistance to your young companion.

- Always make sure any life jacket or vest you buy is a good fit.

HOW TO COPE IN A FLOOD

Reports of flooding are on the increase; some blame climate change, others the fact that in most developed and developing countries we are building an increasing number of homes, factories and offices in high-risk flood areas and not successfully managing rivers and their flood plains. It's likely that increased flooding is due to a combination of several factors – but that's scant consolation as the flood water is rising in your kitchen.

INDISPENSABLE THINGS

- Emergency first-aid kit
- Food
- Drinking water
- Radio (batteries)
- Torch (batteries)
- Clothes
- Any prescribed medication
- Mobile phone

PRACTICAL TIP

In the majority of flood incidents, there is usually a fair amount of warning given before the flood waters arrive. If you live in a high-risk area and are concerned about flooding, listen to the local radio station and watch local news bulletins for flood warnings. This should give you ample time to undertake the following before you evacuate the area. It's always best to secure your home, putting as many essential items upstairs as possible, and leave if you can.

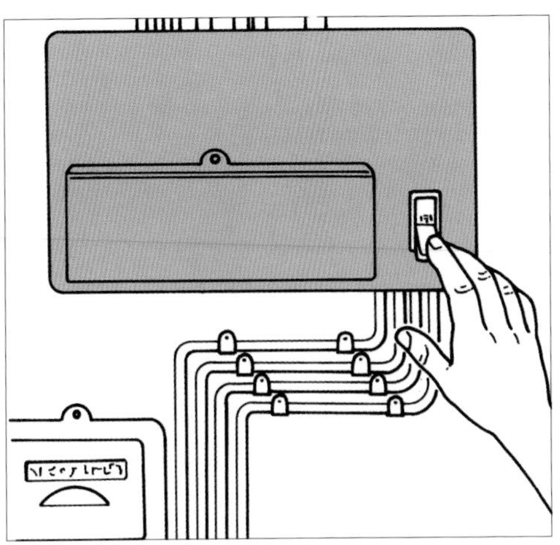

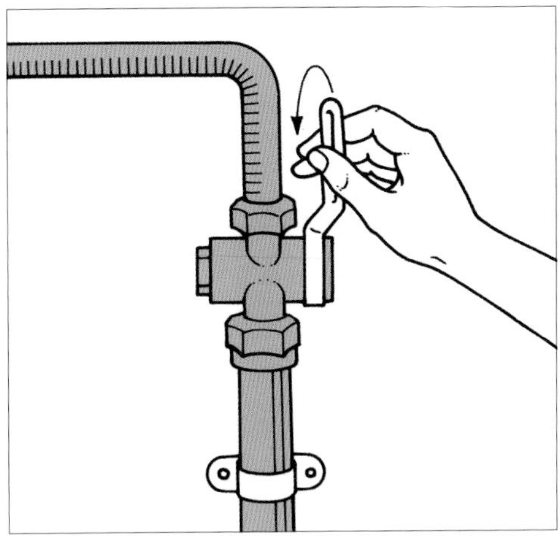

1 Turn off the main electricity supply to your house and unplug all electrical appliances. This will help protect your property as well as making it safer when you return after the flood waters have receded. However, never touch any electrical appliances if you're standing in flood water.

2 Along with the electricity supply, also turn off any gas supply you have to the house. Again this will protect your home and make it easier to recommission the supply after the flood.

3 If you don't have time to secure your home and leave the area, gather together the things listed on page 302, along with important documents, such as birth certificates and insurance policies, and any easily portable valuables, and move to a higher floor away from the flood waters. Keep listening to the radio for information.

4 As an extra precaution in extreme flood conditions, wash out baths and sinks with antibacterial cleaning products or bleach, rinse well and then fill with cold water – that way you'll have something to drink if the emergency services can't get to you for a couple of days.

INDISPENSABLE WARNING

Don't evacuate if it means having to drive through flooded roads; you may get swept away in your car. Don't walk through fast-flowing flood water; even 18cm (6in) of water can topple you over. Don't go near any downed power cables.

HOW TO REACT IN A CAR ACCIDENT

According to the UK's Department for Transport, in recent years around 3,000 people each year lose their lives on Britain's roads, while in the US that figure is around 41,000, according to the Federal Highway Administration – 115 every day, or one every 13 minutes. Fortunately, the majority of the 6.4 million accidents that occur on US roads or the 300,000 on UK roads result in minor or no injury, but you still need to know what to do if you're involved in an accident, otherwise you might jeopardize your insurance policy.

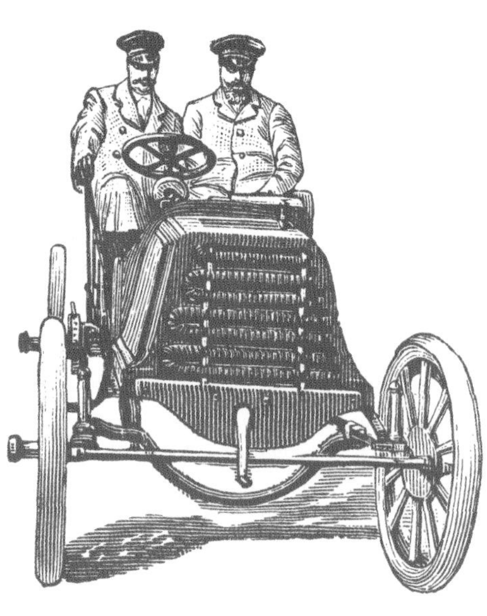

INDISPENSABLE THINGS

- Emergency first-aid kit
- Disposable/inexpensive camera
- Breakdown kit
- Pen and paper
- Mobile phone

PRACTICAL TIPS

If you are in an accident involving another car, motorcycle, cyclist or pedestrian you must stop. You should then exchange the following information:

- Name, address and phone numbers
- Name, address and phone numbers of any witnesses
- Licence plate numbers
- Details of insurance companies
- Year, model and make of cars.

Use a camera to take photos of any damage sustained to all vehicles. Try to avoid discussing who was responsible for the accident with anyone other than the police. As soon as you can, contact your insurance company and they will begin to process the accident claim by contacting the other parties' insurance companies.

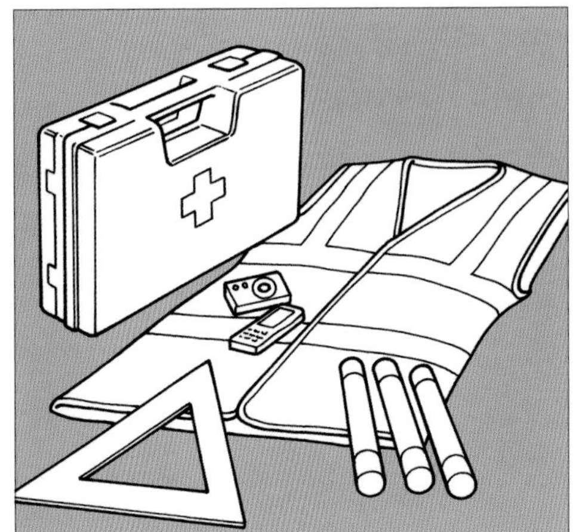

1 Today, most cars come with some accident/break-down equipment, such as warning triangles and a basic first-aid box. However, we strongly recommend that you assemble your own kit, comprising an adequately stocked first-aid kit, warning triangles, flares, a high-visibility vest, a camera, pen and paper, and always ensure you have your mobile phone with you.

2 If you're involved in an accident but are still in control of the vehicle, pull safely into the side of the road at the first available opportunity. Turn off the ignition and turn on your hazard warning lights.

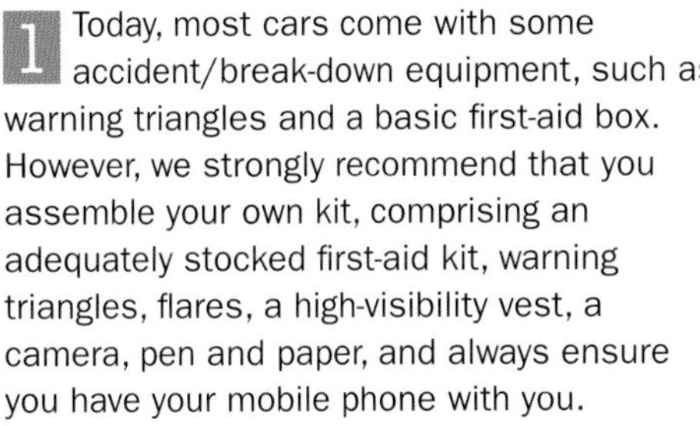

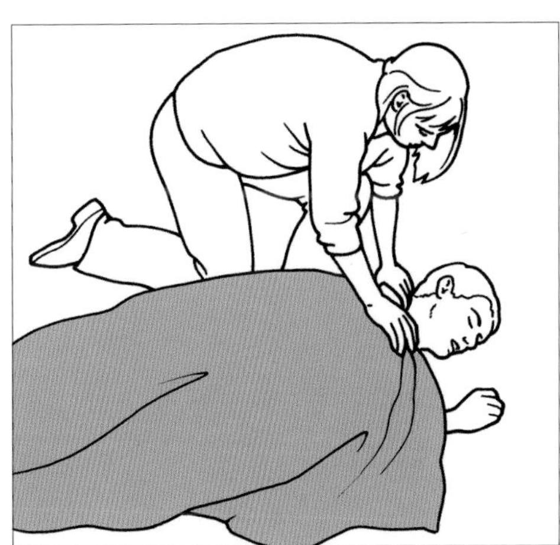

3 Assess any passengers in the car for signs of injury. If anyone appears injured, phone the emergency services immediately. Do not move the casualty. Assess them using ABC (*see pages 266–7*) and if necessary begin CPR (*see pages 268–9*). Reassure the casualty while waiting for assistance, and if necessary reduce any bleeding by pressing a lint pad or a clean towel against the wound.

4 Having attended to any passengers in your car, approach any other vehicle involved in the accident and ask the driver and passengers if they are injured. If necessary, call the emergency services.

HOW TO REACT IN A BOMB BLAST

Thanks to the work of national security services and their cooperation with the services of other countries, domestic terrorist attacks, although a real and constant threat, are mercifully few. Of course, this is no guarantee that terrorists won't successfully detonate a bomb in a busy city centre sometime in the future; and for those working or living in countries with significant terrorist activity, explosions can be an almost daily occurrence. We should try not to let the threat, perceived or otherwise, affect our lives and continue with normal routine as best we can.

INDISPENSABLE THINGS

- Cool head
- Nerves of steel

1 Of course, much easier said than done, but immediately following an explosion try to remain as calm as possible. If you can, find something solid to hide under, such as a sturdy table, to protect you from collapsing ceilings or walls; there may well be further explosions. Assess whether you personally have sustained any injuries – surprisingly, it may not always be obvious.

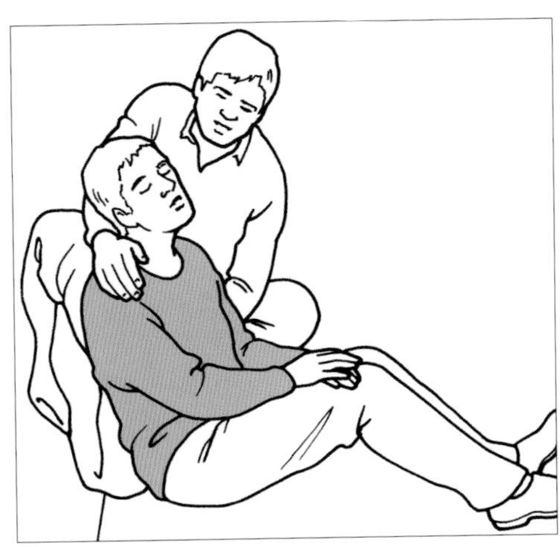

2 If you are sure it is safe to do so, go to the aid of others. If someone is seriously injured but conscious, do not attempt to move them unless not doing so will result in further injury. If someone appears seriously injured and is unconscious, assess them using ABC (*see pages 266–7*) and if necessary begin CPR (*see pages 268–9*). For any minor injuries, implement any first-aid you can.

3 Under no circumstances should you use a lighter or matches immediately following a blast. Gas supply pipes may well have broken in the explosion and you don't want to cause another one.

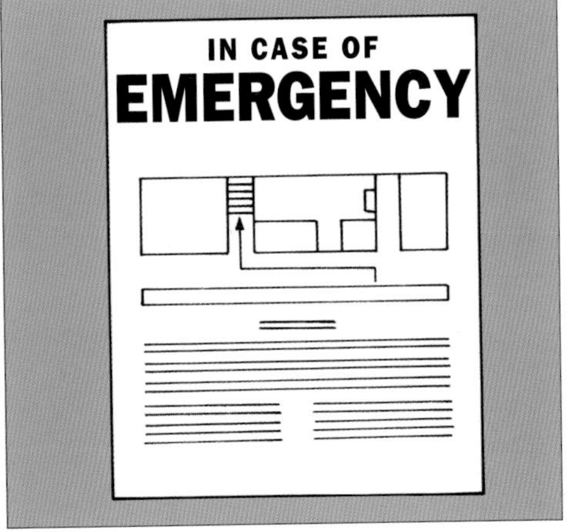

4 Most public buildings will have emergency information signs posted. Read these carefully as they may offer valuable information on how to evacuate the building as safely as possible. Given the potential risk of subsequent explosions, you should consider carefully whether or not to evacuate immediately. Again, if not doing so will endanger your life, evacuate; but if you're not in any immediate danger, it may be safer to wait under the shelter until emergency services reach you, or you are given the OK to evacuate by members of staff.

HOW TO SURVIVE A HURRICANE

Hurricanes have hit the headlines a lot in recent years, notably Katrina in August 2005, which was responsible for flooding around 80 per cent of New Orleans, resulting in the loss of some 1,500 lives. Fortunately, not all hurricanes are as devastating as Katrina, but every year, during the Atlantic hurricane season (June–November), vast areas of the Caribbean and much of the coast around the Gulf of Mexico live under the threat of potentially deadly tropical storms.

INDISPENSABLE THINGS

- Emergency first-aid kit
- Food
- Drinking water
- Radio (batteries)
- Torch (batteries)
- Clothes
- Any prescribed medication
- Mobile phone

INDISPENSABLE ADVICE

Thanks primarily to the meteorologists of the US National Hurricane Center, it's impossible for a hurricane to form and gather impetus without being spotted. So, in the vast majority of cases, people are given adequate warning to board up and lock up their homes and evacuate the area before the hurricane strikes.

Hurricanes can, however, change course quite drastically in a very short period of time, and in these cases people can get caught out. In other cases, if a hurricane is of a low category, many people will choose to sit out the storm. Here are a few steps to take to make life a little more bearable.

1 It's likely that you'll have some time before the hurricane is actually upon you. Use this time to cut down any weak-looking branches in the garden, and put inside any garden ornaments or objects, such as dustbins, that are likely to get caught up by the wind and potentially smash into your own or your neighbours' property.

2 Board up your windows with specially made hurricane shutters or at least home-made shutters made out of strong plywood nailed to the frames. If you live in a hurricane area, you should have these made in advance. Some people tape their windows to stop the glass shattering, but recent evidence suggests that this will offer little protection. Shutters are most effective.

3 Assemble items on the list given on page 308. It may be a day or two before you can get to any shops, so ensure you have plenty to eat and drink. A radio will keep you informed about the status of the storm.

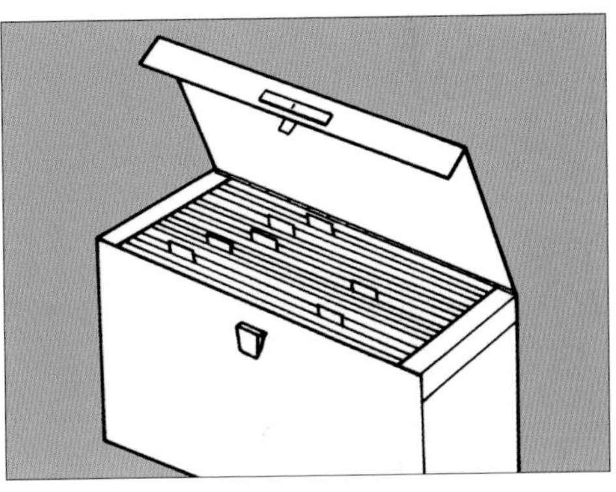

4 Put all your important documents, such as medical records, insurance policy details and bank account details, together in one safe place and carry them with you.

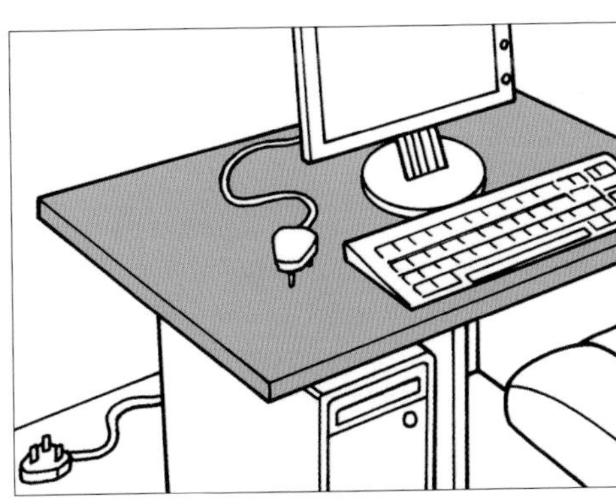

5 It's a wise precaution to unplug all your electrical appliances as lightning strikes may cause a power surge in your home that will damage such items.

HOW TO SIGNAL SOS

Although now superseded by other systems, for much of the 20th century 'SOS' was the generally accepted international maritime distress signal. A popular misconception is that the letters were an abbreviation for 'Save Our Ship' or 'Save Our Souls', but such phrases were used to help people remember the letters themselves. The reason SOS was used is because in Morse Code S is '...' (or dit/dit/dit) and O is '— — —' (or dah/dah/dah), and easy to signal when icy cold water was pouring into a ship, and also easy for anyone listening to decipher and realize a ship was in trouble.

INDISPENSABLE THINGS

- Whistle
- Foghorn
- Torch
- Anything that makes a noise

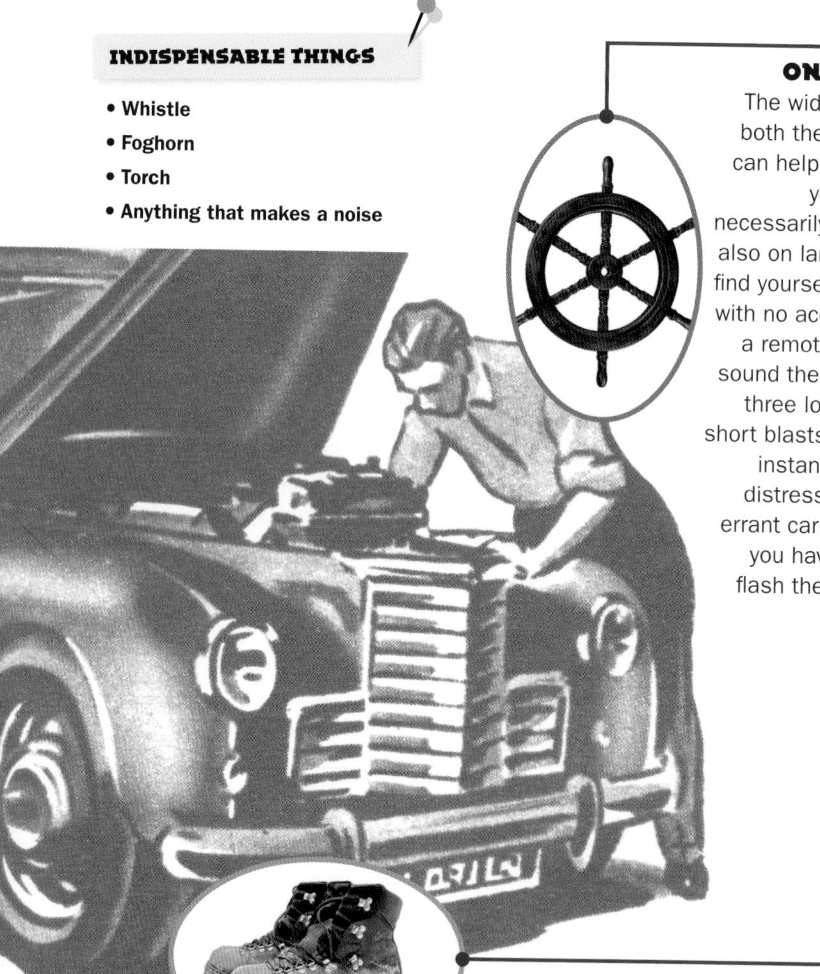

ON LAND OR AT SEA

The widespread recognition of both the signal and the letters can help enormously if you find yourself in difficulty, not necessarily while on the sea, but also on land. For example, if you find yourself stranded in your car with no access to a telephone in a remote location, periodically sound the horn with three short, three long and a further three short blasts. Anyone listening will instantly recognize that as a distress signal rather than an errant car alarm. Alternatively, if you have a torch, periodically flash the SOS signal to attract someone's attention.

IN POOR VISIBILITY

Similarly when hiking, if you or a member of your party is injured and cannot walk to safety and visibility is poor or it's getting dark, signalling SOS on a whistle with three short, three long and three short blasts will alert any potential rescuers and help them to locate you. No whistle? Use anything that will make a distinctive and penetrating sound, such as metal on metal or a hollow wooden object. Keep repeating the SOS signal, and anyone who hears it is likely to recognize it as a cry for help.

HOW TO SIGNAL SOS WITH SMOKE

You might instantly think of Native Americans, and why not? They knew a thing or two about signalling over great distances. Seeing smoke signals rising into the sky must have been an eerie sight for those adventurous folk heading West. So if you find yourself stranded and lost in the wilderness, take a metaphorical leaf out of the collective Native American book and signal for help using smoke.

INDISPENSABLE THINGS

- Matches or lighter
- Dry kindling
- Blanket or coat

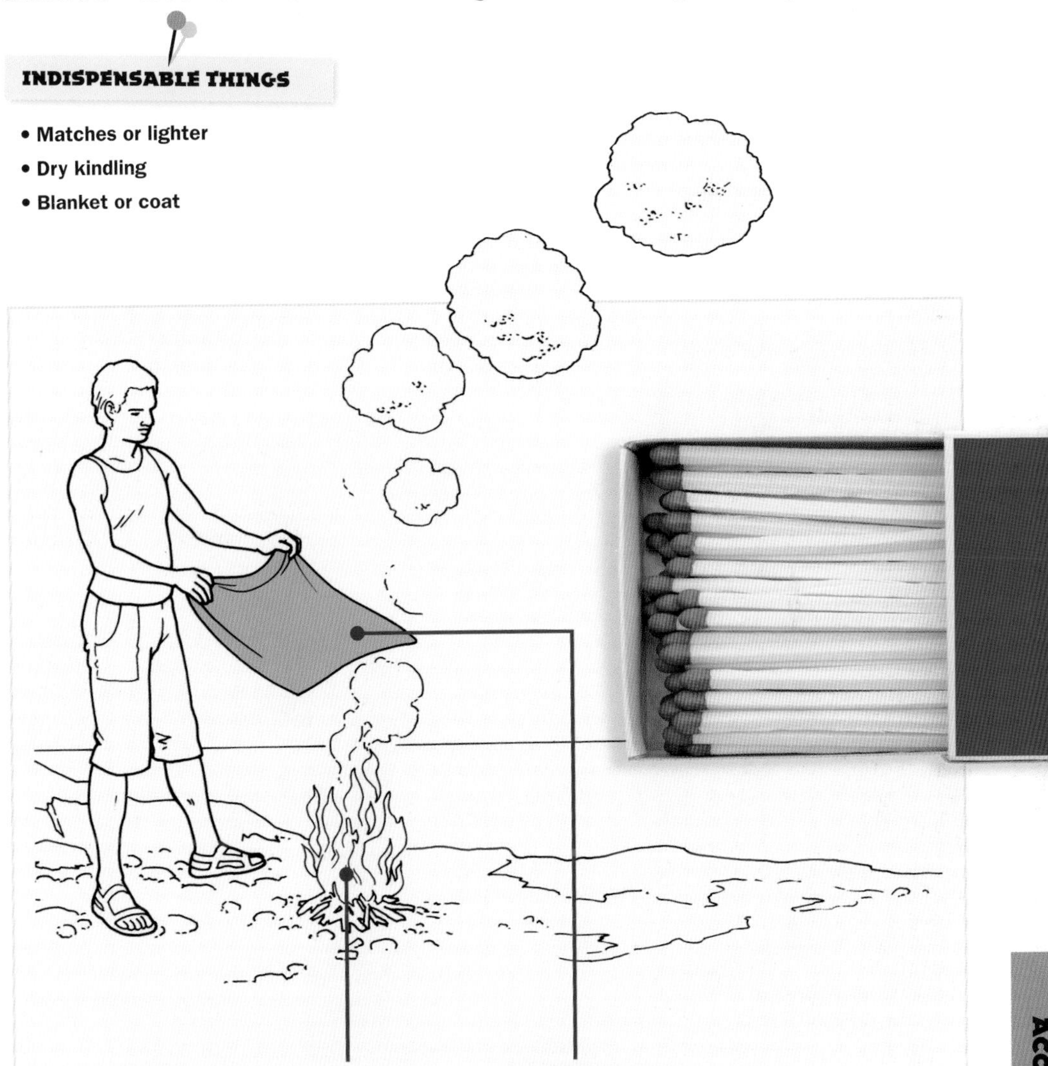

MAKING A SMOKY FIRE

The first thing you need to do is to make a fire (*see page 234*). Start your fire with good, dry kindling to generate lots of heat. Once your fire is burning steadily, add handfuls of damp grass or leaves – anything wet that will make the fire smoke.

SIGNALLING

When the fire's really smoking, use a blanket or a coat to carefully cover the fire periodically to prevent the smoke rising. Try signalling three 'puffs' at a time – this is the universal number for help and will alert people to the fact that it's not just a natural scrub or forest fire.

HOW TO SIGNAL SOS WITH LETTERS

So what at first seemed like a really great idea, to get away as far as possible from all human contact, has backfired horribly – either you're in the middle of nowhere with a broken 4x4 or truly stranded on a desert island with a boat that won't start. There's nothing with which to start a fire, but at least you know that after two or three days people will start wondering where you are.

INDISPENSABLE THINGS

- Large rocks or stones
- Flatish area of cleared land
- Book to read

USING ROCKS

It's likely that your rescuers will first start to look for you from the air; but without any decent firewood, how can you attract their attention? Easy, make a sign. Using large stones or rocks (or anything else that comes to hand), spell out the letters 'SOS' and you'll quickly grab the attention of any eagle-eyed pilot. Make the letters large!

BE VISIBLE

Remember to choose rocks or other objects that are easy to distinguish in terms of colour or texture from the ground, otherwise your cry for help won't be sufficiently visible from above.

HOW TO SIGNAL SOS WITH MATERIAL

'No good,' you cry. There's nothing to make a fire with and there aren't enough rocks to spell out S, let alone SOS. Don't panic: there is another way of attracting an aerial search party. This one utilizes the shape of the internationally recognized distress flag used by ships all over the world. All you need are blankets, rugs or any largish piece of material – even a newspaper would do.

INDISPENSABLE THINGS

- Blankets or rugs
- Newspaper
- Rocks or stones

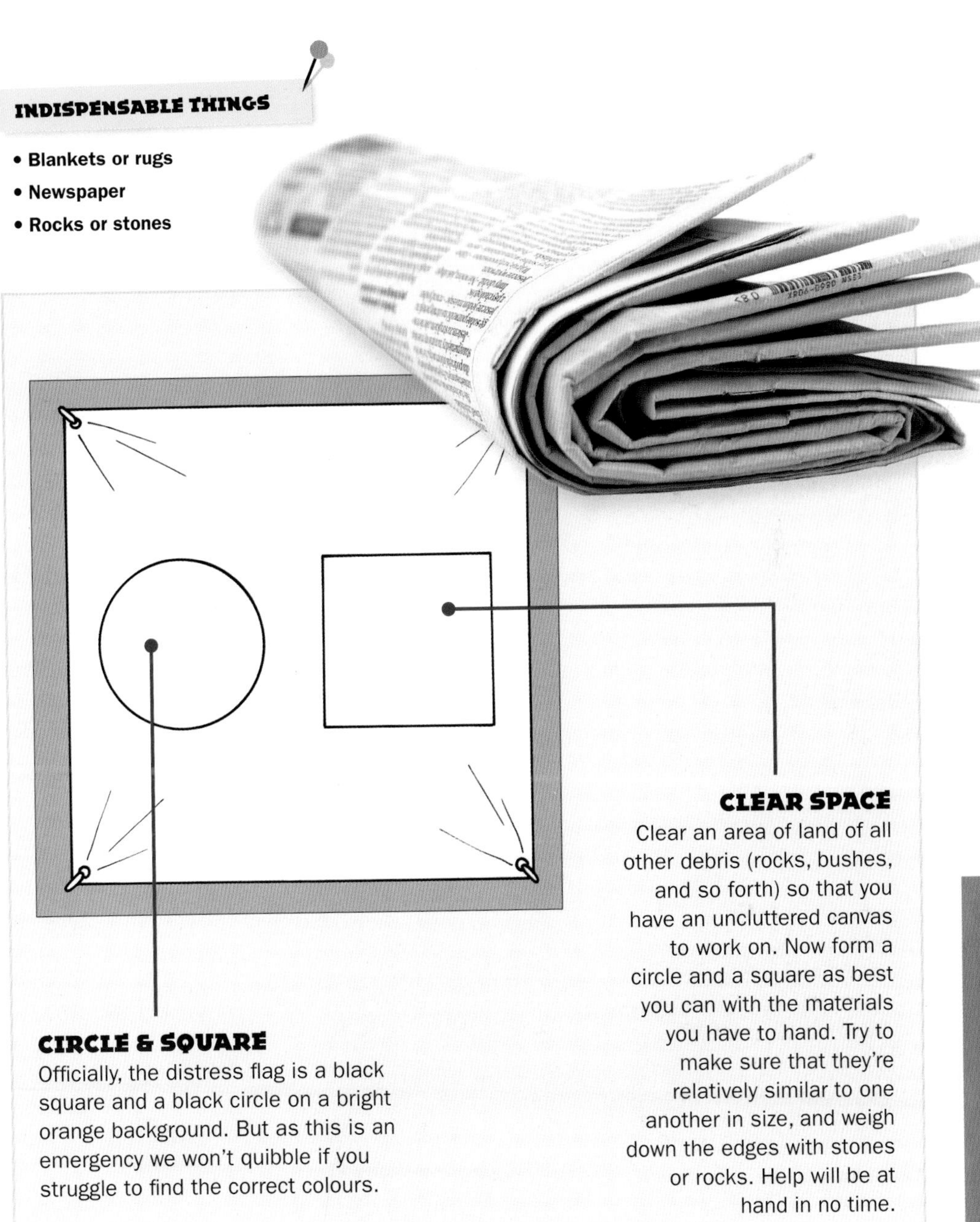

CLEAR SPACE

Clear an area of land of all other debris (rocks, bushes, and so forth) so that you have an uncluttered canvas to work on. Now form a circle and a square as best you can with the materials you have to hand. Try to make sure that they're relatively similar to one another in size, and weigh down the edges with stones or rocks. Help will be at hand in no time.

CIRCLE & SQUARE

Officially, the distress flag is a black square and a black circle on a bright orange background. But as this is an emergency we won't quibble if you struggle to find the correct colours.

HOW TO SURVIVE A BLIZZARD IN YOUR CAR

OK, so when you set off there was just a flurry of snow and you couldn't possibly miss your great-aunt's special Christmas Eve celebrations – anyway it was only supposed to be a 30-minute drive as you were taking the back roads to avoid the traffic; and now where did all this snow come from? – you can barely see the road! And where's everybody else gone? Suddenly the festive spirit has deserted you and you feel very alone. Here's what to do, and what not to do, if you're caught in a blizzard while driving.

INDISPENSABLE THINGS

- Mobile phone
- Torch
- Water
- Something to eat
- Blankets
- Gloves
- Extra clothes
- Roadside emergency kit
- Signal devices

1 As tempting as it might be to 'just keep going', it's not worth it. In poor visibility you run the risk of either crashing into an object by the side of the road or having a head-on collision with another vehicle. Pull over to the side of the road and stop. If you have a mobile phone, call 999 to alert the emergency services to your situation and provide them with as much information as you can about your whereabouts.

2 Having stopped, unless you can see a building very close to you, don't be tempted to walk for help. You'll get lost in a blizzard, particularly at night, and may end up with hypothermia or freezing to death. There are likely to be emergency services in operation and they're much more likely to find a car than an individual, especially if you keep the hazard lights on; these will also act as a warning to other vehicles.

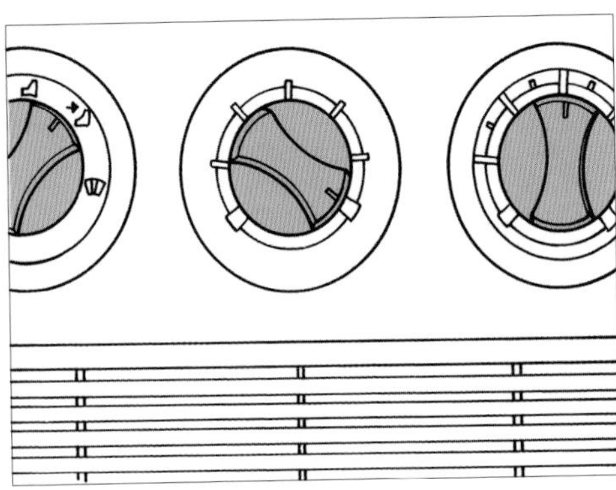

3 To keep yourself warm, run the car with the heater on for about 10 minutes at hourly intervals. It's tempting to run it for longer, but you could run out of petrol before you're rescued, or inadvertently introduce carbon monoxide into the car. As a safety precaution open a window very slightly.

4 Depending on how heavily the snow is falling, every so often go to the rear of the car to check that the exhaust is still free of snow. If the exhaust should become blocked, again you may find that carbon monoxide will find its way into the car when you're running the engine to stay warm.

5 In very cold conditions it's essential to maintain good circulation. To do this either clap your hands or stamp your feet. You don't need to move much at all to keep the blood flowing freely around your body.

PRACTICAL TIP

As well as staying in the car (apart from getting out to check the exhaust), it's also recommended that you keep your seatbelt on in case you're hit by another car.

HOW TO BUILD A SHELTER

Somehow you've miscalculated the time needed to complete the trek; the sun's going down and you've still got another three hours hiking before you make it back to the car. You estimate that it will be dark in an hour, so there's no alternative but to spend the night in the woods, and it looks like rain. The first thing is not to think about *The Blair Witch Project* (if you haven't seen it that shouldn't be hard – just be pleased you haven't) and the next is to go about making a shelter – here are a couple of ideas.

INDISPENSABLE THINGS

- Dead wood, branches and leaves
- Length of rope
- Tarpaulin

PRACTICAL TIP

No matter how convinced you are that your hike in the woods won't involve an overnight stay, always carry a tarp in your backpack. It's portable, lightweight and you never know when you might need to rig up a makeshift shelter.

DEBRIS HUT SHELTER

1 The debris hut shelter is very simple to make, but you need access to a good supply of dead wood, branches and leaves. The basic structure utilizes a long central pole supported at one end by two shorter branches crossing over one another near the top. Alternatively, you could simply rest one end of the pole in the crook of a tree. (If there's a strong wind consider where the opening will be.) Now find or cut suitable lengths of shorter branches to rest against the central pole to form the structure shown.

2 Once you have completed the basic structure, next cover it with any suitable material that you can find lying around, such as large fern leaves, leafy branches, pine boughs, grass, earth sod – literally anything that won't fall between the branches or won't get blown away too easily. You'll need to lay on and overlap quite a lot of material to ensure the shelter is watertight. Use a coat to block the entrance to the shelter to help you keep warmer if necessary.

TARP SHELTER

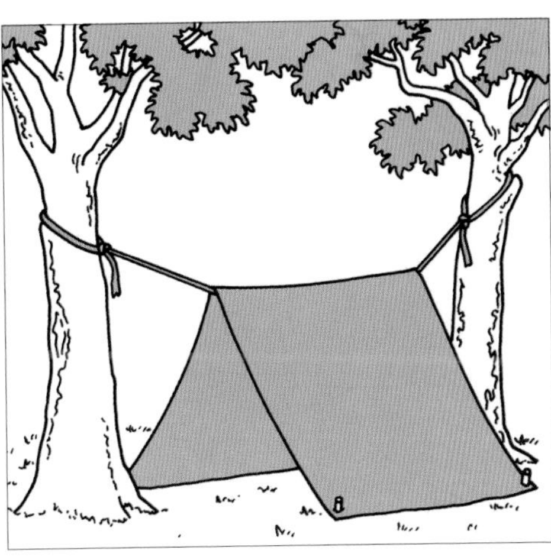

1 The tarp shelter is one of the easiest and quickest of emergency shelters to put up. Begin by tying the length of rope between two trees. Again, ideally consider where you want the two openings to be. Also, you can make the shelter lower at one end if that will help protect you from the wind.

2 Next simply throw the tarp over the rope and secure the corners. You could use sharpened sticks as pegs to do this, although it's probably best not to puncture the tarpaulin as it may tear or let in water. Better to use heavy rocks to weigh down the corners.

HOW TO SURVIVE AN AVALANCHE

With the largest examples moving some 10 million tonnes (9.8 million tons) of snow at speeds of up to 300kph (190mph), avalanches are a serious force of nature. Of course the best way to survive an avalanche is to avoid them altogether, by steering clear of steep slopes with thick powder snow. If you are about to be engulfed by an avalanche, the following procedures may help you to survive.

INDISPENSABLE FACT

The authorities responsible for the safety of the numerous people who go skiing each year take their responsibility very seriously. In 1999, the mayor of Chamonix, France, was convicted of second-degree murder for not evacuating an area that was subsequently hit by an avalanche, killing 12 people.

INDISPENSABLE THINGS

- Ski clothing and equipment fitted with RECCO reflectors

STAY ON YOUR FEET

Try to stay on your feet for as long as possible. If you're caught in the snow, try to remove your skis and any other heavy equipment as this will drag you deeper into the snow.

HOLD ON

Hold on to any nearby branches for as long as possible.

KEEP TO THE SIDE

If you have time, try to ski or walk to the side of the avalanche slope. The centre of the avalanche carries the highest risk because it's where the snow is at its greatest volume and speed.

'SWIM'

Once subsumed by moving snow, try to make swimming motions with your arms and legs to keep as close to the surface as possible before the snow settles around you.

CUP YOUR HANDS

As the avalanche is about to stop, but before it has done so, cup one hand in front of your nose and mouth to create a pocket of air. The majority of people die of suffocation when caught in an avalanche, so creating a region of air may buy you valuable time. With the other hand reach up so that it is visible to rescuers.

SURVIVING IN EXTREMES

Just think how dull life would be without a little risk; it's good for us to put ourselves in a bit of danger every now and again – particularly you adrenaline junkies, you know who you are. So what if every now and again you have to fight off sharks or survive a riot – we've got all the answers here.

HOW TO DEFEND YOURSELF

Hopefully you'll never be in a situation in which you have to defend yourself against attack. Of course there are things that you can do to avoid the scenario altogether, such as being aware of your surroundings, not going into high-risk areas alone, and using public transport or taking a taxi in areas you're unsure about – but however careful you are, there is still an outside possibility that one day you may have to confront an attacker.

INDISPENSABLE THINGS

- Small can of hairspray
- Pepper spray (where legal)
- Car keys or pen
- Personal attack alarm

PRACTICAL TIP

If you think you're going to be attacked, ascertain as quickly as possible whether you're being attacked for your money or whether it's an intentional physical attack. If the attacker just wants your money, hand it over and tell the assailant to leave. If it's clear, however, that the attack is going to lead to an assault, you'll need to physically deter your attacker.

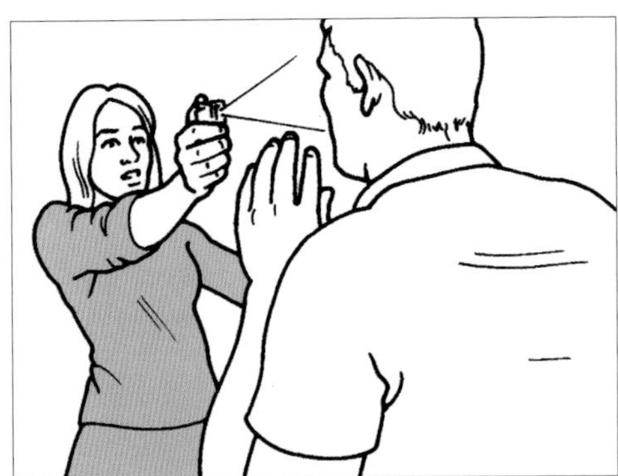

1 In countries where pepper spray is legal, by all means use this if you're absolutely certain you're about to be assaulted. In other countries, including the UK, pepper spray is classified as a firearm and you'll be breaking the law if you use it, even to defend yourself. One alternative is to carry a small can of hairspray and spray that in the attacker's face – it should give you enough time to run away.

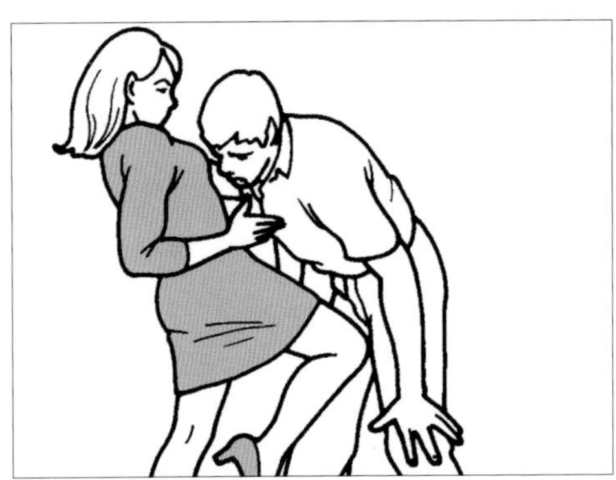

2 If the attacker has grabbed you by the arms or around the neck, lift your knee as hard as you can into his groin. If well aimed, you will inflict severe pain on the assailant, giving you time to escape.

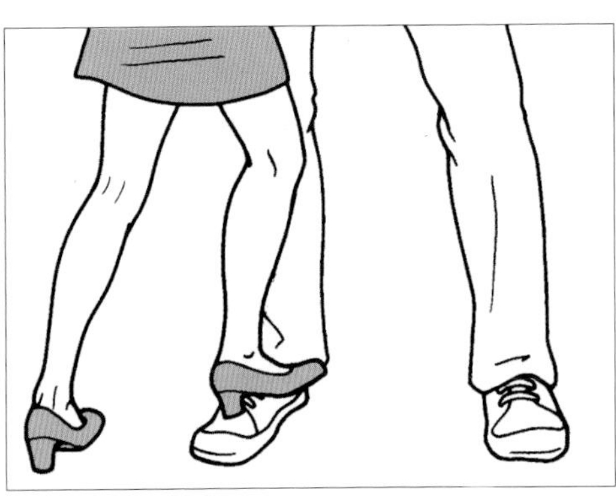

3 An alternative to kneeing the attacker in the groin is to stamp as hard as you can, ideally with the heel of your shoe, on the attacker's ankle or foot. Again, this will cause quick, sharp pain.

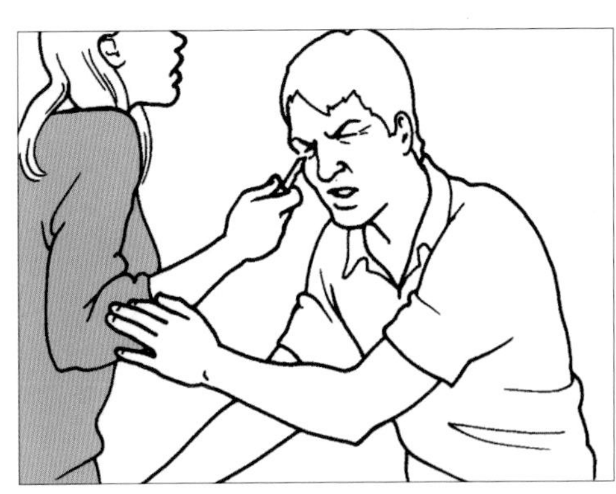

4 Use anything sharp you have to hand to poke into the attacker's eyes, such as your car keys, a pen or even your fingers.

5 Remember that your prime objective is to get away – once you've inflicted any form of pain that has forced your attacker to release you, run away as fast as you can. Use a personal attack alarm to attract the attention of passers-by; this should also help to deter your attacker.

HOW TO SURVIVE A BEAR ATTACK

With an ever-increasing number of us enjoying outdoor pursuits, whether at home or on holiday, it's logical that the number of encounters with bears is also on the rise. Bears have very wide-ranging territories and will eat just about anything. The number-one rule, therefore, if you want to avoid running into a bear is not to leave food lying around your campsite – that really would be one teddy bears' picnic you'd best avoid.

INDISPENSABLE THINGS

- Bear pepper spray (where legal)
- Whistle
- Air horn

PRACTICAL TIP

The best way to defend against a bear attack is to avoid an encounter altogether. Find out from local sources if there are bears in the area; if there are, and particularly if it's the breeding season, find an alternative place to camp. If you must stay in the area, make your presence known by talking loudly, singing or clapping your hands periodically. Unless feeling threatened or very hungry, bears will avoid contact with humans.

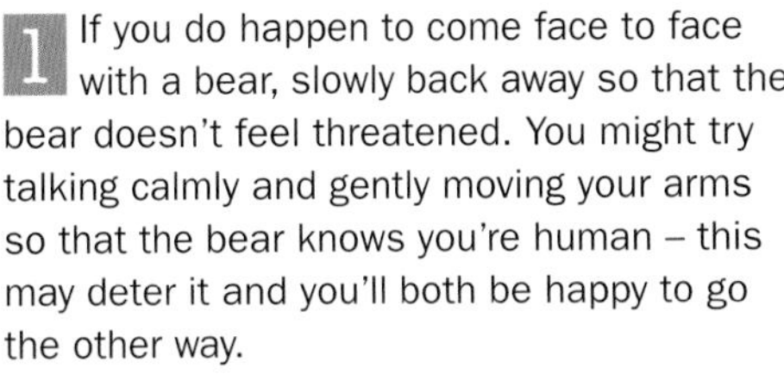

1 If you do happen to come face to face with a bear, slowly back away so that the bear doesn't feel threatened. You might try talking calmly and gently moving your arms so that the bear knows you're human – this may deter it and you'll both be happy to go the other way.

2 If you accidentally stumble upon a bear and her cubs, she will certainly perceive you as a threat and may react by standing up on her hind legs. Remain as calm as possible; don't shout and wave your arms as this may further upset her. Simply back away, talking quietly. Hopefully that will diffuse the situation and the bear will back down.

3 If the bear looks as if she is about to charge and there are trees nearby, one option is to climb a tree, although black bears are proficient climbers. Again, hopefully by climbing a tree you'll have indicated you're not a threat and the bear won't bother to pursue you.

4 If you're going to be attacked, it's important to know which species of bear you're dealing with. If it's a black bear, your best chance of survival is to fight back as fiercely as possible with any weapon you have to hand, making as much noise as possible. If you're confronted with a grizzly bear, the only option is to play dead. Curl up into a ball and try to protect your neck and stomach. A backpack will provide some protection.

HOW TO SURVIVE A SHARK ATTACK

OK, so we know the odds of being attacked by a shark are pretty small – in fact, 1 in 11.5 million according to the International Shark Attack File – but as a gruesome end, being attacked by a shark has to rank in the top 10. So what, practically, can you do if this disturbing nightmare should turn into stomach-churning reality one day as you're enjoying the holiday of a lifetime in the warm waters of South Africa or North America?

INDISPENSABLE THINGS

- Anything solid or sharp with which to hit the shark
- Diving or swimming buddy

1 If you see a shark coming straight towards you, don't try to swim for safety straight away, unless you're certain you can get out of the water before the shark reaches you. Stay calm and vertically still in the water (vertical because it makes it harder for a shark to bite you, as its nose will get in the way). The shark will hopefully realize you're not it's usual prey and leave.

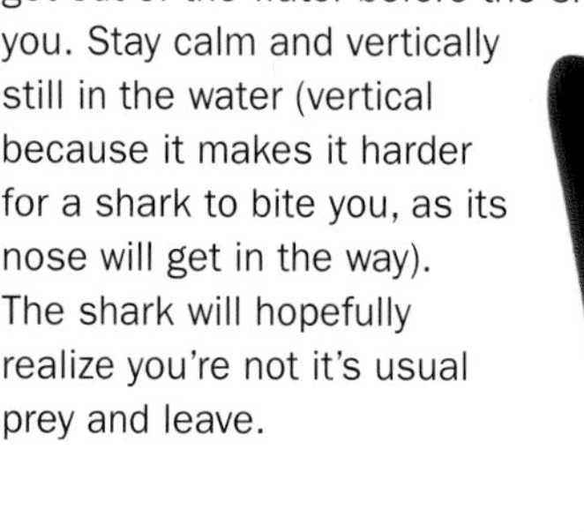

2 If the shark approaches in a zigzag fashion, that indicates it's likely to attack. Get back-to-back with your swimming partner (you're not swimming alone, are you?) so that one of you can always see what the shark is doing. If you are on your own in the water, stay as calm as possible and try to keep watching the shark. If there's a reef nearby, put your back towards it.

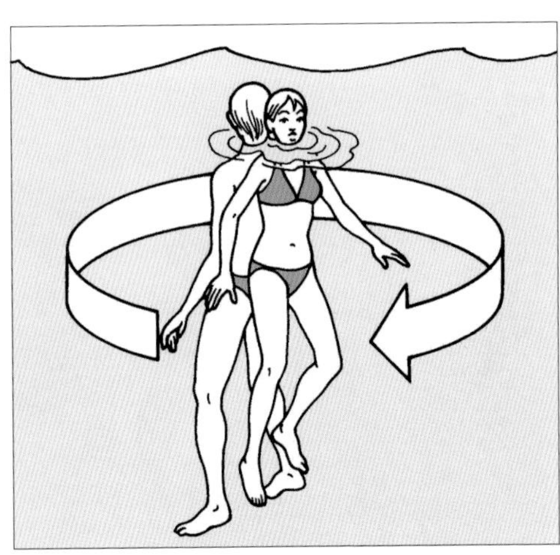

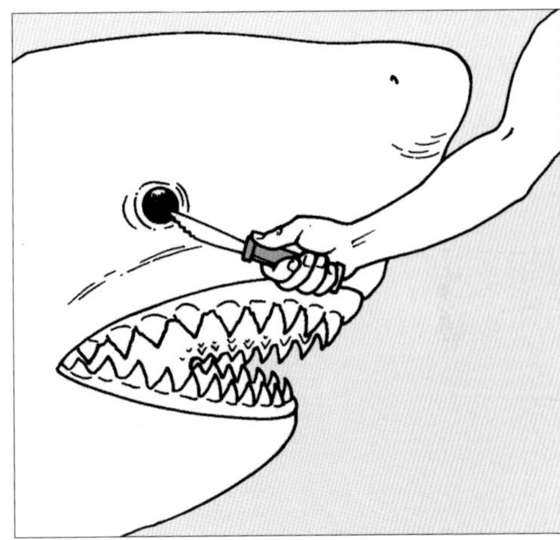

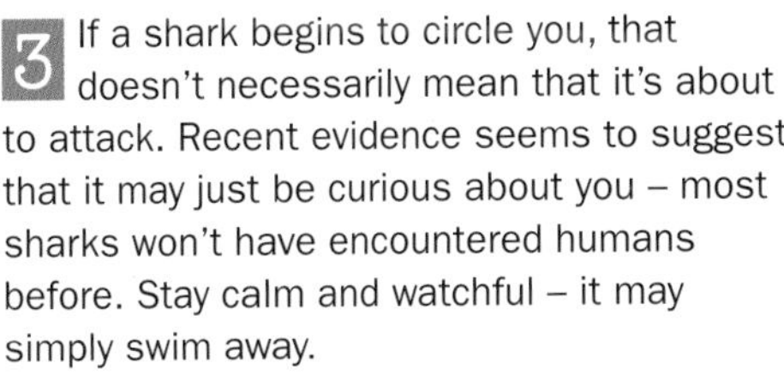

3 If a shark begins to circle you, that doesn't necessarily mean that it's about to attack. Recent evidence seems to suggest that it may just be curious about you – most sharks won't have encountered humans before. Stay calm and watchful – it may simply swim away.

4 If you are actually attacked by a shark, fight back as aggressively as you can. Don't play dead, as the shark will only attack further. The best option is to hit the shark in the gills or the eye with any appropriate object. Punching a shark on the nose may also deter it. If you have a spear gun or a knife, use it. Again, aim for the gills and eyes. Whatever happens, keep fighting back, remembering to breathe when you get a chance to surface.

HOW TO SURVIVE A DOG ATTACK

Although not as exotically terrifying as being attacked by a shark or bear, attacks by dogs are naturally far more numerous and can often result in horrific injuries and even death. In 2007, 33 people in the US died as a result of being attacked by dogs. Most people who require serious medical treatment following a dog attack are children, many of whom are bitten in the face – if not trained or well cared for, man's 'best friend' can readily become a savage wild animal reverting to basic attack instincts.

INDISPENSABLE THINGS

- Pepper spray (where legal)
- Thick coat or jacket
- Rocks/sticks

POLICE DOGS The easiest dogs to 'defend' against are well-trained police dogs – as long as you give yourself up. If you find yourself caught up in a disturbance where police dogs have been deployed, face the dog (but do not engage in eye contact), stand still and keep your arms by your side. Police dogs are trained to recognize these submissive gestures and will simply stand guard until their handler calls them off.

SINGLE UNTRAINED DOG If a single, untrained dog begins to bark and snarl at you, shout and make yourself appear large and powerful. At the same time throw rocks or anything else appropriate. The majority of untrained dogs will run away if confronted by something that appears more powerful than them. If possible, try to put an obstacle or barrier between you and the dog, such as a dustbin lid, a gate or a large plant pot.

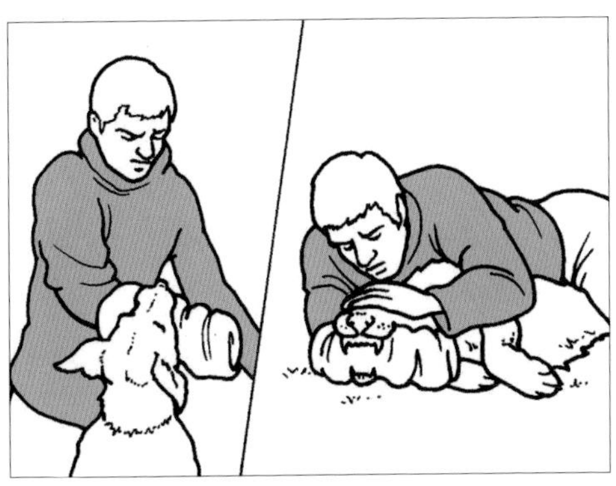

GUARD DOGS Poorly trained guard dogs are usually the hardest to defend against. They may not recognize submissive gestures, and will simply be trained to attack. Try offering your arm (preferably the one you don't normally use) wrapped in a coat. Just over half of all dogs will bite on this. With your arm in its jaws, fall as heavily as you can onto the dog in order to disable it.

A GROUP OF DOGS If you're being attacked by more than one dog, try to back up against something solid to stop them encircling you, and fight them off with anything you can lay your hands on until help arrives. If they get behind you, you're in big trouble.

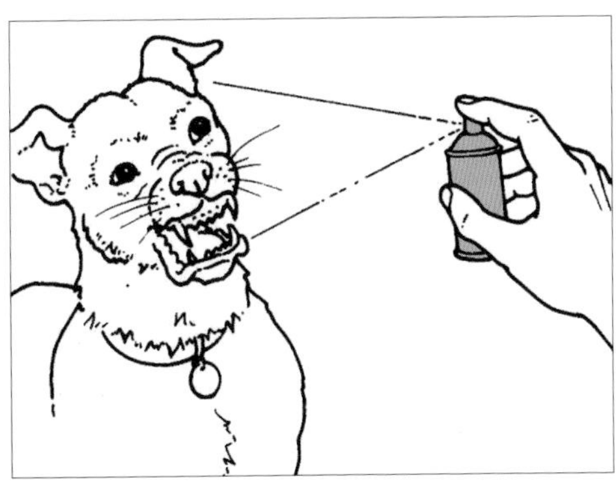

PEPPER SPRAY In countries where it is legal, carry a pepper spray with you if you live in an area where dogs roam freely. This will temporarily disable any dog.

HOW TO ESCAPE FROM A SINKING CAR

While for the inhabitants of some countries the risk of running off the road into a river or canal may seem remote, in others it's a real danger – in Holland, for example, people pay £100 to be dropped in a large tank while in a car in order to practise escaping, that's how seriously they view the risk. In the US, instances of drivers leaving the road and ending up in the water reach around 10,000 each year and subsequent fatalities average 300. Here's how to give yourself the best chance of survival.

INDISPENSABLE THINGS

- Autoglass-breaking hammer

1 In most cases when cars enter the water the impact, fortunately, is slight. Of course, this depends on the speed at which the car was travelling before leaving the road and whether there was any significant drop to the water. Usually cars aren't travelling at excessive speed and the water, whether river, canal or levee, is only slightly lower than the road. One victim compared it to entering the water in a log-plume amusement ride.

2 Having entered the water the priority is to open the window and release the seat belt. (Trying to open the door will be futile due to the water pressure on the outside and will only waste valuable time.) If you have electric windows, opening the window before releasing the seatbelt makes more sense as the water will at some point interfere with the car's electrical systems (some cars have wind-up windows in the back). Ask any passengers to do the same.

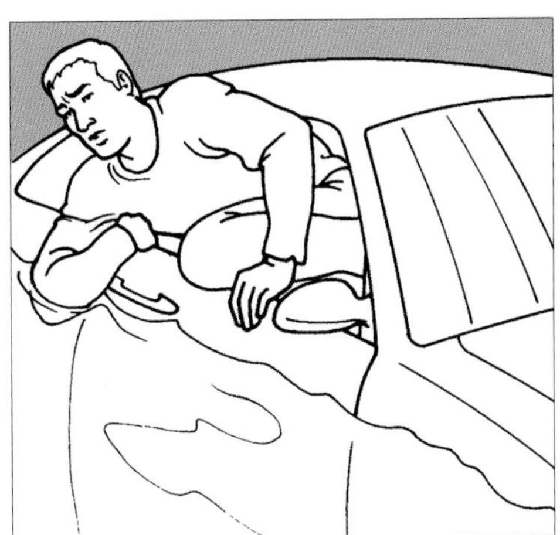

3 With the window open you should be able to climb out relatively easily and swim to dry land. Only go back to the car if someone is in difficulty and needs help escaping through the window. Under no circumstances re-enter the car for any possessions. If for whatever reason you cannot open the windows, try breaking a side window with anything with a pointed end. Car windows are extremely tough so may need an autoglass-breaking hammer, which you may want to keep in the glove compartment at all times. Don't try the windscreen as it's very unlikely you'll be able to break this.

4 As a last resort, if there's no way of escaping through the windows, you'll have to wait until the car is submerged and filled with water, at which point the pressure inside and outside the car will be equalized, enabling you to slowly push the door open. Take a deep breath at the very last minute before the car is entirely filled with water. Ensure the door is unlocked and push it open. You will need to push quite hard, as, although the pressure is equal inside and out, as you push the car door you'll also be pushing against a heavy body of water – but it will open.

HOW TO ESCAPE FROM A HOUSE FIRE

No matter how carefully we guard against a fire in the home, there is always the possibility that we become victim to one – whether through an accident in the kitchen, a poorly maintained electrical appliance or from smoking. And while domestic fires can break out at any time, perhaps the most alarming and distressing, and potentially the most life-threatening, are those that start in the middle of the night when the occupants are asleep. According to one set of statistics, around 25 per cent of casualties of house fires were asleep when the fire broke out.

PRACTICAL TIP

It's essential that your house is fitted with a sufficient number of well-maintained smoke alarms. These, above everything else, are likely to save your life. In addition, make sure everyone in the house knows which route to take in the event of a fire (and an alternative route, should the principal route be inaccessible) and a convenient place to meet outside.

INDISPENSABLE THINGS

- Well-maintained smoke alarms
- Torch
- Mobile phone

1 Keep a torch by your bed in case the fire has disabled the lights. It can be very disorientating and not a little scary to wake up to the smell of smoke and a smoke alarm screeching. Try to stay calm. You may have inhaled smoke in your sleep already so it's essential that you stay as low to the ground as you can when you get out of bed to avoid as much smoke as possible.

2 When moving around the house to alert all the other occupants to the fire, continue to stay close to the floor where the air is cleaner and cooler. Find something appropriate, such as a cloth, to cover your mouth to help reduce smoke inhalation.

3 Always test to see how hot a door is by feeling with the back of your hand before opening it. A fire may be blazing on the other side and opening the door will introduce further oxygen, causing the fire to spread more rapidly, if not causing a minor explosion. If anyone's clothes catch fire, drag them to the ground before they start running (which will only serve to fan and spread the flames) and roll them, ideally in a rug or large towel, to smother the flames.

4 When a room has been safely evacuated, always close the door behind you. This will slow the rate at which the fire spreads around the house. Make for the emergency meeting place and phone the fire service.

HOW TO SURVIVE IN THE DESERT

You were told by your guide that the 4x4s they use were the most reliable on the market, and so yours has proved – if only your guide had been as reliable, perhaps the vehicle would not have become stuck in sand while you were still three hours away from civilization without any means of contacting anyone. There's nothing else for it but to go by foot, and you're not exactly swimming in water.

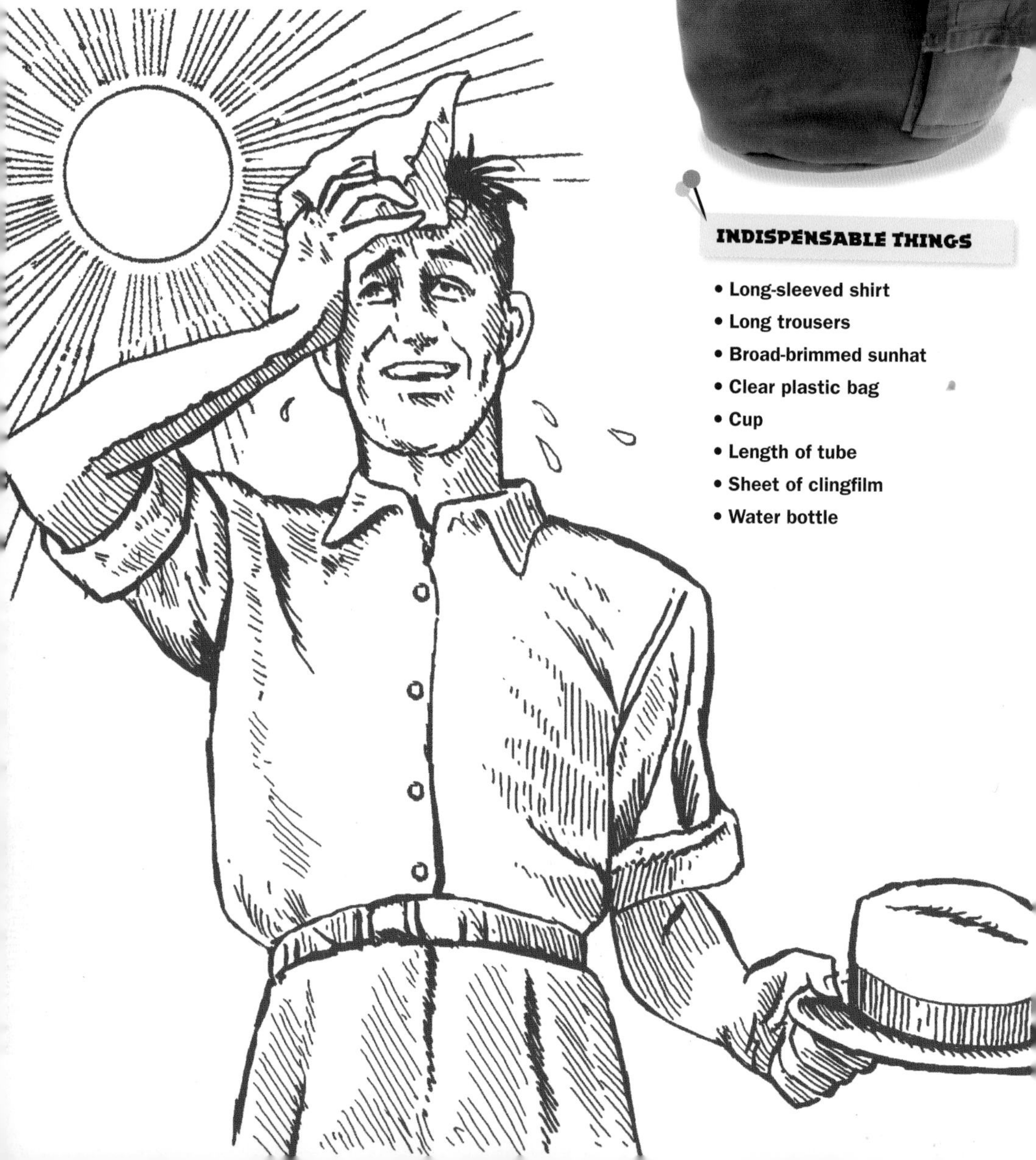

INDISPENSABLE THINGS

- Long-sleeved shirt
- Long trousers
- Broad-brimmed sunhat
- Clear plastic bag
- Cup
- Length of tube
- Sheet of clingfilm
- Water bottle

1 Surviving in the desert is all about the relationship between air temperature, physical activity and water consumption. It's essential to lose as little water as possible from your body, so if you have to walk in the desert, wear a long-sleeved shirt and long trousers. You may feel hotter, but the material will retain your sweat for longer than your exposed skin, from which any moisture is likely to evaporate almost instantly. Wear a broad-brimmed hat to protect your head from the sun.

2 If you can, find a sheltered place in which to rest during the heat of the day; only walk at night when it will be a great deal cooler than during daylight hours. Again, doing any physical activity in the cooler air temperature will reduce the rate of necessary water consumption. Visibility in the desert at night is usually sufficient to walk by, owing to the lack of moisture in the air.

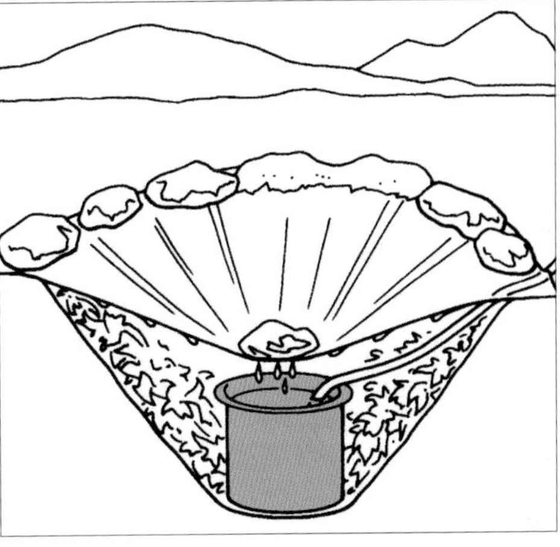

3 If you're running out of water in the desert, tie a clear plastic bag over the end of a plant or small branch of a tree, ensuring that the bag is sealed as tight as possible. During photosynthesis the plant will transpire, releasing water vapour, which will collect in the bag. Keep the bag attached to the plant until after sunset in order to collect as much moisture as possible.

4 If there aren't any plants growing in the vicinity, try building a sun still. Dig a hole in the ground until you reach the moist subsoil. Place a cup in the bottom of the hole and run a plastic tube from the cup to the edge of the hole. Cover the hole with a taut sheet of clingfilm held in place by stones or sand. Ensure there is a good seal all the way round. Place a small stone in the centre of the sheet so that it dips over the cup. The moisture in the subsoil will evaporate under the heat of the sun and collect on the inside of the sheet. From here it will flow down to the centre and drip into the cup. You can then suck the water through the tube.

HOW TO PERFORM A FIREMAN'S LIFT

How come it's the firemen who seem to get all the fun? In fact the fireman's lift, or fireman's carry as it's also known, is no longer the recognized method by which to carry someone out of a burning building. This is due to the fact that toxic fumes could potentially asphyxiate someone being carried at shoulder height. The preferred method is now to drag someone along the ground (away from potentially harmful fumes) – but the lift can still come in handy in numerous other situations.

INDISPENSABLE THINGS

- Relatively strong back

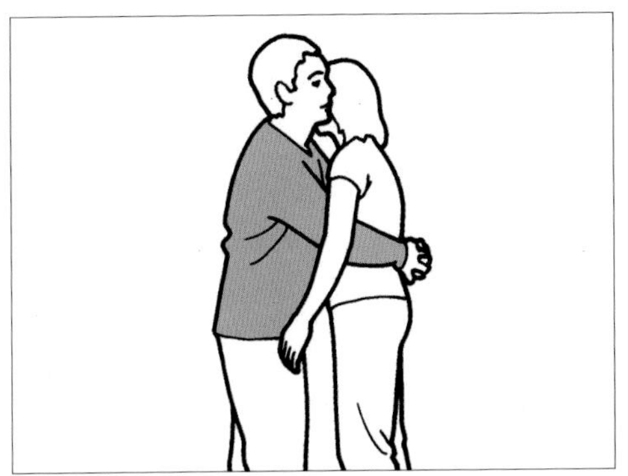

1 Lift the casualty into a standing position with both arms wrapped around his or her waist so that you are facing one another. This position will also prevent the casualty from falling backwards.

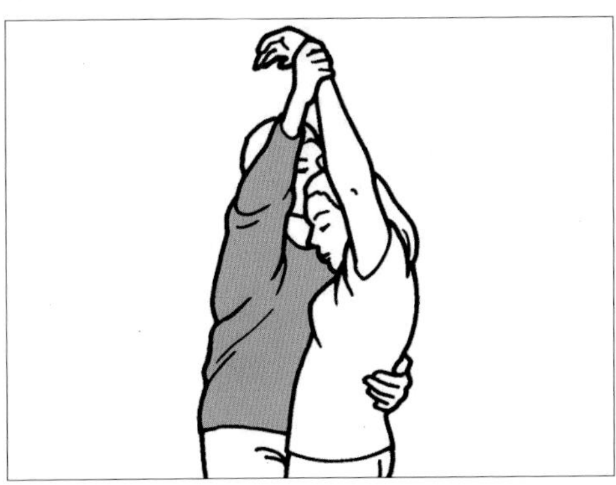

2 While still supporting the casualty with one arm around the waist, with your other hand lift one of the casualty's arms by the wrist so that the arm is fully extended.

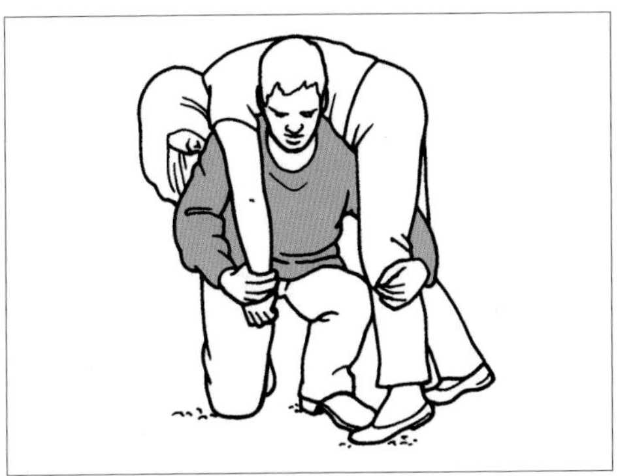

3 With the casualty's arm extended, quickly duck under the raised arm and hold it by the wrist, while going down on one knee to start supporting the weight on your shoulders. Pass the other hand through the victim's legs and hold him or her by the back of the knee.

4 Pass your arm further through his or her legs so that you can take hold of the casualty's wrist, which should now be released by the hand that was originally used to raise the arm. This frees up your arm and so helps you keep your balance as you're about to stand up.

5 Ensuring that the casualty's weight is evenly balanced across both of your shoulders, now stand up – you may need to lean forward a little to help you do this. Once you're standing you should be able to carry the casualty quite easily over a fairly long distance before having to set him or her down. To do this, crouch down and gently roll the victim off your shoulder onto his or her back.

PRACTICAL TIP

When performing the fireman's lift, or fireman's carry, it's important that the carrier uses his or her legs to lift the casualty, instead of the back. That way the carrier will avoid any injury to his or her back.

HOW TO PREVENT HYPOTHERMIA

Essentially, hypothermia is a cooling of the body's core temperature as it drops below 35°C (95°F). There are three recognized phases of hypothermia, each increasingly more severe than the last, starting with numb hands and goose bumps, going through blue lips and mild confusion, and culminating in a point when walking is almost impossible and the pulse and respiration are dramatically lowered; death will happen when the main organs can no longer function normally, which will usually occur when the body temperature dips below a teeth-shattering 30°C (86°F).

INDISPENSABLE THINGS

- Blankets
- Dry clothes
- Someone with whom to share body heat
- Shelter
- Hot, sweet tea

1 Of course, as with so many things, avoiding hypothermia altogether is the best cure. Always dress appropriately for cold weather, even if you intend only to be outside for a few minutes. Lots of layers, a warm hat, gloves and warm boots are essential if you intend to spend time outdoors in cold weather.

2 Anyone participating in outdoor sports in a cold environment should be aware of hypothermia, particularly if there's a chance of them becoming wet in the process. Wet clothes, particularly cotton, will increase the rate at which hypothermia advances, because they lose about 90 per cent of their insulating properties. Don't stay out in the cold in wet clothes, but change into dry ones at the earliest opportunity.

3 Shivering is a sign of the onset of hypothermia – do not ignore it. If you can't get back to camp or your car, try to find a natural shelter from the wind and rain, somewhere where you can perhaps start a fire and dry out wet clothes. Along with wet conditions, wind will also speed up hypothermia as it drives cold air through and under your clothes, so taking valuable heat away from the core of your body.

4 If you're in a really exposed location with no natural shelter to escape to, you must at least erect a makeshift camp using anything you have to hand in order to combat the worst of the conditions. On pages 318–19 we showed you how to make some primitive types of shelter using the most basic materials. If there are two of you, share body heat once you're in the shelter by clinging to one another. And a thermos of hot, sweet tea will literally be a life saver – just sip it slowly.

HOW TO STOP A PANIC ATTACK

Usually caused by major anxiety, hyperventilation brought on by a panic attack will cause the sufferer to feel out of control with a sense of impending terror, accompanied by the physical symptoms of numb hands and feet, red face, tingling fingers, chest pains and light-headedness. The cause of all this is the intake of too much oxygen due to unnaturally fast deep-breathing.

INDISPENSABLE THINGS

- Calming manner
- Removal of all onlookers

REASSURANCE IS VITAL

It is important to approach someone having a panic attack with a calm and confident demeanour (even if you don't feel that way). Separate the casualty from any bystanders or passers-by – it is easier to calm a patient down one to one. If possible, sit the him or her down on a chair in a quiet room. Reassure the patient and gradually encourage him or her to slow their breathing down. Do not expect him or her to answer any questions immediately. Be calm and reassuring. The symptoms (tingling fingers, feeling faint, chest tightness, dizziness) should start to abate after around 5 to 7 minutes.

IF SYMPTOMS PERSIST

If, however, symptoms persist or indeed should the victim lose consciousness, call the emergency services and monitor the casualty's breathing and pulse.

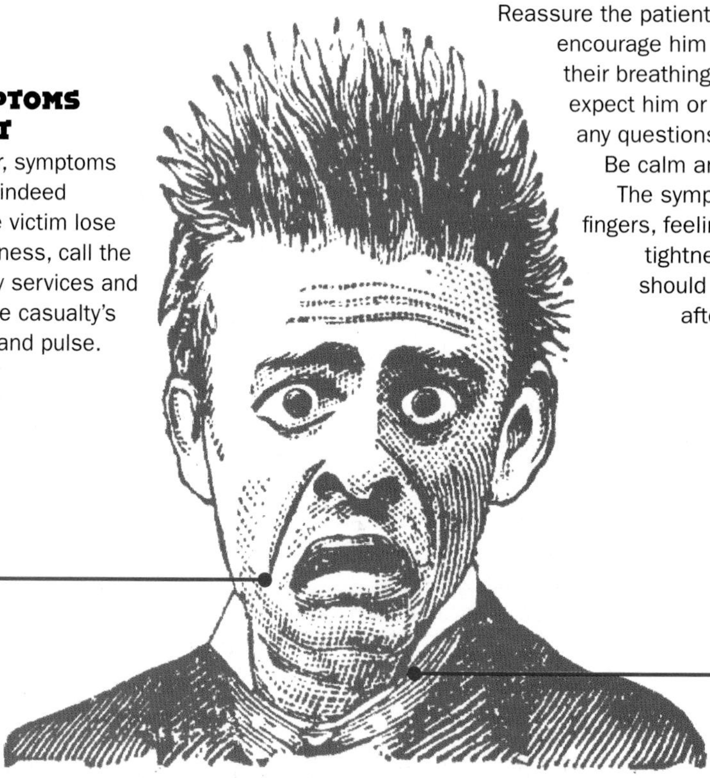

INDISPENSABLE WARNING

If the patient's appearance is pale and clammy instead of flushed, then call an ambulance immediately. They may be suffering from something more than a panic attack.

HOW TO SURVIVE A RIOT

What initially sounded like a carnival procession coming up the road, on closer inspection is really a baying mob smashing windows, setting fire to cars and generally causing a bit of a commotion – who are you kidding, it's a fully fledged riot and you're about to get caught up in all the action. Assuming that you're unwilling to join in with all the looting, tear gas, water cannons and other festivities, here's how best to extricate yourself.

INDISPENSABLE THINGS

- Mobile phone

CALL SOMEONE

At the first sign of trouble, surreptitiously phone someone to let them know where you are and what's happening. Try to avoid getting caught in the middle of the riot by looking for side roads down which you can quietly walk – don't run. Running will attract attention to yourself and may cause people to chase you.

LOOK FOR REFUGE

Look for refuge in a hotel, large apartment block or ideally an embassy – make it absolutely plain to anyone on the door that you're not part of the disturbance and are looking for safety.

IF YOU'RE IN A CAR

If you're in a car, drive slowly away from the disturbance if you can, looking for back roads rather than the main streets. Reverse away from the trouble rather than taking time attempting to turn the car around.

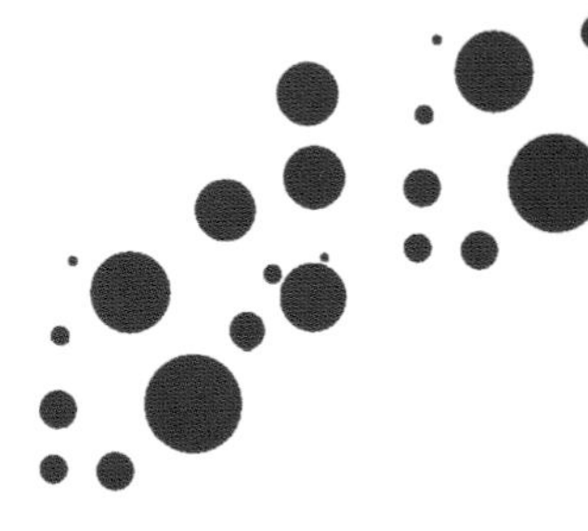

HOW TO SURVIVE A BIOLOGICAL OR CHEMICAL ATTACK

It's an unsavoury fact of modern life, but we're living in turbulent times when international terrorism appears to be a constant threat in most regions of the world. Terrorists exist whose aims are to cause widespread fear among the public and to seed self-doubt in established governments. To achieve this they will attempt any form of atrocity, including the use of biological and chemical weapons, to inflict as many casualties and generate as much fear as they can. We should all be prepared.

INDISPENSABLE THINGS

- Duct tape
- Damp towels
- Radio (batteries)
- Mobile phone
- Emergency kit
- Tinned food
- Bottled water

PRACTICAL TIP

Terrorist activity, by its very nature, does not come with a warning. So you're unlikely to be able to choose where to be when an attack takes place. If you're outside when an attack occurs, enter the nearest safe, accessible building and aim to get up as many storeys as possible – gas used in such attacks is usually denser than air and will therefore stay low to the ground.

1 If you're at home and near the vicinity of the attack, quickly gather together the items listed on page 340 and move to the highest, least accessible room – that is, the one with fewest windows and doors. Lock the door to prevent others who may have been contaminated from entering the room.

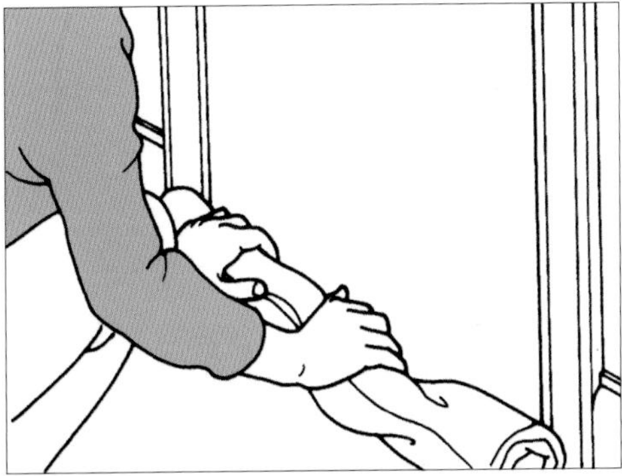

2 Turn off any air-conditioning units and ventilation systems and use the duct tape to tape any gaps in doors and windows. Use damp towels to block any large gaps under doors. This will help to stop gas or a biological agent such as anthrax from entering the room.

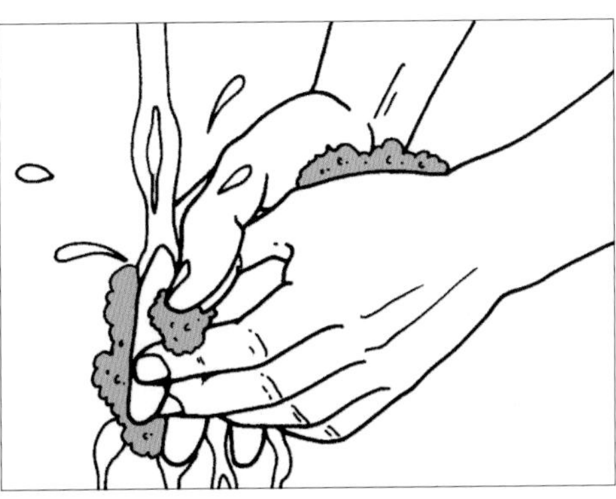

3 In the case of a biological attack, follow standard hygiene practice. Thoroughly wash yourself, especially your hands, and don't come into close contact with anyone who may have been contaminated.

4 Wash all surfaces and clothes that have been in contact with someone you suspect of being contaminated, and under no circumstances rub your eyes.

5 Stay indoors and listen to the radio for any information that will help you determine the severity of the attack and whether or not you need to evacuate the area. Use your mobile phone to stay in contact with other members of the family who may have been elsewhere at the time of the attack.

HOW TO SURVIVE AN EARTHQUAKE

Earthquakes can happen pretty much anywhere in the world, but there are recognized regions where the incidents and risk of earthquakes, due to the local instability of the Earth's crust, are much greater. Our knowledge of these regions has, in most cases, led to the implementation of 'quake-proof' construction techniques. However, every now and again the failure to use such construction techniques can result in horrific loss of life, as witnessed on 12 May 2008 when an estimated 69,000 people lost their lives in Sichuan Province, China, many of them children trapped in poorly constructed schools.

PRACTICAL TIP

If you live in a region recognized as a high-risk earthquake zone, have a plan. Decide which room is likely to be the safest in which to take shelter – remember you're looking for something sturdy under which to hide, and avoid rooms with lots of heavy objects such as shelves and cabinets that could easily topple over during the quake.

INDISPENSABLE THINGS

- Sturdy table or desk

1 As soon as you feel the room begin to shake, seek shelter under a sturdy table or desk. Even a large chair, if you can fit under it, will afford you some protection against falling masonry or other large objects. Make yourself as small as possible and tuck your head in, covering your head and neck with your arms.

2 If there is nothing suitable under which you can take shelter, go to the nearest interior wall and take cover there in the same position. When ceilings fall in, they are more likely to collapse in the centre of the room than at the edge. Only shelter under an internal doorway if you know it is strongly constructed.

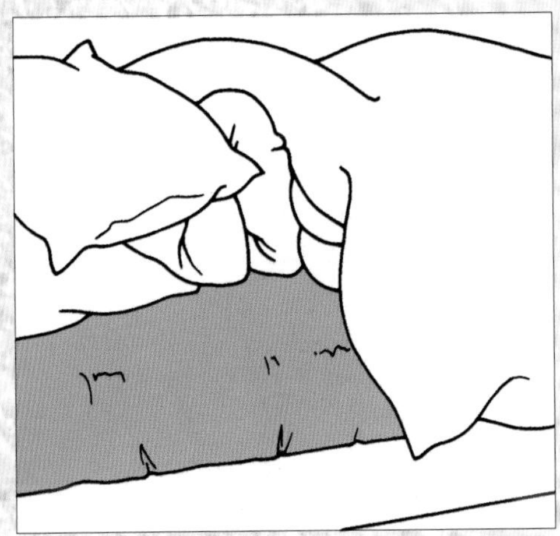

3 If the earthquake strikes while you're in bed, it's often best to stay in bed, curl up into a ball, and cover your head with a pillow or two. Evidence suggests that people who get out of bed to seek shelter are more likely to get injured. If, however, you can quickly roll out of bed and under a table, this is the best option.

4 If you're outdoors when an earthquake starts, try to make for open ground away from tall buildings and other constructions. This way you will avoid being hit by falling masonry and other debris.

HOW TO AVOID A LIGHTNING STRIKE

The risk of being struck by lightning is far greater in some regions of the world than in others, but it's something that we should all take seriously. In the US between 80 and 90 people die each year from lightning strikes, while in the UK the figure is around three. However, the number of people suffering from burns and other injuries is far greater in both countries.

INDISPENSABLE THINGS

- Cool head
- Car

PRACTICAL TIP

If you find yourself outside in a thunder storm with lightning present, the first thing is to assess the risk of a lightning strike. Count the seconds between hearing thunder and seeing lightning – if it's less than 30 seconds there's a risk of a lightning strike.

1 Avoid high ground and don't take shelter under a tree. Lightning will strike tall, isolated objects such as trees, and the current can easily pass from the tree through you to the ground. In addition, trees have been known to literally explode when struck by lightning.

2 If you're out camping and a storm is approaching, don't take shelter in your tent, particularly if it's in an exposed location. The tent is likely to have metallic components that will attract lightning.

3 If you're caught out in the open, make yourself as small a 'target' as possible. Crouch down low to the ground (but do not lie flat) and minimize the amount of contact you have with the earth.

4 If you can get to your car, do so. Put all the windows up and don't touch any metallic element inside the car. If the car is struck by lightning, the metallic body of the car will take up the charge and conduct it safely to the ground.

5 If you're inside during the storm, stay well away from all electrical appliances, wall sockets and don't use the telephone. If the house is hit, the current may well surge through these objects.

PRACTICAL TIP

If someone with you is struck by lightning, they may well be rendered unconscious. If so, check that they are breathing and that they have a pulse. If not begin CPR (*see pages 268–9*). If they are breathing but unconscious, place them in the recovery position (*see page 285*). Don't worry about touching someone who has been struck by lightning, for they will not be carrying a charge.

INDEX

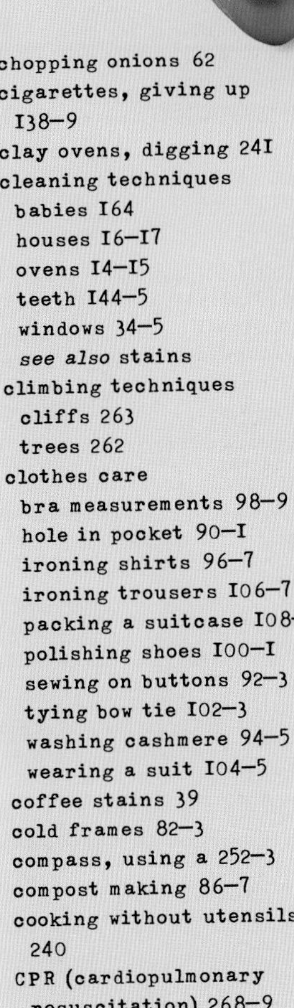

INDEX

INDEX

ACKNOWLEDGEMENTS

The publishers would like to thank Christine Evans, Marie-Eve Foisy, Martin Lusk, Vivienne Macey, Colin Richardson, Dr Christopher Van Tilburg, Tony Wafer and Professor Greg Whyte for their invaluable advice.

ABOUT THE AUTHORS

HOME & GARDEN: Sara Rose has written many books on nutrition, health and fitness, and is the best-selling author of *Vitamins and Minerals*. A busy mother of two and proud possessor of an allotment, her indispensable advice will help you maintain your home, impress others with your culinary skills and make the most of your garden in a practical, time-saving way.

HEALTH & BEAUTY: Kim Davies is a writer, adventurer and practical mother who has changed nappies in moonlit lay-bys, crossed India on a shoestring, and applied emergency first-aid to jellyfish stings. She practises yoga and knows how to tie a bow-tie. Her published titles include *Go Green, Save Money* and *The Baby and Toddler Meal Planner*.

TRAVEL & SPORTS: Nic Compton was brought up on boats in the Mediterranean and one of his earliest practical memories is of his father teaching him to tie a bowline knot at the age of six. He has worked as a carpenter and shipwright, and rebuilt bicycles before turning his attention to more academic matters. He has written six books, including *Sailing Solo* and *The Great Classic Yacht Revival*.

ACCIDENT & EMERGENCY: David Martin is an adventurer and explorer whose favourite pastimes include sailing, motorcycle touring, trekking and camping. To pursue safely his love of the outdoors, David has undergone a number of first aid and other sport-related safety courses, as well as developing a good understanding of field craft and how to react in adverse conditions.

PICTURE CREDITS

The publisher would like to thank the following individuals and organizations for their kind permission to reproduce the images in this book. Every effort has been made to acknowledge the pictures, however, we apologize if there are any unintentional omissions.

CORBIS: 84/Brand X.

GETTY IMAGES: 7/Rubberball; 8, 226/Stockdisc; 136/Stockbyte; 160/Dorling Kindersley; 298/Riko Pictures.

DAVID MELLOR DESIGN (www.davidmellordesign.co.uk): front cover image (green dessert spoon).

PHOTOLIBRARY: 70/Denkou Images.